Looking back at Stanier Locomotives

Strathwood

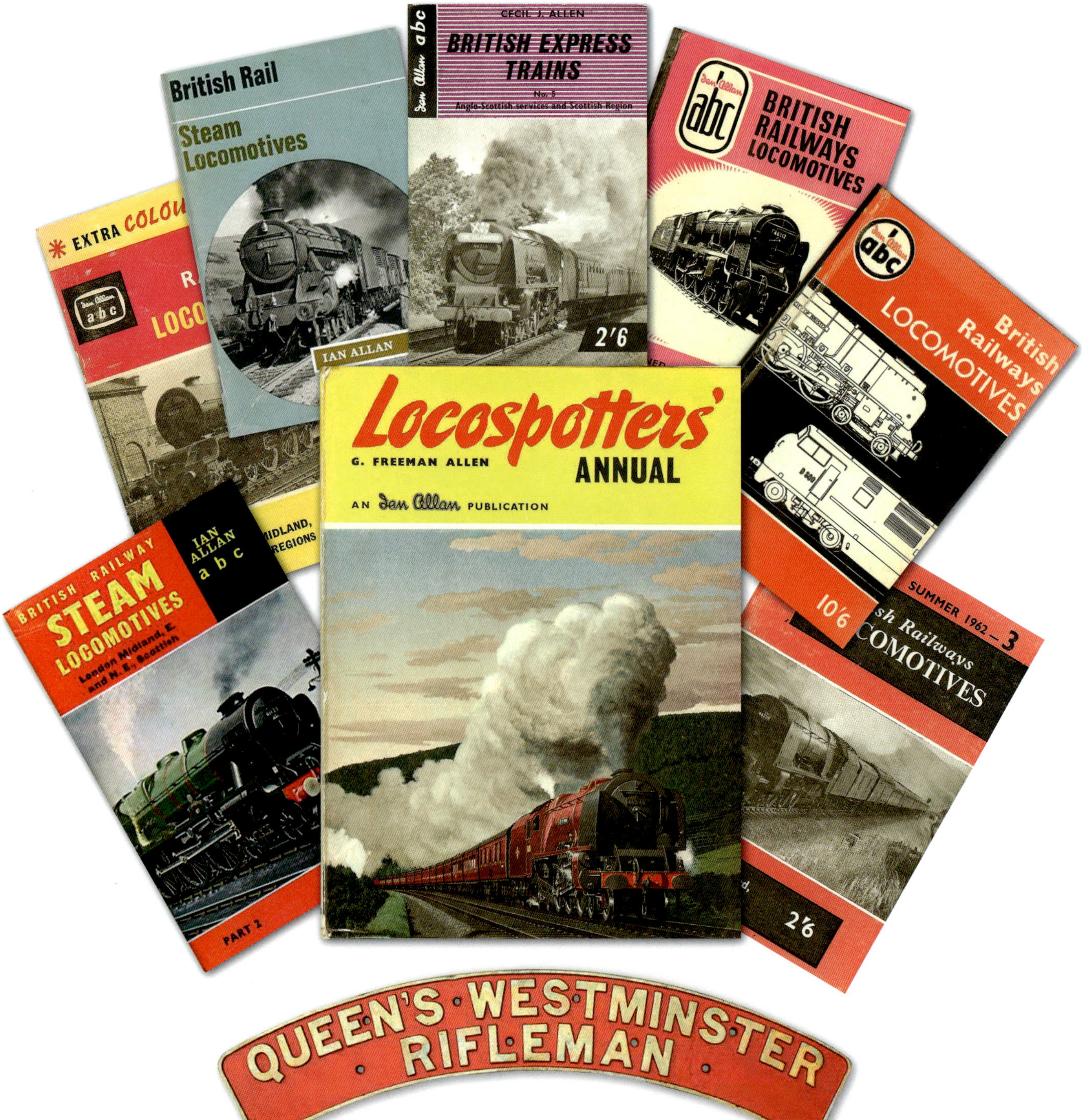
CECIL J. ALLEN
BRITISH EXPRESS TRAINS
No. 5
Anglo-Scottish services and Scottish Region
2'6
British Rail
Steam Locomotives
IAN ALLAN
BRITISH RAILWAYS LOCOMOTIVES
British Railways LOCOMOTIVES
10'6
EXTRA COLOU
Locospotters' ANNUAL
G. FREEMAN ALLEN
AN Ian Allan PUBLICATION
IAN ALLAN a b c
BRITISH RAILWAY STEAM LOCOMOTIVES
London Midland, E. and N. E., Scottish
PART 2
SUMMER 1962 – 3
COMOTIVES
2'6
QUEEN'S WESTMINSTER RIFLEMAN

Looking back at Stanier Locomotives

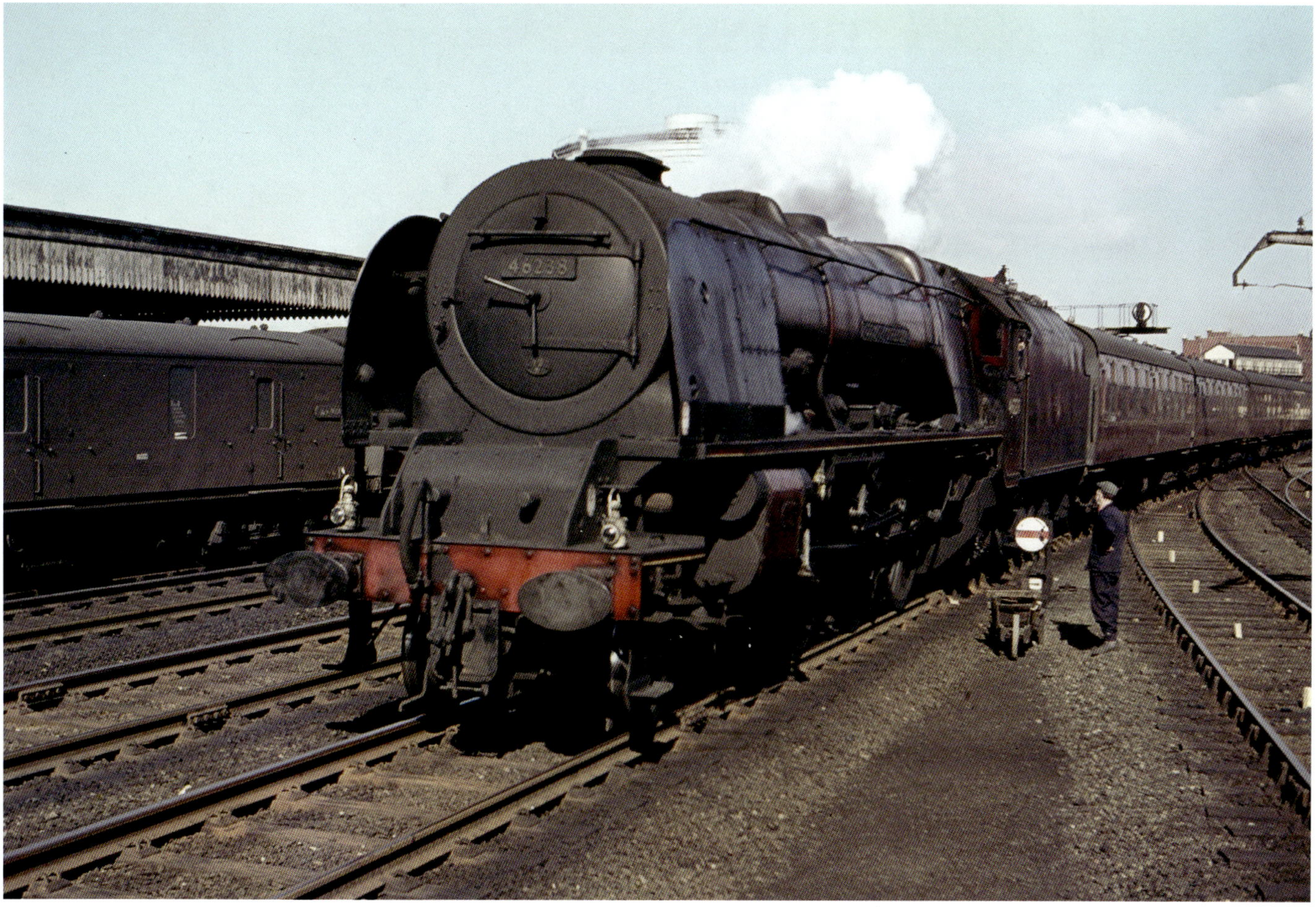

A moment to savour as 46238 City of Carlisle arrives at Lancaster in 1963 stopping at the city to exchange passengers under the watchful eye of a ganger diligently carrying out his duties. ***Strathwood Library Collection***

Kevin Derrick

Strathwood

Looking back at Stanier Locomotives

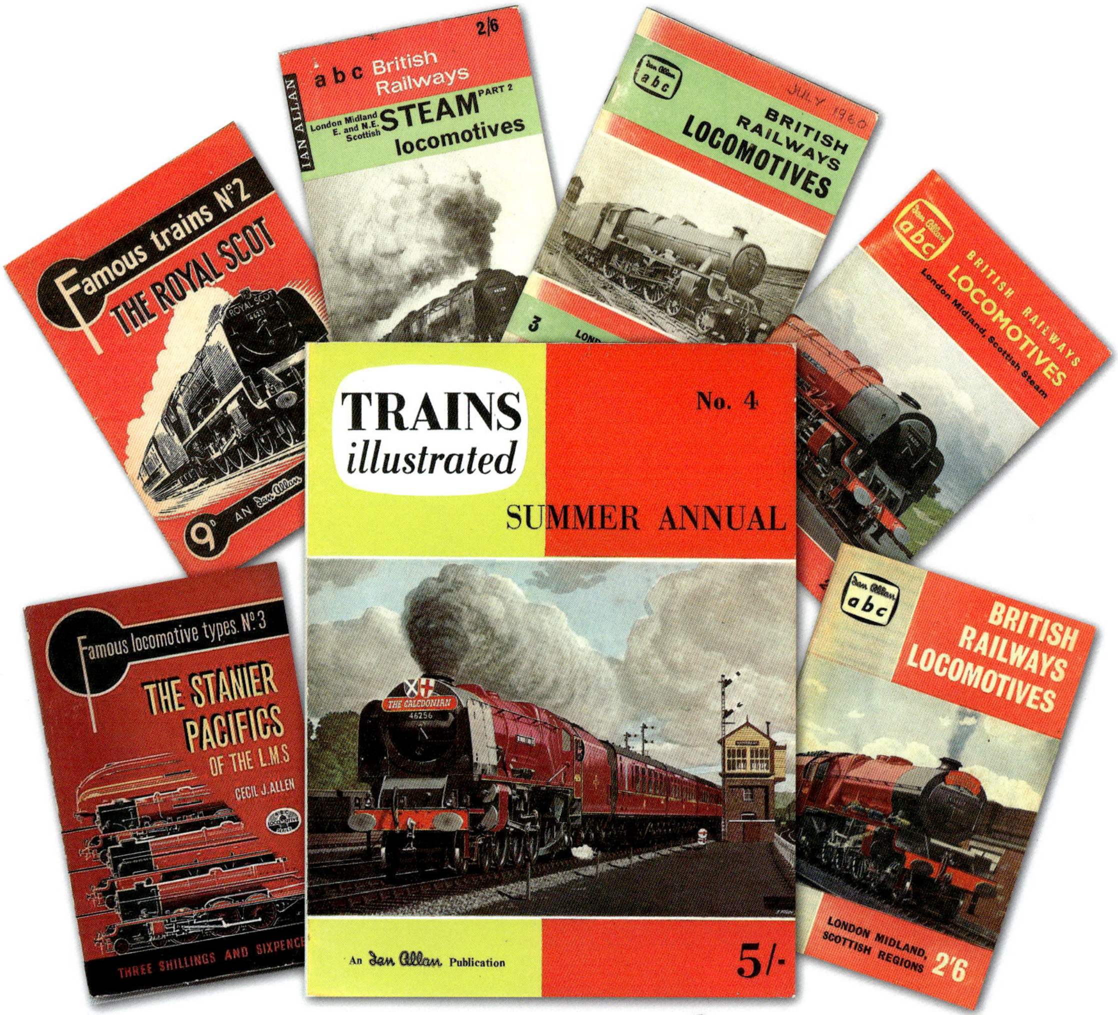

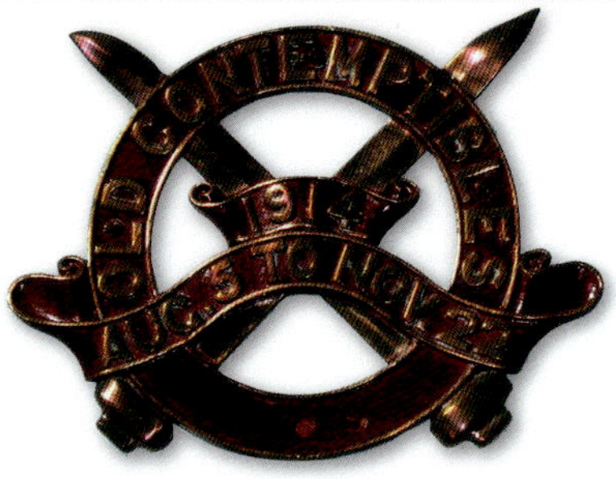

First published 2009

ISBN 1-905276-25-7
ISBN 978-1-905276-25-7

Published by Strathwood Ltd, Glenavon House, Kinchurdy Road, Boat of Garten, Inverness-shire, PH24 3BP. Tel 01479 831139

Proudly printed in the United Kingdom

Contents **Page**

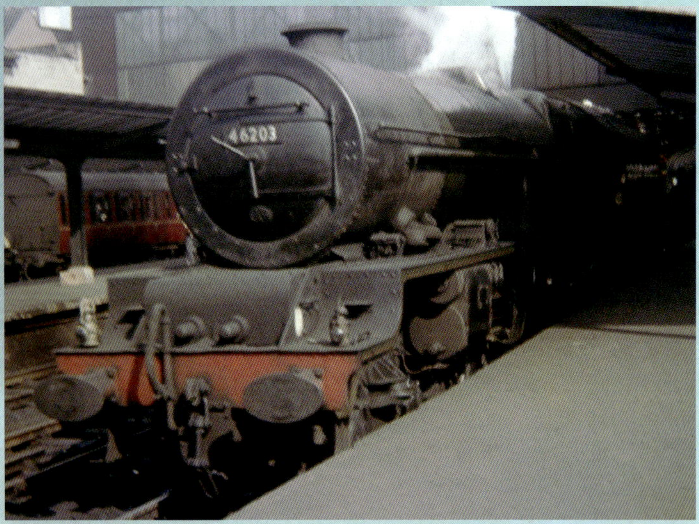

Above: A lucky Lizzie 46203 Princess Margaret Rose stands at Carlisle Citadel in July 1962. ***Strathwood Library Collection***

This page; Another hard working Stanier 8F 48329 plods past Heaton Mersey on 17 January 1964 with a rake of empty sixteen ton coal wagons rattling behind the drawbar. ***Dave Down***

Introduction

The great man was born in Swindon on 27 May 1876 where his father worked for the Great Western Railway as Chief Clerk to the then Chief Mechanical Engineer William Dean. He was educated at Swindon High School, and also for a single year at Wycliffe College.

Stanier followed his father into a career with the Great Western Railway and between 1897 and 1900, he worked as a draughtsman, before becoming Inspector of Materials in 1900. In 1904, George Jackson Churchward as Chief Mechanical Engineer appointed him as Assistant to the Divisional Locomotive Superintendent in London. After eight years in this post his career took another step forward, when in 1912 he returned to Swindon to become the Assistant Works Manager. Six years passed and he was promoted to the position of Works Manager in 1920.

Considering the experience he must have gained the Board of Directors of the rival London Midland and Scottish Railway appointed Stanier as their Chief Mechanical Engineer with effect from New Years Day 1932, succeeding Sir Henry Fowler in this important post.

His first efforts involved overseeing the construction of ten 0-4-4Ts for push and pull working already ordered, while he considered what to do about an acute shortage of heavy express passenger and freight locomotives, which he met by developing a stock of capable, reliable and efficient engines. Over 2,000 were built in the period 1932-47, combining many characteristics of Great Western Railway practice, such as tapered boilers, but now with LMS features such as outside Walschaerts valve gear which improved accessibility. His early boiler designs, with low-degree superheat and other Swindon characteristics were unsatisfactory and which he quickly rectified by revising the design with larger superheaters.

In 1942 he was appointed as Scientific Adviser to the Ministry of Production and ceased to take an everyday role in the locomotive affairs of the LMS, concentrating his energies on the war effort, although he remained as a valued consultant to the company.

He was knighted in 1943 in recognition of his achievements and was elected a Fellow of the Royal Society in 1944 on his retirement becoming the only railway engineer other than George Stephenson himself to receive the honour. He was also President of the Institution of Mechanical Engineers in 1944.

Sir William Arthur Stanier, FRS passed away on 27 September 1965 aged eighty nine having left a magnificent legacy in the development of the steam locomotive within the United Kingdom.

The Looking Back at series is fast developing into a collectable account using colour photographs of the various designs and specific classes in the era since nationalisation. A further dip into the archives is planned to look at various types in more detail. If you can help with even a single shot of any of the classes covered in this volume, please get in touch.

Kevin Derrick
Boat of Garten 2009

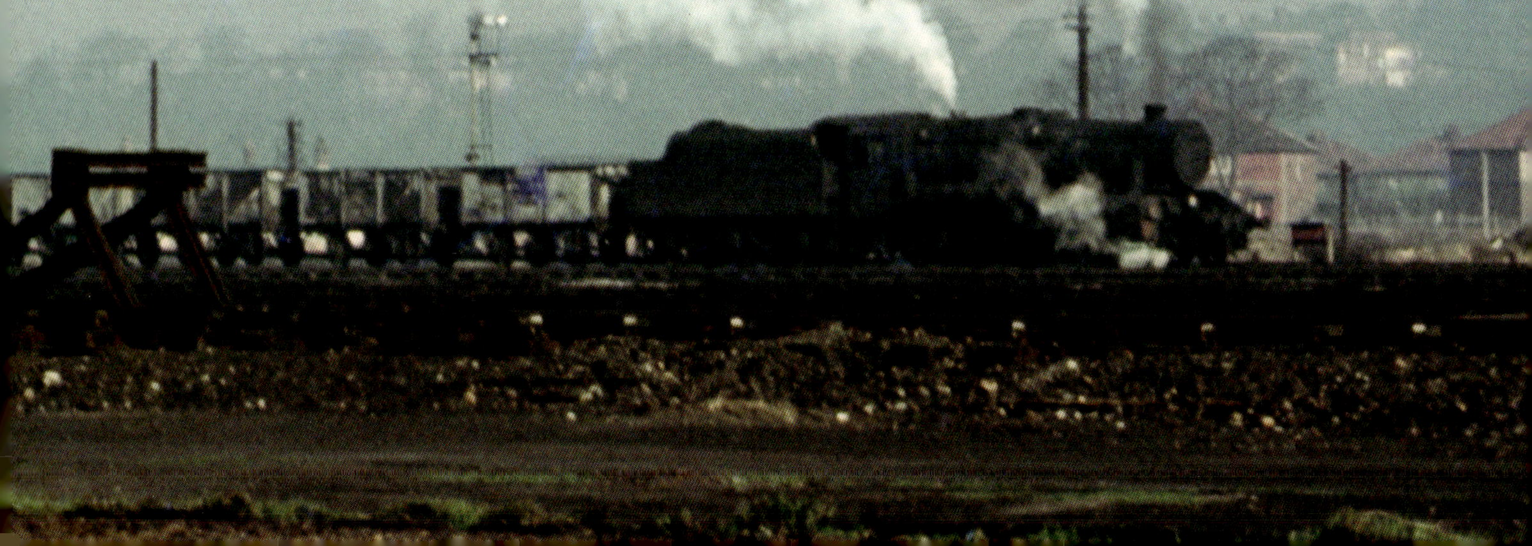

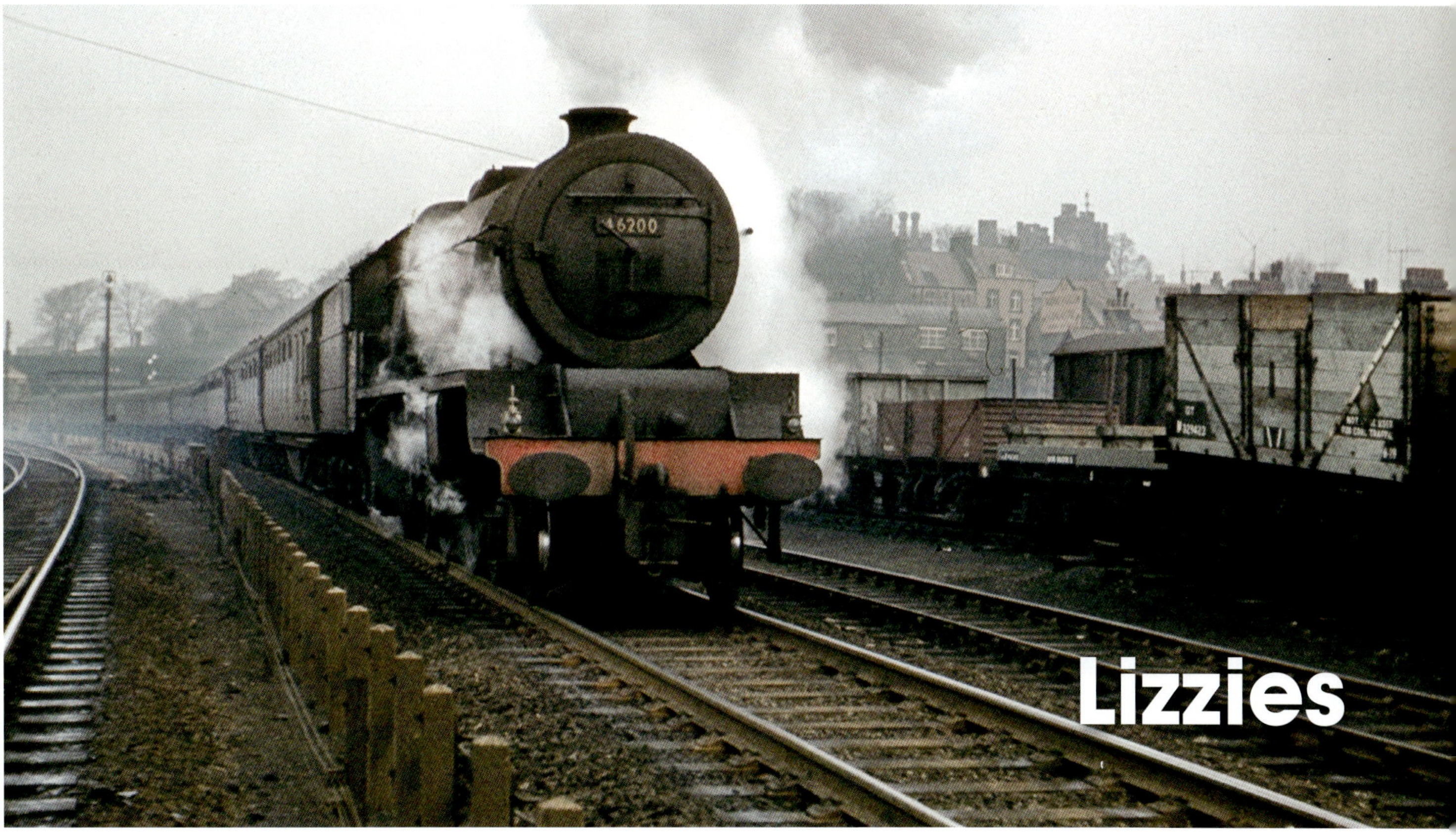

Lizzies

Although the first two of the class were a disappointment when built in 1933, they would go on with improvements to become fine locomotives. The first built 46200 The Princess Royal gets a long rake of coaches away from Lancaster in the winter of 1961/2, her last year of service. Originally classified as 7P when built by the LMS, until British Railways deemed the class to be 8P in their new system. ***Late Ray Helm/Strathwood Library Collection***

When built the first of the production locomotives 46203 Princess Margaret Rose like its sister the Turbomotive 6202 Princess Anne were fitted with then new Mark I tenders. However it was soon found that in traffic on heavy Anglo-Scottish trains their hunger for coal would require increased capacity. Therefore all except 6202 were paired with Mark III tenders with higher side sheets affording an extra ton of coal lifting the capacity to ten tons. When our cameraman recorded 46203 at Carnforth in the summer of 1962 she was stored serviceable it would seem, although withdrawn that October. ***Late Ray Helm/Strathwood Library Collection***

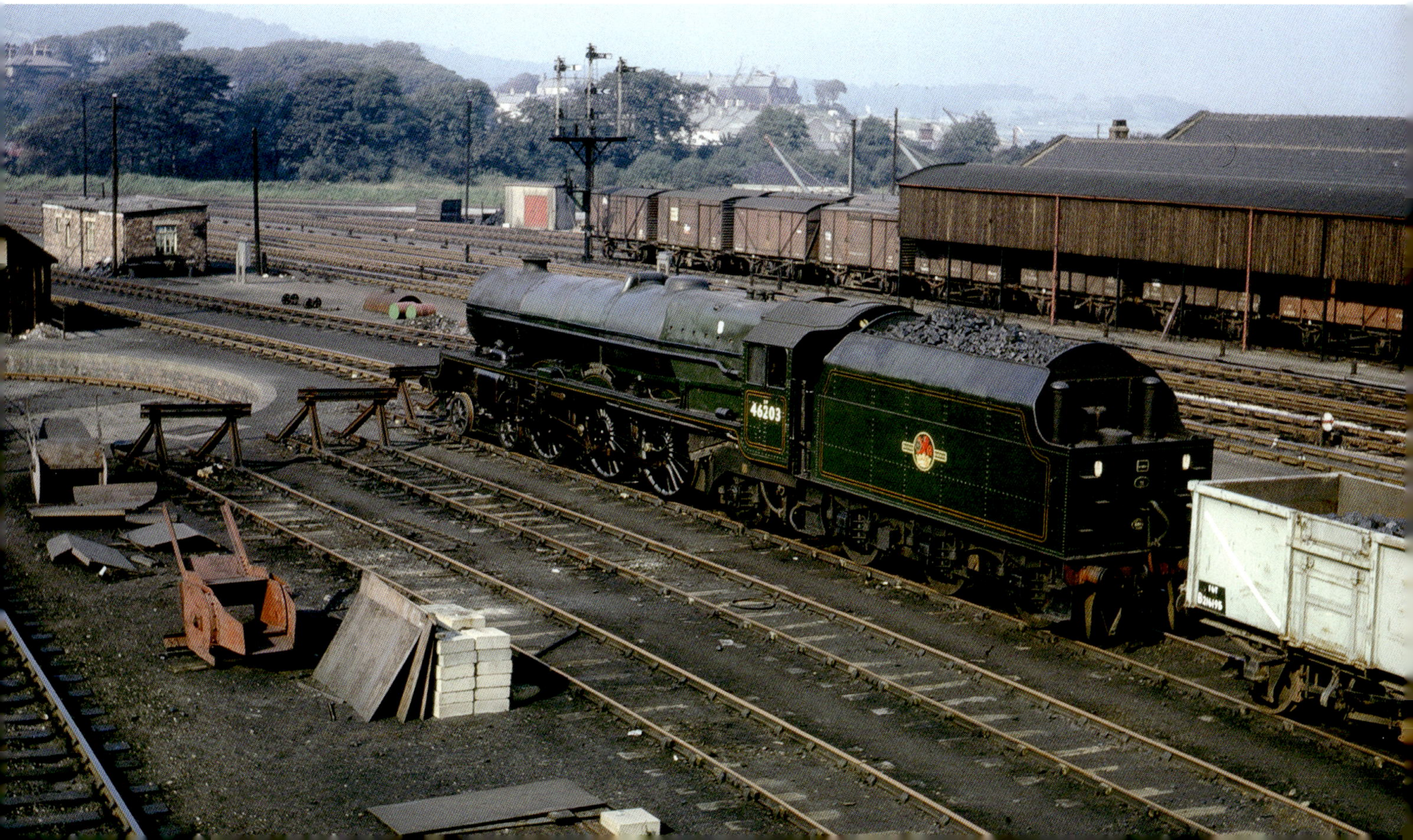

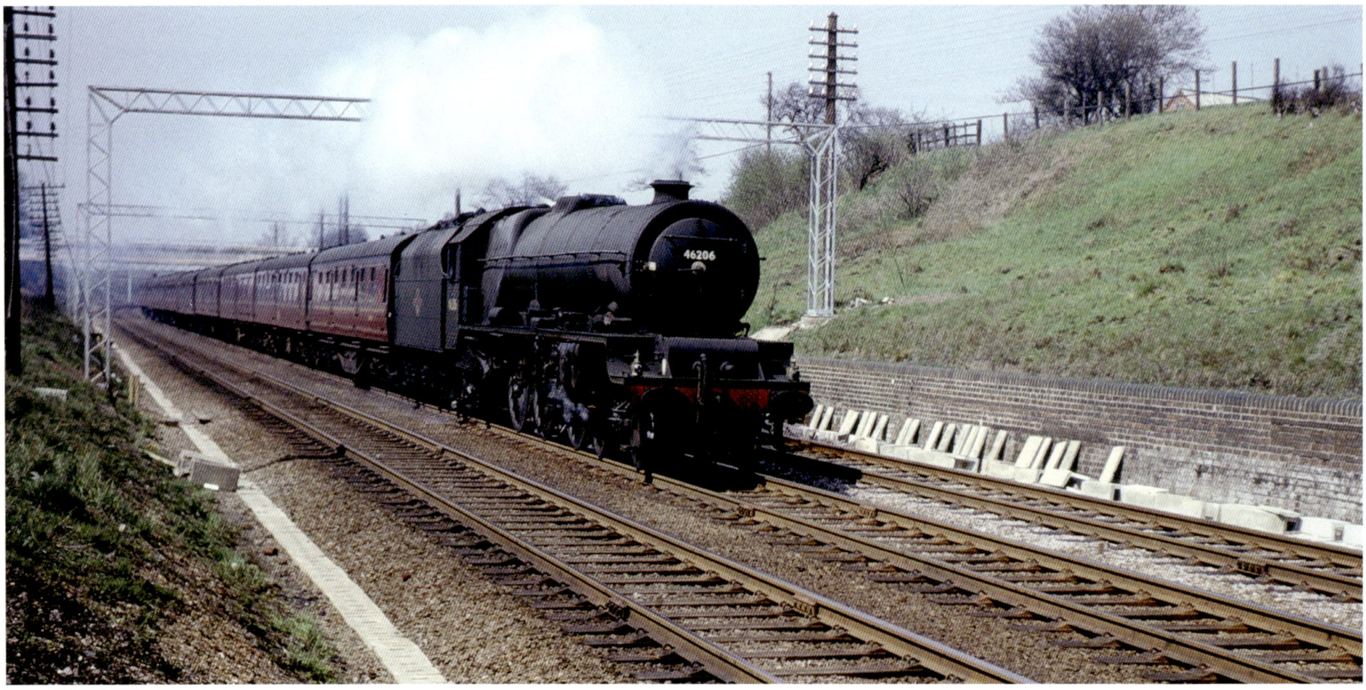

The erection of overhead masts and gantries for electrification would help to see off the class along with arrivals of English Electric Type 4s. Seen again in that last summer of service for the six serviceable engines in 1962 was 46206 Princess Marie Louise roaring along near Tamworth. ***John Gill***

The first two locomotives of the class remained easily identifiable at a distance when introduced, until well into the British Railways era as they were the only ones with domed boilers. Also their fireboxes were longer than the production locomotives. In the early 1950s most of the class were adapted in order that the boilers could be exchanged as required during works overhauls with the now modified shorter boiler barrel variety which had been fitted with domes and top feeds by now. This view shows 46200 The Princess Royal stabled in front of 71000 Duke of Gloucester at Crewe in 1961. The latter engine came into existence to fill the perceived gap in 8P power left after the withdrawal of the Harrow smash victim 46202 Princess Anne which had been rebuilt into more conventional form by 1952. ***Strathwood Library Collection***

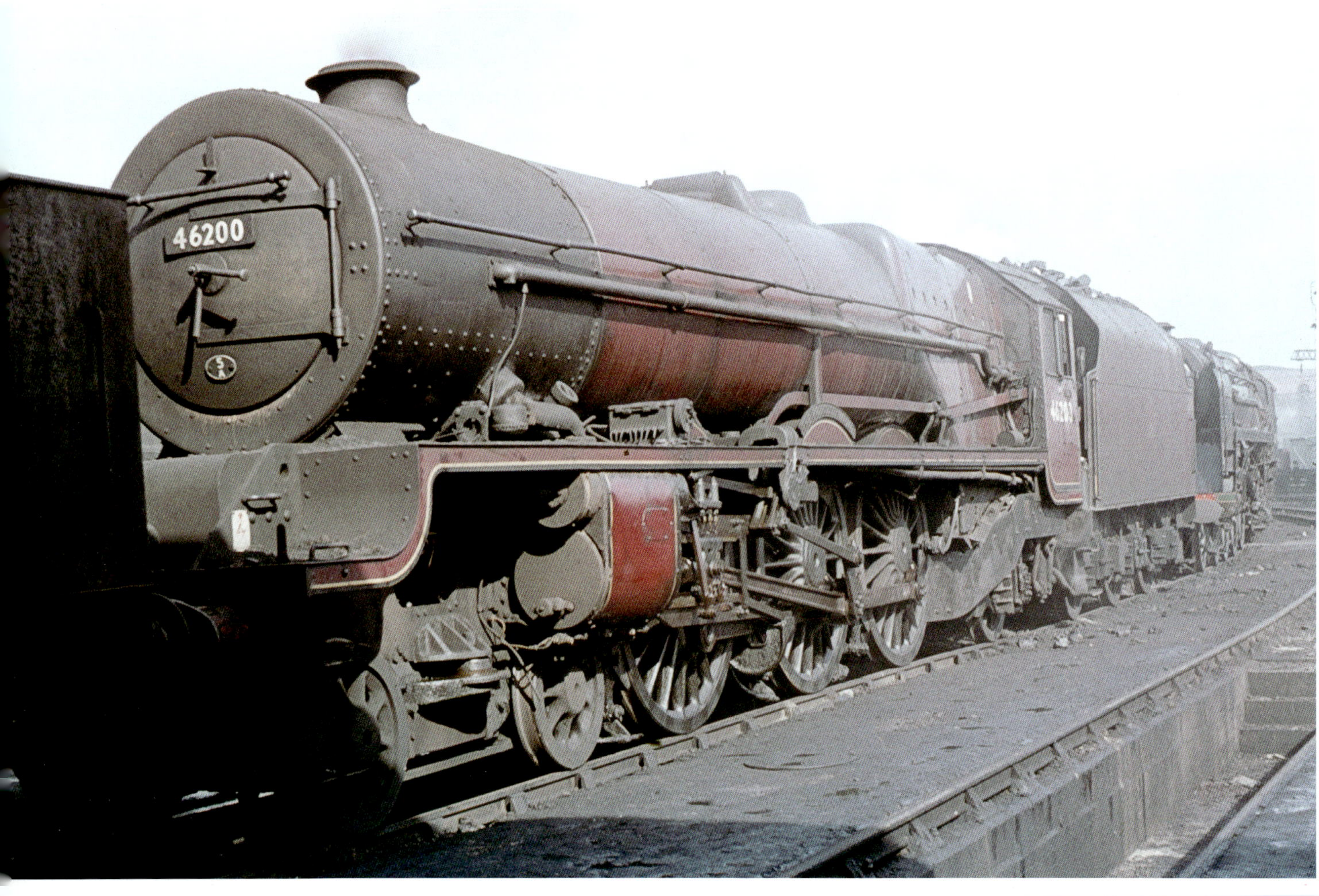

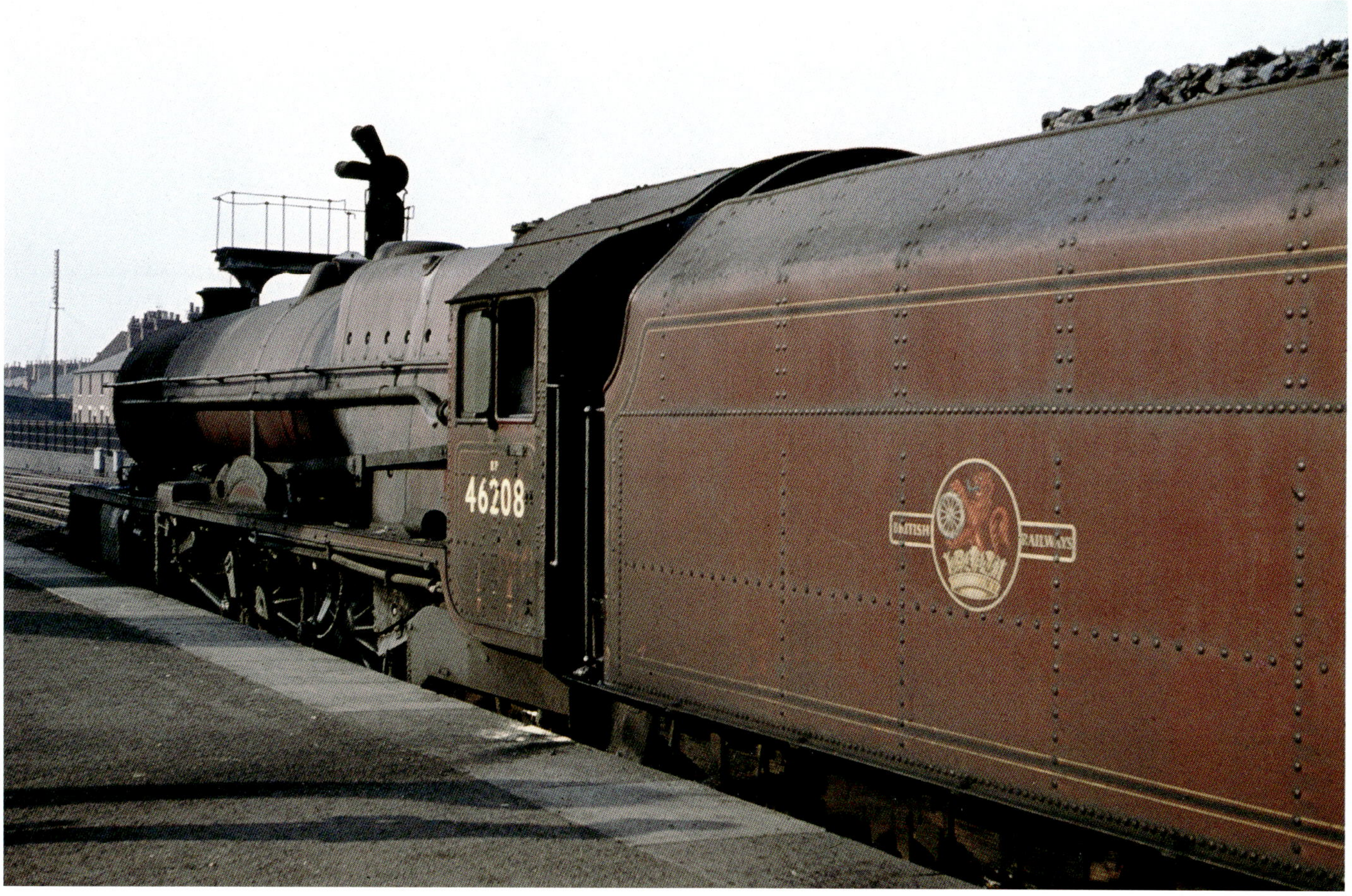

Although several livery variations were tried in the British Railways era such as blue, which did perhaps make them look like Gordon the blue engine from the Thomas stories, 46208 Princess Helena Victoria models the fully lined version of maroon whilst halted at Stafford in 1959. This engine was the first to be repainted back into maroon in 1958 and was unique in this style of lining. ***Strathwood Library Collection***

Another example repainted by Crewe Works into lined British Railways green was 46211 Queen Maud awaiting a call back to service at Crewe in 1960. Comparison with the photograph opposite of 46200 shows the different crosshead arrangement fitted to the production engines. ***Strathwood Library Collection***

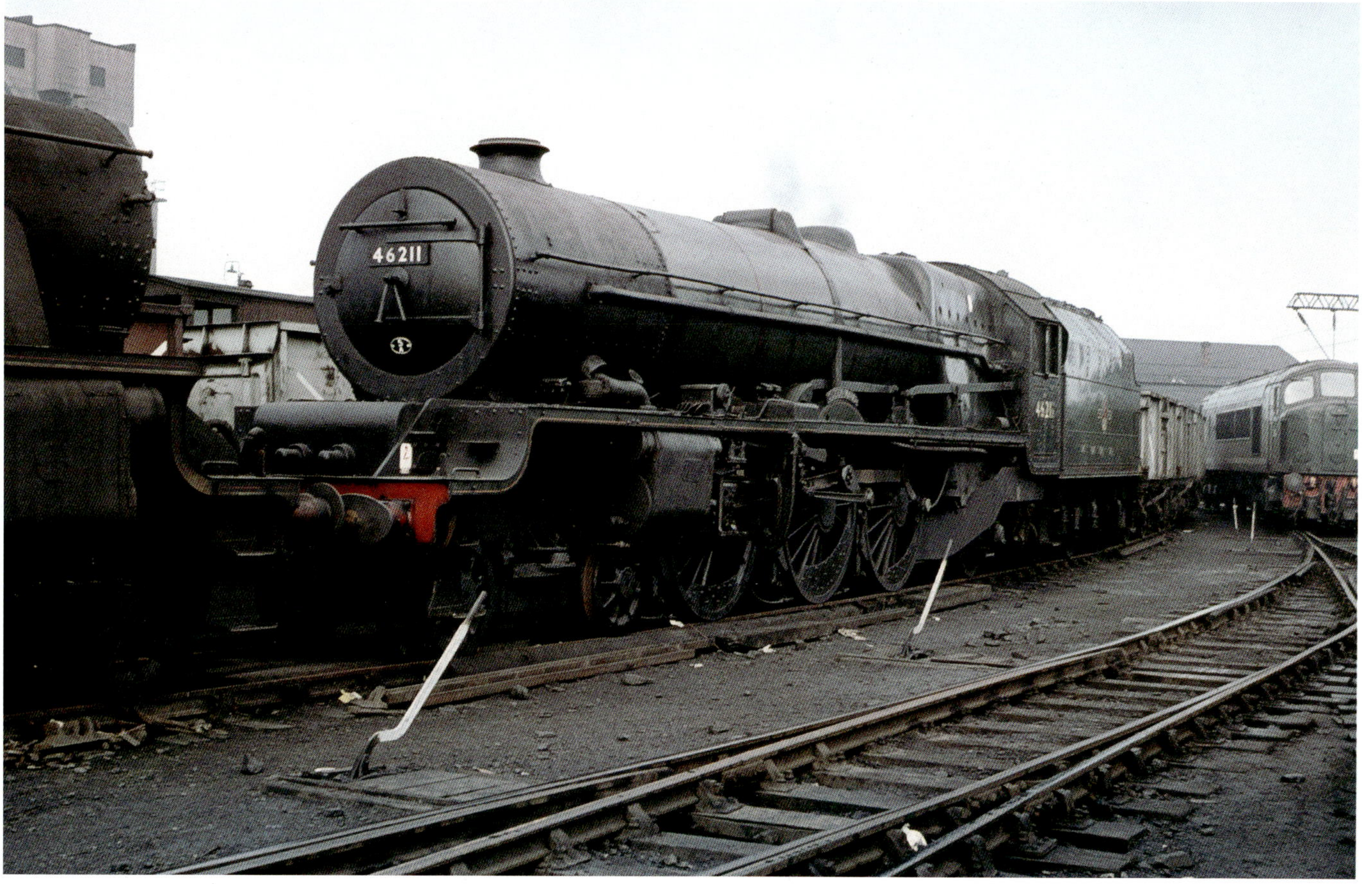

Churchill's 8Fs

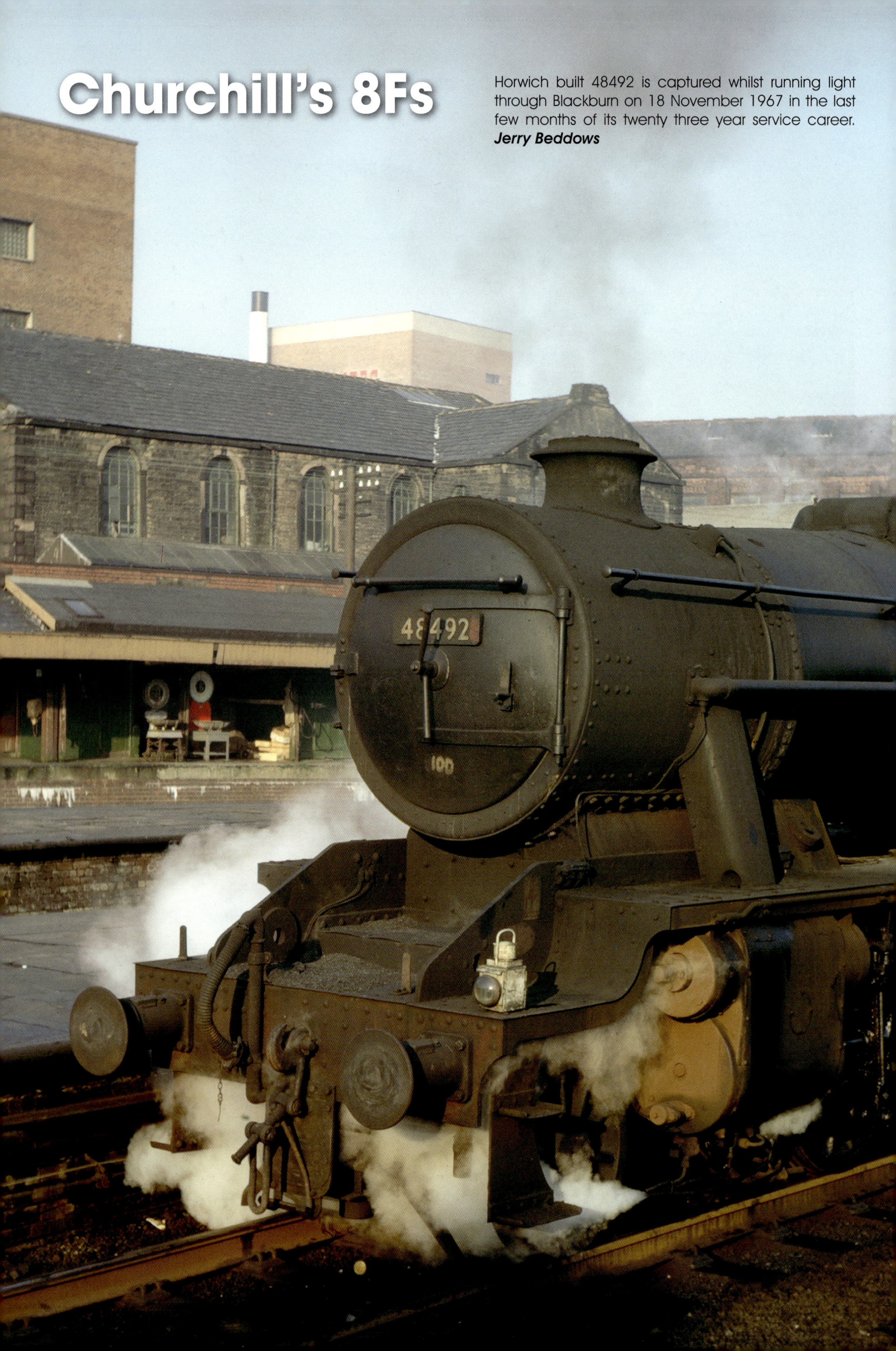

Horwich built 48492 is captured whilst running light through Blackburn on 18 November 1967 in the last few months of its twenty three year service career. ***Jerry Beddows***

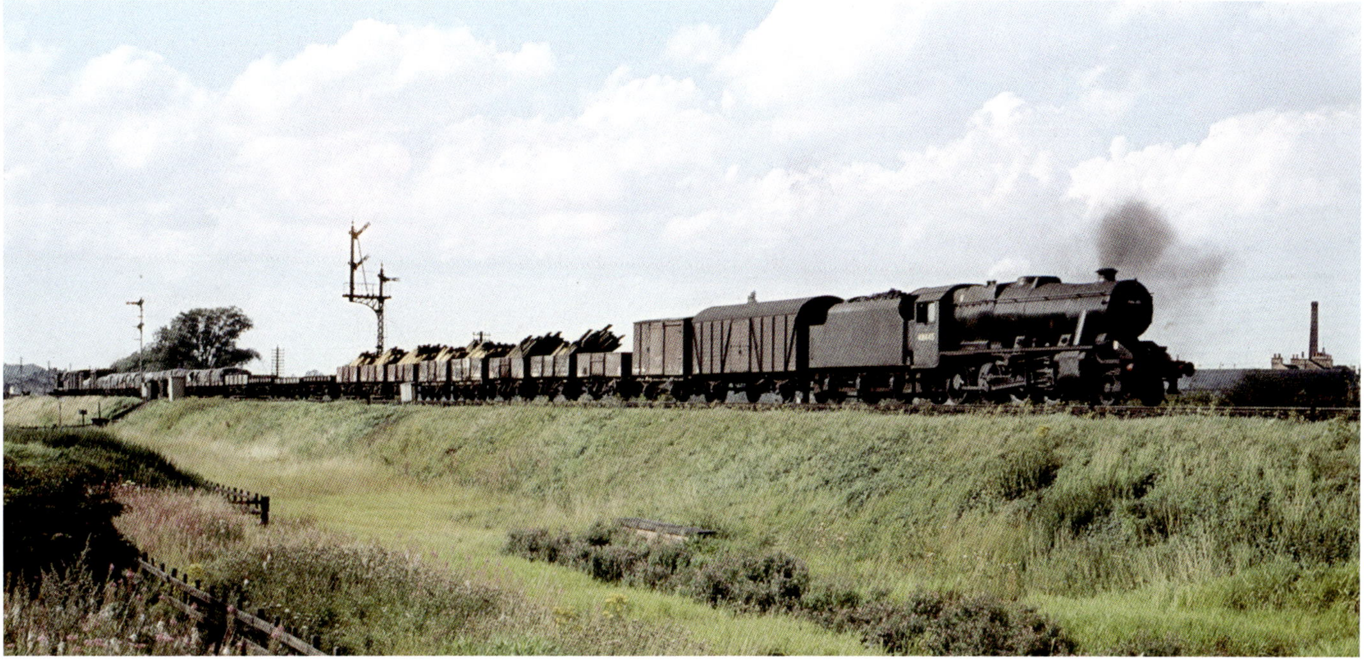

At the outset of World War Two less than one hundred and fifty of Stanier's design of 2-8-0 were in service since their introduction in 1935. With the onset of hostilities it was clear that the shortage of heavy freight locomotives both within Great Britain and the Commonwealth would be a problem if not speedily dealt with by Mr Churchill's War Cabinet. Whilst it would become clear that additional savings of materials would be needed and Robin Riddles would head the design team with the Austerity 2-8-0s, the gap would be filled in the short term with a rapid build of Stanier's design. So it was that the workshops of the big four companies would begin building these superb heavy freight locomotives to fulfil orders for the War Department and to help fill the needs of all of the companies. Among these orders were two batches built at Swindon and from the second build in 1944 from the GWR's works was 48445 seen here near Gamston on the East Coast Main Line in 1958. ***Strathwood Library Collection***

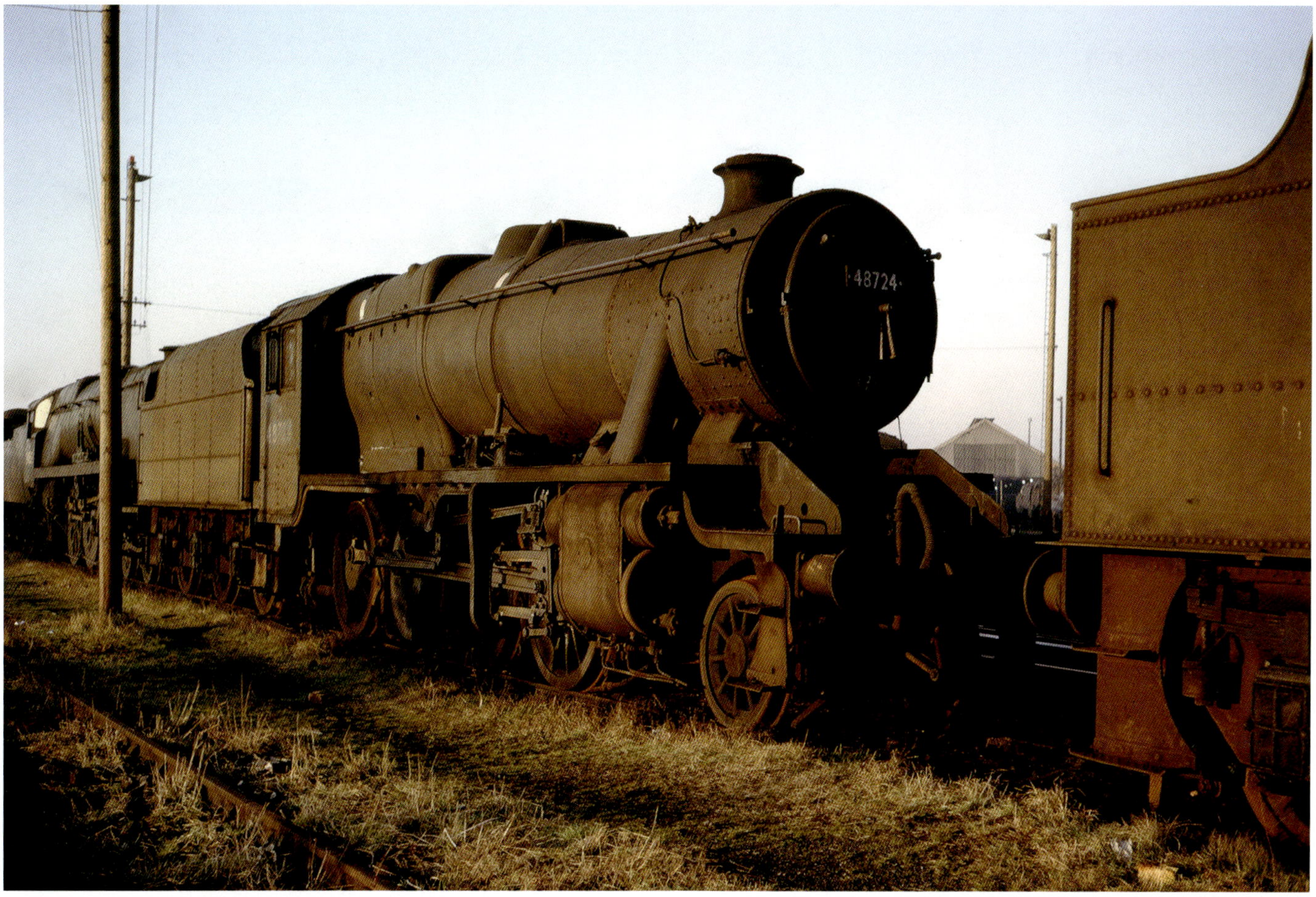

Also built in 1944 at the time of the Normandy invasion was 48724 in the Southern Railway's workshops at Brighton. Along with another rusty and weary stablemate it returned to former Southern Railway metals at Eastleigh in November 1964 to undergo a works overhaul and a return to traffic for another three years life. ***Late Norman Brown/ Strathwood Library Collection***

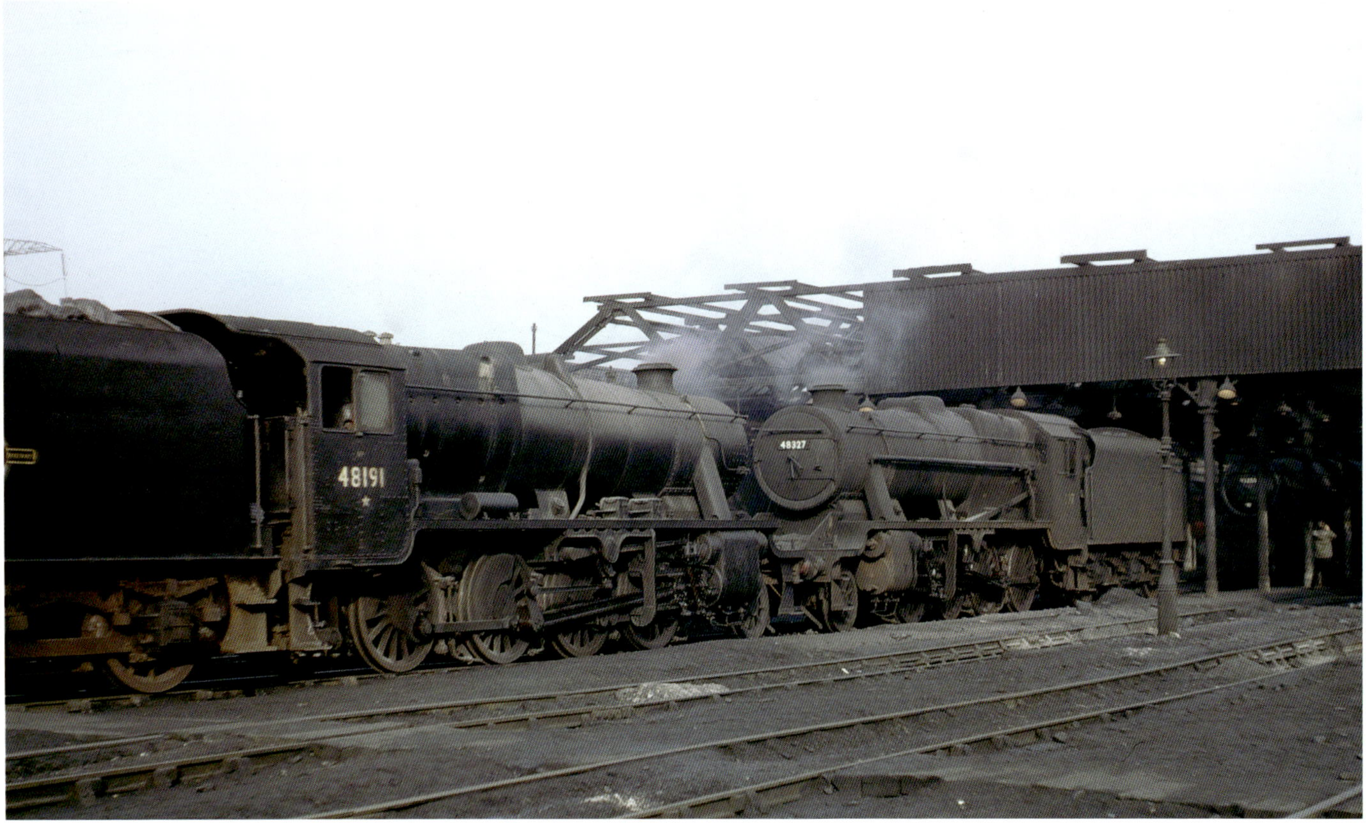

The painted star marking on the cab sides of 48191 at Heaton Mersey on 3 March 1968 denotes that this locomotive has been modified with integral cast balance weights to the wheels to enable it to be operated in theory at least, at speeds of up to 50mph on express freights. Hopefully for the crew without too much uncomfortable longitudinal shuttling of the locomotive at speed. ***Jerry Beddows***

When first introduced Stanier had specified a domeless boiler which was fitted to the first twelve of the class, nor were they fitted with a vacuum brake at first unlike the later engines. Another of the Brighton built locomotives was 48677 picking up speed running light through Bagulay on the former Cheshire Lines Committee route on 9 September 1967. ***Jerry Beddows***

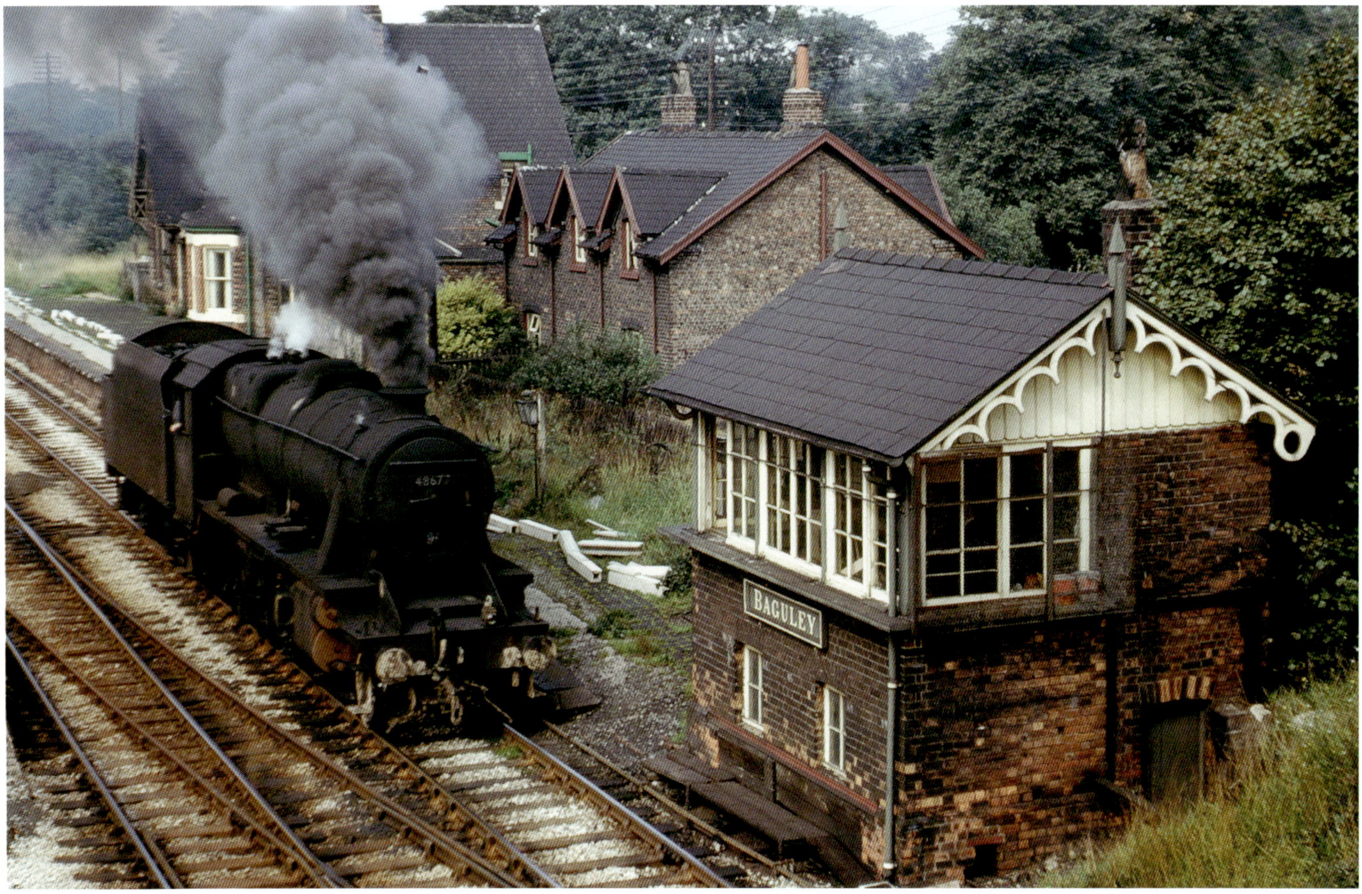

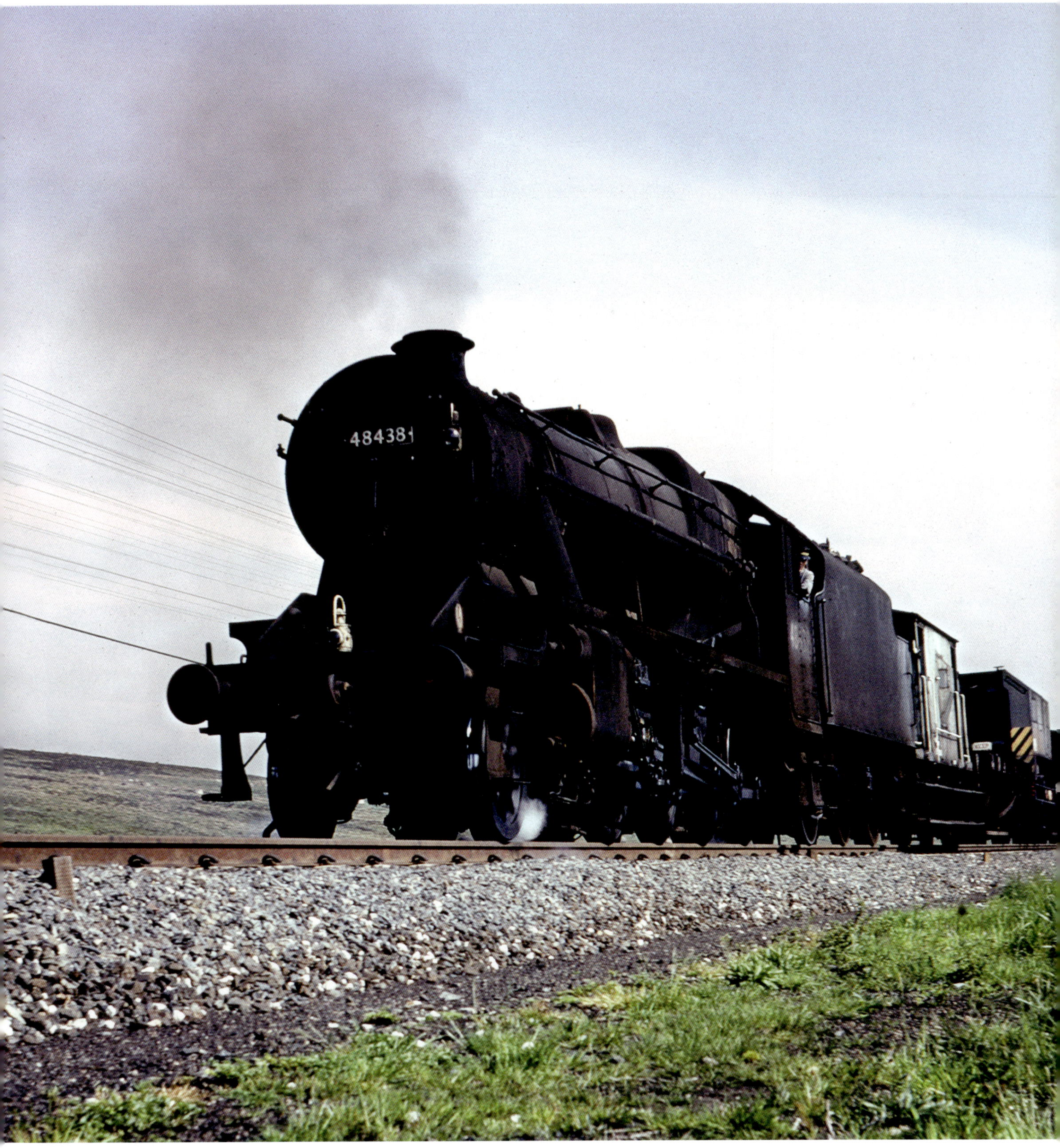

When production of the class ended at Darlington Works in the autumn of 1946, 852 locomotives had been built to this basic design for use around the world. This example 48438 passing Scout Green on 2 June 1967 was another product from Swindon, whilst the works of Crewe, Horwich, Doncaster, Eastleigh, Ashford and Brighton all chipped in with production along with outside contractors North British, Vulcan Foundry and Beyer Peacock. With such a large number built, it makes the class the most numerous of all of the Stanier designs and the fourth largest class of steam locomotives built within the United Kingdom, although the maximum number in British Railways stock was 666 from 1957 until 1960. This was after the repatriation of three War Department locomotives to become 48773-5, the first casualty within the British Railways fleet was 48616 in October 1960. It should be remembered that several locomotives were lost at sea on their way to war service when their transport ships were sunk by enemy action. ***Strathwood Library Collection***

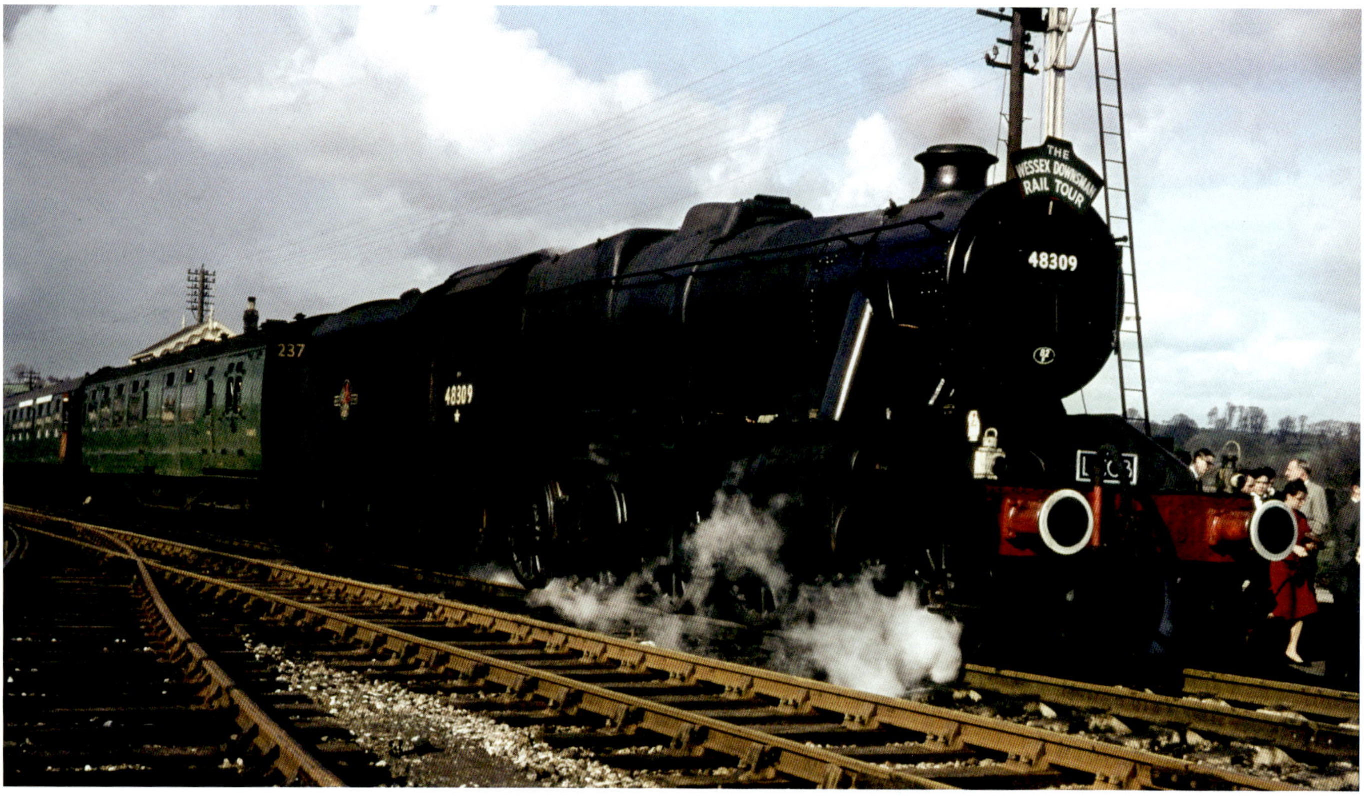

During 1955 two Stanier 8Fs, 48309 seen here on the Somerset & Dorset at Shepton Mallet on 4 April 1965 and 48707 were specially fitted with steam heating equipment with hoses at the tender end only in order that the pair could work a Royal Train over the Central Wales line. ***Late Vincent Heckford/Strathwood Library Collection***

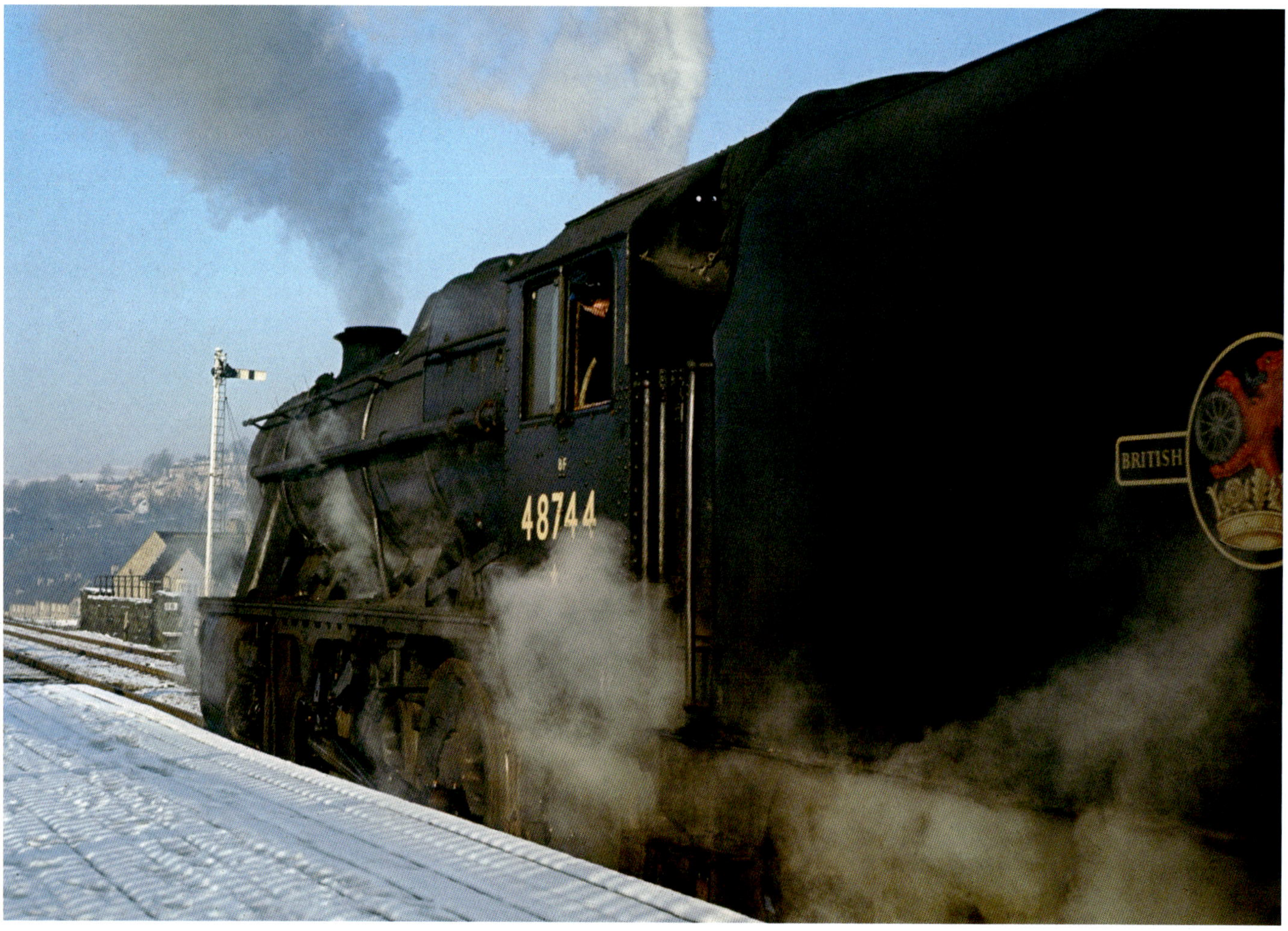

The numbering history of 48744 seen drifting through Hathersage in the winter of 1966 is interesting. When built at Darlington in 1946 it was taken into stock as an LNER locomotive in their classification as an O6. This batch was quickly renumbered in 1947 under Thompson's new scheme, then ironically transferred to the LMS who gave the batch their own numbers also in 1947. With Nationalisation in 1948 a further renumbering took place again, it must have been confusing for early spotters! ***Win Wall/Strathwood Library Collection***

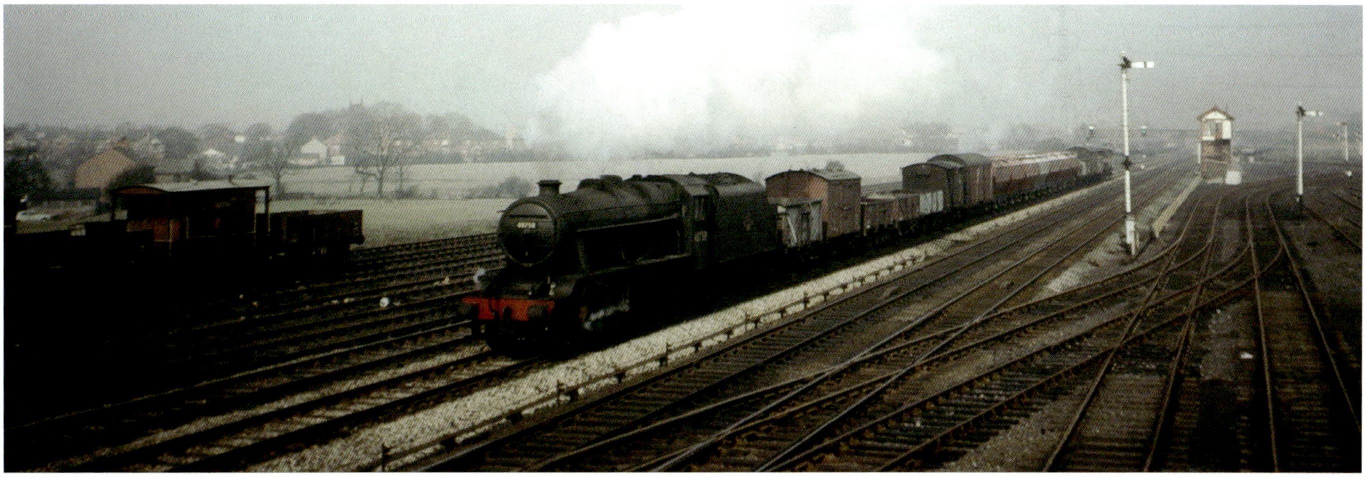

One of Doncaster's build of 8Fs 48758 passes Farrington in April 1965. This particular locomotive would be withdrawn by christmas 1967 and quickly broken up the following March. ***Chris Forrest***

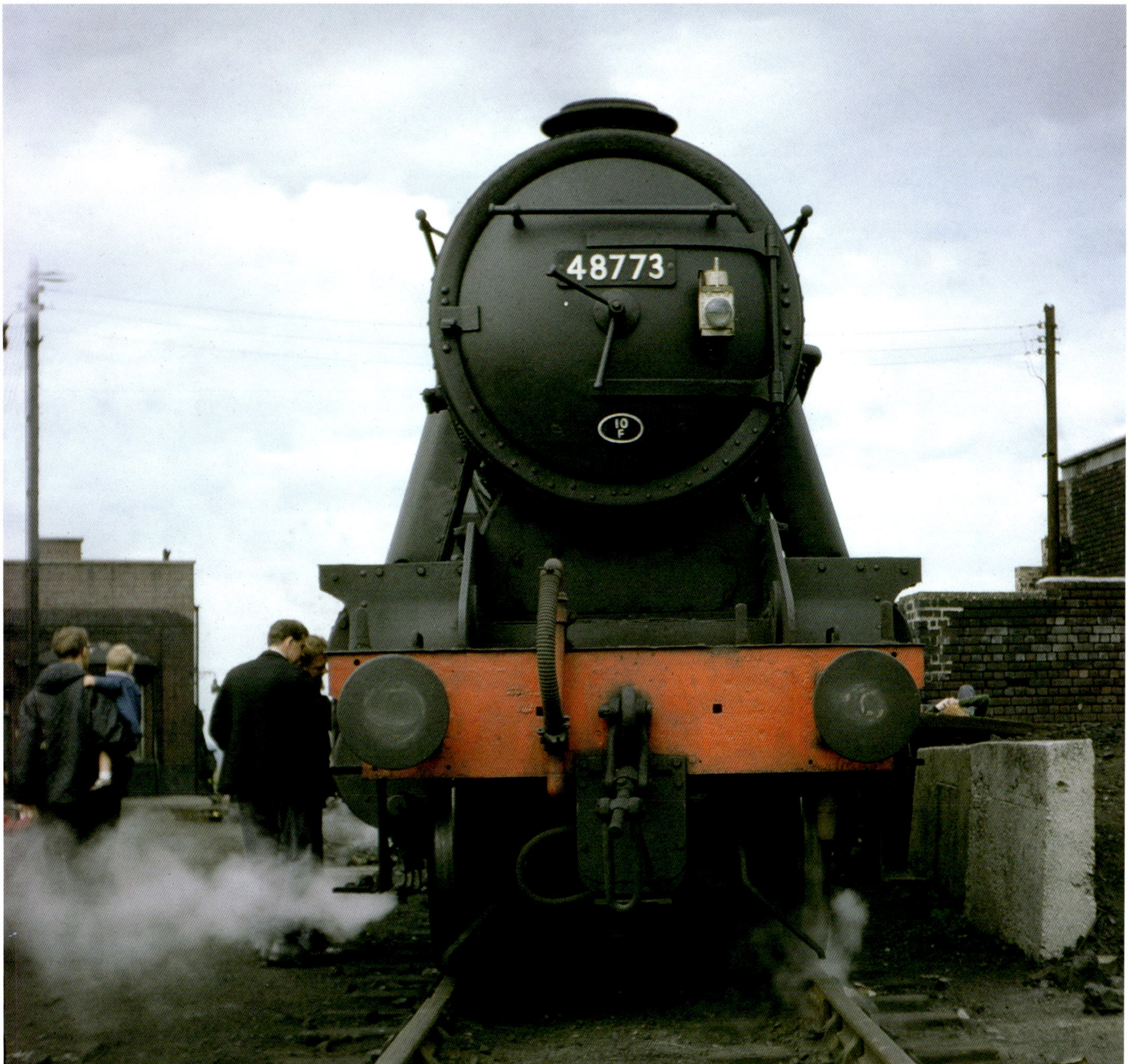

Of the three repatriated War Department 8Fs, 48773 seen at Rose Grove 3 August 1968 also lays claim to several numbers in its career. Built by North British it became LMS 8233 in 1940, and when transferred into national service it became WD 307. Sent overseas in 1941 to Iran it took the identity of their State Railways No. 41-109. Return to the UK as WD 70307 followed in 1952, when it was taken to Derby for overhaul emerging as WD 500 and sent to the Longmoor Military Railway and later Bicester. It was among the three engines absorbed into British Railways stock in 1957 as 48773. In preservation it has adopted its former LMS guise as 8233 for a number of years. ***Mick Farrer***

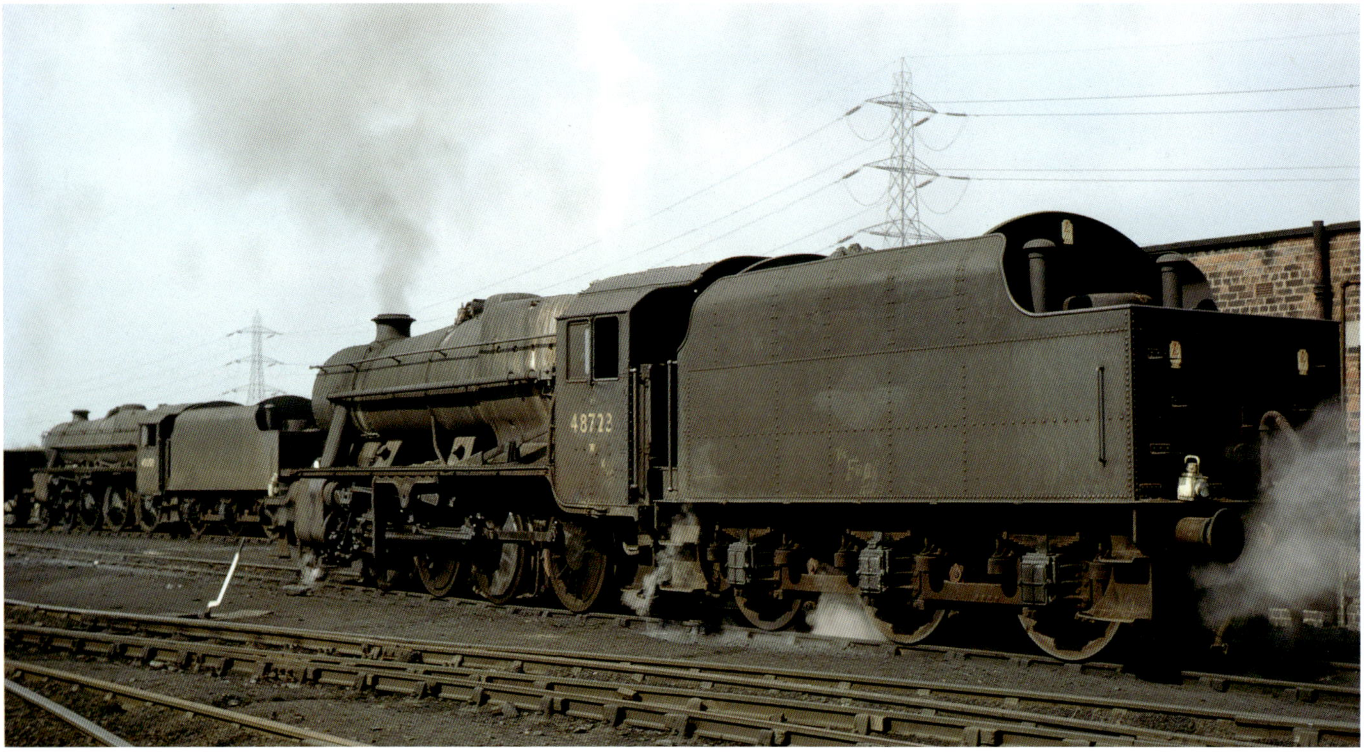

The standard 8F tenders have been constructed variously with both riveted construction and welded methods through the years. All of the Southern Railway built locomotives were initially built with welded tenders this Brighton example 48723 has acquired a riveted tender in its travels by the end of its days at Heaton Mersey in April 1968. ***John Gill***

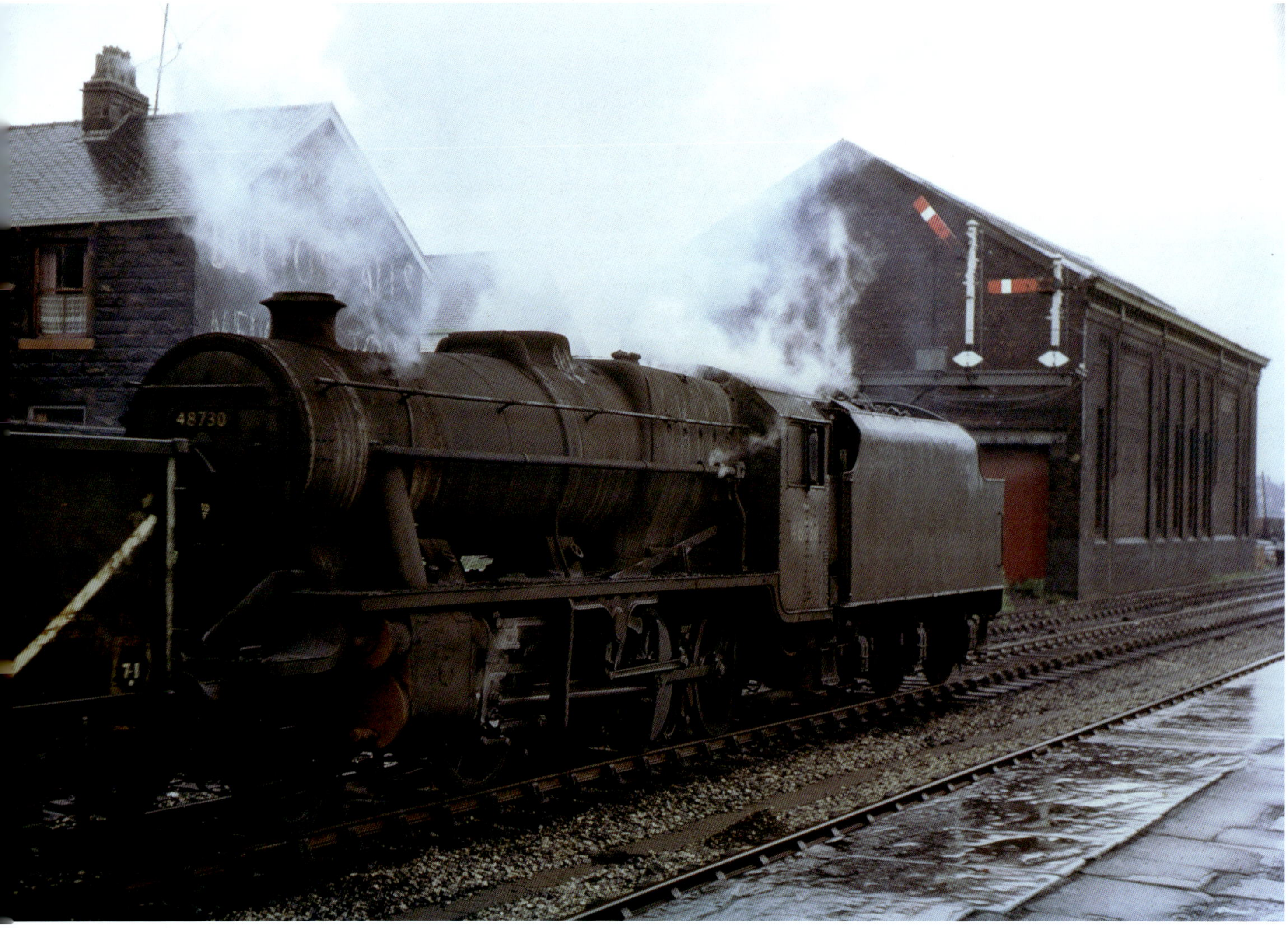

Darlington built 48730 working tender first through Rose Grove in the rain on 3 July 1968 has been switched from a riveted tender to a welded one since it was built. ***Jerry Beddows***

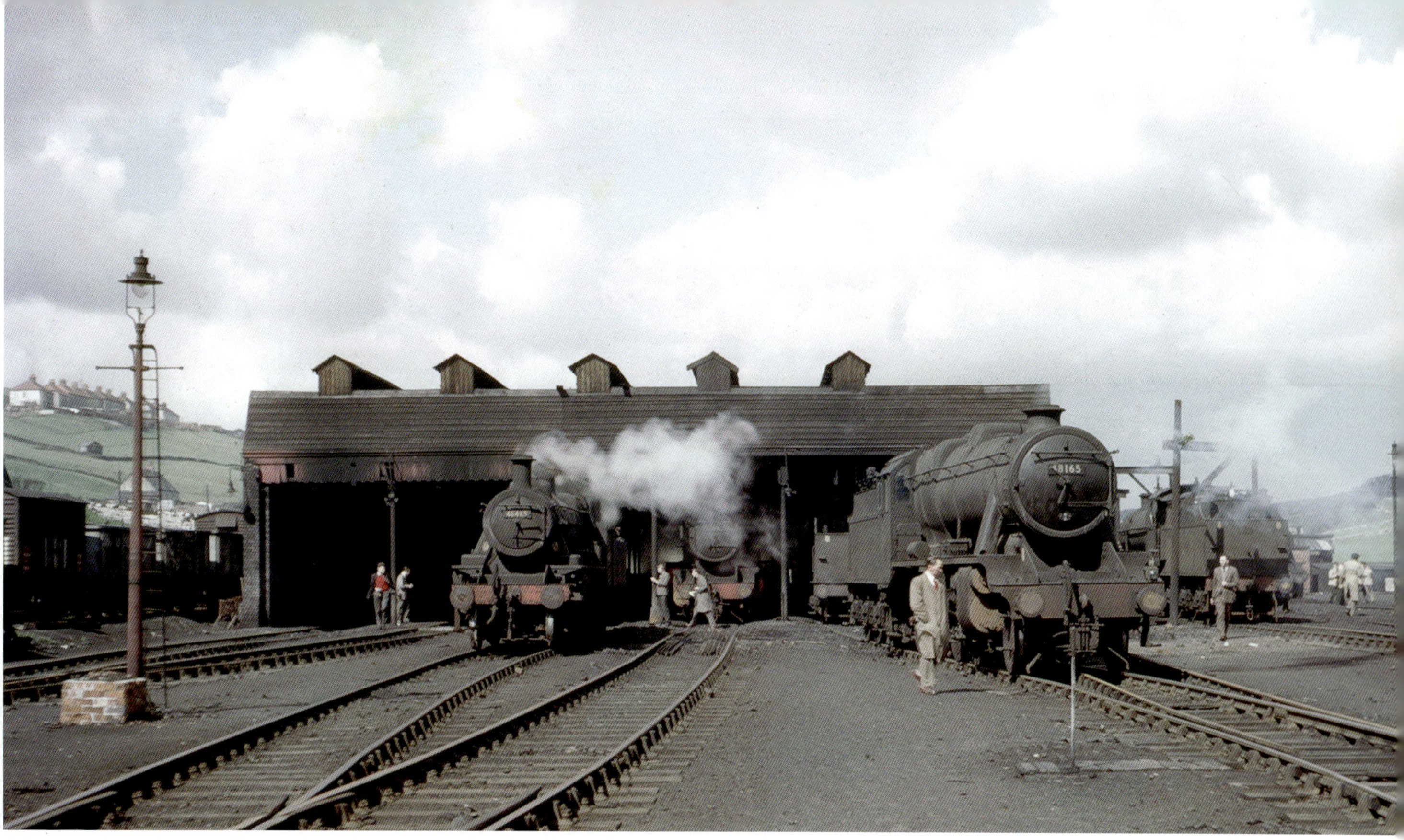

In the late 1950s a number of Jubilees originally paired with the Fowler type of 3500 gallon narrow tenders were exchanged with Stanier 8F 4000 gallon tenders, such as 48165 on shed at Buxton in 1964. ***Win Wall/Strathwood Library Collection***

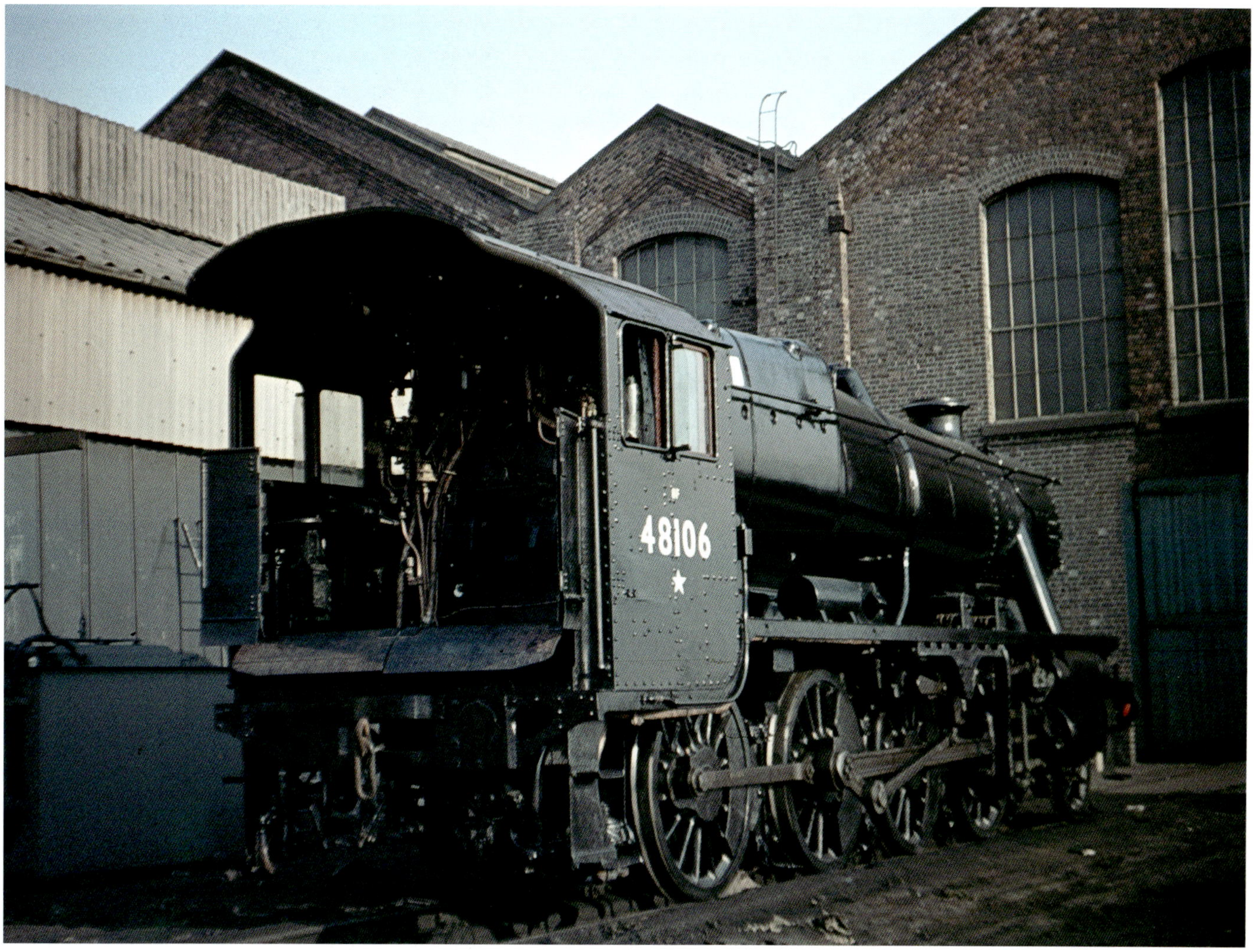

Ex works at Crewe in April 1965 and awaiting pairing up with the next available tender was 48106 which shows how class members often swapped designs. ***Noel Marrison***

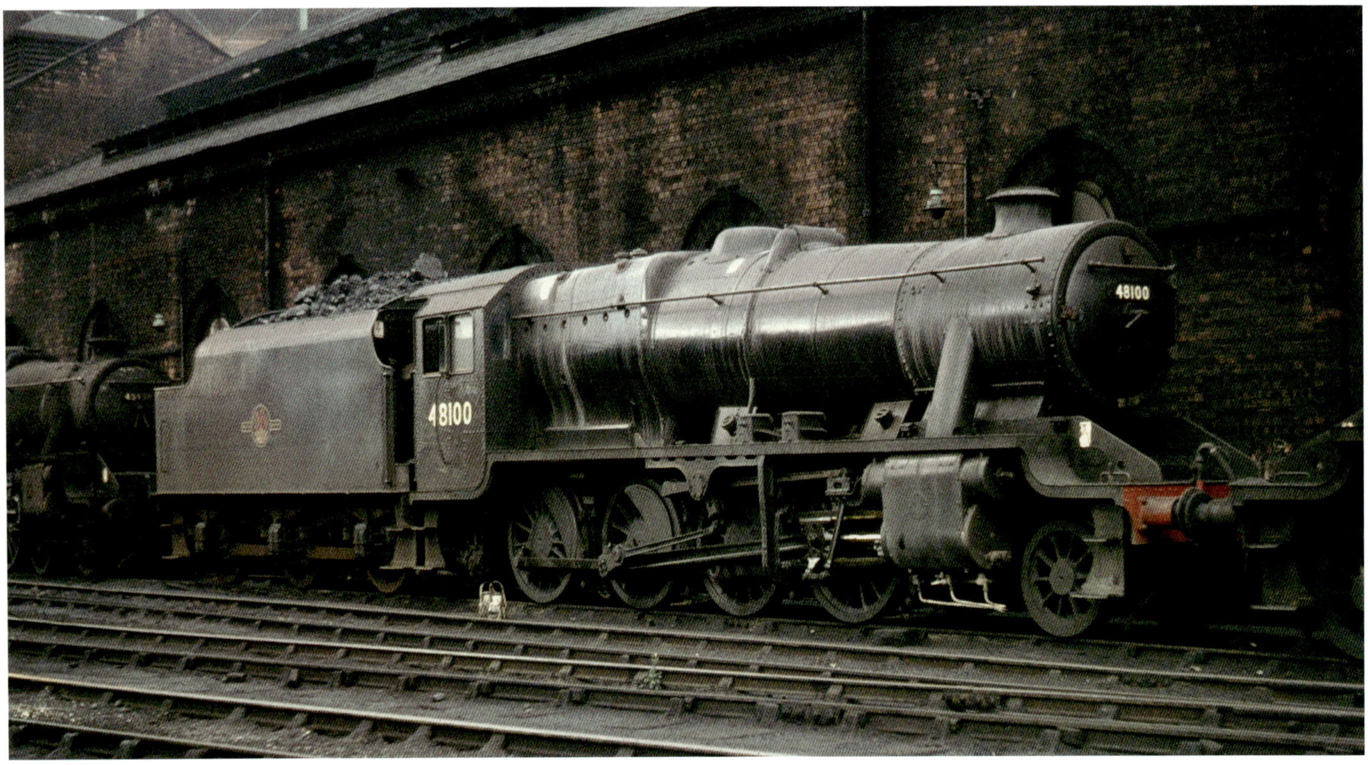

Having been most likely outshopped last by Darlington Works after overhaul was 48100 at Bristol Barrow Road in 1964 wearing the former North Eastern Railway's works favoured larger numbers. ***Strathwood Library Collection***

During the 1950s a number of the former Swindon built locomotives were transferred to the Western Region. Swindon being Swindon, it was decided to modify these engines and remove the LMS style of vacuum ejectors in front of the cab to their own favoured type with a shorter cranked exhaust pipe from the smoke box, as seen here on 48410 at Old Oak Common on 20 March 1960. ***Frank Hornby***

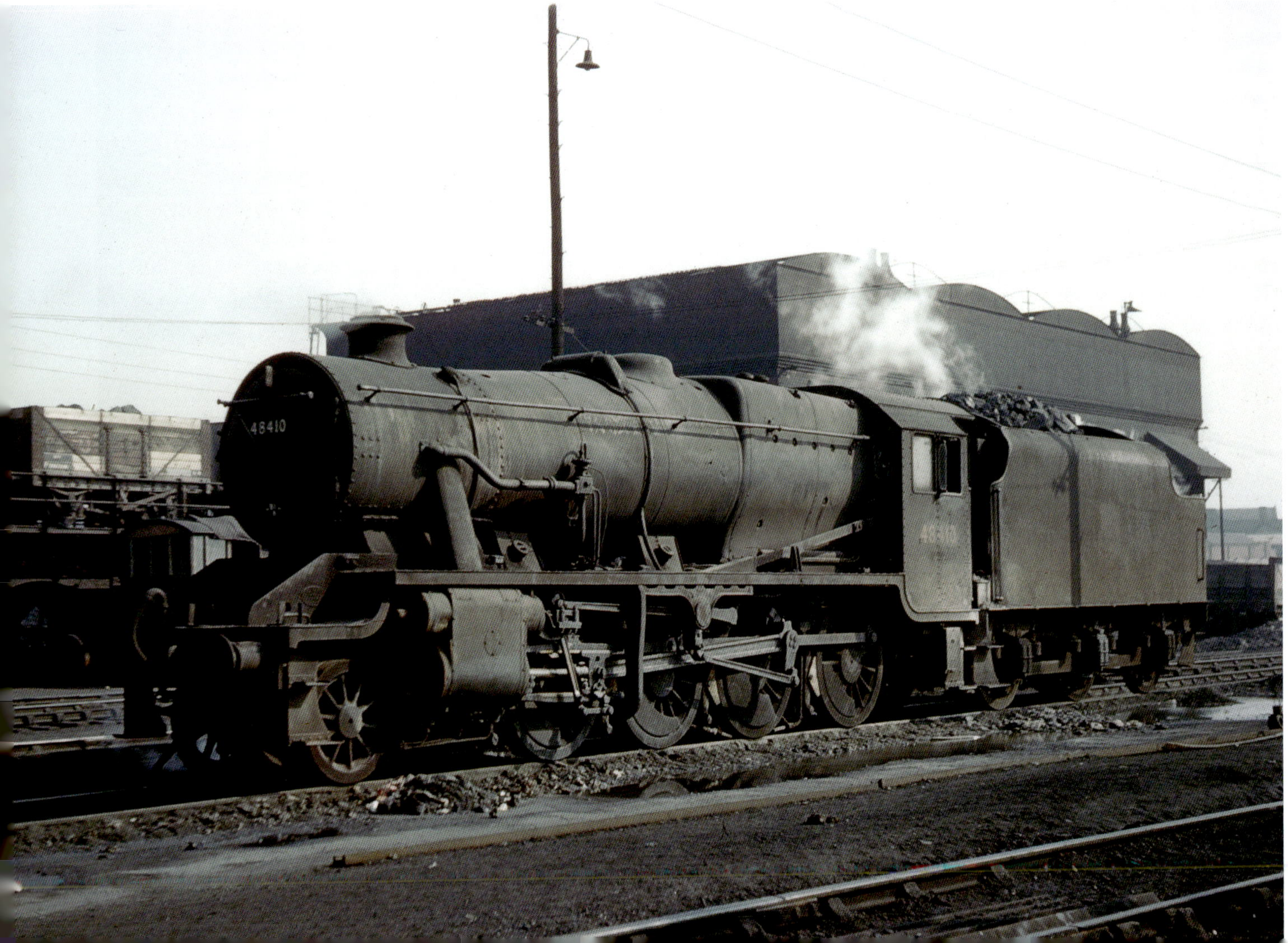

Rebuilt Scots

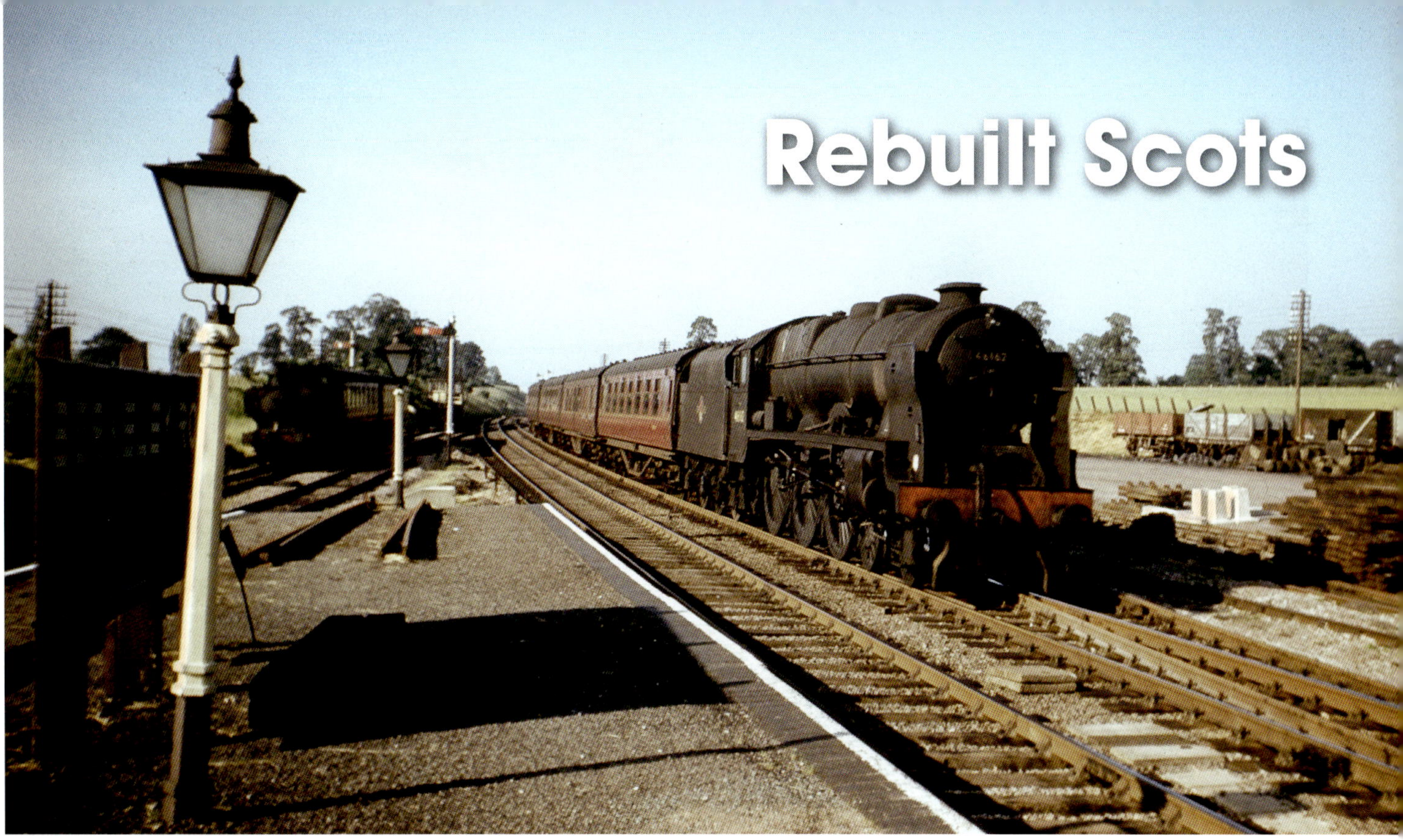

Rolling southbound into Berkeley Road in 1962 we find 46162 Queen's Westminster Rifleman in its last year in service. ***Gerald Peacock***

In August of the following year fellow rebuilt Scot 46126 Royal Army Service Corps makes a brief stop at Aylesbury Town on Great Central service. This locomotive previously carried the name Sanspareil recalling the Rainhill trials until June 1936. ***Win Wall/Strathwood Library Collection***

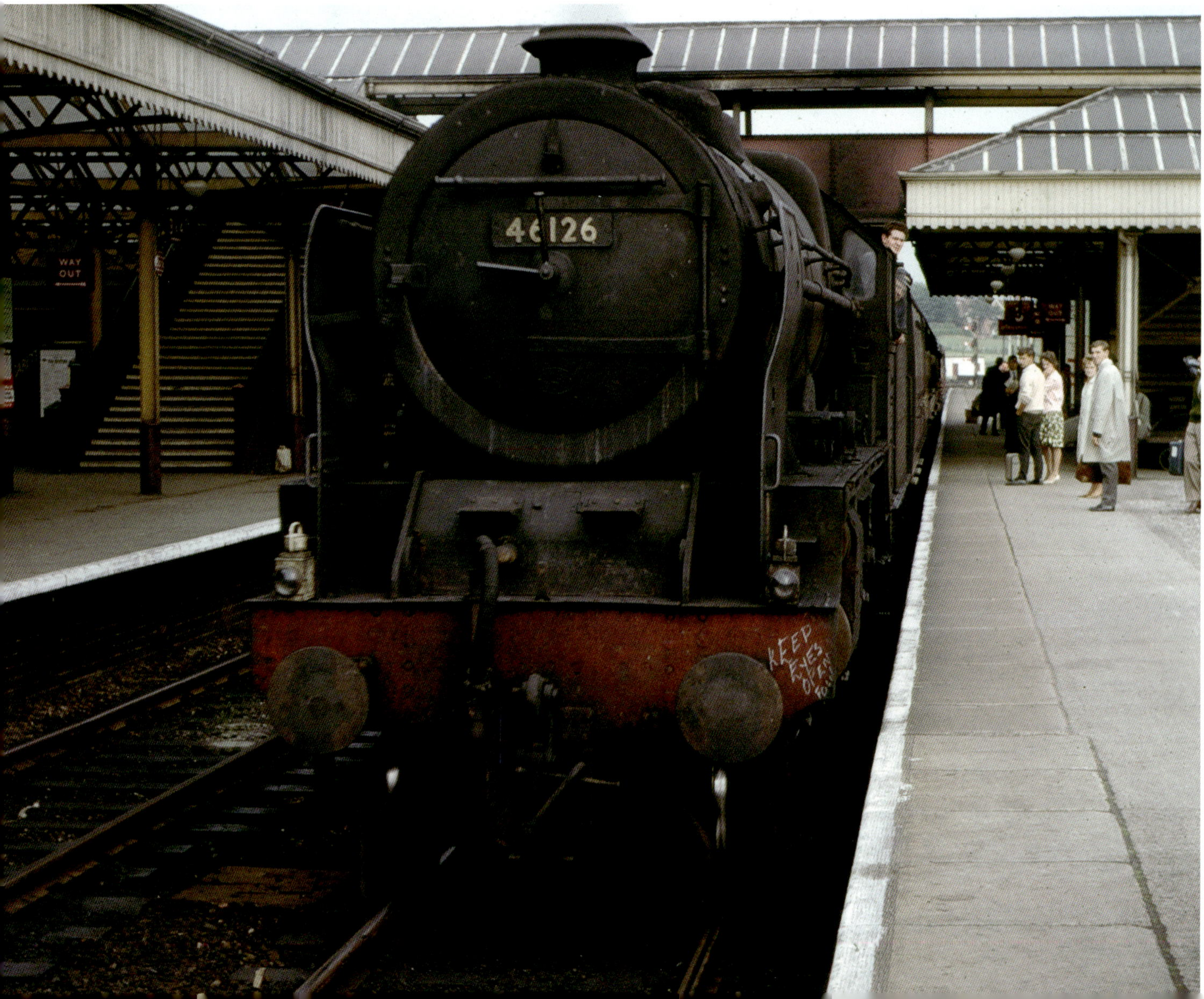

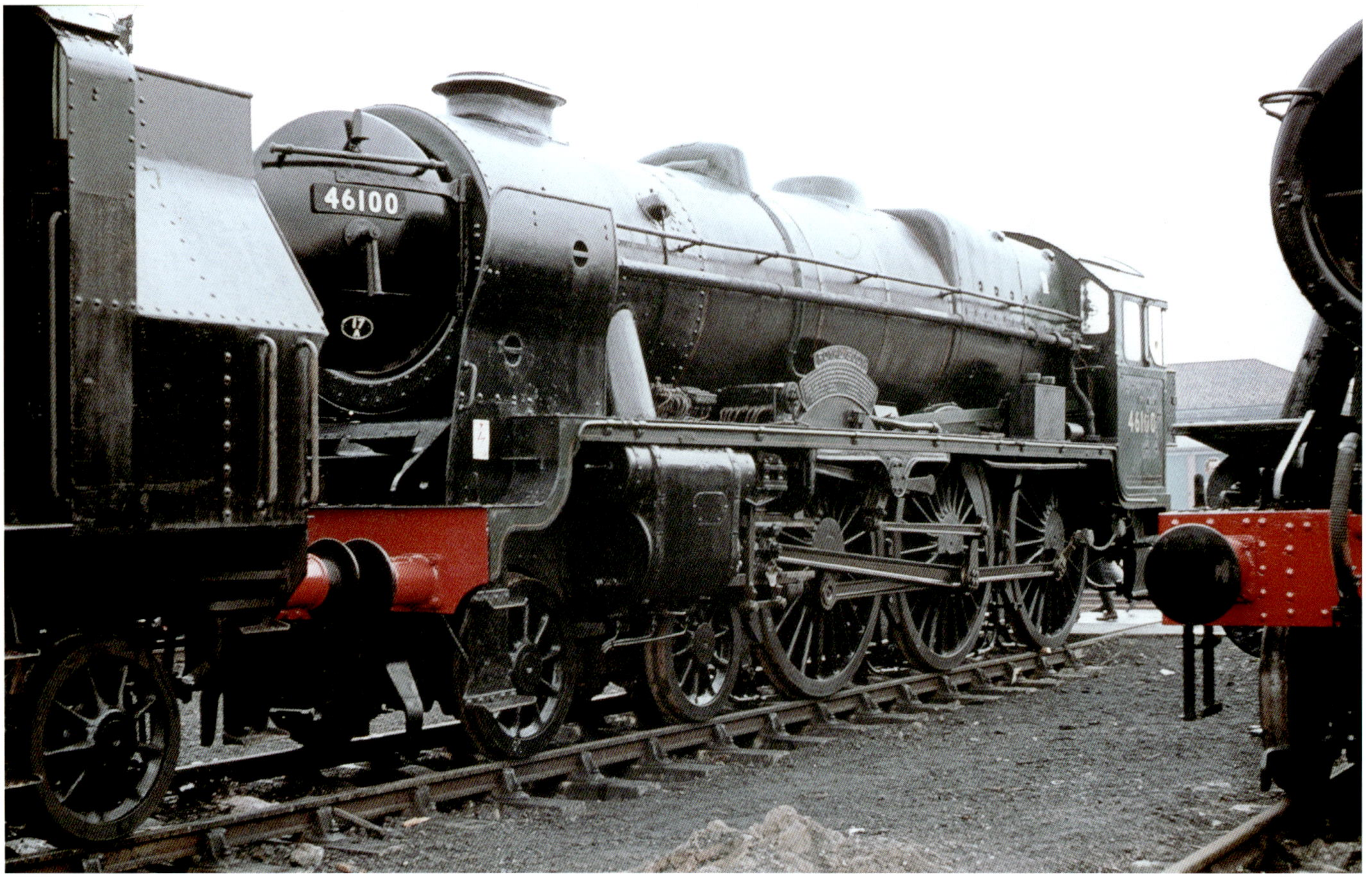

The original 6100 Royal Scot was built to a design by Sir Henry Fowler in 1927. Then in 1933, 6152 swapped identities with 6100 and masqueraded as Royal Scot as an exhibit at the Chicago World Fair across the Atlantic in America. Whilst in the USA the locomotive made a successful 11,194 mile tour of the country recalled on the plaque affixed under the engine's nameplate seen here. The locomotives did not revert to their original identities even after being rebuilt when 46152 was dealt with in 1945 and 46100 followed in 1950. The impostor is seen at Crewe awaiting a return to traffic in the late 1950s. ***Strathwood Library Collection***

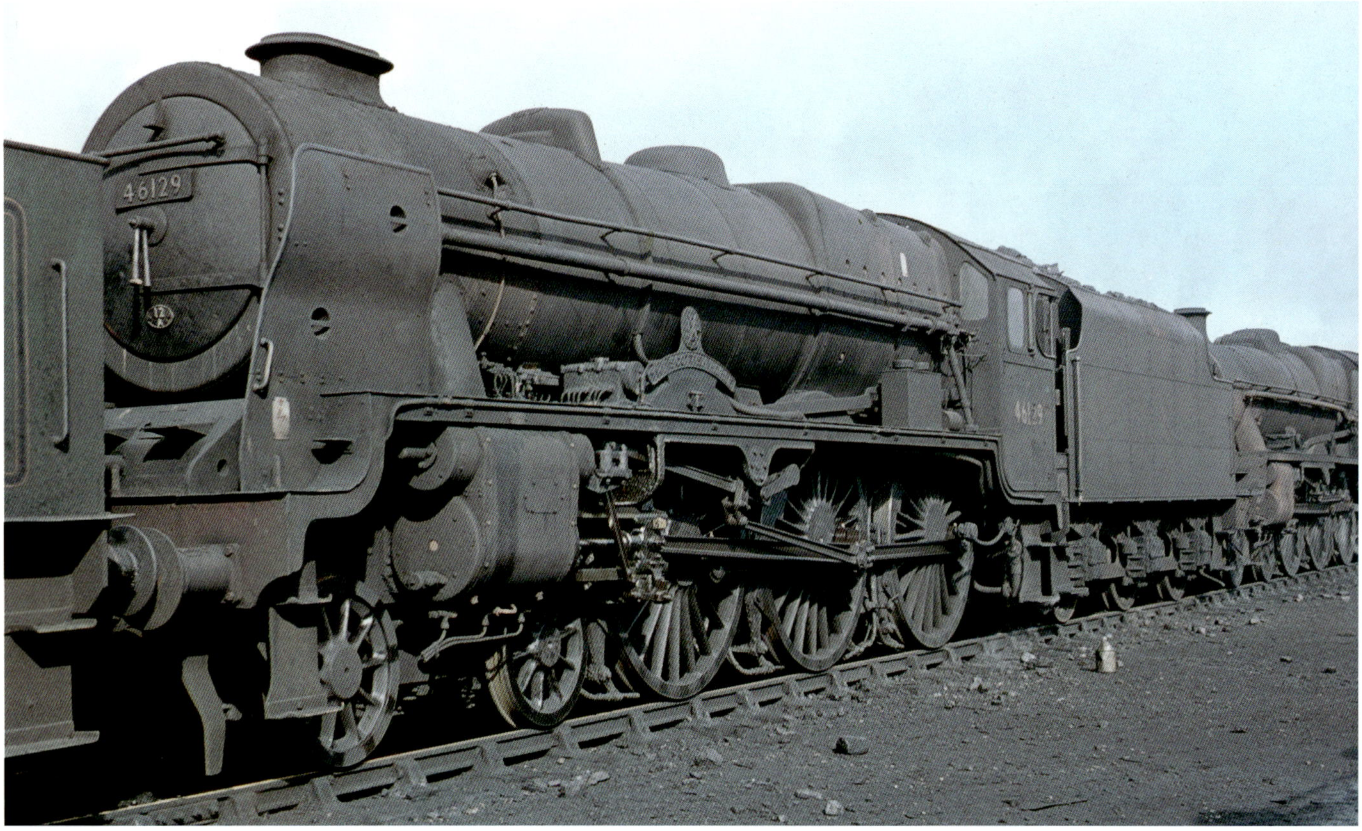

Built by North British in Glasgow in 1927 and originally named Comet, another change of identity to become The Scottish Horse in 1935 for 46129 seen in the lines again at Crewe at the end of the 1950s. ***Strathwood Library Collection***

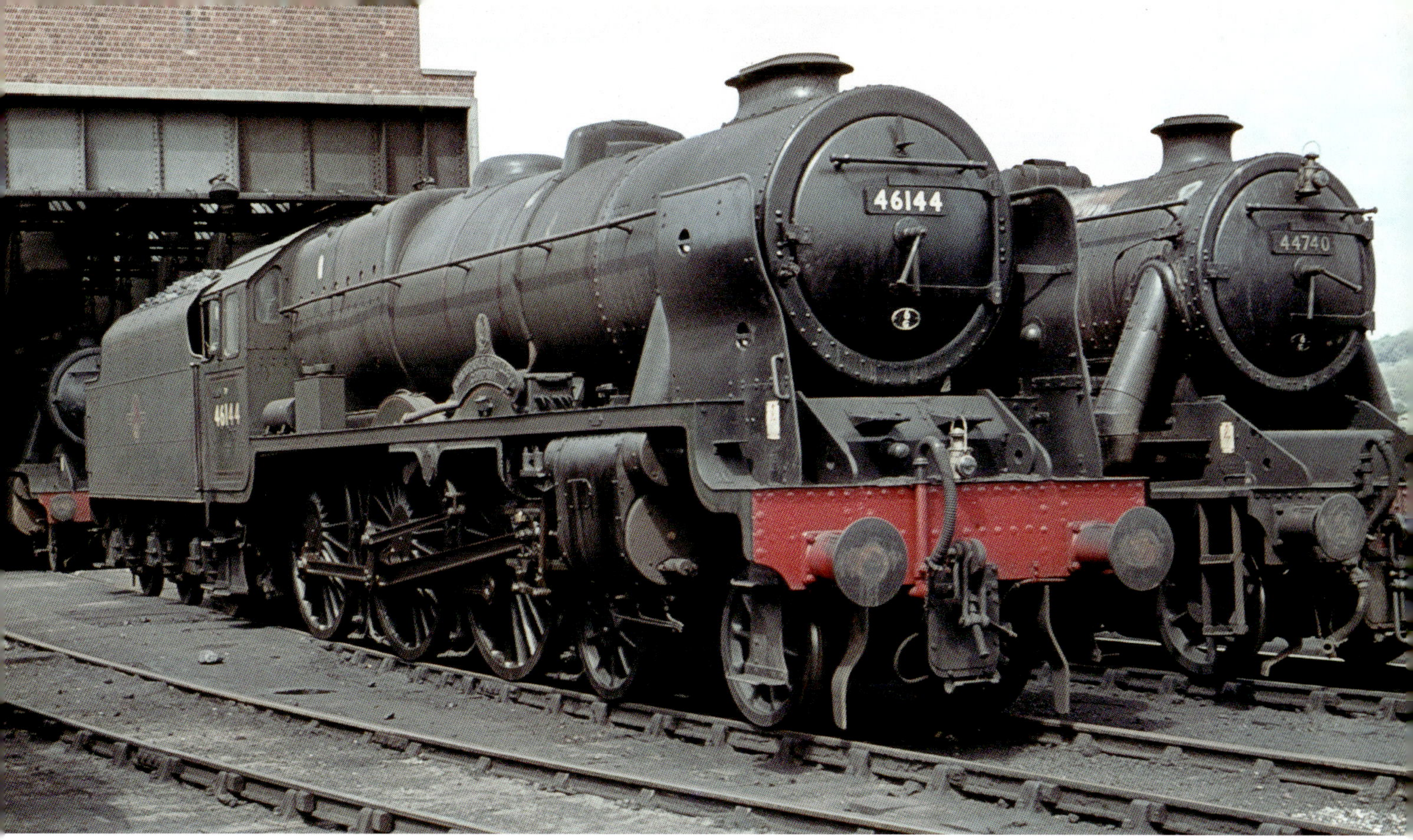

The rebuilding of the class was given the go ahead in late 1942 for the first twenty Royal Scots to be rebuilt with Stanier's developments. Although the war meant materials were at a premium, many of the engines had been in service for a dozen or more years and their boilers and cylinders would require renewal. Couple this with problems over leaking smoke boxes it made sense to make the best of what was there and rebuild the engines in most need of attention. It would be 1945 when 46144 Honourable Artillery Company seen at Llandudno Junction in 1962 was so treated. ***Strathwood Library Collection***

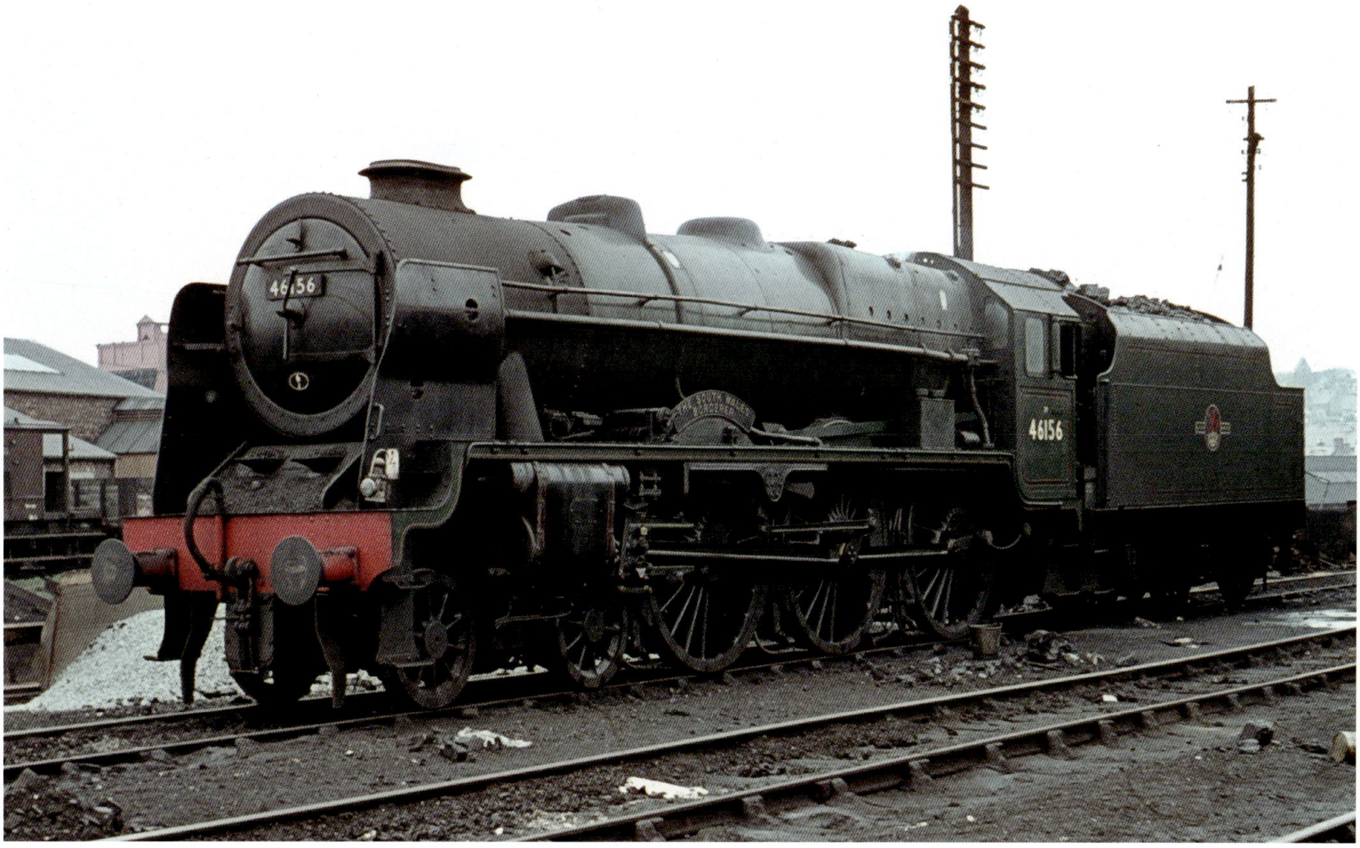

Among the last to be rebuilt would be 46156 The South Wales Borderer standing on shed at Holyhead in 1960. The honour of the last original Royal Scot would be 46137 The Prince of Wales's Volunteers South Lancashire which returned to traffic in March 1955. This work being carried out in the reigns of both Ivatt and Riddles as successive CMEs. ***Strathwood Library Collection***

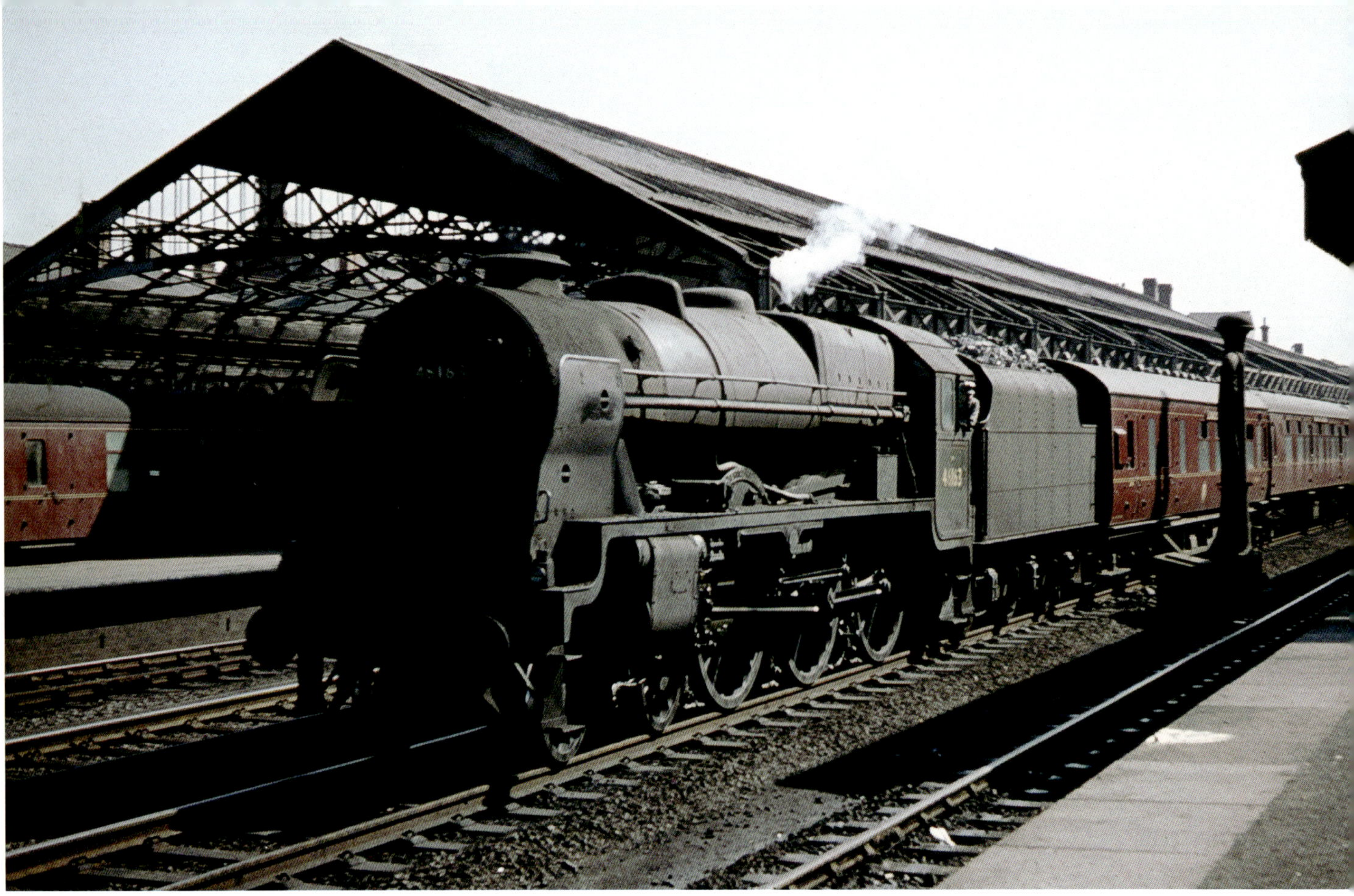

Twenty of the class were built in the LMS's own workshops at Derby including 46163 Civil Service Rifleman here passing through Stafford in 1959. ***Strathwood Library Collection***

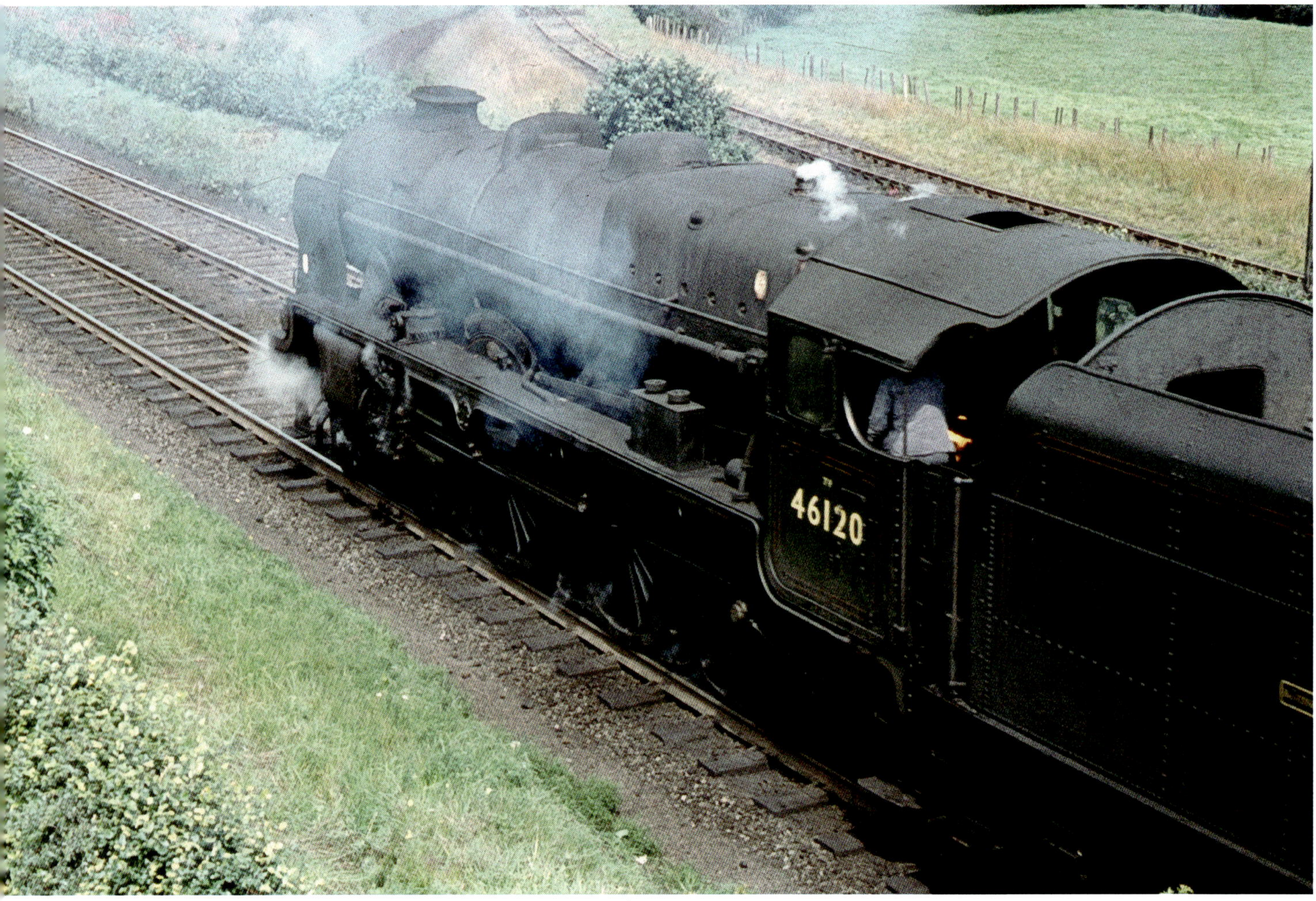

As part of the extensive rebuilds, new tenders were provided giving 9 tons coal capacity which the crew of 46120 Royal Inniskilling Fusilier seem to have great faith in, their engine heading away from Beattock in 1958 with a much depleted tender. ***Strathwood Library Collection***

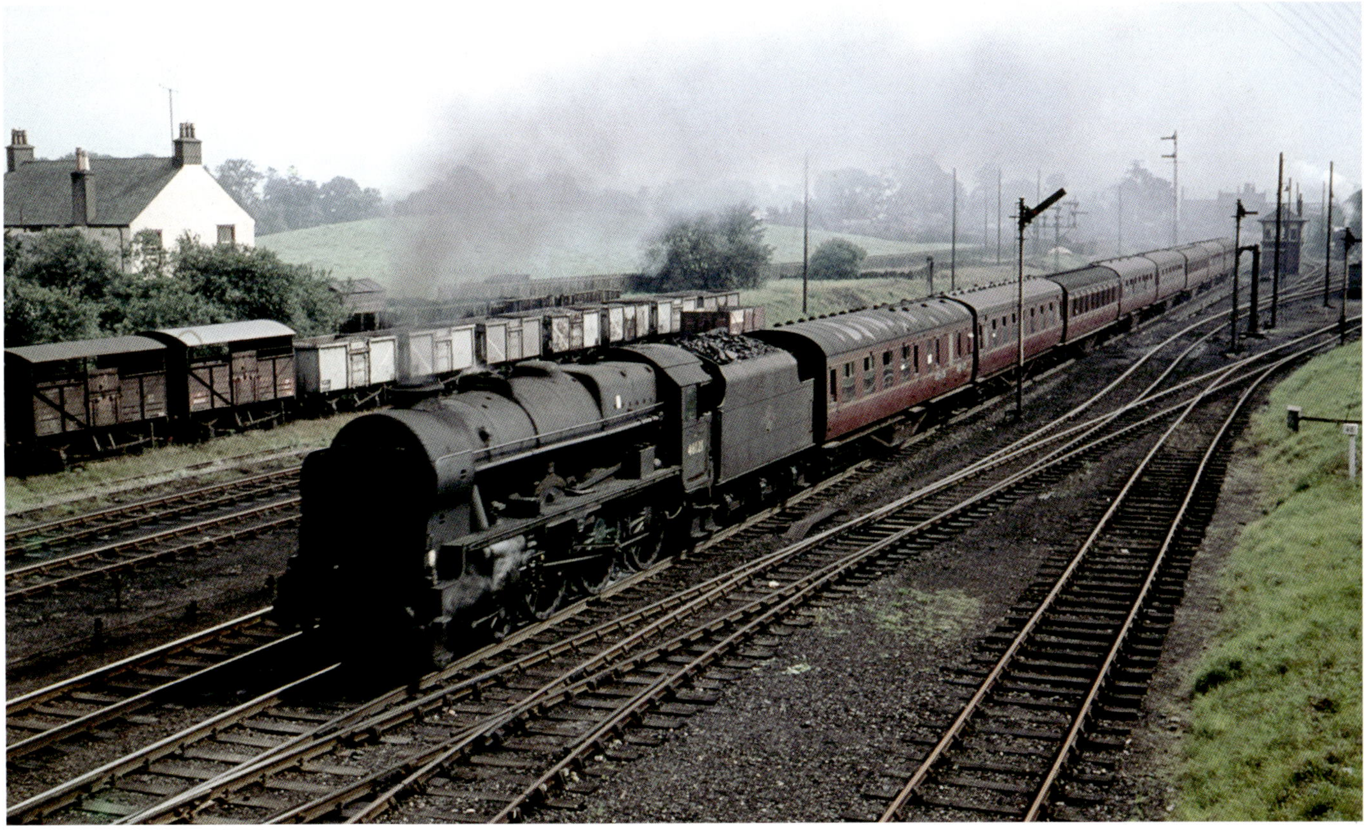

Also heading away from Beattock in the same year was the next built 46121 Highland Light Infantry, City of Glasgow Regiment with a healthier stock of coal going forward. ***Strathwood Library Collection***

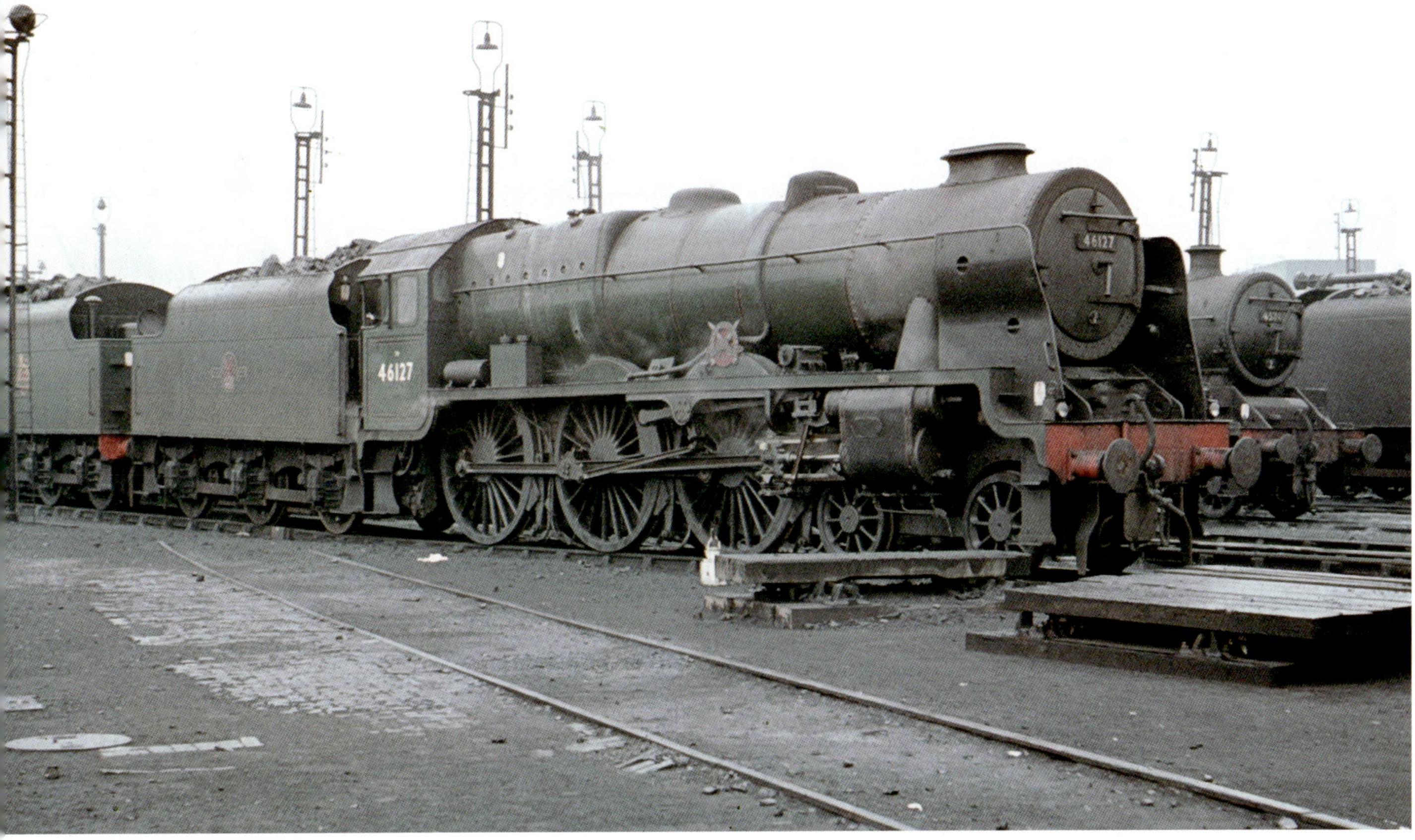

With a distinctive nameplate 46127 Old Contemptibles 1914 Aug 5 to Nov 22 waits patiently for the next action at Crewe around 1960. The name derives from a comment by the German Kaiser Wilhelm at the start of the First World War " It is my Royal and Imperial Command that you concentrate your energies for the immediate present upon one single purpose, and that is that you address all your skill and all the valour of my soldiers to exterminate first the treacherous English [and] walk over General French's contemptible little army" Sadly for the Germans The British Expeditionary Force held their ground valiantly. ***Strathwood Library Collection***

Lobsters and Camels

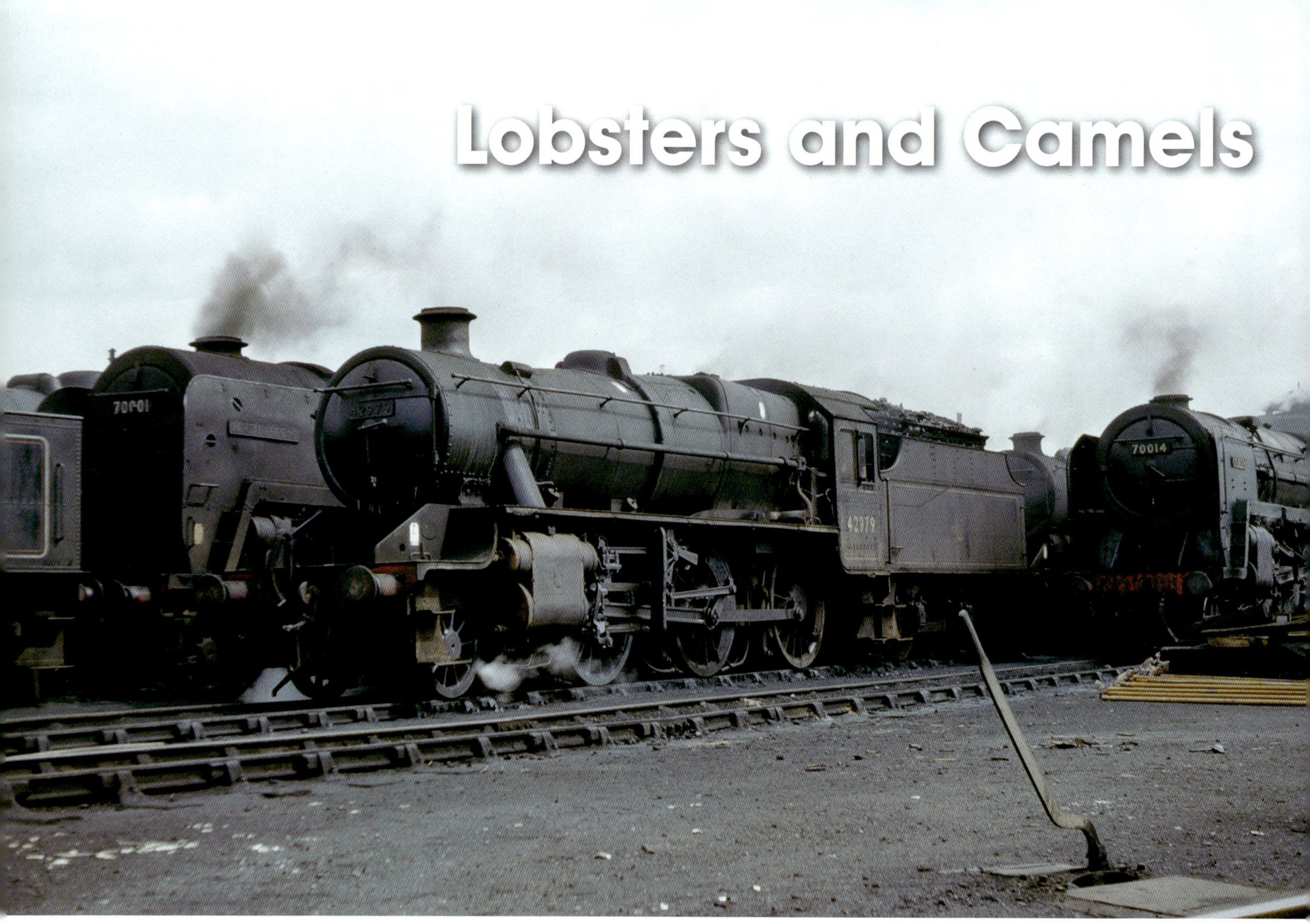

Although there were 245 mixed traffic Moguls already in successful service to a design by Hughes and Fowler, Stanier decided that when a need arose for a further build it would be to his own design and not to Horwich's Crabs. Built in four batches at Crewe between 1933 and 1934 they preceded the Black Fives which were to be far more successful as a design. Among the final order was 42979 sandwiched by Britannias at Willesden on 18 August 1963. ***Frank Hornby***

Running light engine through Guide Bridge in the early sixties was 42977 which would survive into 1966 and be among the last of the forty engines in service. ***Strathwood Library Collection***

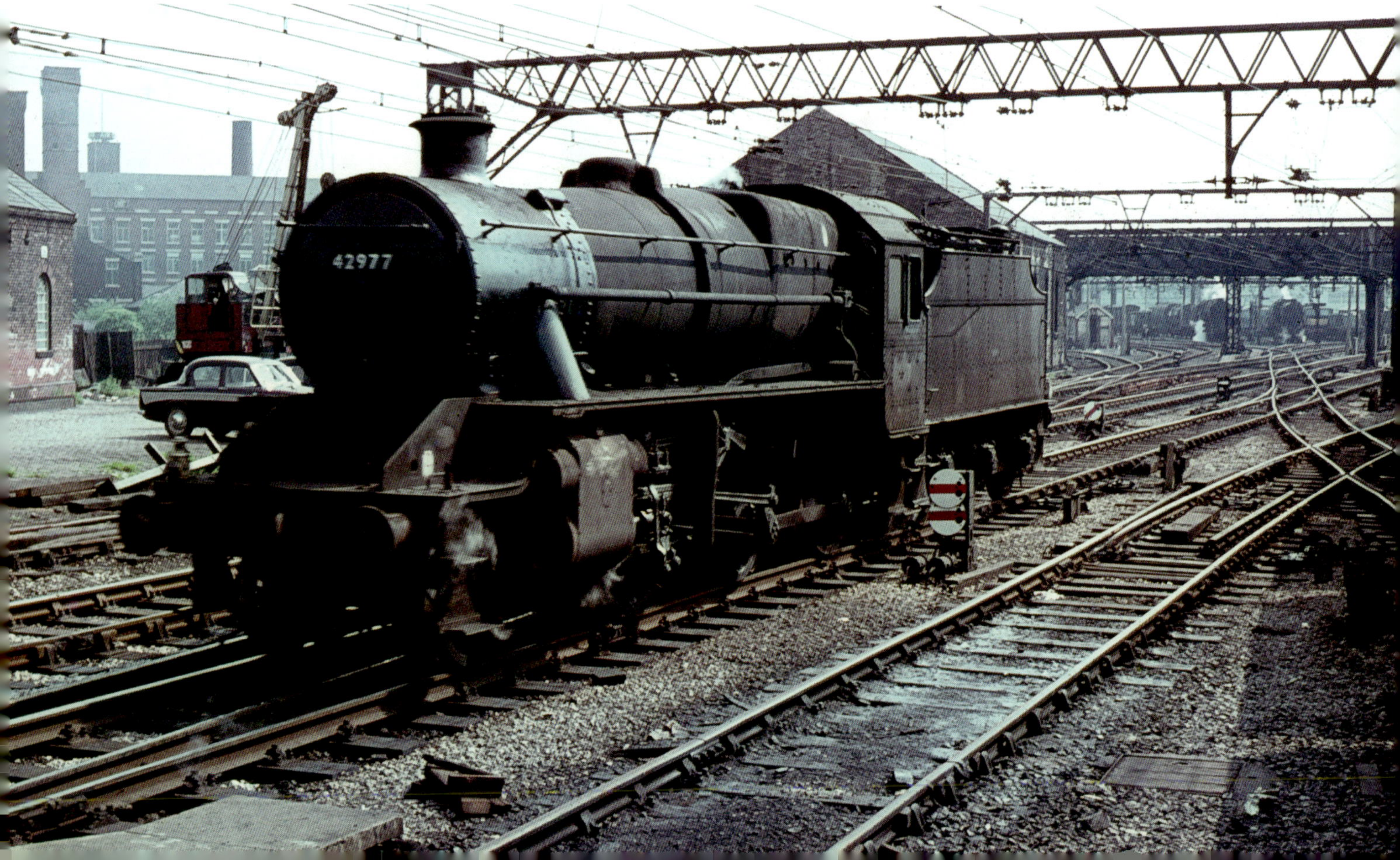

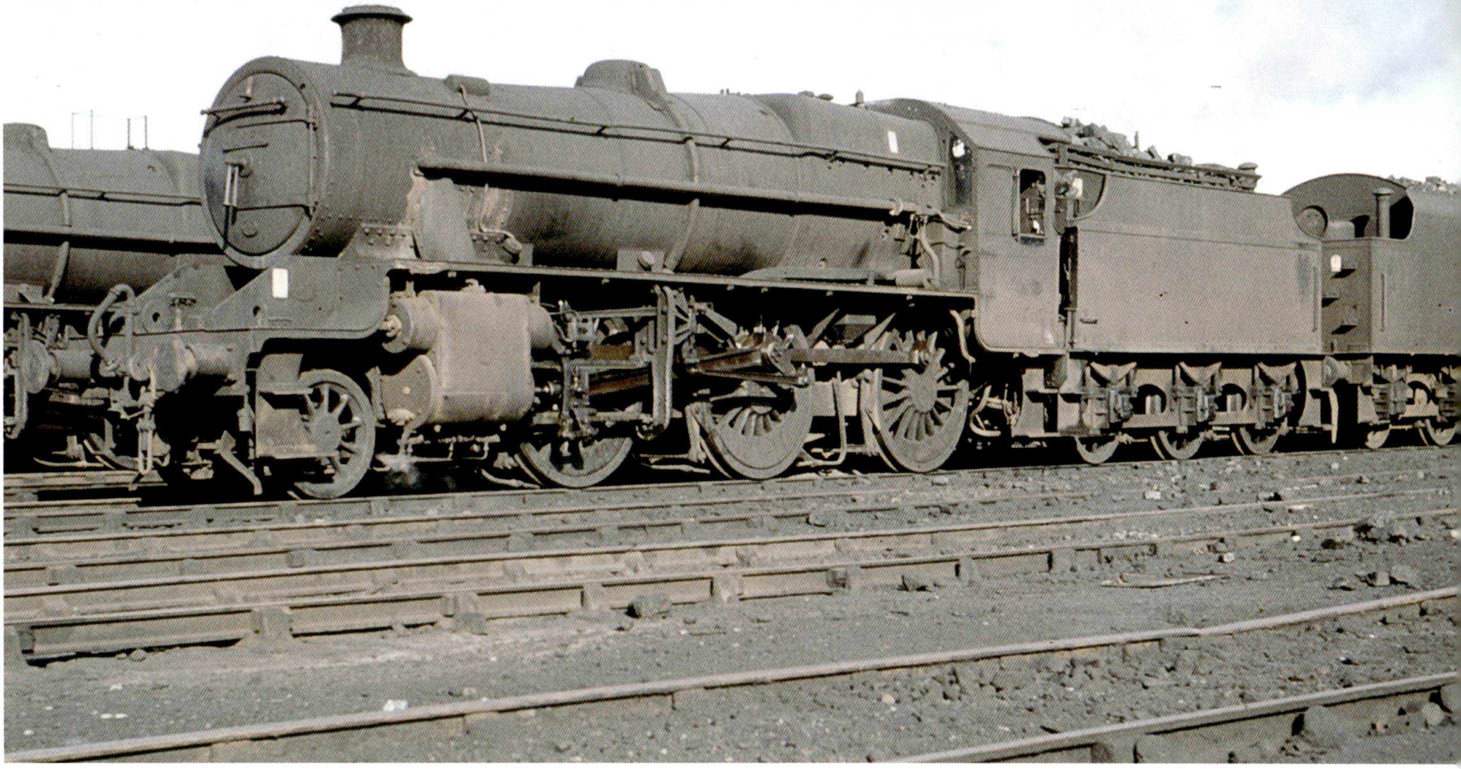

When first introduced the class had a distinctive tall dome and top feed which replaced the almost Great Western style which Stanier ordered to be removed. This was replaced by a quite large (in proportion) dome cover before giving way to the design seen in these pictures as typified by 42952 at Gorton in 1963. ***Strathwood Library Collection***

It was this unusual design of dome that led some LMS men to call the class Camels while others preferred Lobsters after the Horwich Crabs. Bringing the goods through Stafford in 1959 was 42950 which lasted until 1965, the first withdrawals starting in 1963. ***Strathwood Library Collection***

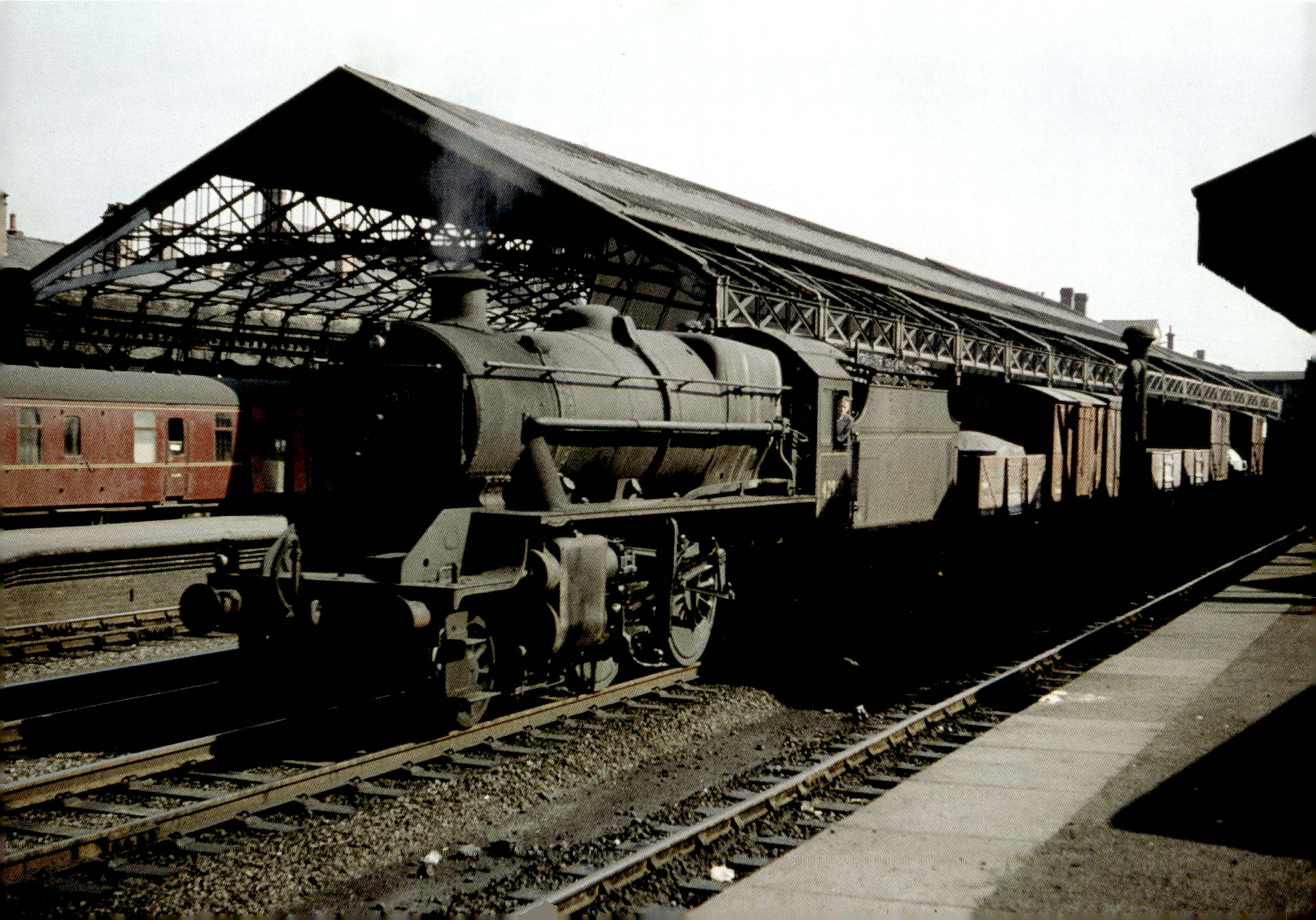

Semis

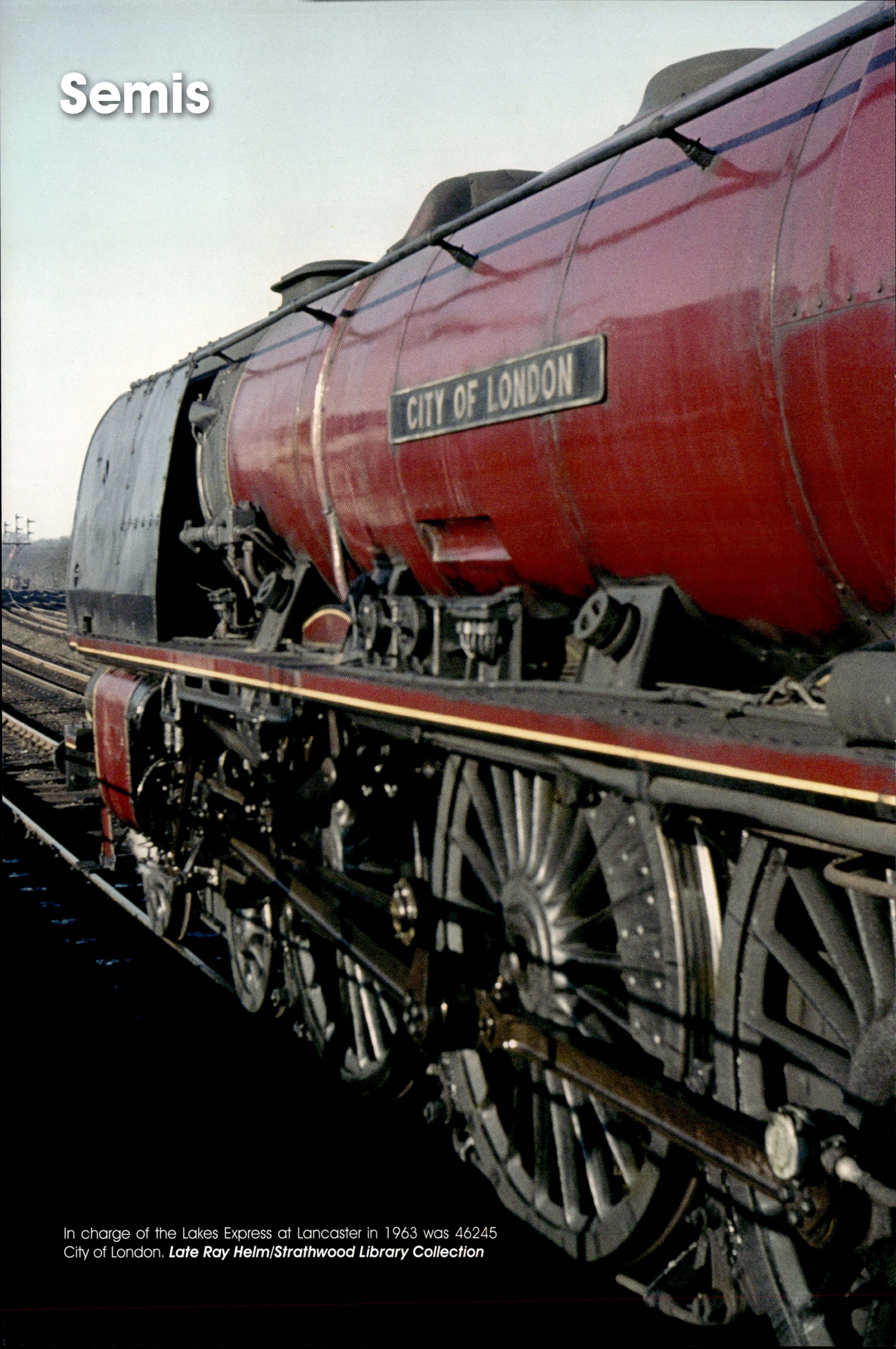

In charge of the Lakes Express at Lancaster in 1963 was 46245 City of London. ***Late Ray Helm/Strathwood Library Collection***

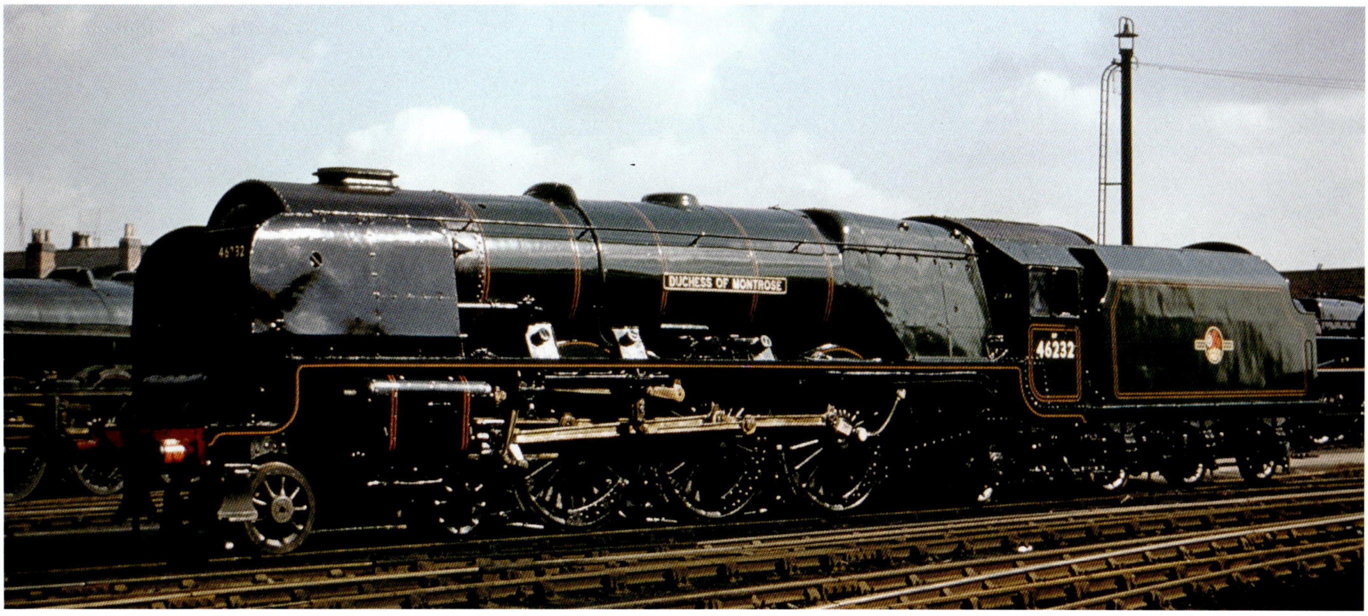

Sparkling ex paint shop at Crewe in 1959 was 46232 Duchess of Montrose in lined green which might be a bit too Swindon for Stanier himself. ***Strathwood Library Collection***

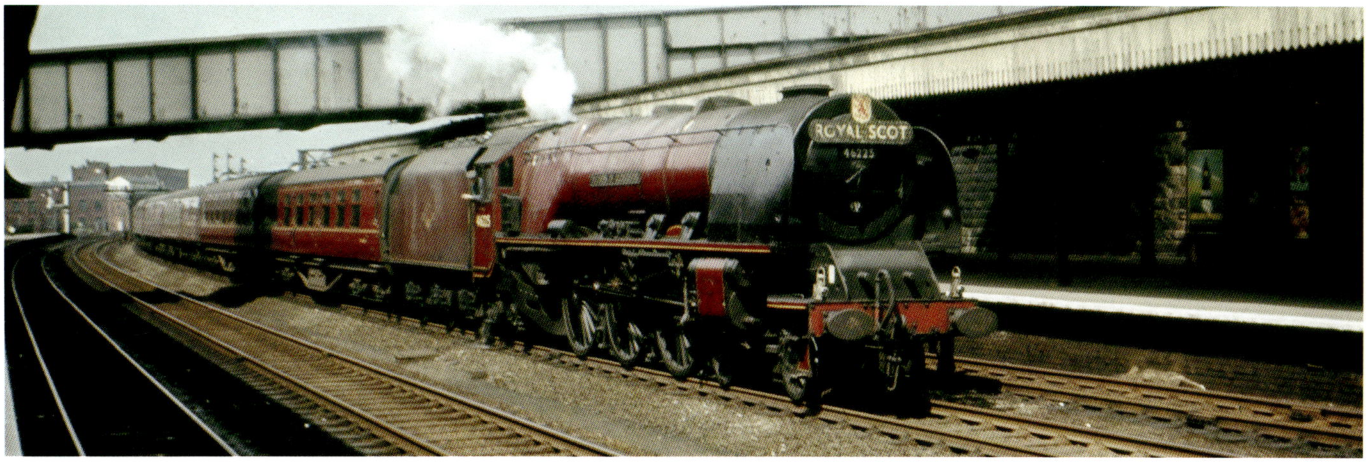

Bringing the Royal Scot through Lancaster in 1963 was 46225 Duchess of Gloucester in a perhaps more acceptable maroon livery. ***Late Ray Helm/Strathwood Library Collection***

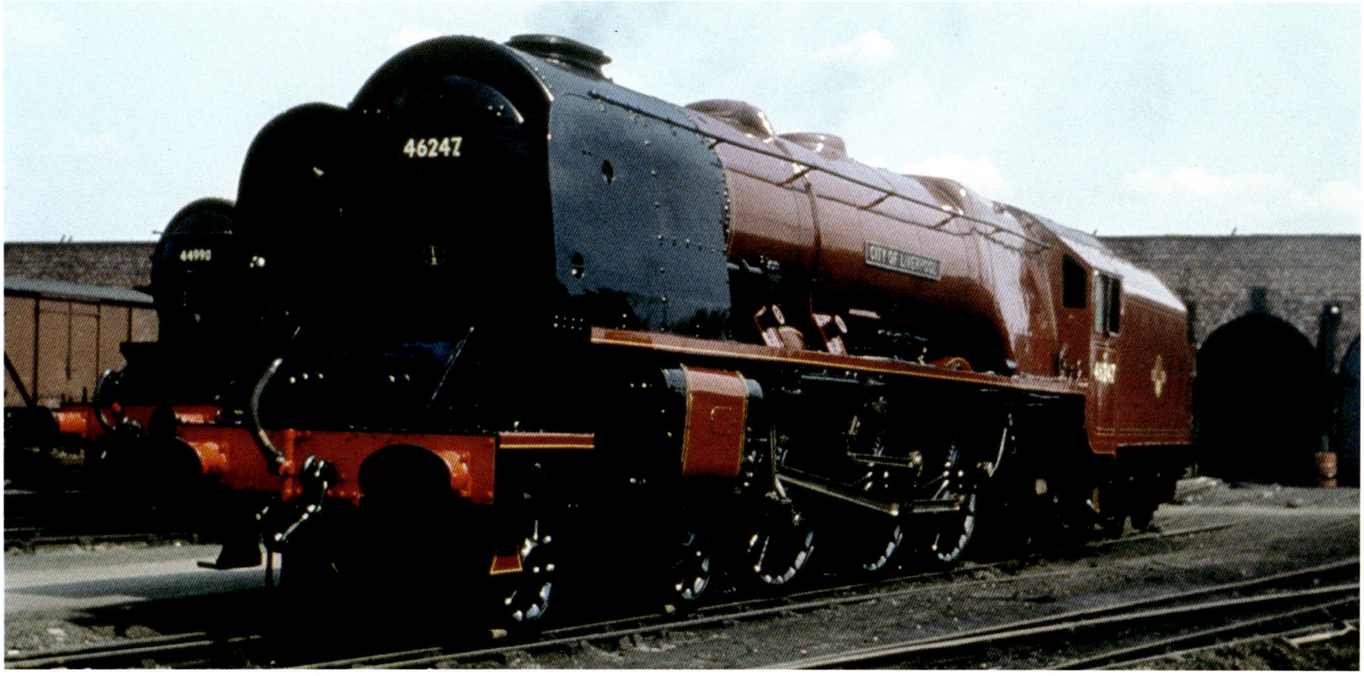

Also ex paint shop at Crewe around 1959 but in a brick red livery was 46247 City of Liverpool awaiting re-entry to service. ***Strathwood Library Collection***

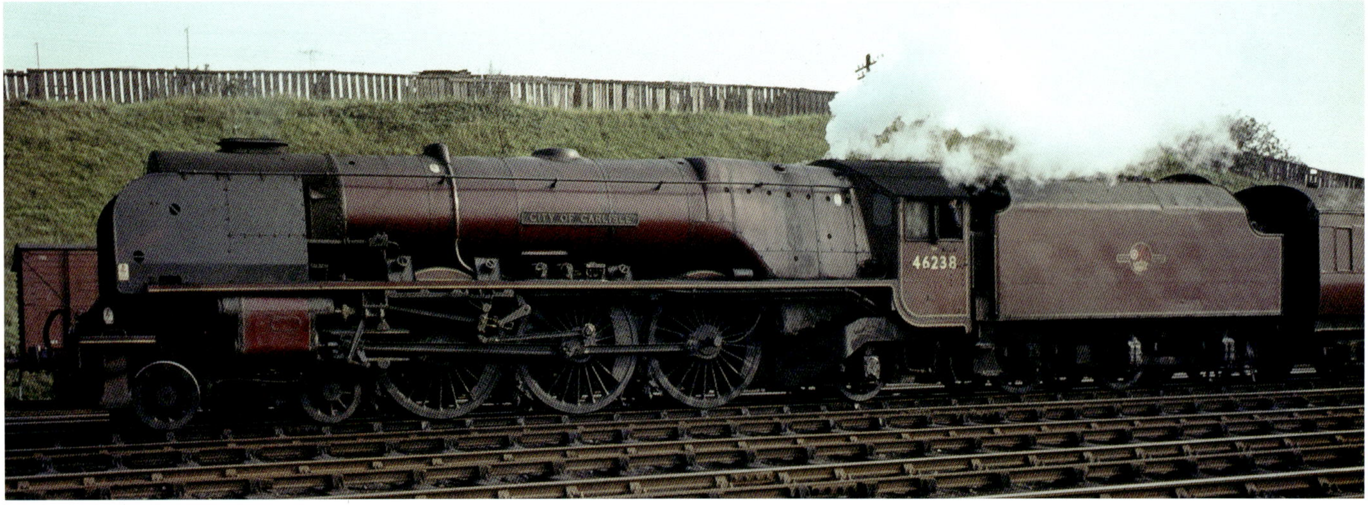

The differences within the class not only with the many livery variations and modifications is beyond the scope of this volume as we concentrate on the classes final few years of service. The distinctive gap on the footpate shows on the once streamlined 46238 City of Carlisle at the head of an empty stock working at Carnforth during 1963. ***Late Ray Helm/Strathwood Library Collection***

Relegated to freight workings by 1963 at Lancaster was 46233 Duchess of Sutherland which was among the non streamlined locomotives when built at Crewe in 1938. The more conventional filled in, stepped up footplate is clear in this view. ***Late Ray Helm/Strathwood Library Collection***

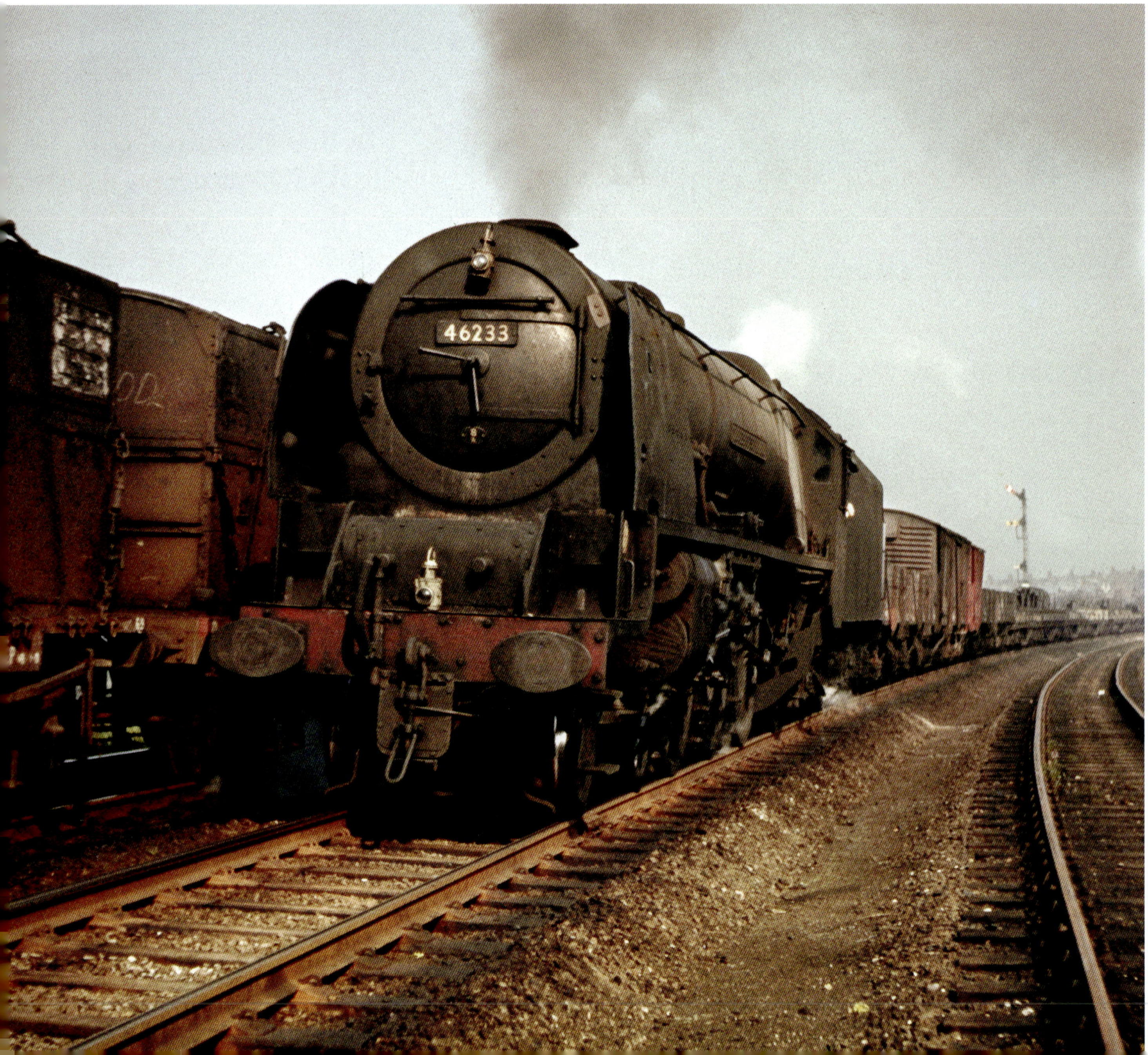

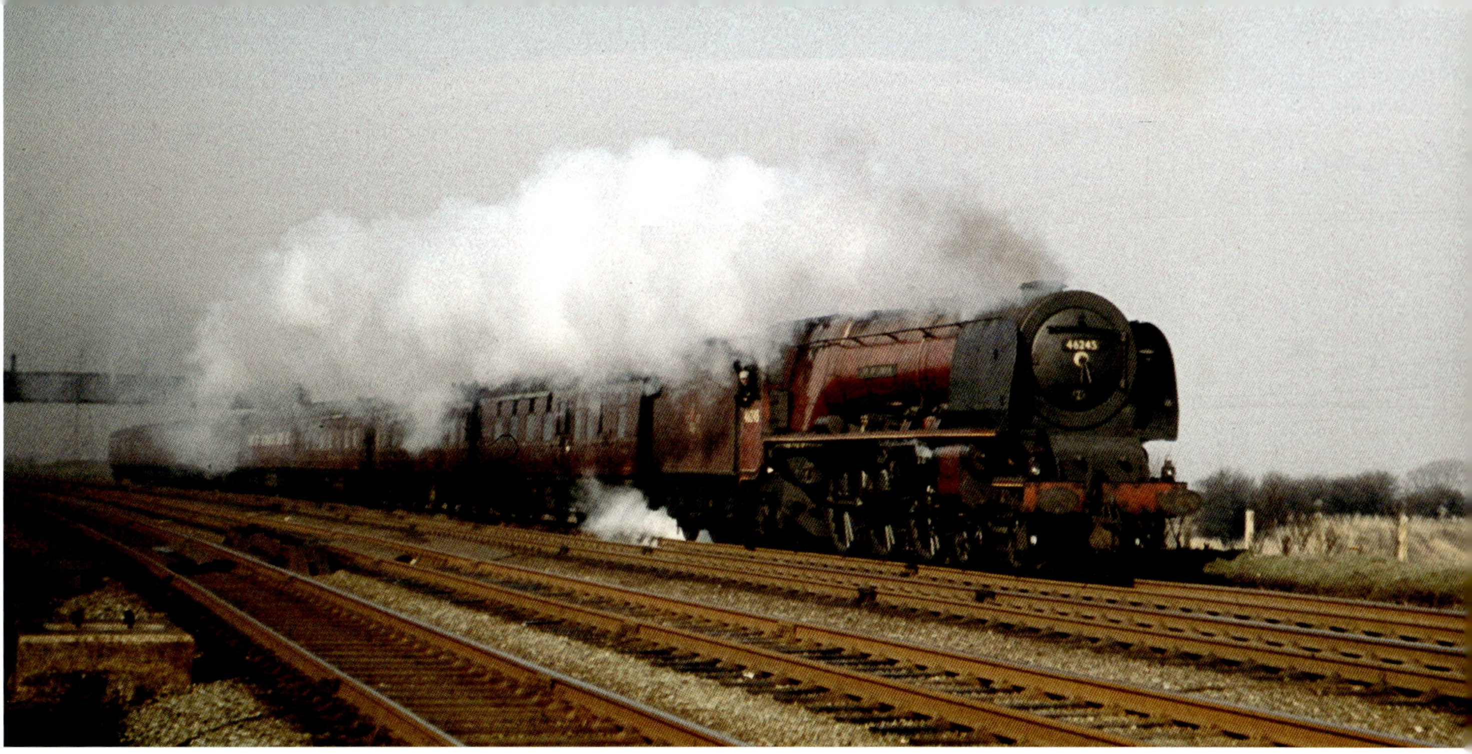

When 46245 City of London was originally built it was to the streamlined design, even though the Second World War was at its height in 1943 with the engine going into service in a wartime black livery. In its final guise the locomotive was seen at Golborne on the up Royal Scot on 5 March 1960. ***Robert Western***

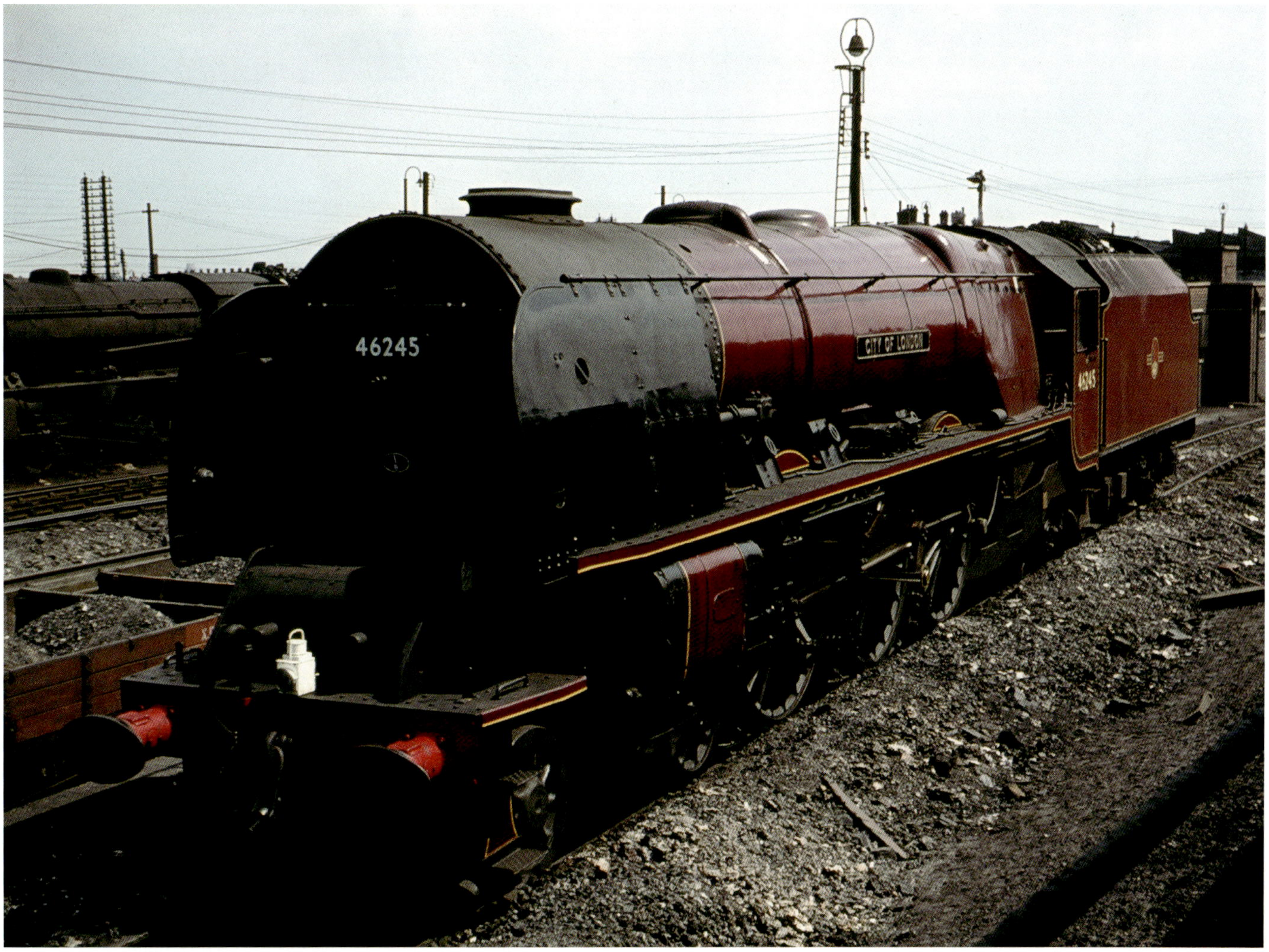

This same locomotive made several excursions into unfamiliar territory towards the last months of its life such as this trip from Kings Cross to Doncaster and return on 9 June 1963, where our cameraman recorded the magnificent machine laying over before the return run on shed at Doncaster. ***John Rowe***

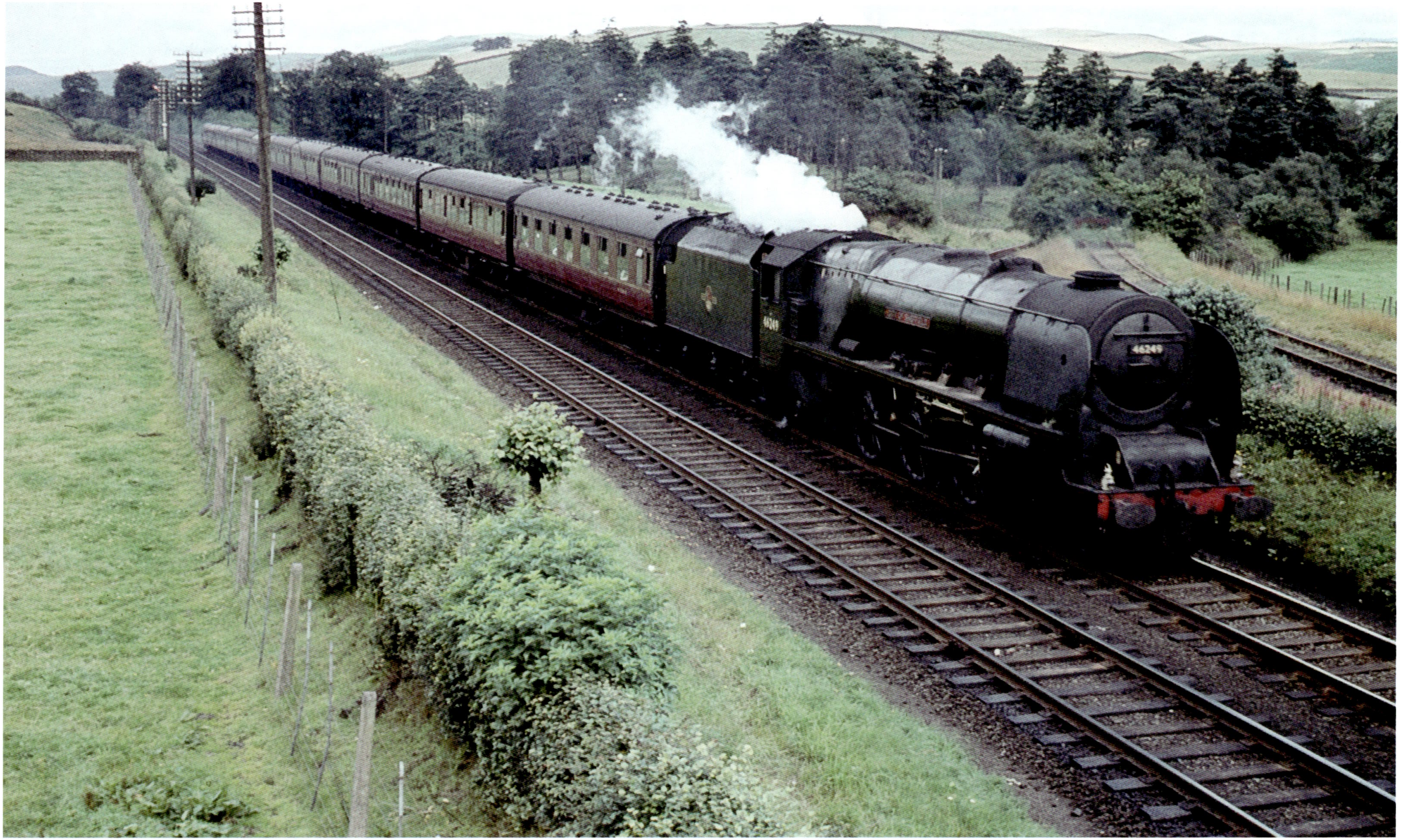

The nameplates of the class have been painted variously over the years with red, black and blue backgrounds. In all of their differing colour schemes the class have had one thing in common throughout, in that they were immensely popular with both railwaymen and enthusiasts alike. Here 46249 City of Sheffield approaches Beattock in 1961 with a typical Anglo-Scottish express before the diesels took over shortly afterwards. ***Strathwood Library Collection***

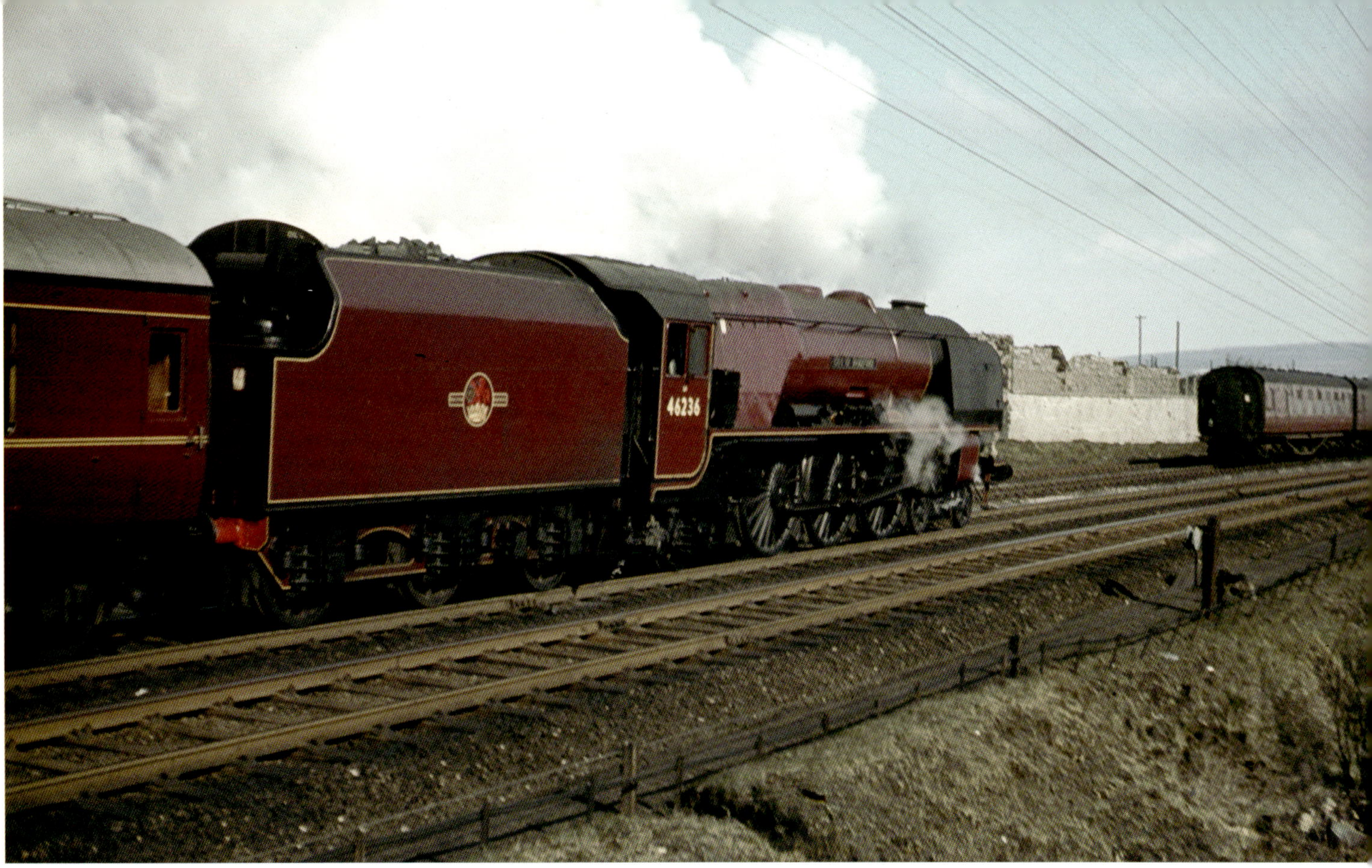

From all angles the class looked right and gave a real impression of power such as here with 46236 City of Bradford near Carnforth during 1963 on a Euston to Glasgow train. ***Late Ray Helm/Strathwood Library Collection***

A low angle view of 46250 City of Lichfield powering a parcels train away from Lancaster in 1963, an easy duty for the engine and her crew perhaps on this Autumn morning. ***Late Ray Helm/Strathwood Library Collection***

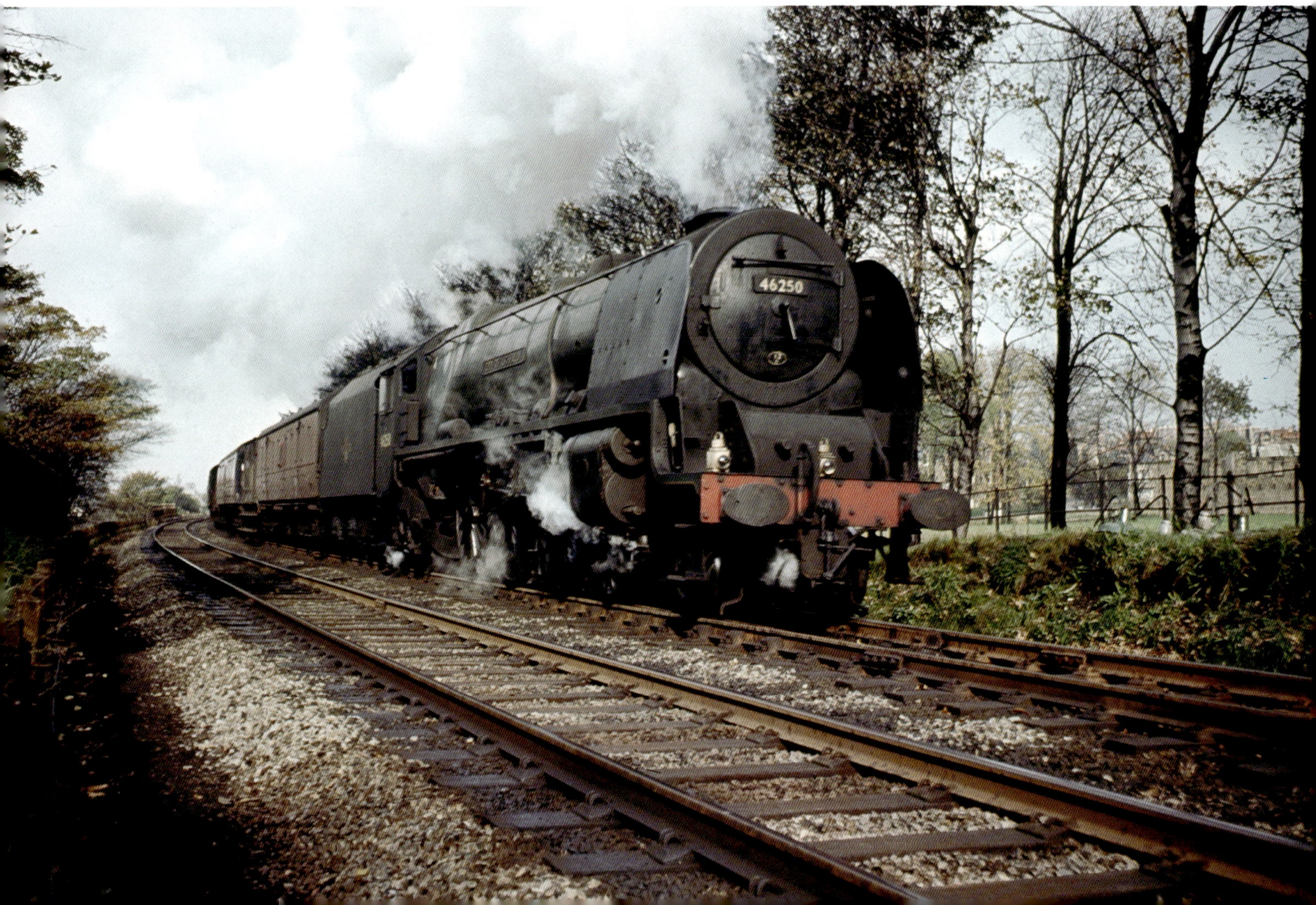

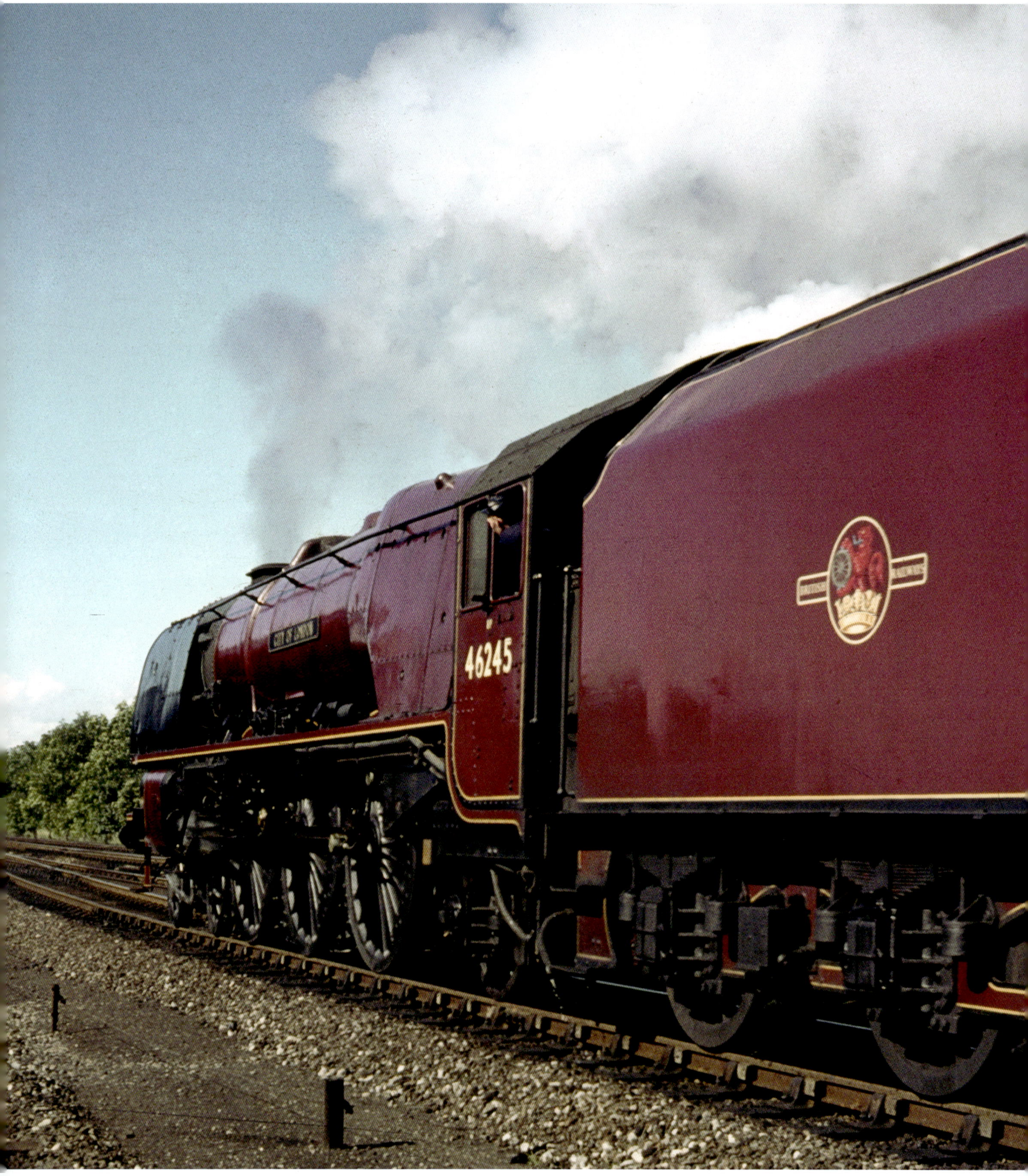

The painting and lining detail applied by both Crewe and Glasgow when outshopping the class extended on the maroon examples to lining the cylinders, steps and under frame of the tender such was the pride in the class as exemplified by 46245 City of London as late as 1963 at Lancaster. ***Late Ray Helm/Strathwood Library Collection***

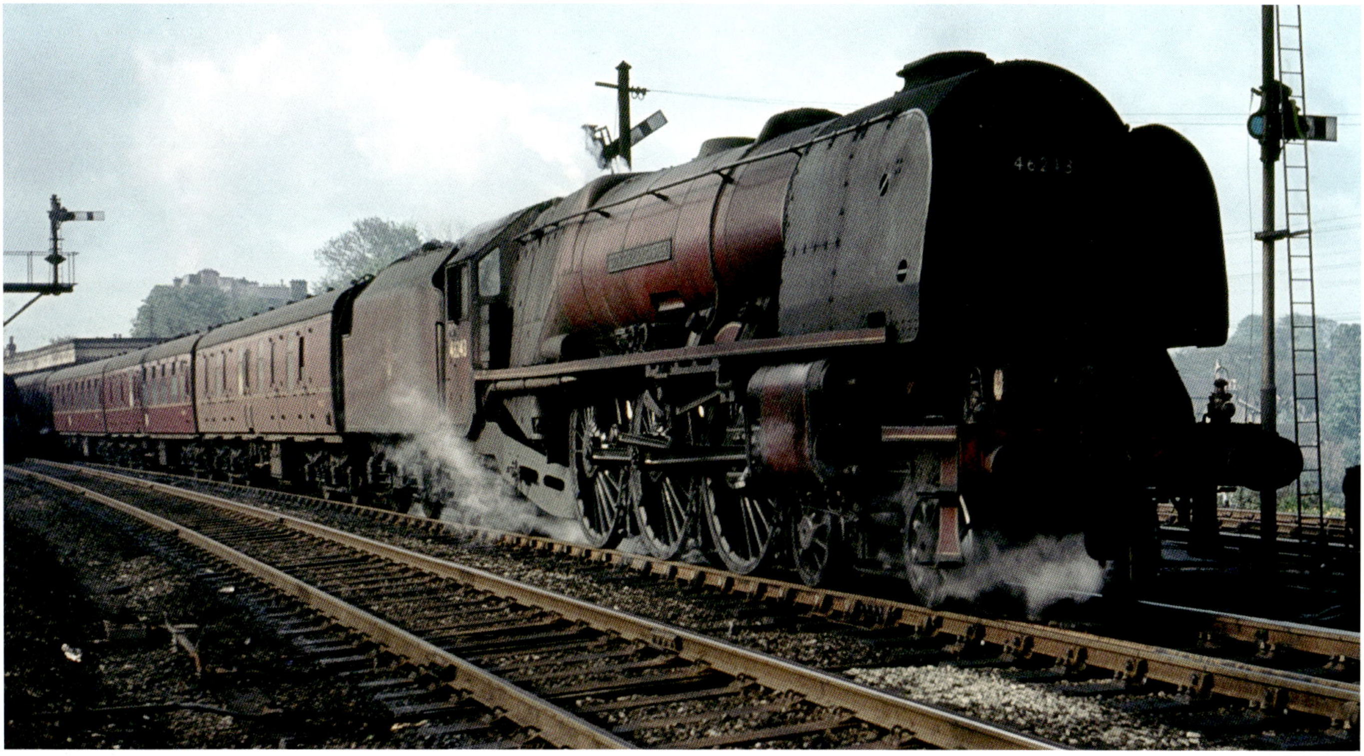

Not all of the class however were to be maintained in pristine external condition at the end as witnessed by 46243 City of Lancaster leaving her namesake with a Warrington to Carlisle semi fast service in 1963. ***Late Ray Helm/Strathwood Library Collection***

Three years previously and 46226 Duchess of Norfolk may be shabby externally but she will tackle Beattock with an immense passenger working, no doubt with the confidence of her engine crew. ***Strathwood Library Collection***

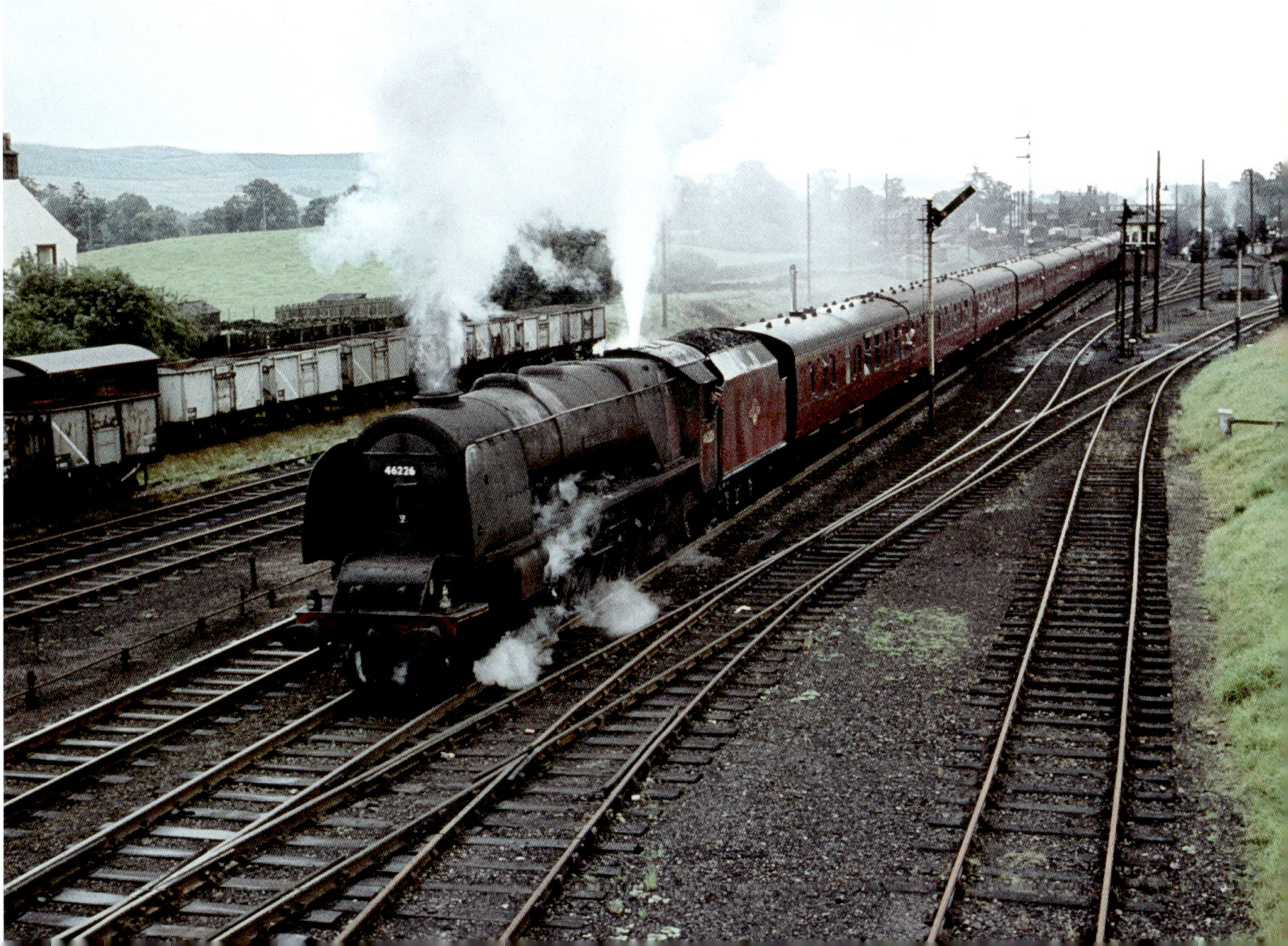

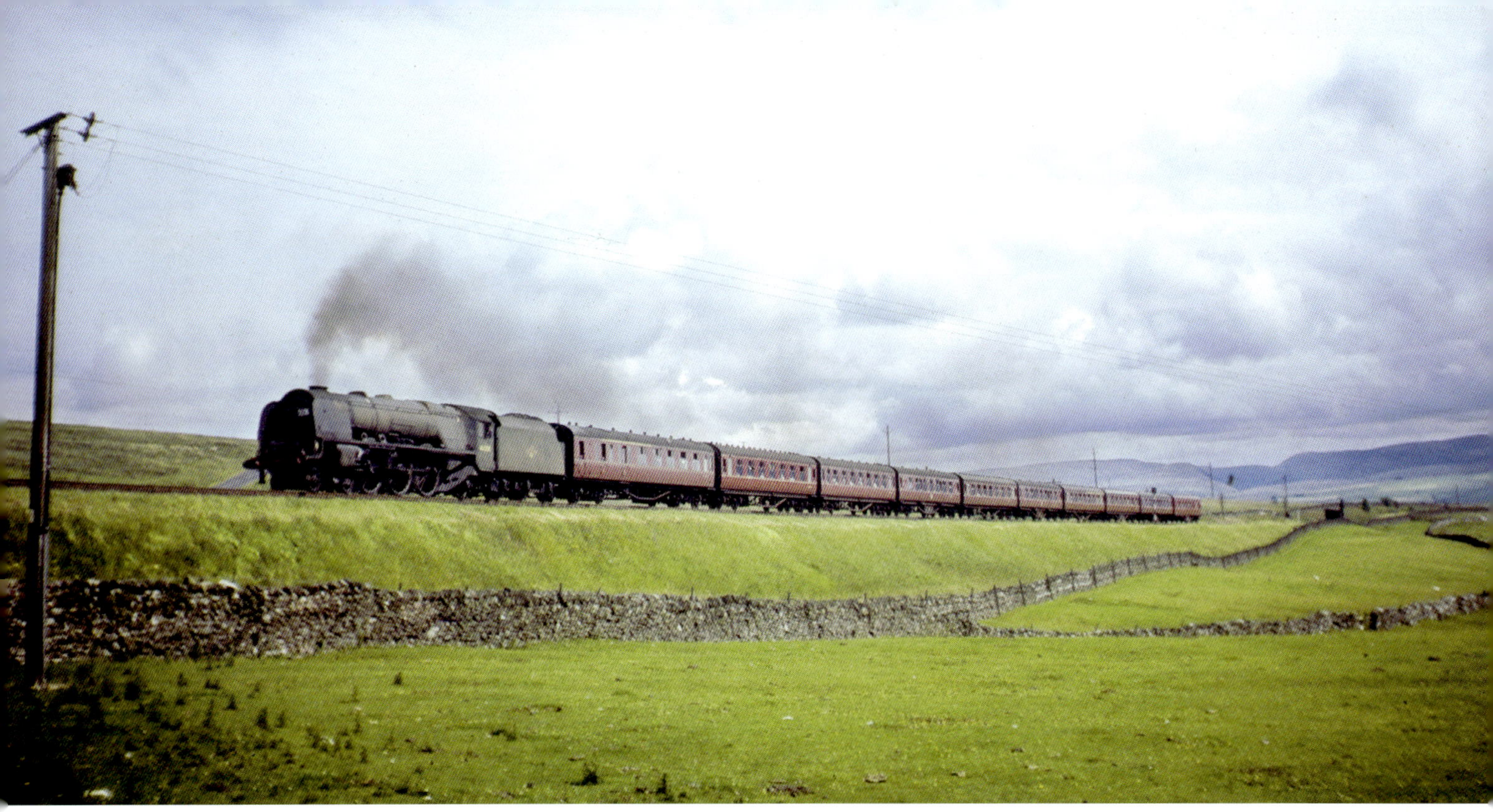

A modest ten coaches behind the tender for 46250 City of Lichfield unaided at Scout Green on 25 July 1964 three months away from being withdrawn from traffic. ***Chris Forrest***

A vantage point from the bridge overlooking Farrington Junction yards on 16 June 1962 affords a fine view of 46234 Duchess of Abercorn striding away with an inter-regional service for the Western Region. ***Chris Forrest***

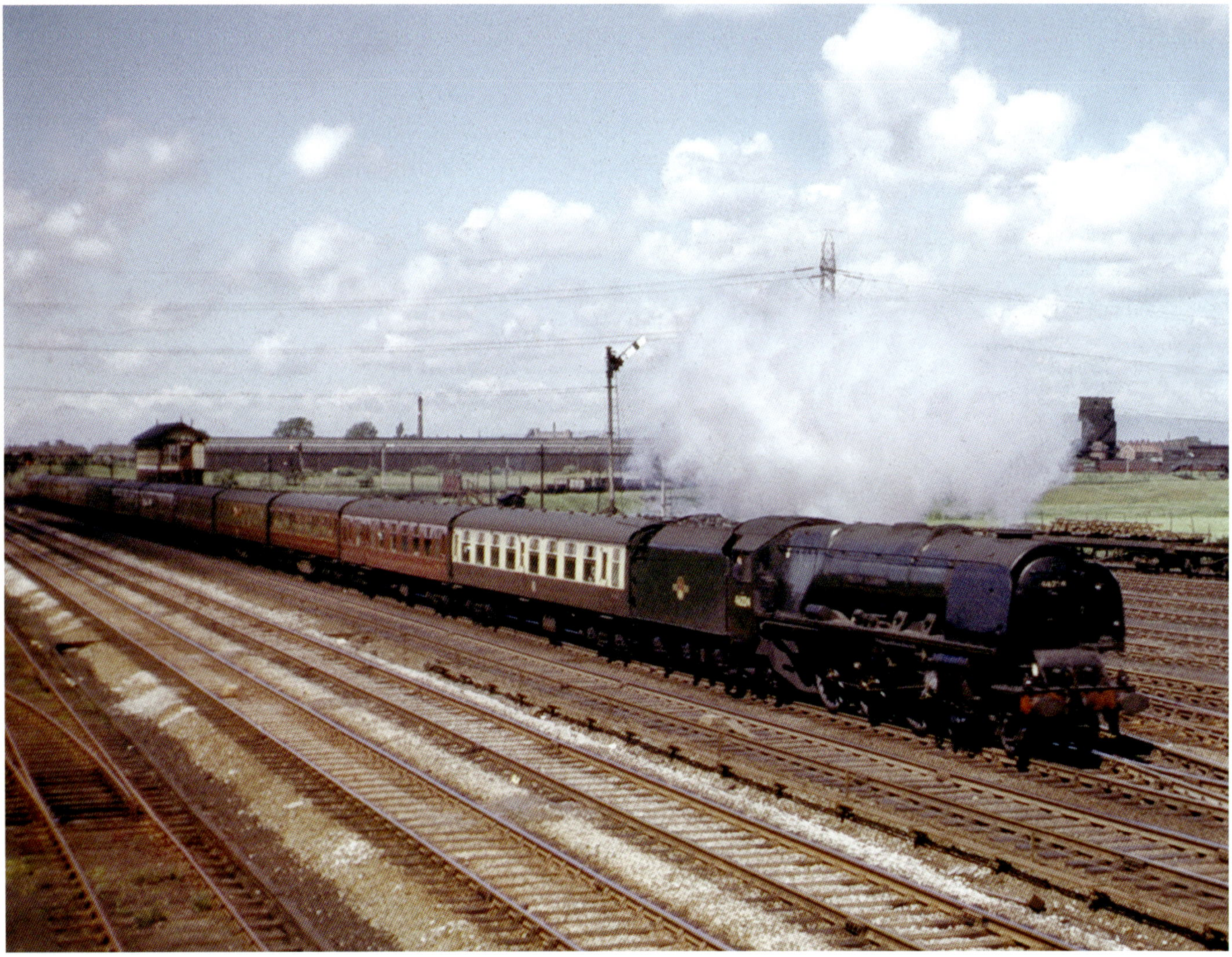

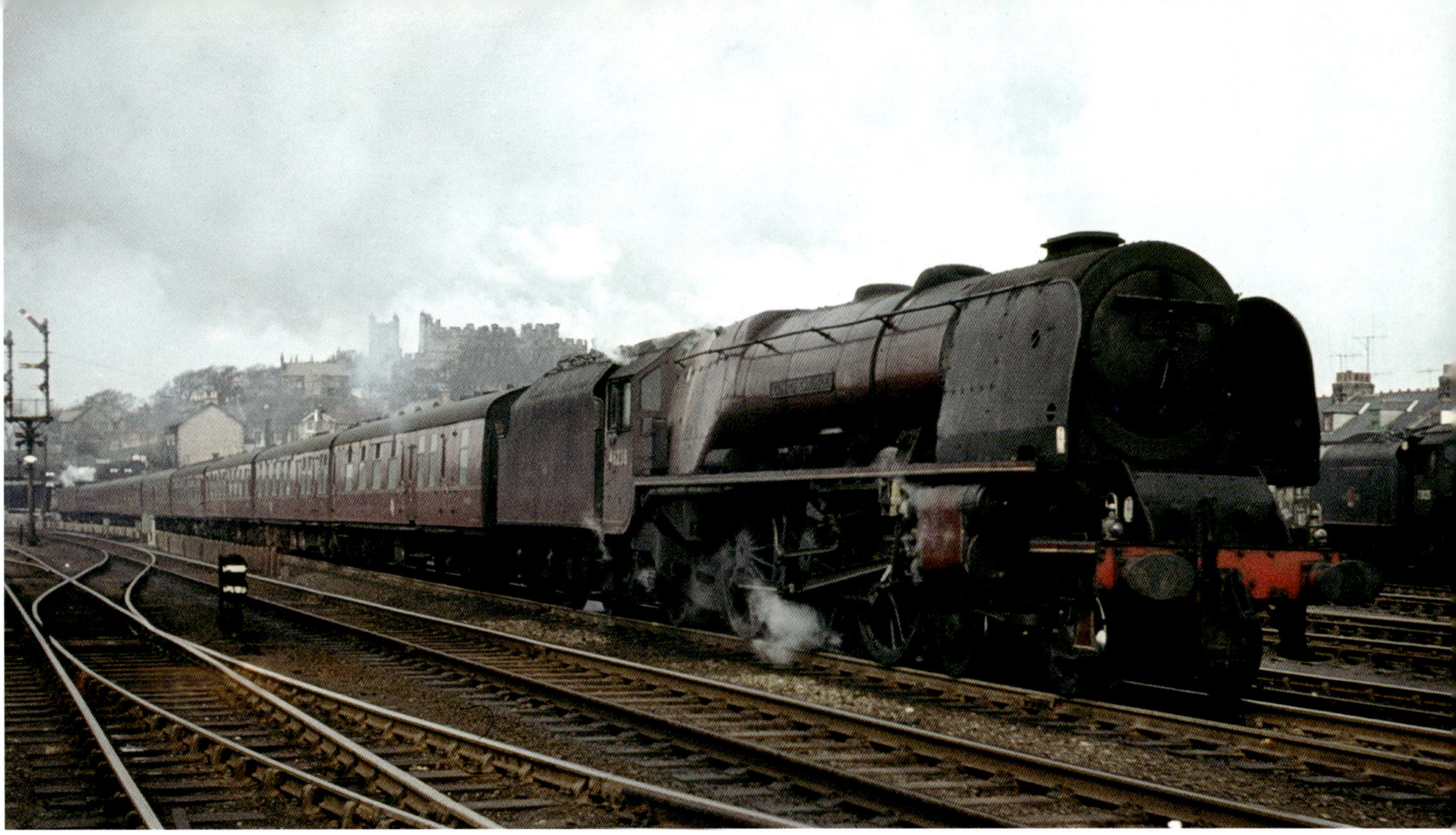

More sterling work on top link services through Lancaster in 1963 for 46238 City of Carlisle far from its days on this route in glittering streamlined maroon and gilt livery in the heyday of the LMS in 1939. ***Late Ray Helm/Strathwood Library Collection***

A number of the class were disfigured by the application of yellow warning stripes to the cabsides such as 46239 City of Chester waiting to leave Holyhead for Crewe but hopefully not beyond as defined by the cabside markings in 1964. ***Strathwood Library Collection***

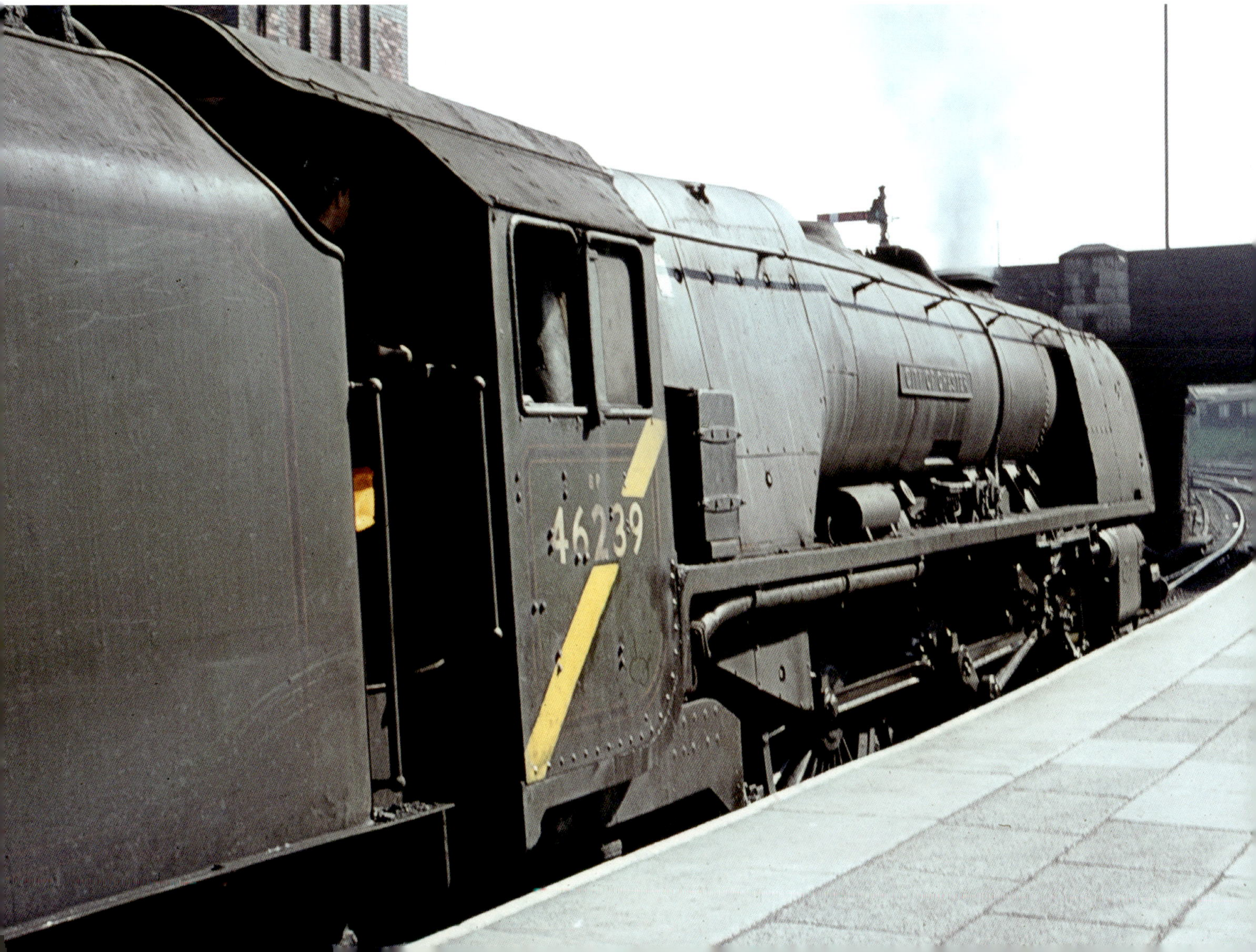

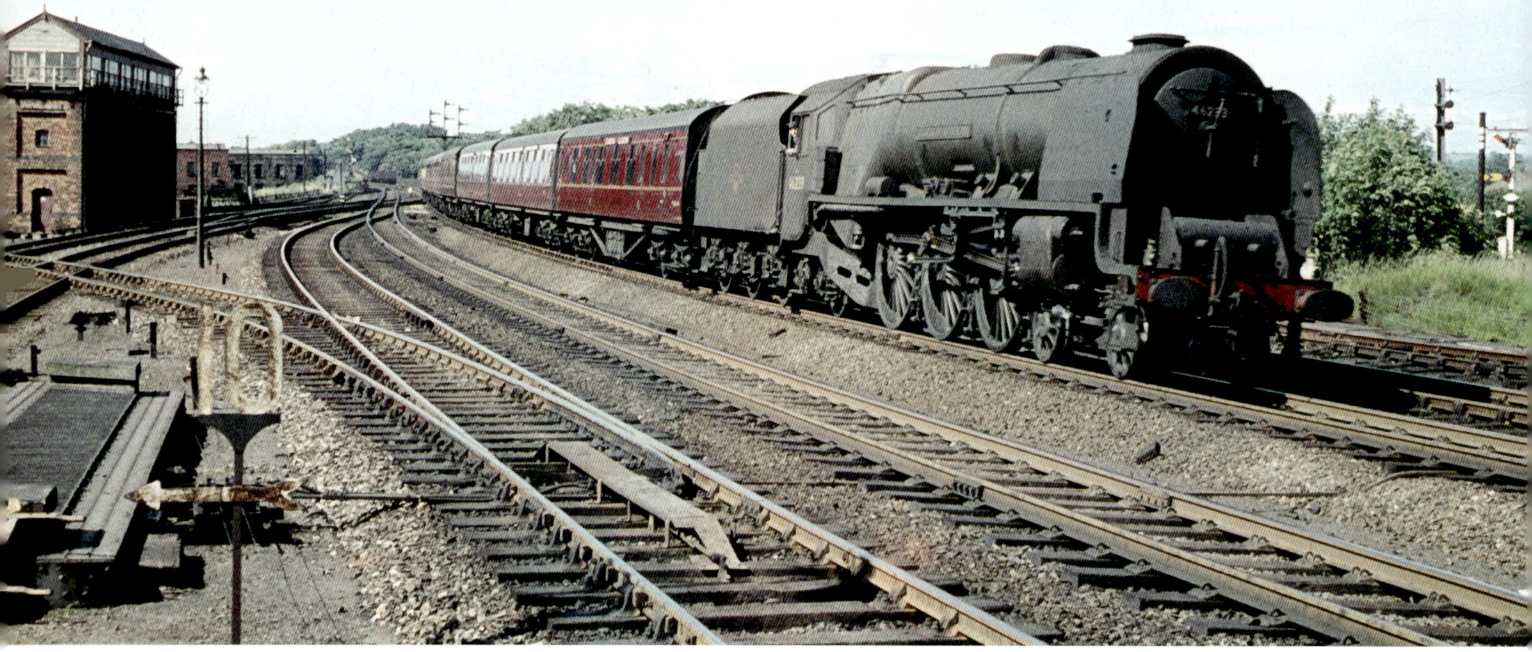

Arriving at Lancaster in 1960 was green liveried 46233 Duchess of Sutherland, one of five non streamlined locomotives built at Crewe in 1938 originally without the smoke deflectors but with a winged back tender. ***Strathwood Library Collection***

The first built was 46220 Coronation released to traffic in a stunning streamlined blue and silver livery and the one time record holder at 114mph on a crazy dash towards Crewe pre-war for the benefit of the press and the publicity men that almost ended in disaster. On a cold frosty morning in early 1963 that brief period of World Record holder was long behind the locomotive now rebuilt into conventional form near Carnforth on an everyday express. ***Late Ray Helm/Strathwood Library Collection***

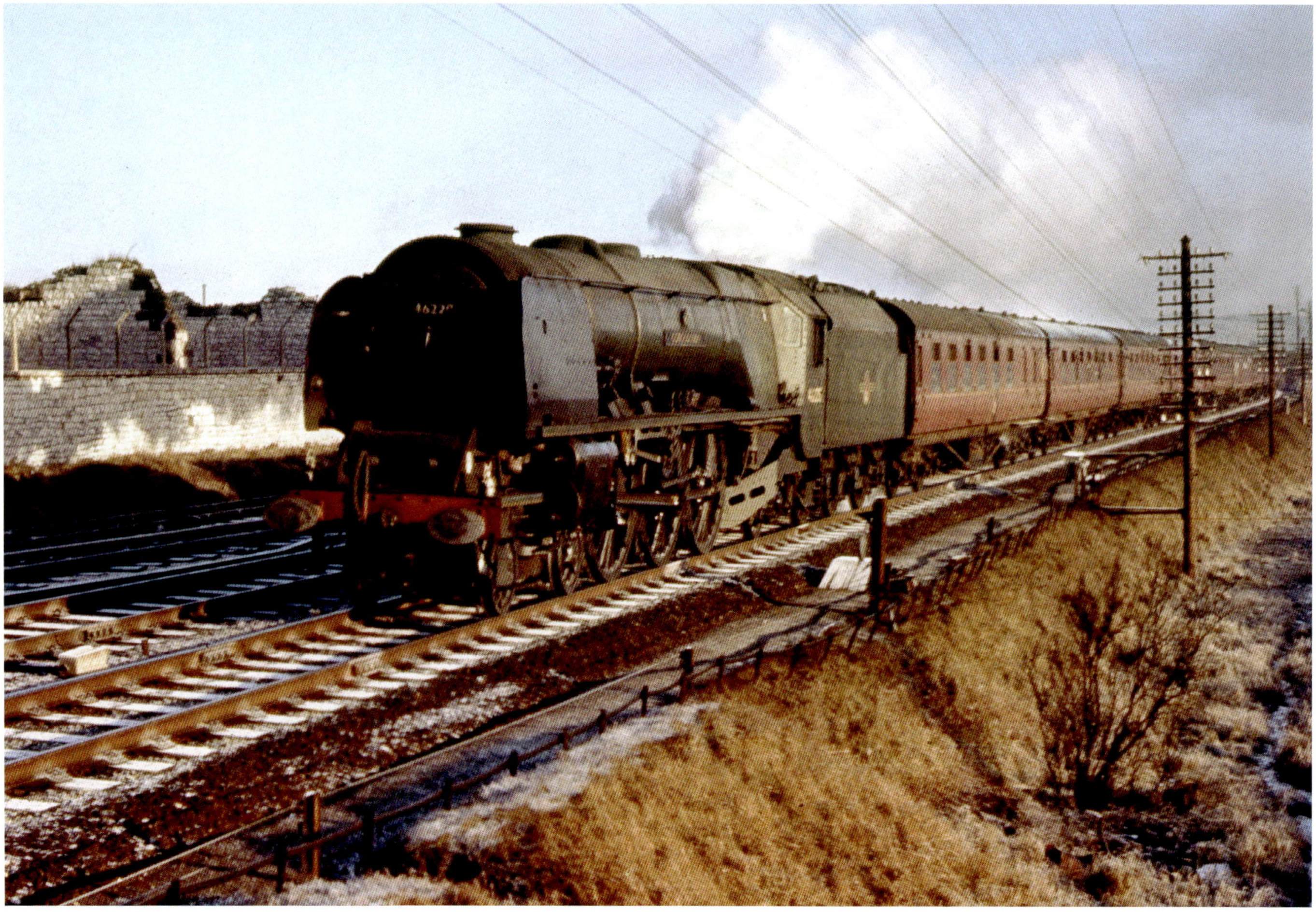

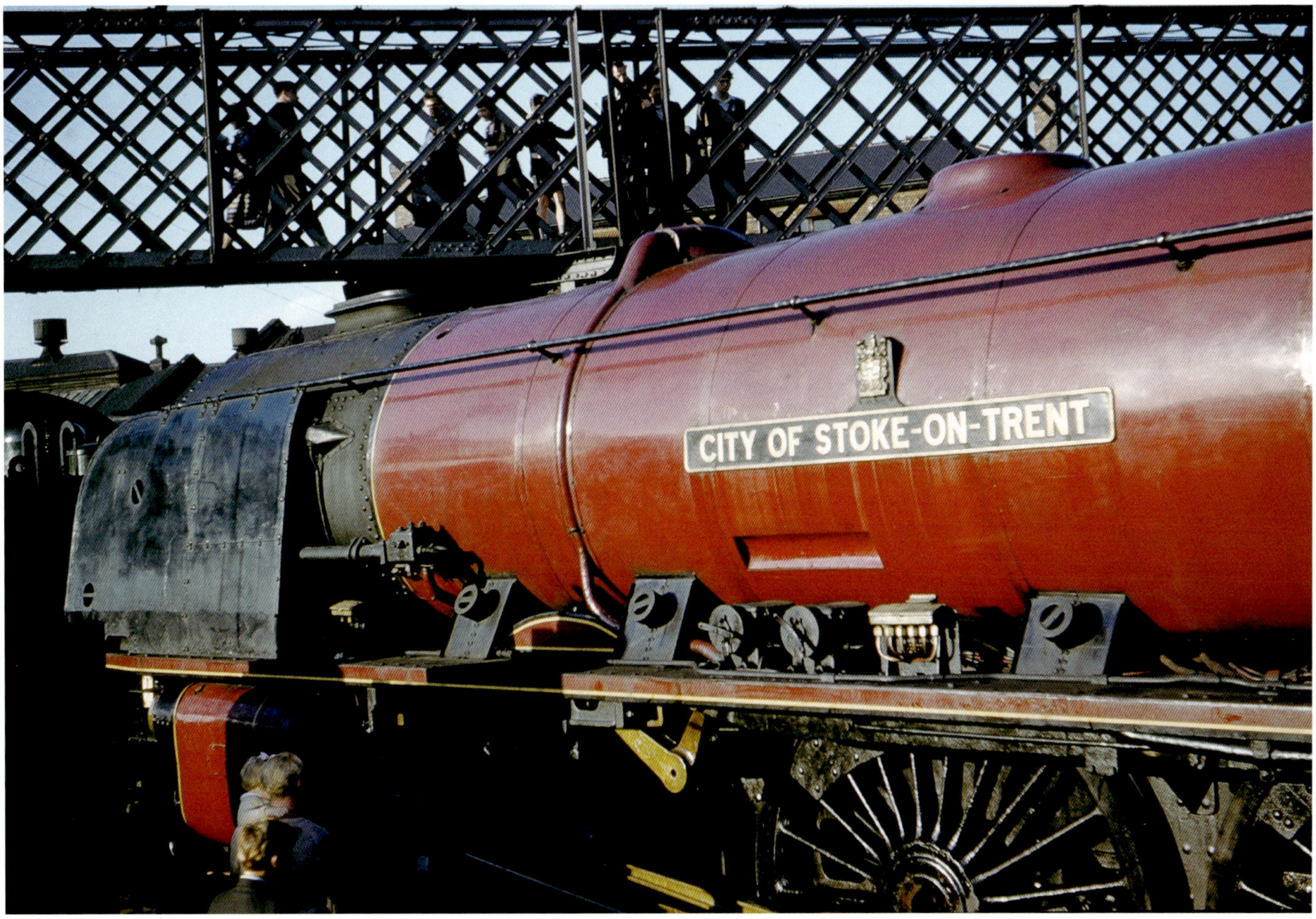

Several of the class were given badges above their nameplates. Among their number was 46254 City of Stoke-on-Trent which made an appearance at Derby for an Open Day in the early sixties. ***Dave Hill***

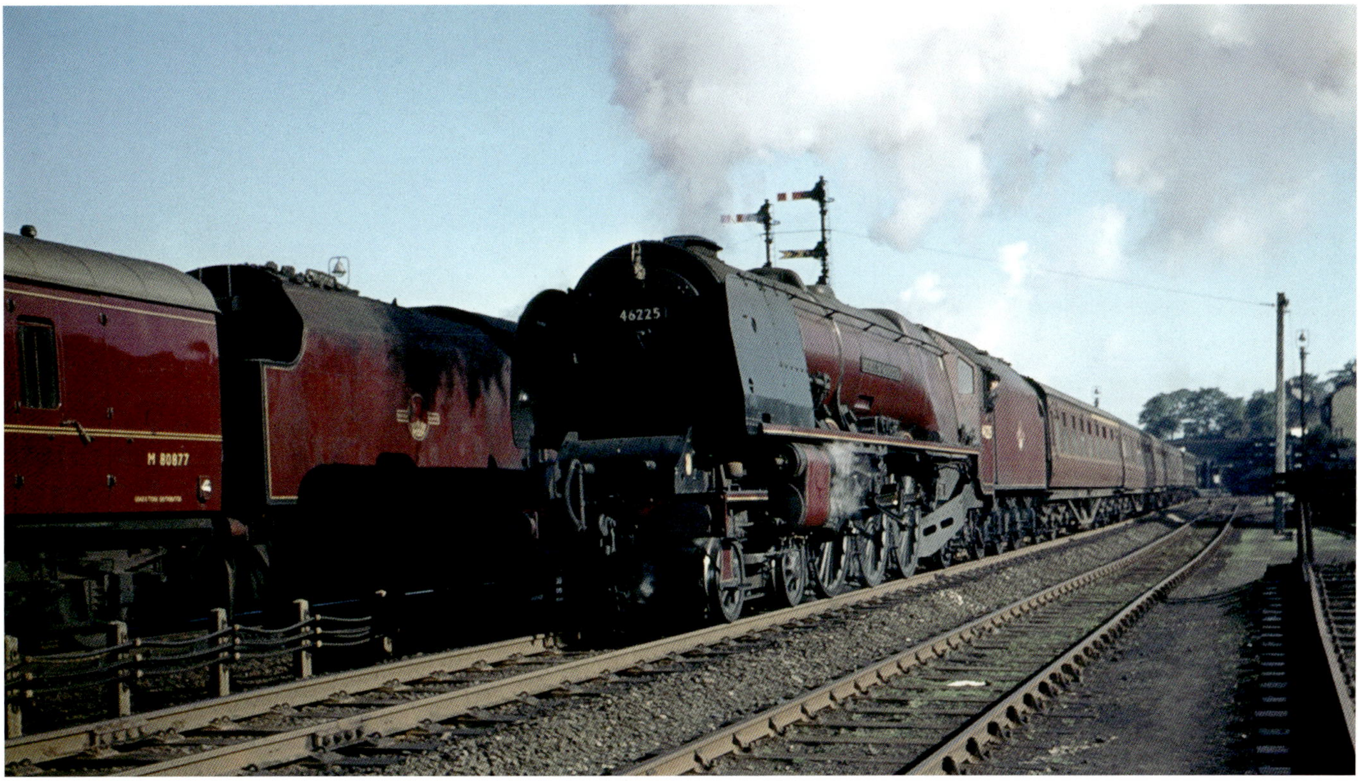

Double Stanier Duchess action at Lancaster as 46225 Duchess of Gloucester passes an unknown maroon sister in 1962. ***Late Ray Helm/Strathwood Library Collection***

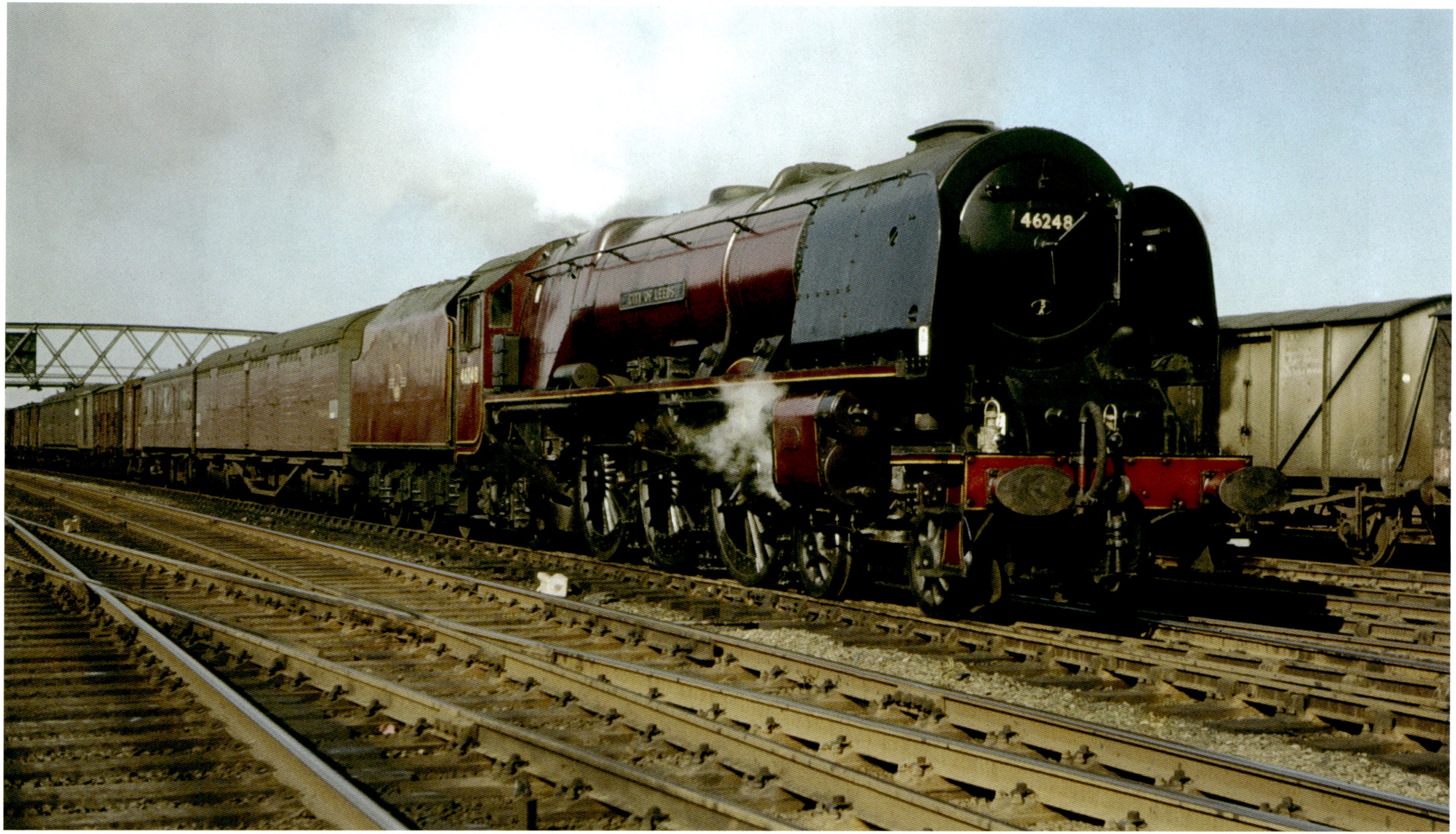

Recently ex works 46248 City of Leeds is ready to depart Carnforth with a long parcels working. As the original streamliners were defrocked beginning with 6235 City of Birmingham in April 1946 and the smoke boxes were in some cases only a few years old, it was decided to retain these original fittings even though they had a pronounced slope to their fronts to save money during those austere times after the war. As smoke box renewals became necessary a program of change began appropriately with 46235 in July 1952 and ending with 46246 City of Manchester in May 1960. However by this time enthusiasts and spotters had nicknamed the class as Semis on account of their semi streamlined nature. ***Late Ray Helm/Strathwood Library Collection***

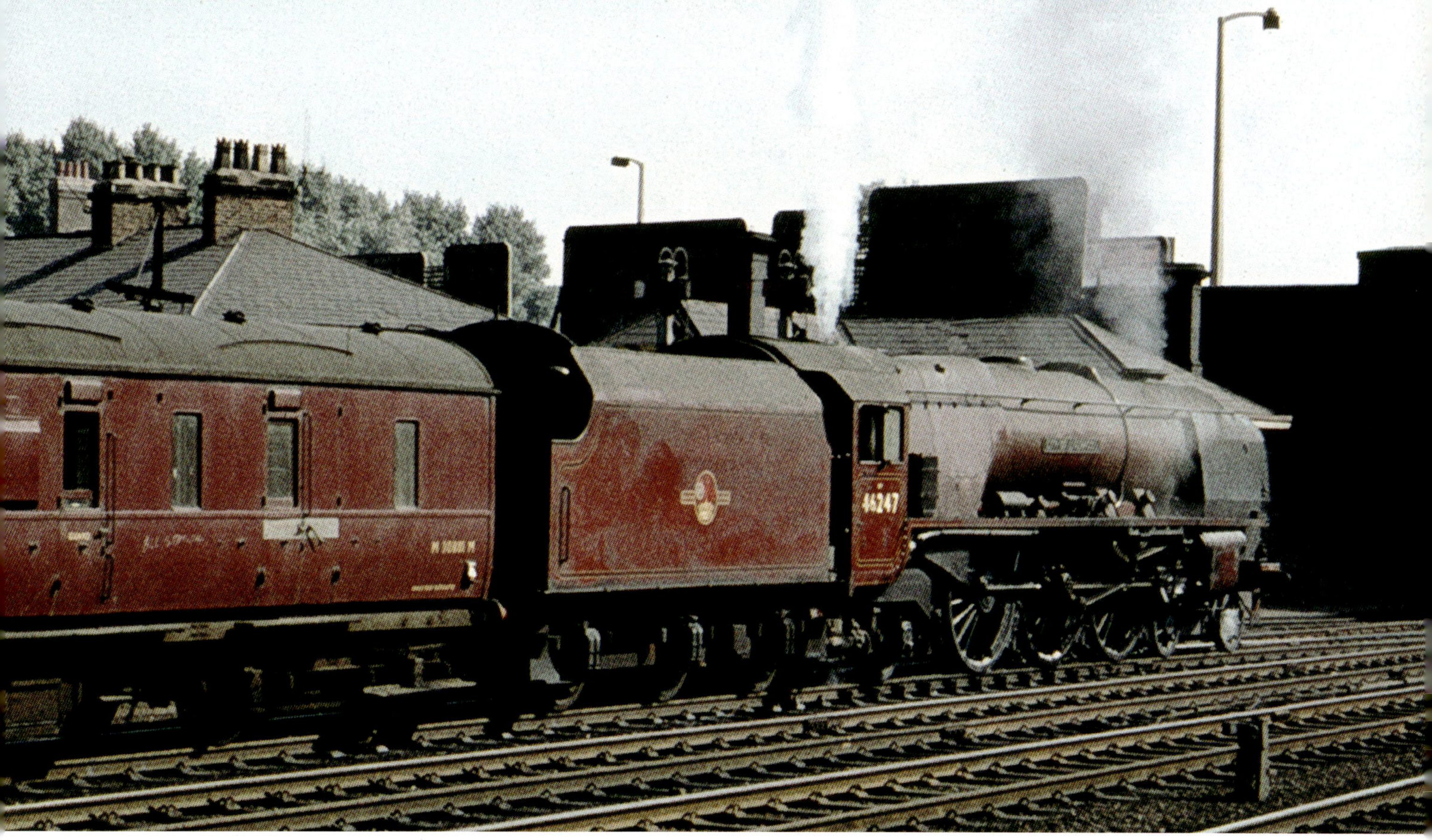

Seen departing Stafford in 1958 was 46247 City of Liverpool in the perhaps appropriate brick red livery, unless you are an Evertonian of course. This locomotive had been one of the streamliners released in wartime black when new in September 1943. During the 1950s the narrow cab front windows of the formerly streamlined locomotives like this example, were replaced with the same style of larger windows as the non streamlined class members to aid visibility. ***Strathwood Library Collection***

The demand for coal and water on the heavy trains associated with the likes of 46250 City of Lichfield pausing for breath here at Lancaster in 1962 was heavy. Stanier introduced a steam operated coal pusher to assist the fireman in fetching the coal forward. At the time of the Modernisation Plan in 1955, thoughts were given towards fitting mechanical stokers to the class and building enlarged eight wheel tenders capable of carrying 12 tons of coal instead of the 10 as designed. The water capacity would have been increased as well from 4000 gallons to 5000 gallons and so adding another 12 tons to the weight of the tender alone! ***Late Ray Helm/Strathwood Library Collection***

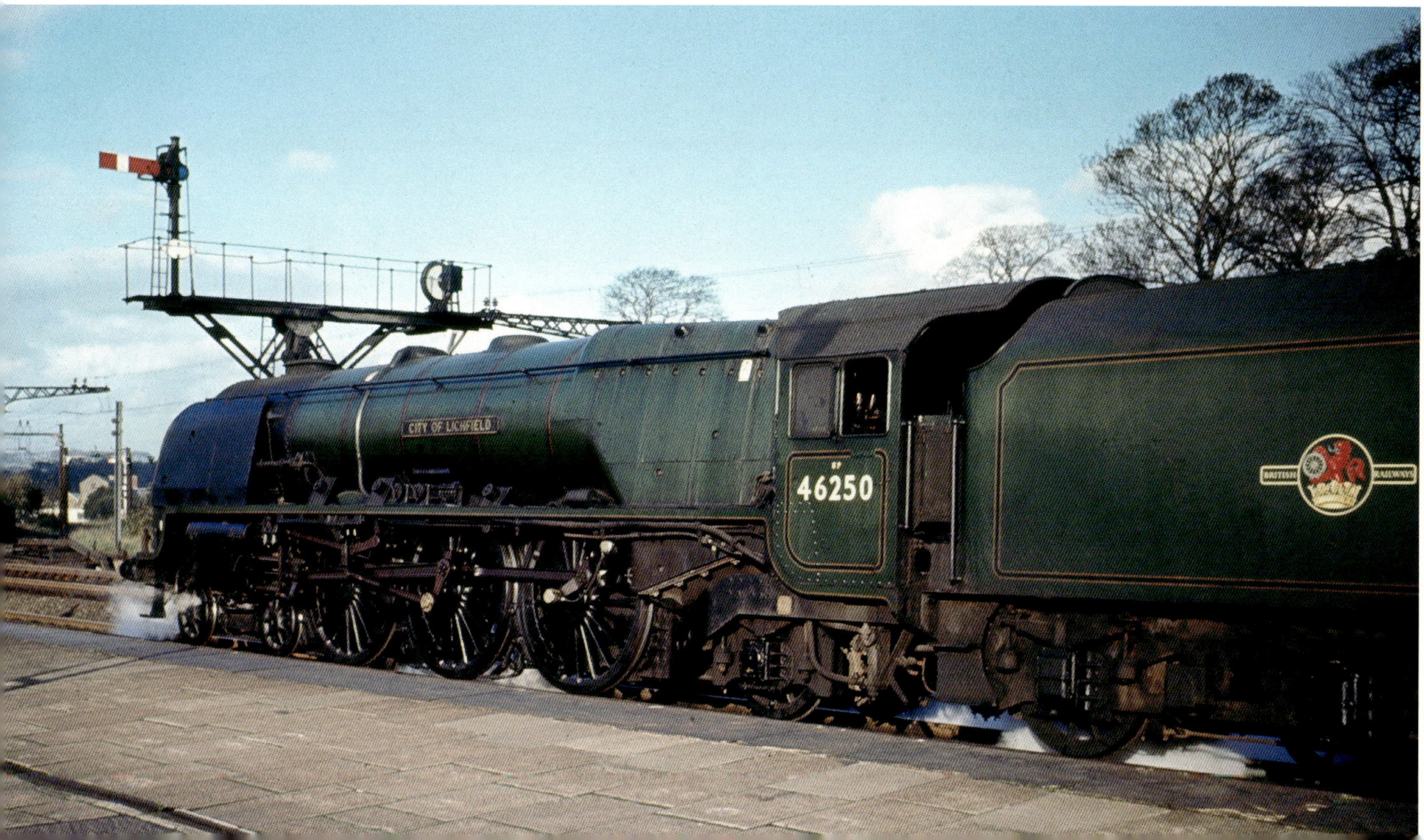

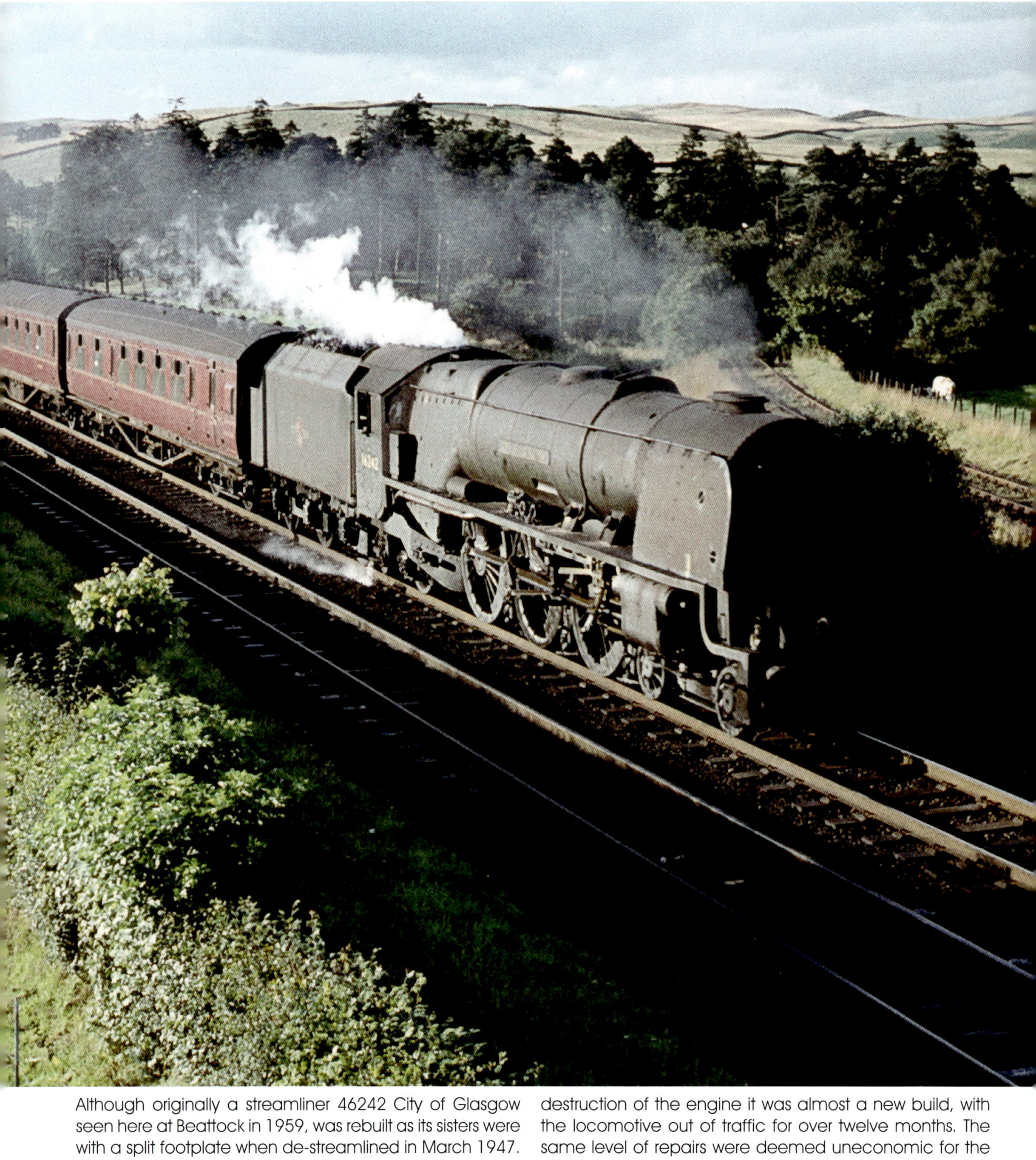

Although originally a streamliner 46242 City of Glasgow seen here at Beattock in 1959, was rebuilt as its sisters were with a split footplate when de-streamlined in March 1947. However after the terrible Harrow tragedy of 1952 which took the lives of 112 souls and left 340 injured, it emerged from works with a continuous footplate and smoke deflectors down to platform level. Such was the level of destruction of the engine it was almost a new build, with the locomotive out of traffic for over twelve months. The same level of repairs were deemed uneconomic for the other two Stanier locomotives involved in this disaster as 46202 Princess Anne and 45637 Windward Islands were both written off. ***Strathwood Library Collection***

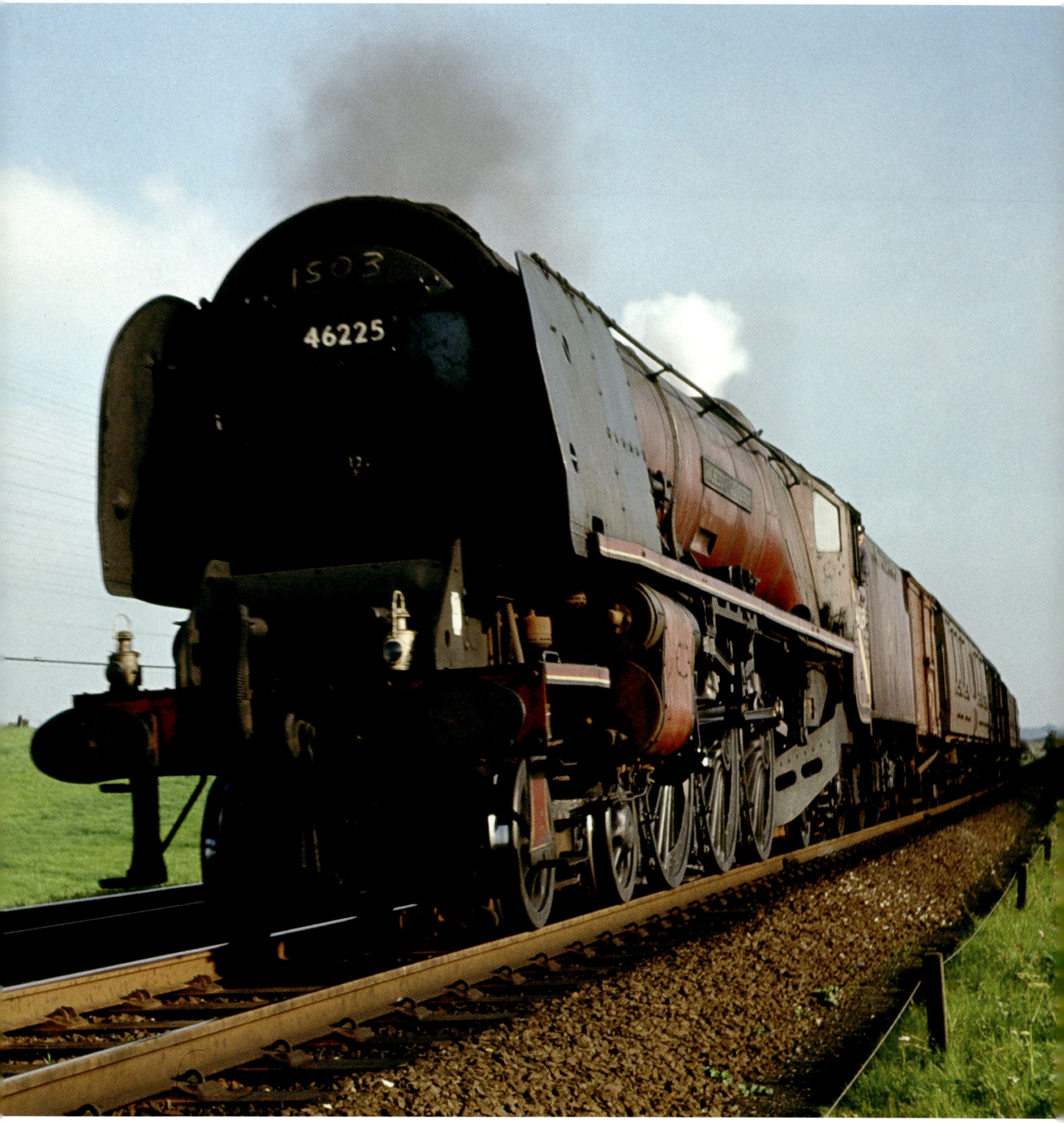

Another Stanier Pacific that had misfortune was 46225 Duchess of Gloucester which was badly damaged in a derailment at Mossland on 15 May 1944 as a result of poorly maintained track work. Three people lost their lives as a result of this incident. Our final view in this chapter is of the locomotive at speed near Lancaster in the early summer of 1963. ***Late Ray Helm/Strathwood Library Collection***

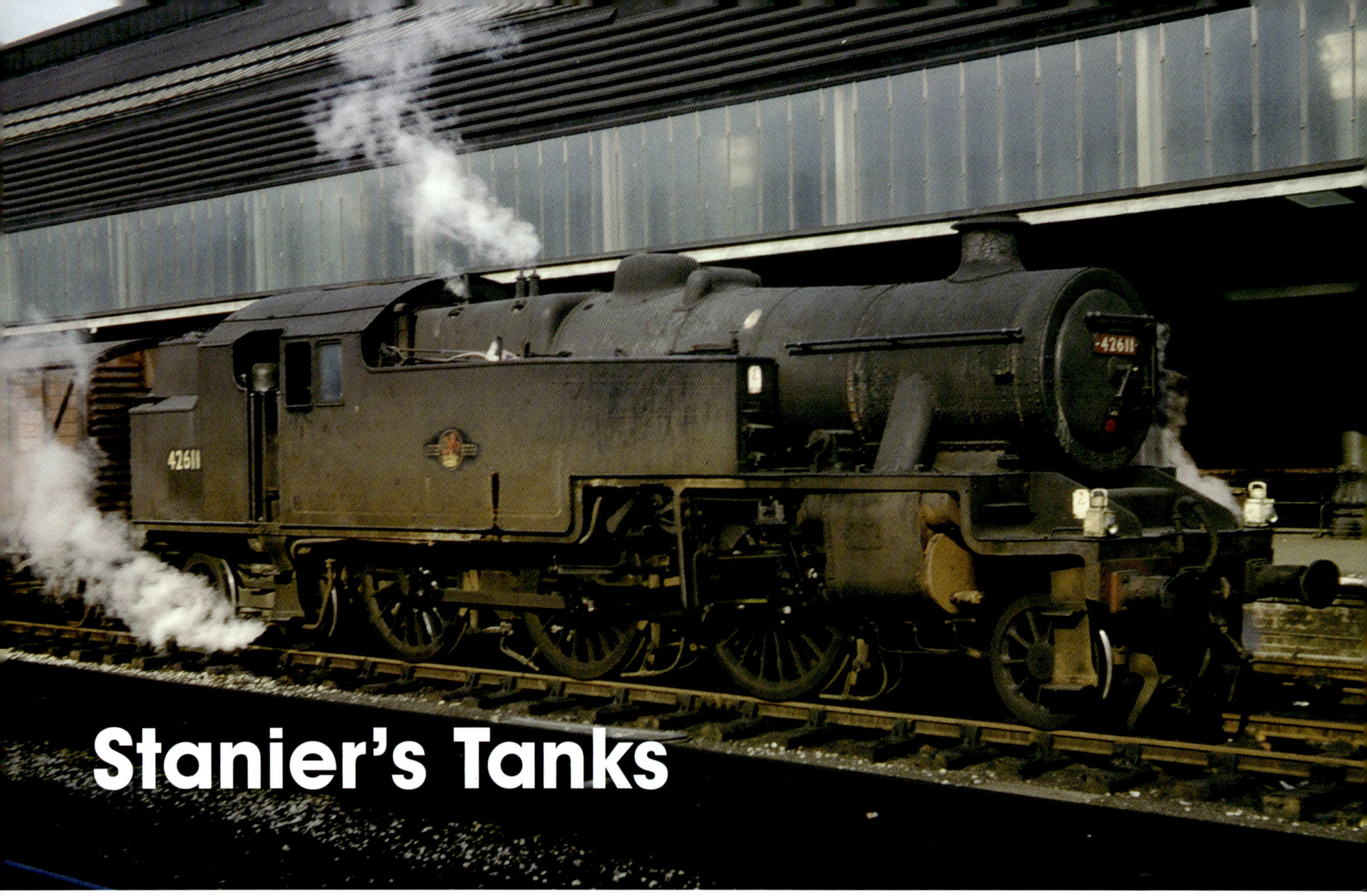

Stanier's Tanks

Such was the success of this design which was really a development of Fowler's earlier design of 2-6-4T that Charles Fairburn ordered further batches be built when he succeeded Stanier with a slightly shorter wheelbase and other detail differences. Among the last survivors was 42611 as the Preston station pilot on 31 March 1967. ***Micheal Beaton***

Lovely sunny conditions on shed at Holbeck in early 1964 shortly before 42618 would be withdrawn. However on this pleasant day she is performing shed duties. ***John Rowe***

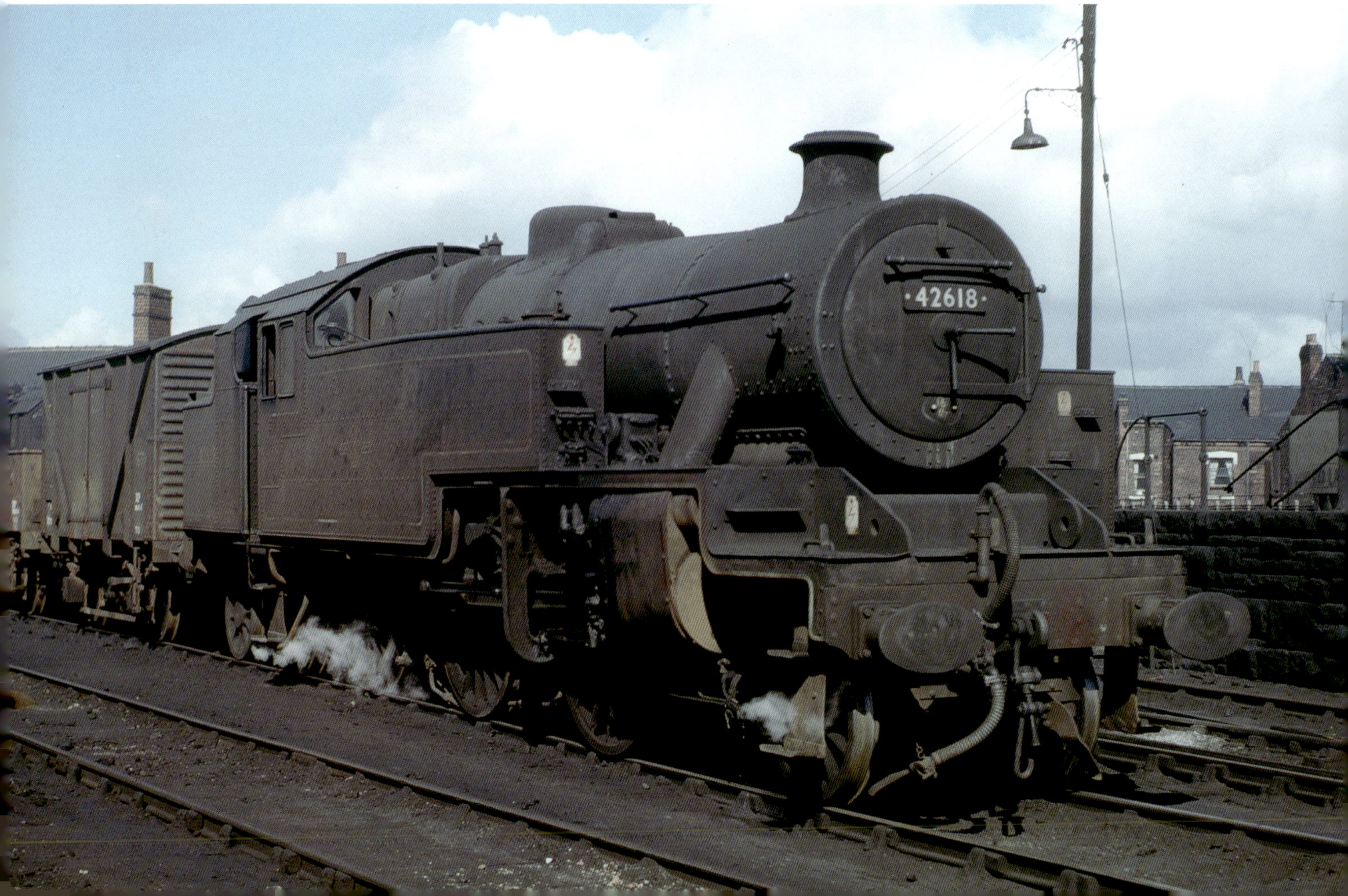

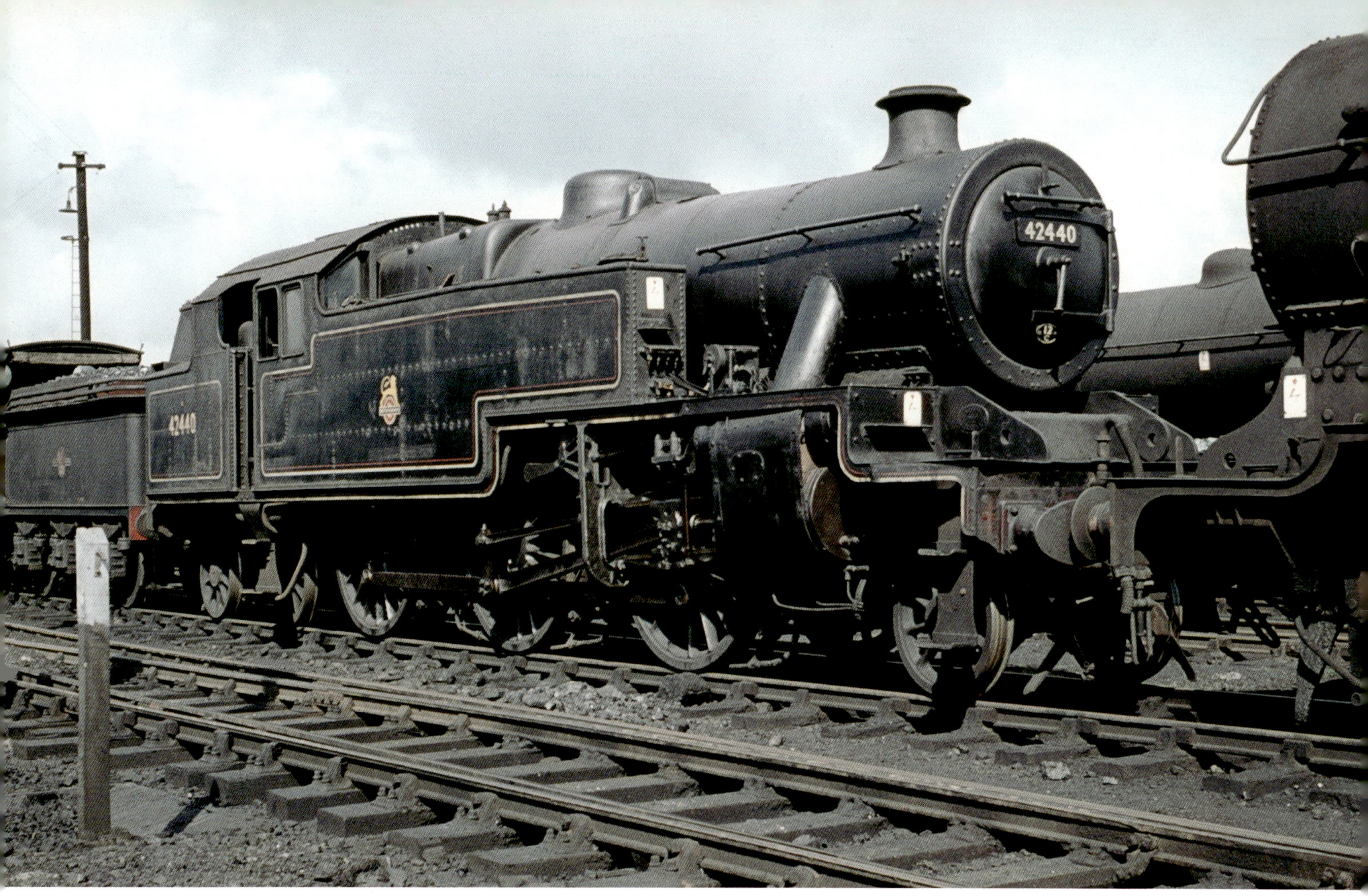

Nine batches of these two cylinder locomotives were built at Derby Works and 42440 was one of these released to traffic in May 1936. Well cleaned at Carlisle Canal shed in 1959, this engine would work on until October 1963. ***Strathwood Library Collection***

This locomotive 42616 would be the last in traffic in 1967 and was withdrawn shortly after this view taken at Bradford Exchange on 29 May 1967. The first to be withdrawn fell upon 42490 in May 1960. ***Jerry Beddows***

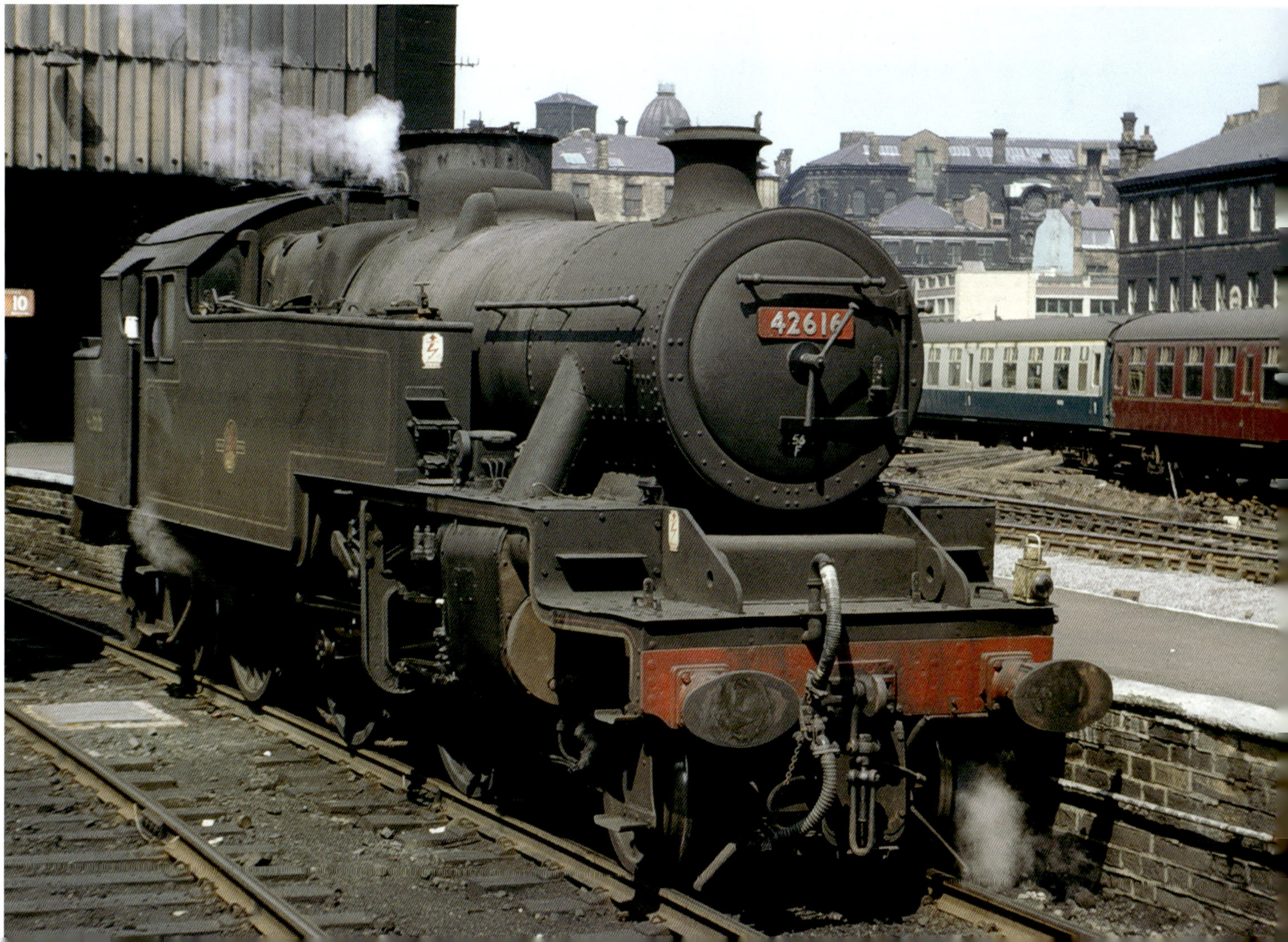

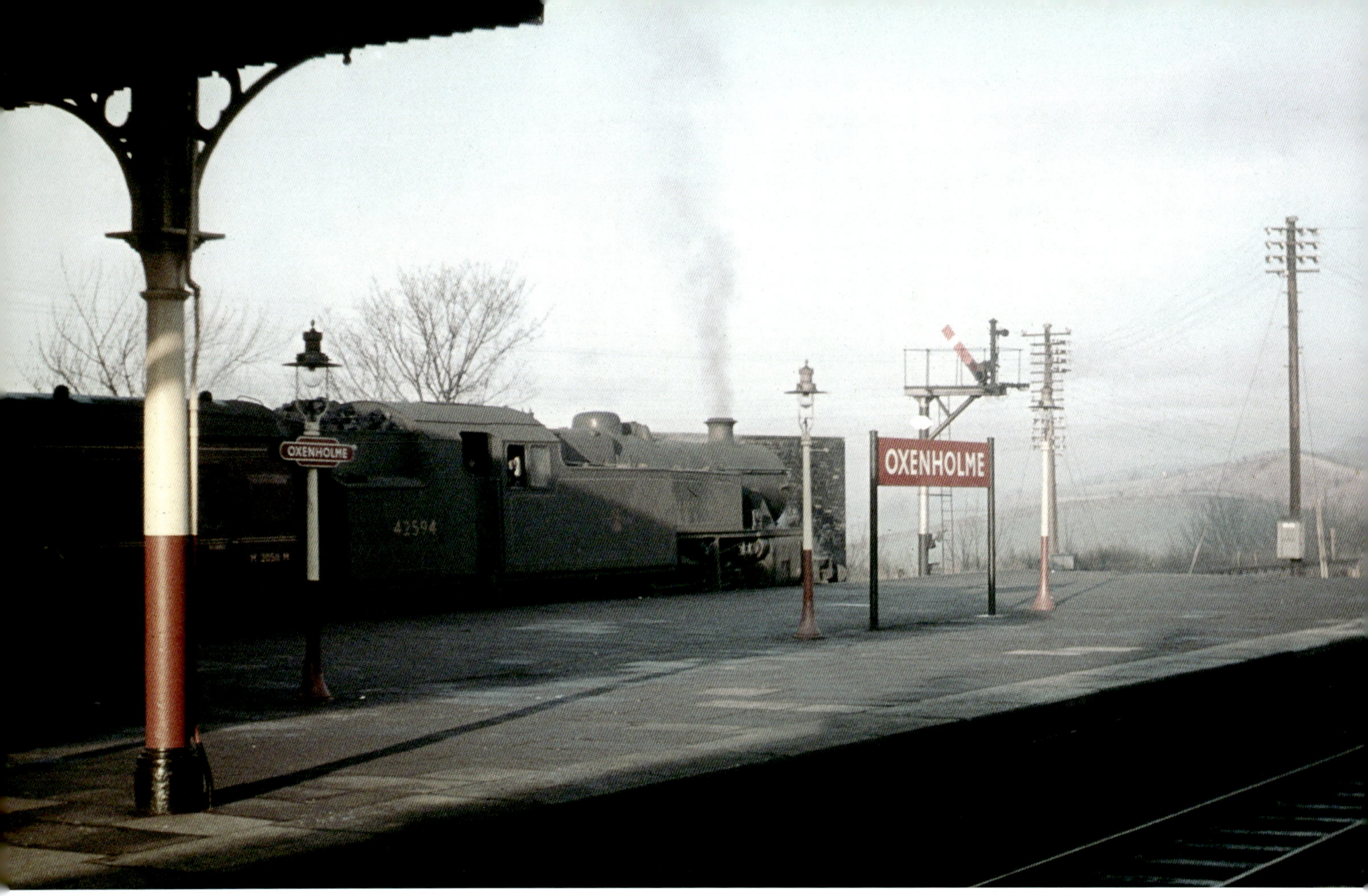

Local passenger duties for North British built 4MT 2-6-4T 42594 with the Windermere branch train at Oxenholme on a misty 19 December 1960. ***Strathwood Library Collection***

Four batches of 3P 2-6-2Ts were built between 1935 and 1938, with construction shared between Derby and Crewe Works. Unfortunately their reputation as poor steamers led to a modified boiler being fitted to a few locomotives as late as 1956. Their reputation was tarnished to the end with the first withdrawal in 1959 and the last by December 1962. In happier times this pair at Southport seem to have steam to spare. ***Strathwood Library Collection***

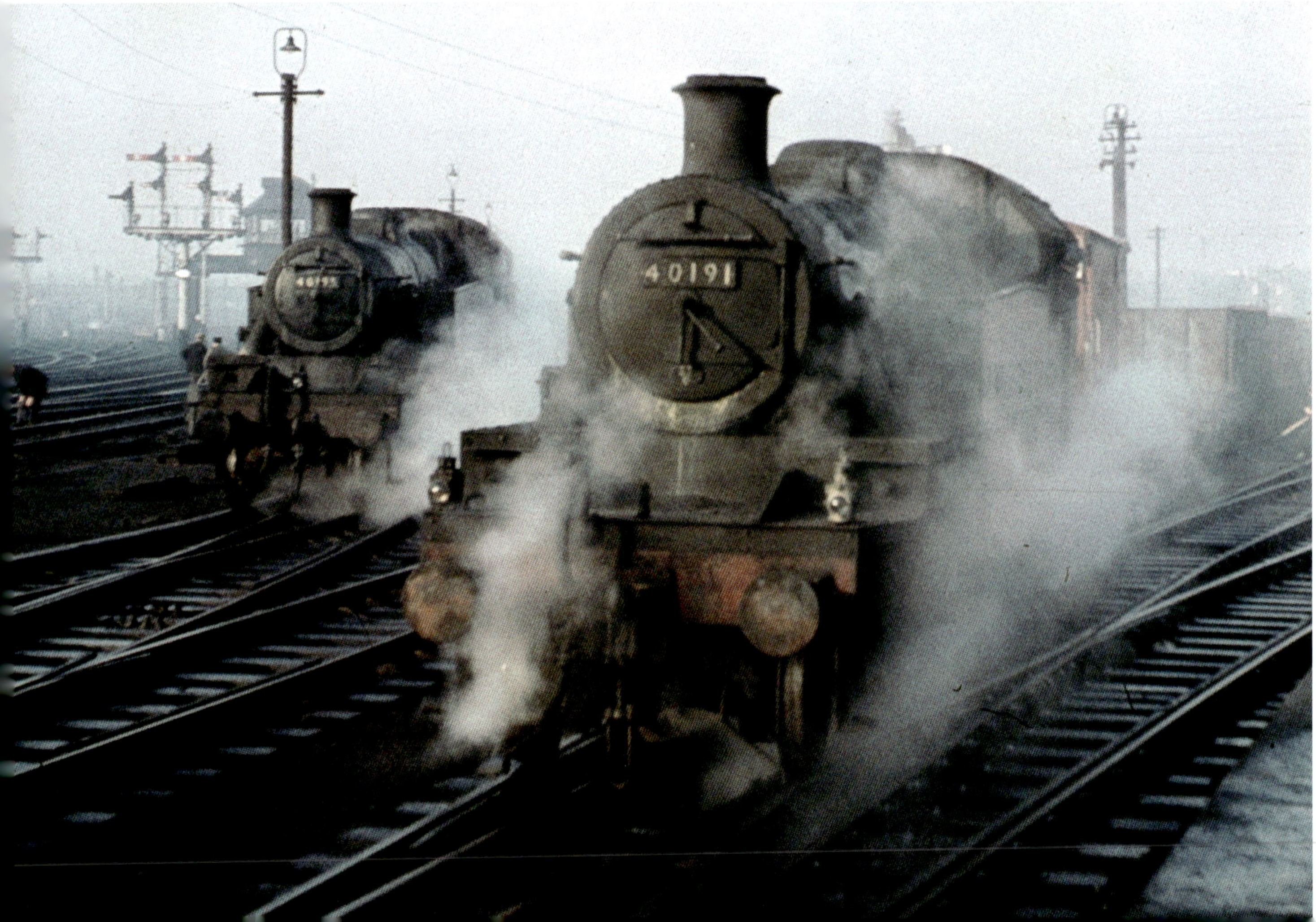

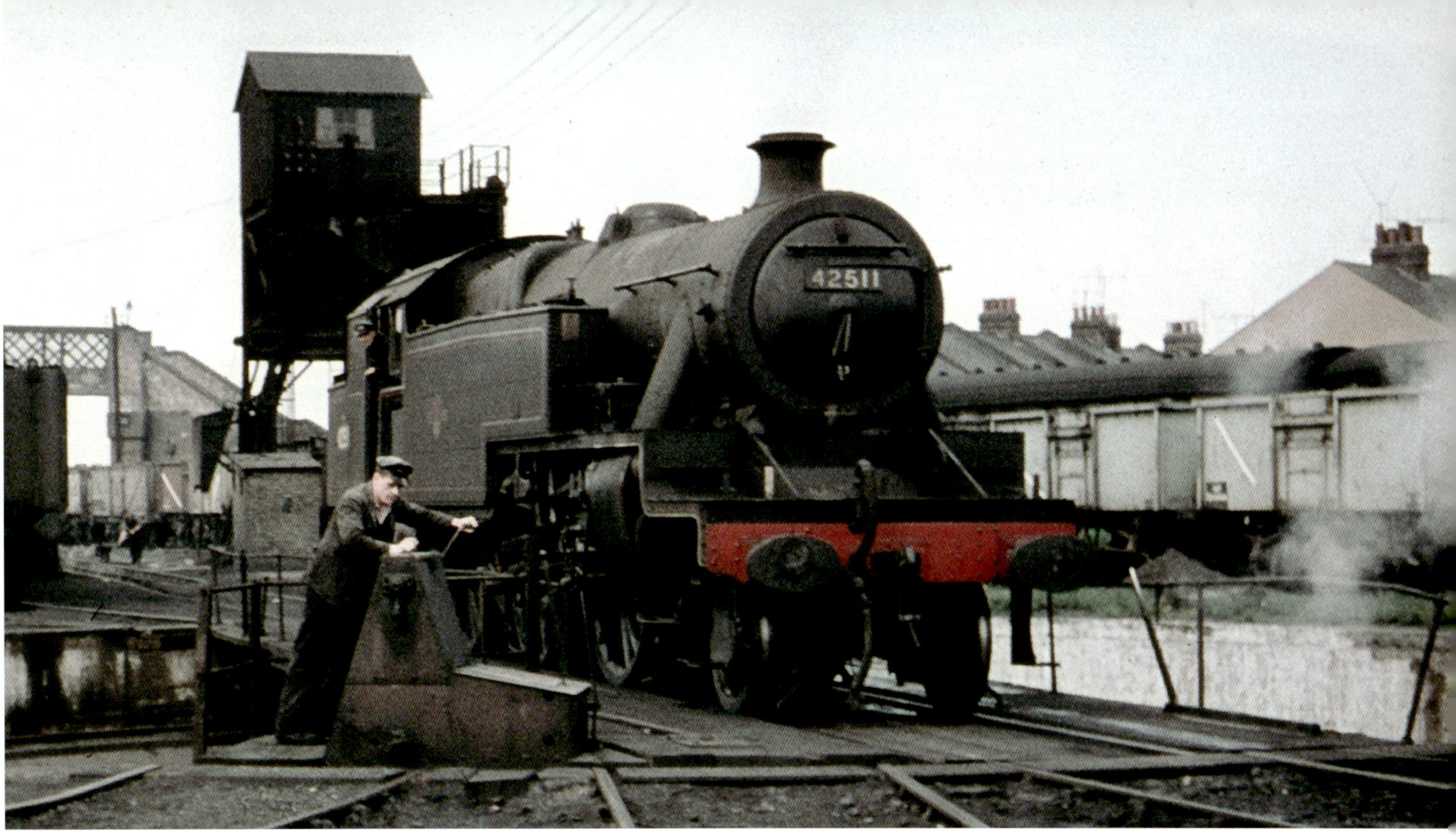

To try and cope with the demands of the heavy and intense services on the former LT&SR routes Stanier developed a three cylinder version of the 2-6-4T design. Thirty seven locomotives were built by Derby Works in 1934. Drivers on this section always preferred traditional running and 42511 is seen being turned the hard way at Shoeburyness on 15 April 1961. ***Late Vincent Heckford/Strathwood Library Collection***

Inside the roofless shed building at Shoeburyness the same day was 42504. The first withdrawn was 42512 in November 1960 and by June 1962 when the full electrification of the routes came into force the remainder were taken out of service en masse. ***Late Vincent Heckford/Strathwood Library Collection***

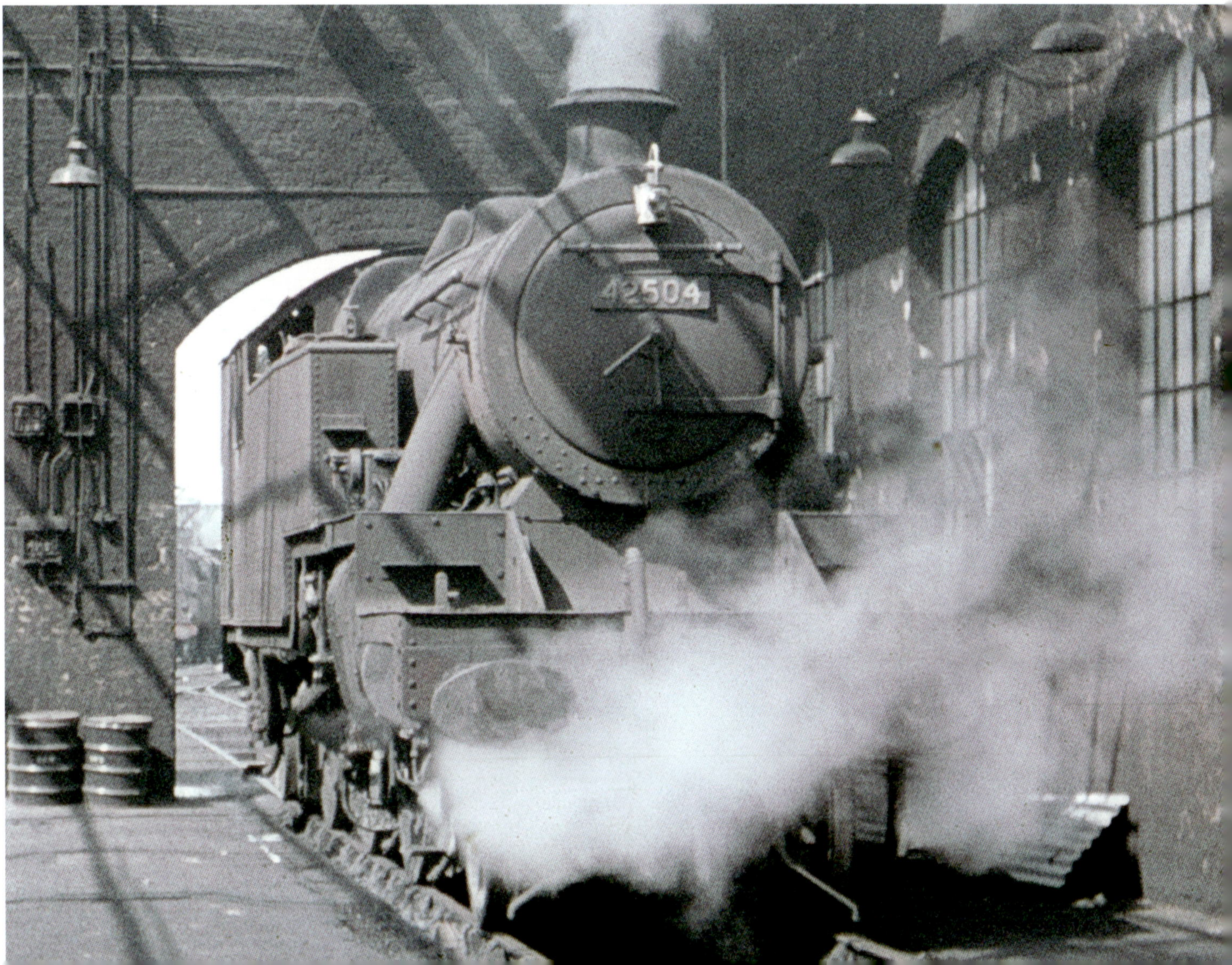

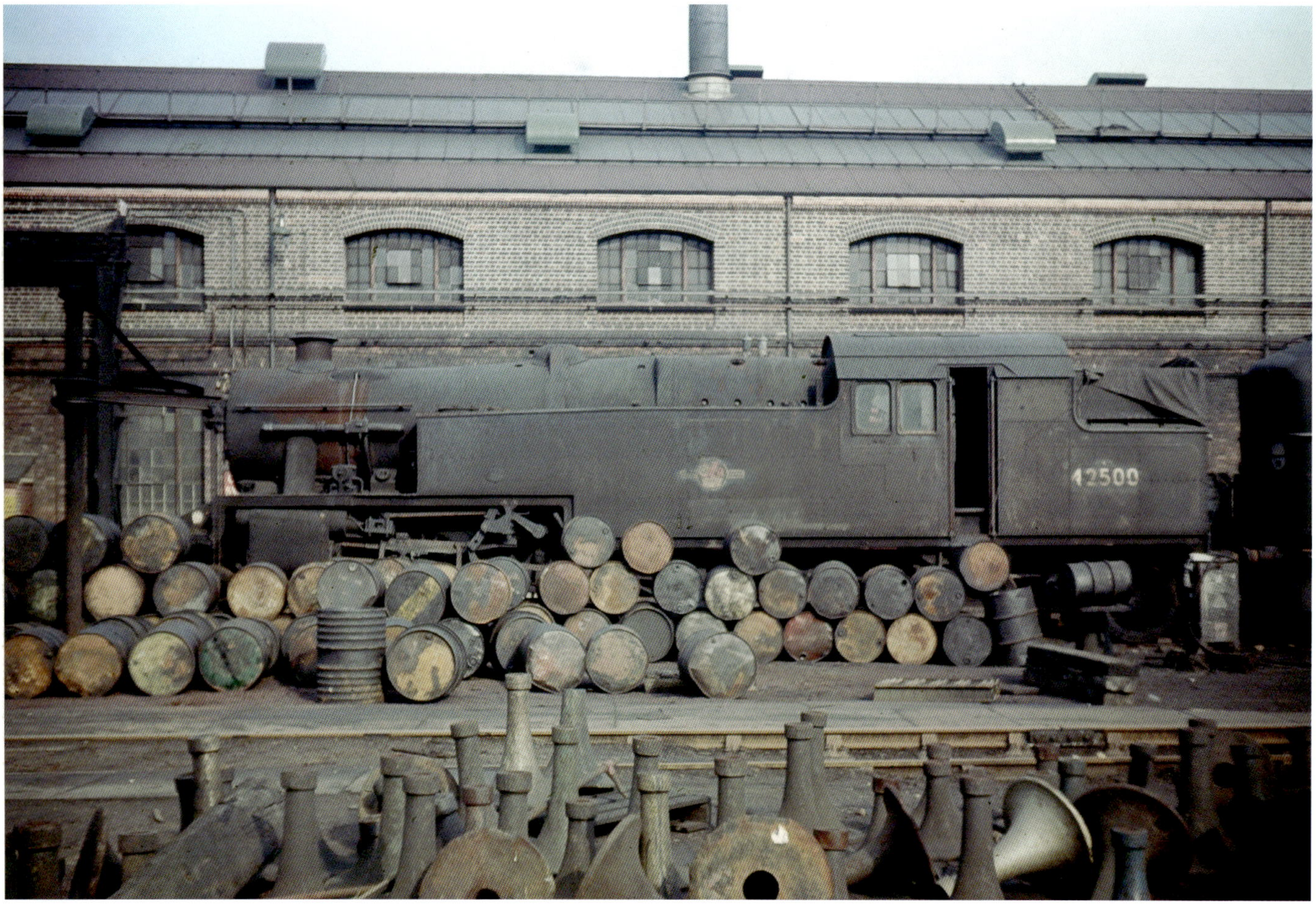

Fortunately the first of the class 42500 was set aside at Derby Works as part of the National Collection, and here it lingered for a number of years until it was restored and sent to Bressingham for display. ***Len Smith***

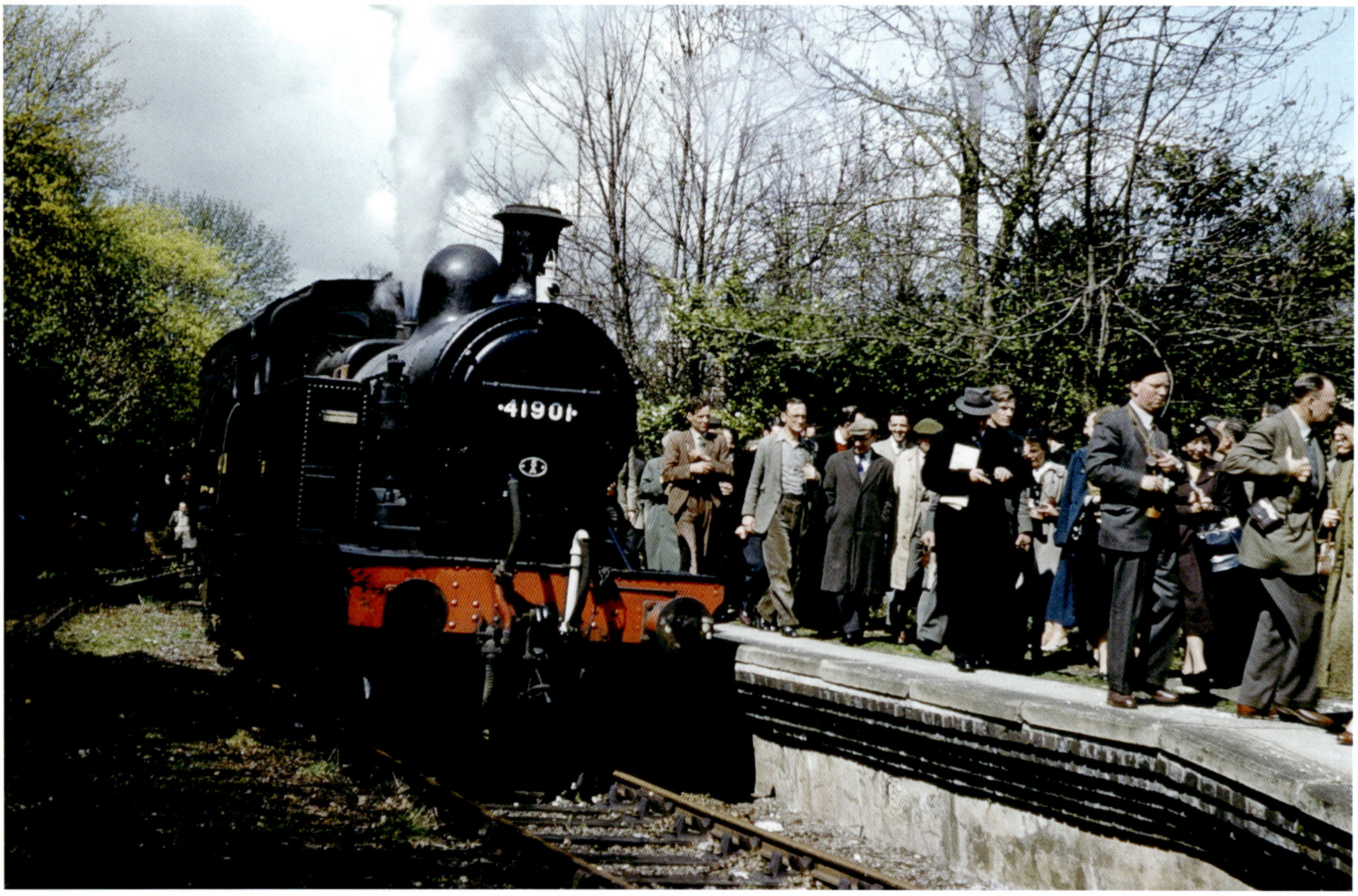

Stanier's first design when he came to the LMS from Swindon in 1932 were ten 2P 0-4-4Ts. Working a special at Stanmore's LNWR station was 41901 in 1958 a year before nine of the ten were withdrawn leaving the 41900 to soldier on alone until March 1962. ***Strathwood Library Collection***

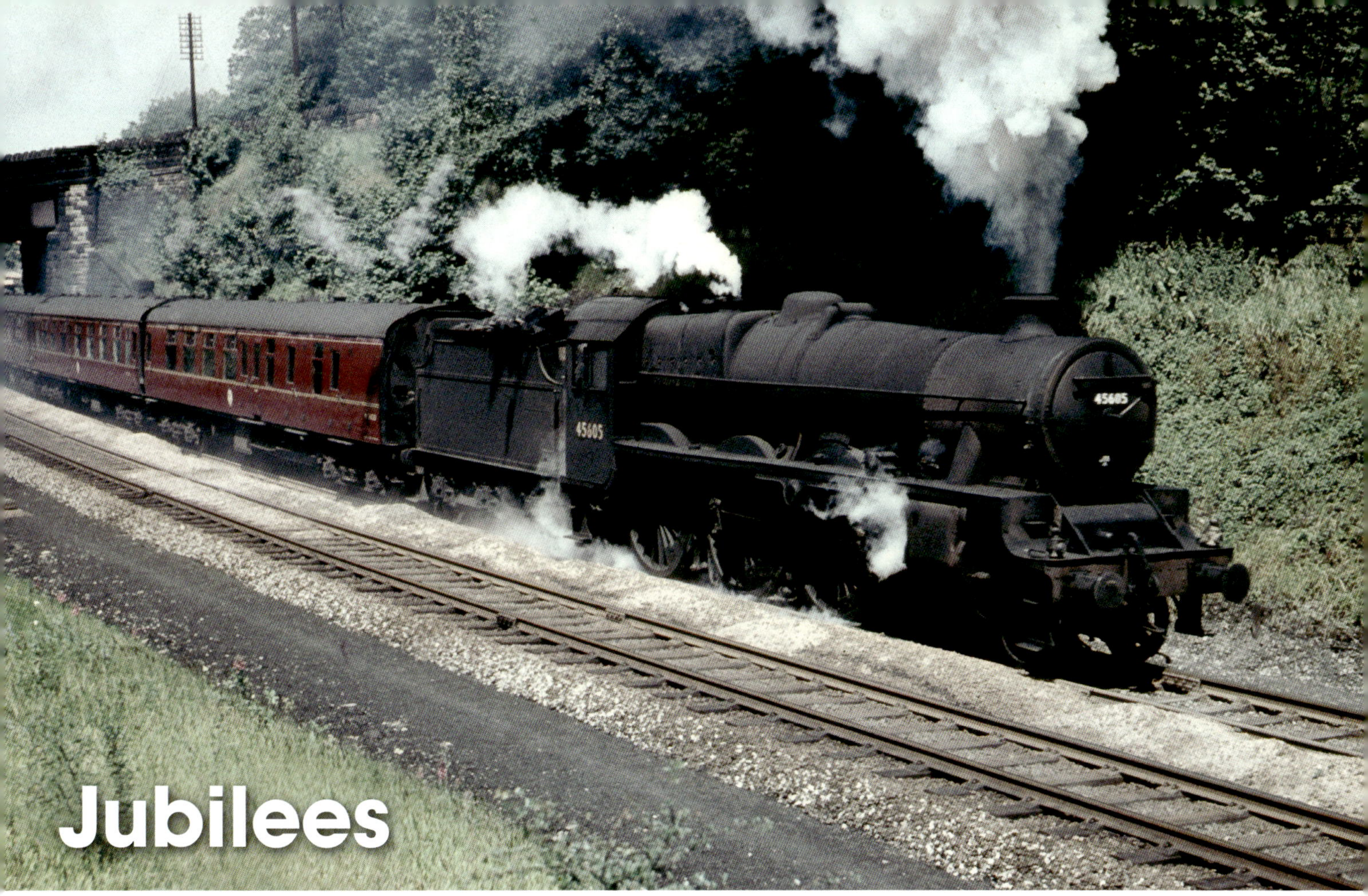

Jubilees

This class although popular with many enthusiasts would leave some enginemen in despair during their history with unreliable steaming at times. However we start with 45605 Cyprus fair tearing through Dore & Totley in 1958 with no such problems today. ***Strathwood Library Collection***

Another filthy machine 45681 Aboukir, this time fitted with the later 4000 gallon tender stands awaiting its next turn away from Blackpool during September 1963. ***John Rowe***

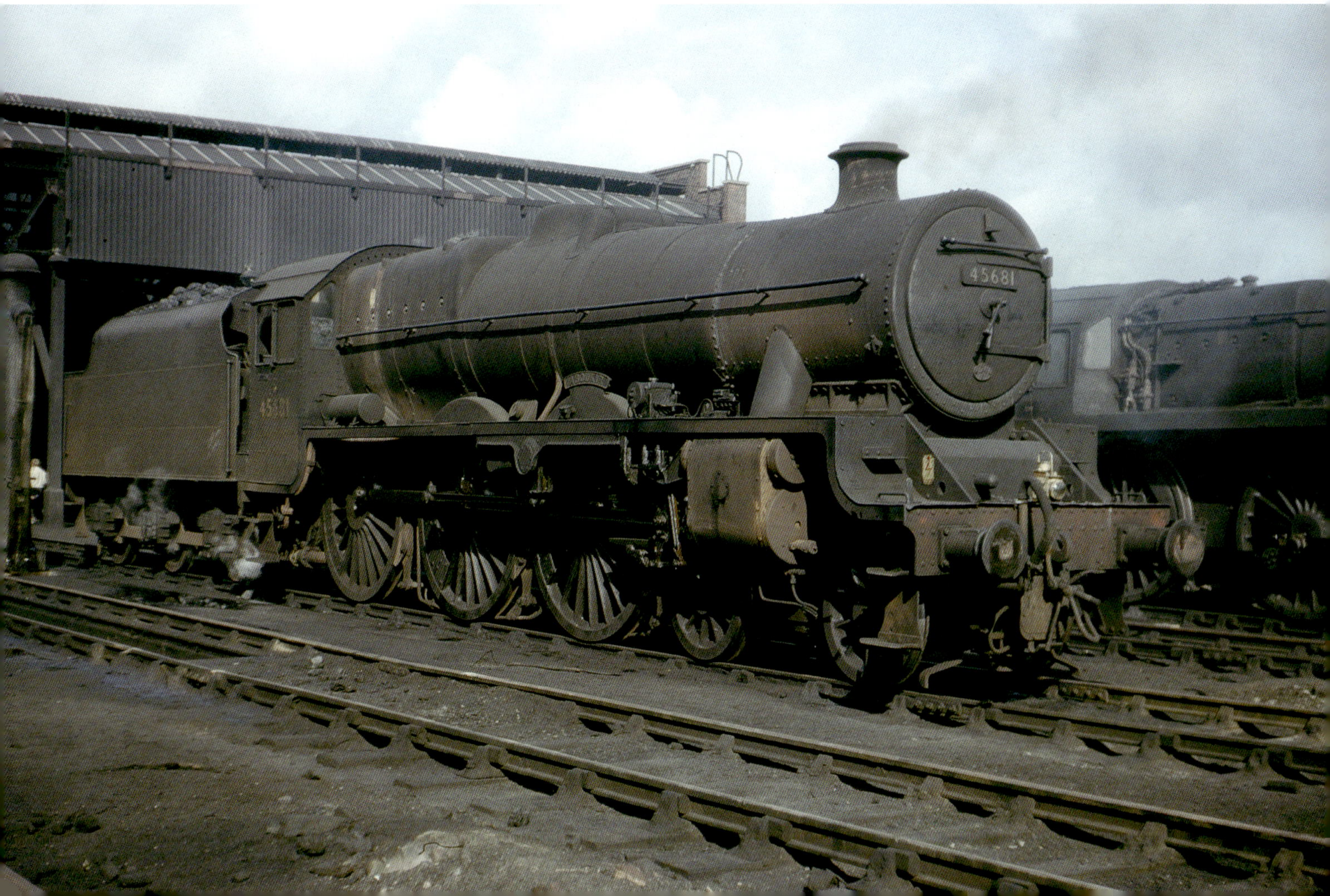

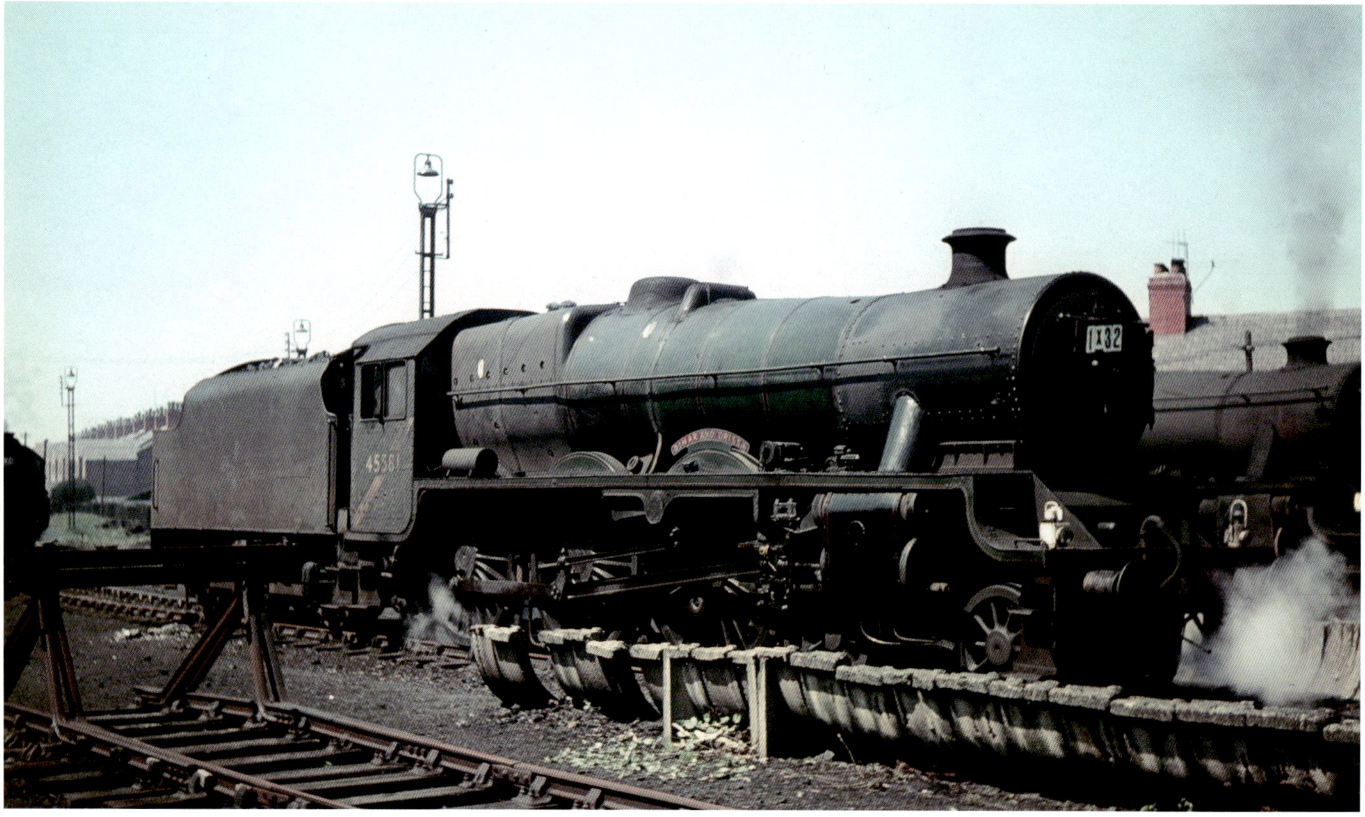

Just fifteen of the one hundred and ninety one Jubilees survived to see the start of 1966 where we see 45581 Bihar and Orissa again at Blackpool North shed on Bank Holiday Monday 30 May of this, their penultimate year in service. By the August Bank Holiday of 1966 this one would be withdrawn too leaving just eight at the year's end. ***Peter Coton***

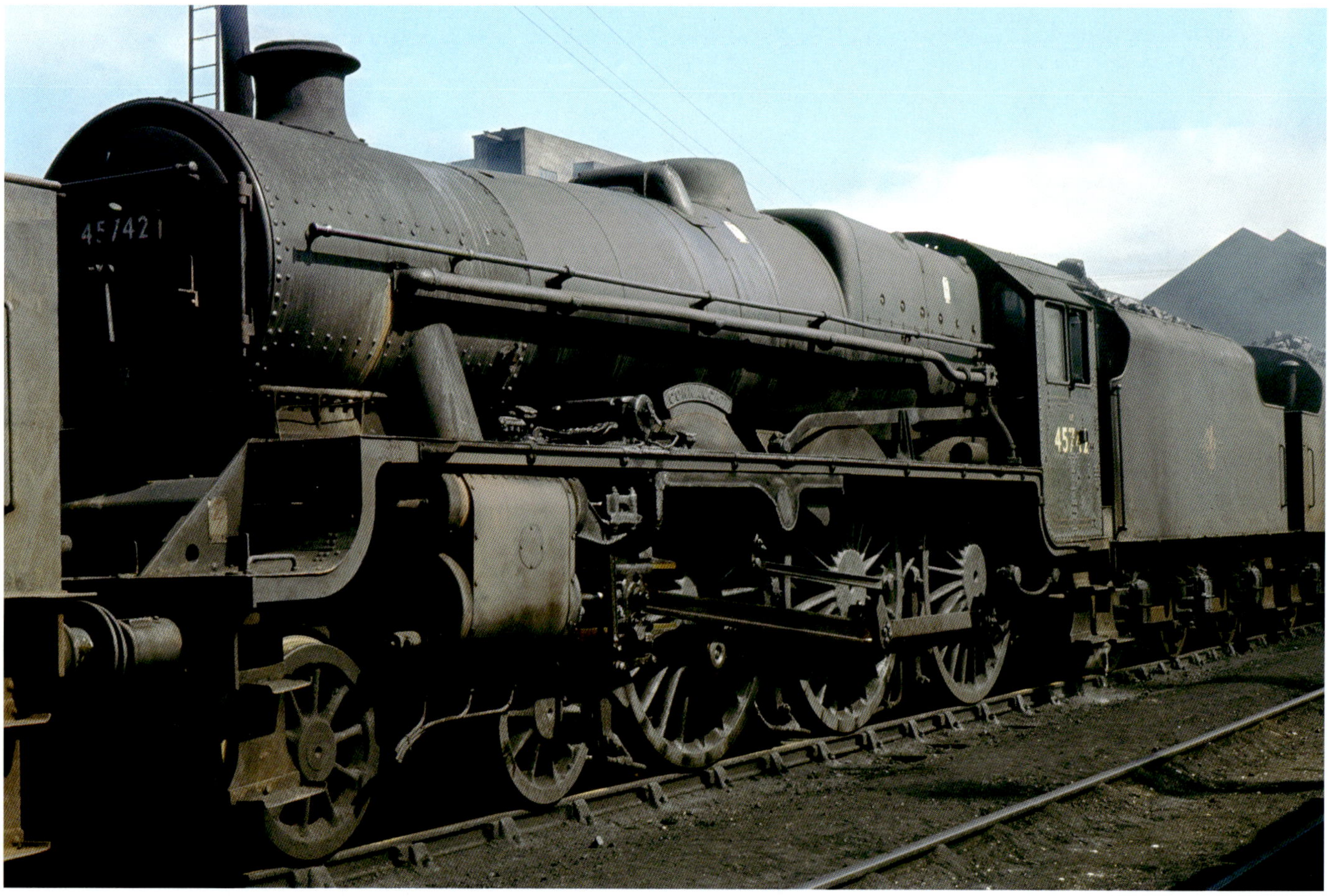

Such was the need for change on the LMS that they ordered batches from four workshops to be built at the same time with Crewe and Derby engaged in construction with the majority including 45742 Connaught the last built from the former LNWR works, whilst North British set about building theirs in both Queens Park and Hyde Park works in Glasgow. This is Connaught as she was at Kingmoor on 12 July 1964. ***Strathwood Library Collection***

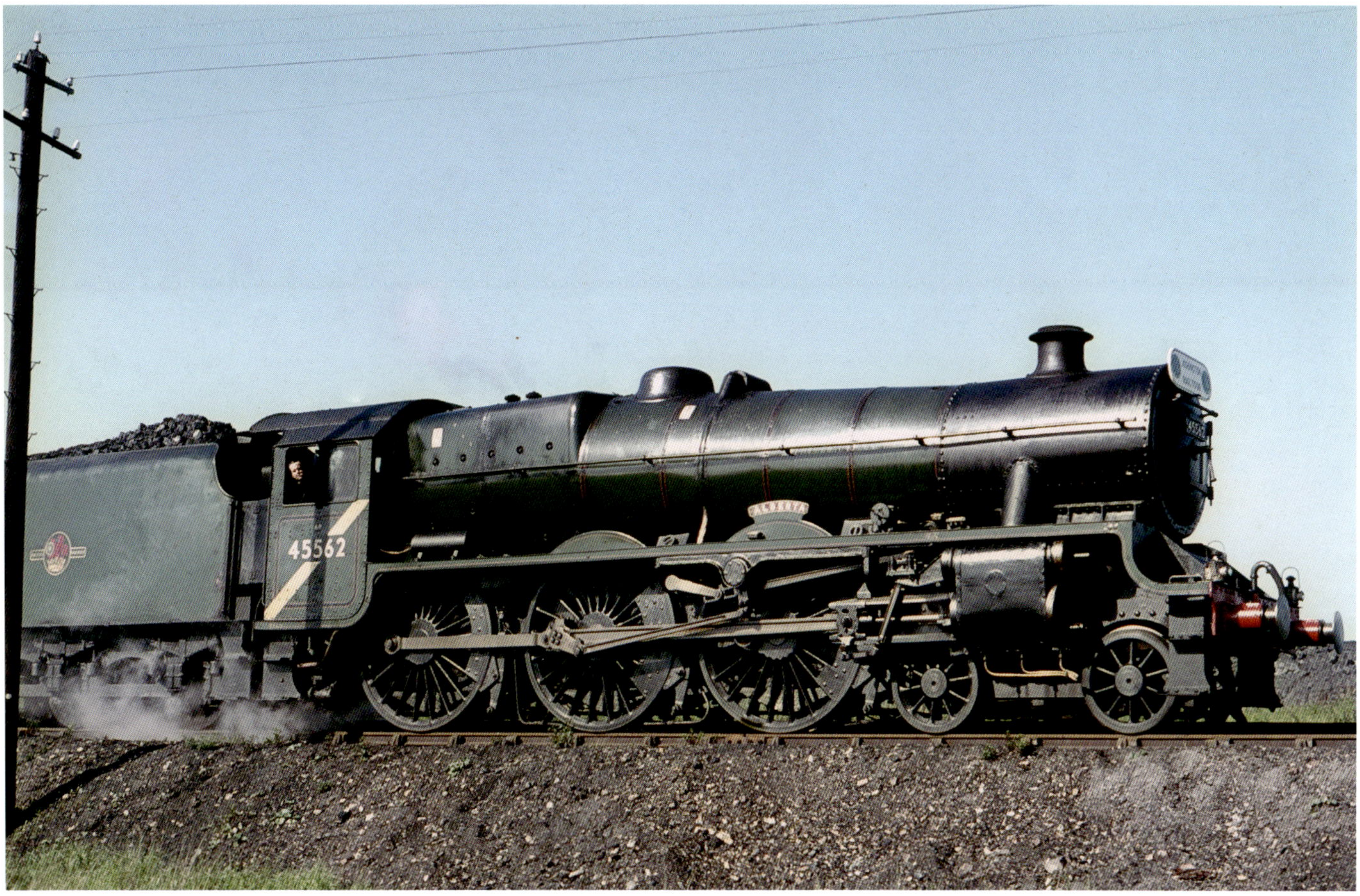

Running with a tender switched from a Black Five and painted in unlined green was 45562 Alberta on a special at Ashington on 10 June 1967. ***Strathwood Library Collection***

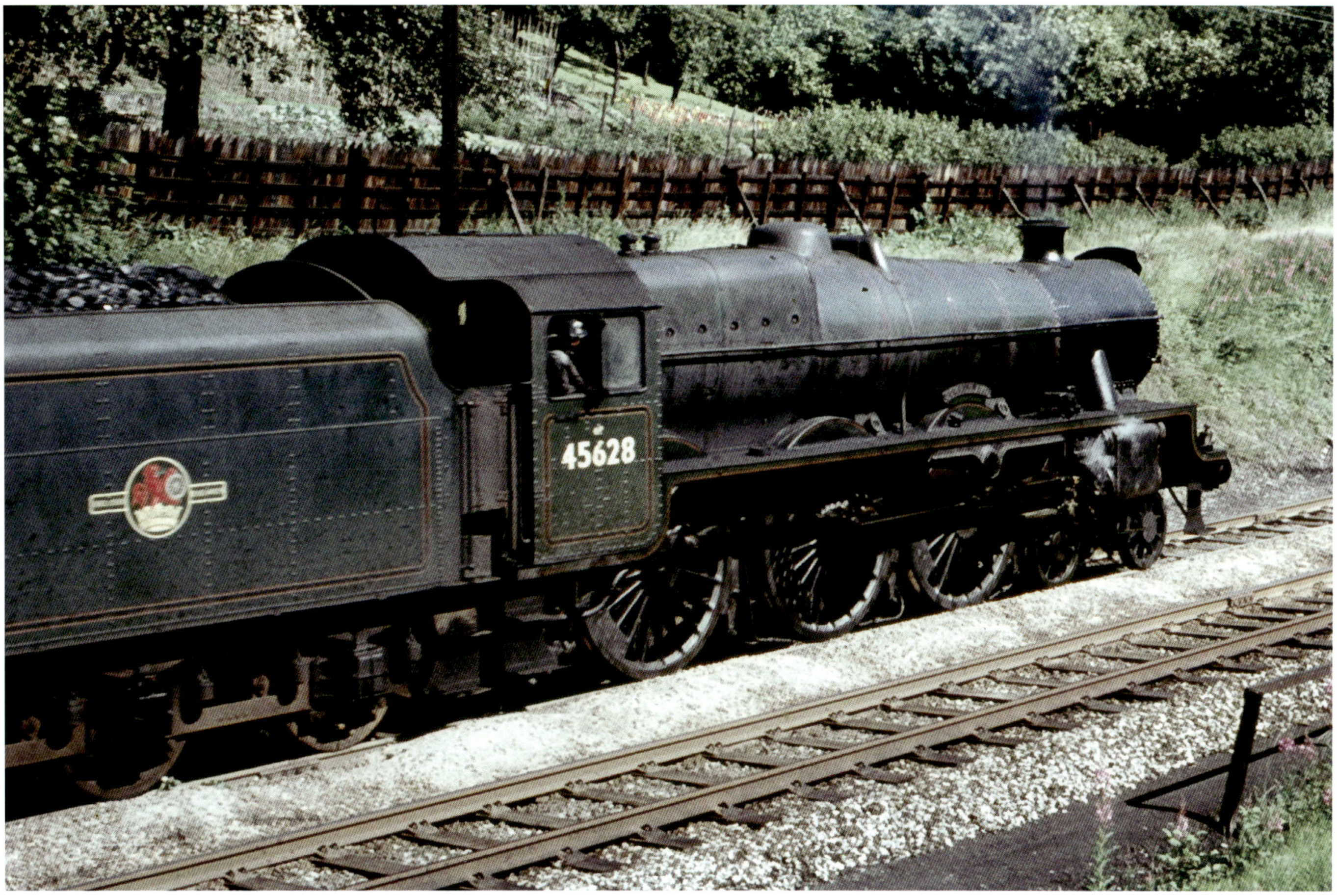

Although two of the class had Stanier 3500 gallon tenders the fitting of both Stanier 4000 gallon welded and riveted tenders would be sporadic through the history of the class with many changes taking place. In 1960 45628 Somaliland was running with rivetted type when recorded at Dore & Totley. ***Strathwood Library Collection***

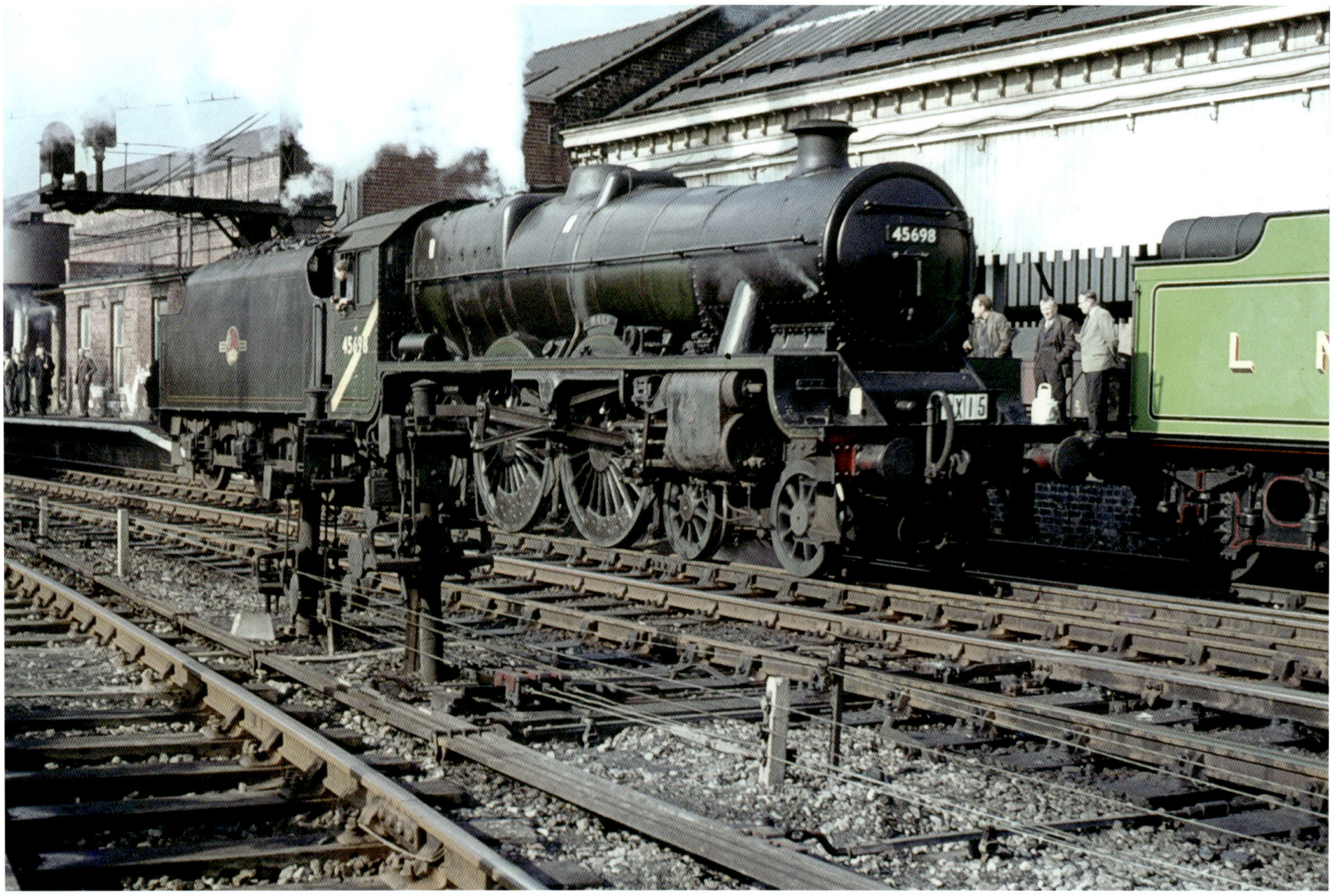

A welded tender is behind 45698 Mars, one of the last survivors on another special duty with The Great Marquess at Wakefield. ***Strathwood Library Collection***

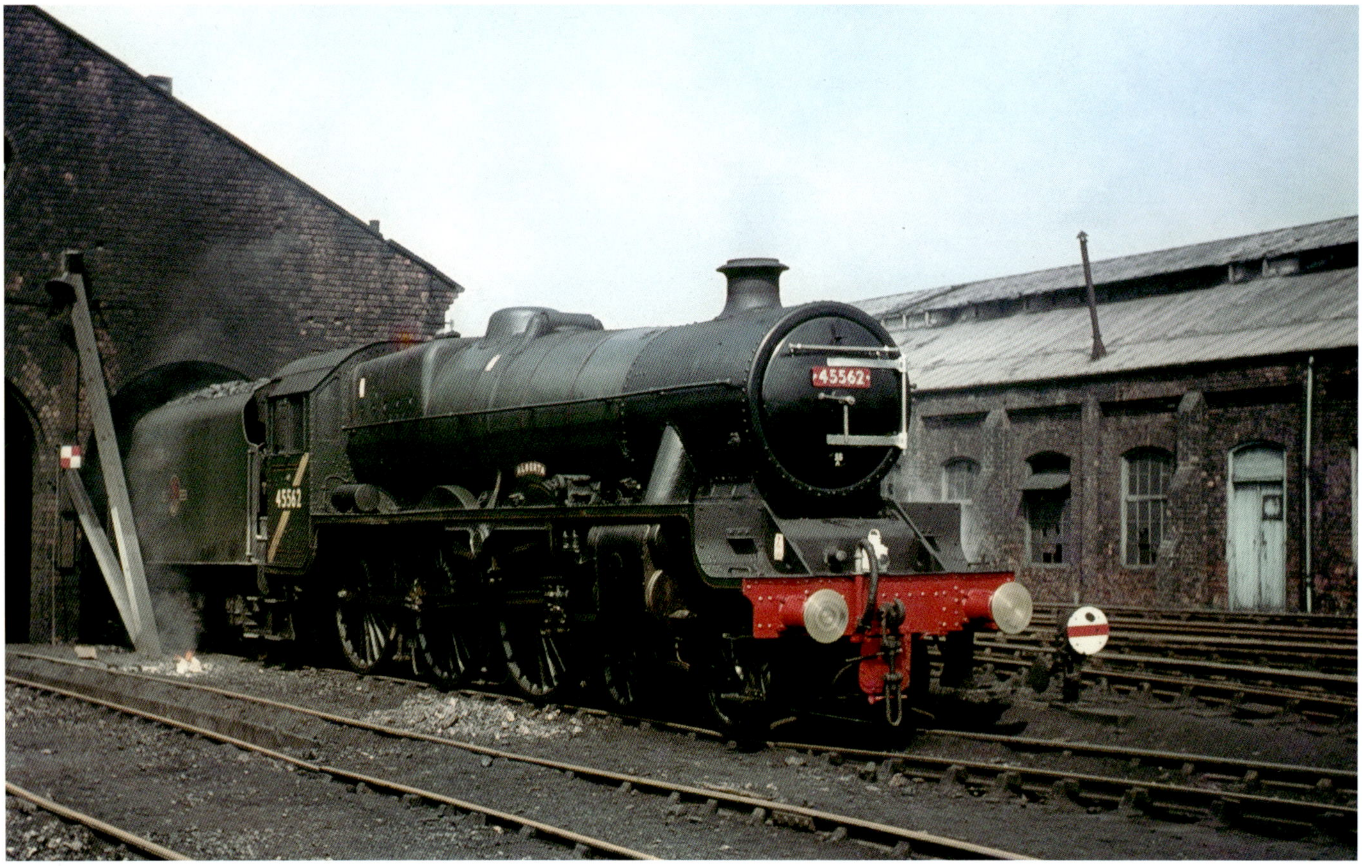

Also engaged on a special 45562 Alberta brings an air of glamour perhaps to West Hartlepool shed with its usual diet of more lowly freight and mixed traffic locomotives in 1967. ***Strathwood Library Collection***

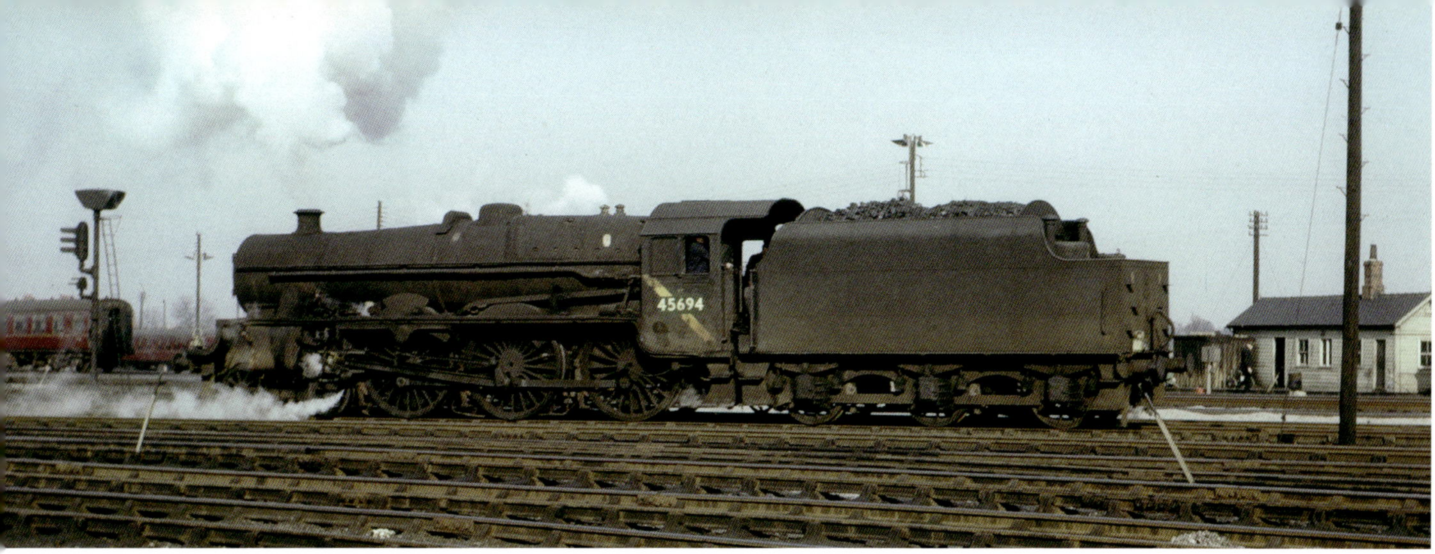

Staying in former North Eastern Railway territory we find 45694 Bellerophon at York in October 1966 where for the majority of their careers they were regular visitors. ***John Gill***

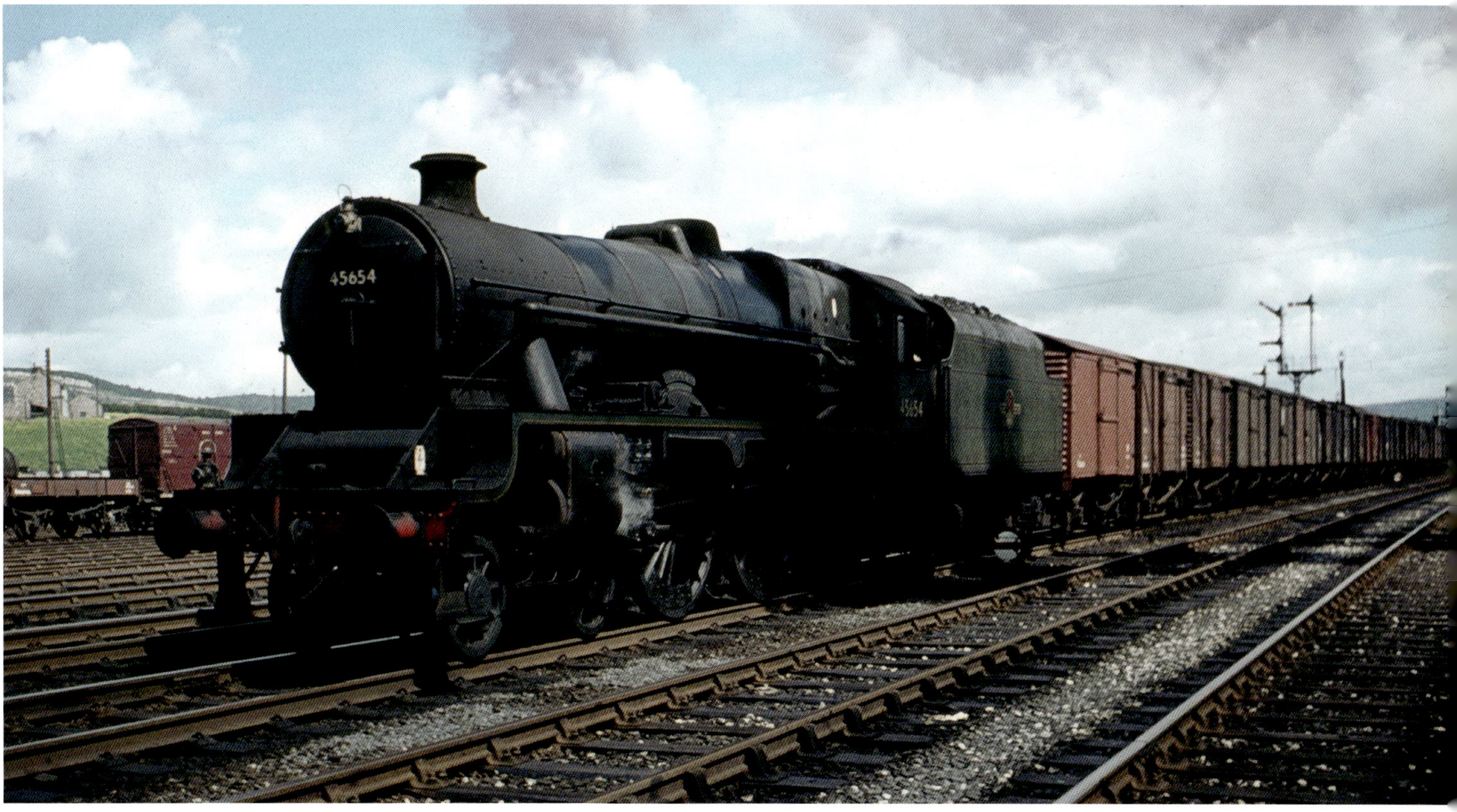

Showing their not uncommon use on fitted freight trains is 45654 Hood getting away from Lancaster in 1962. ***Late Ray Helm/Strathwood Library Collection***

Below: Four years before also at Lancaster we see 45593 Kolhapur arriving with a semi fast passenger working. ***Strathwood Library Collection***

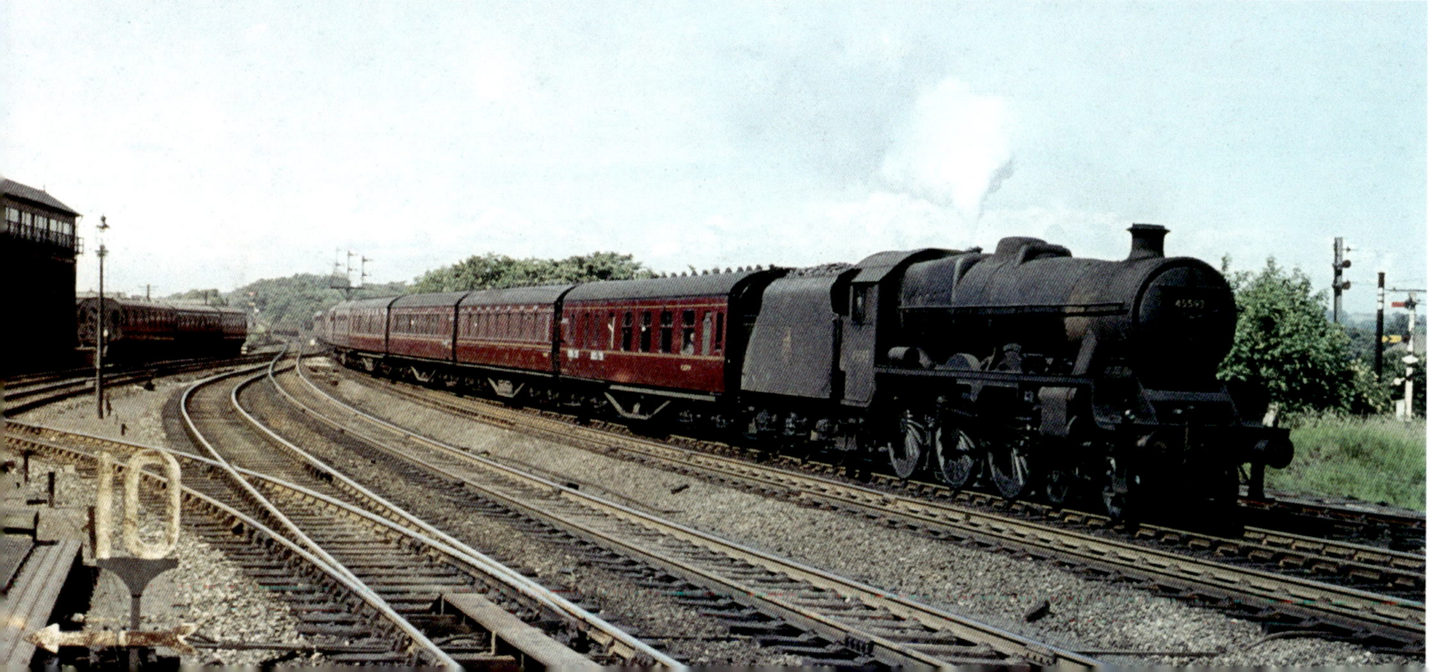

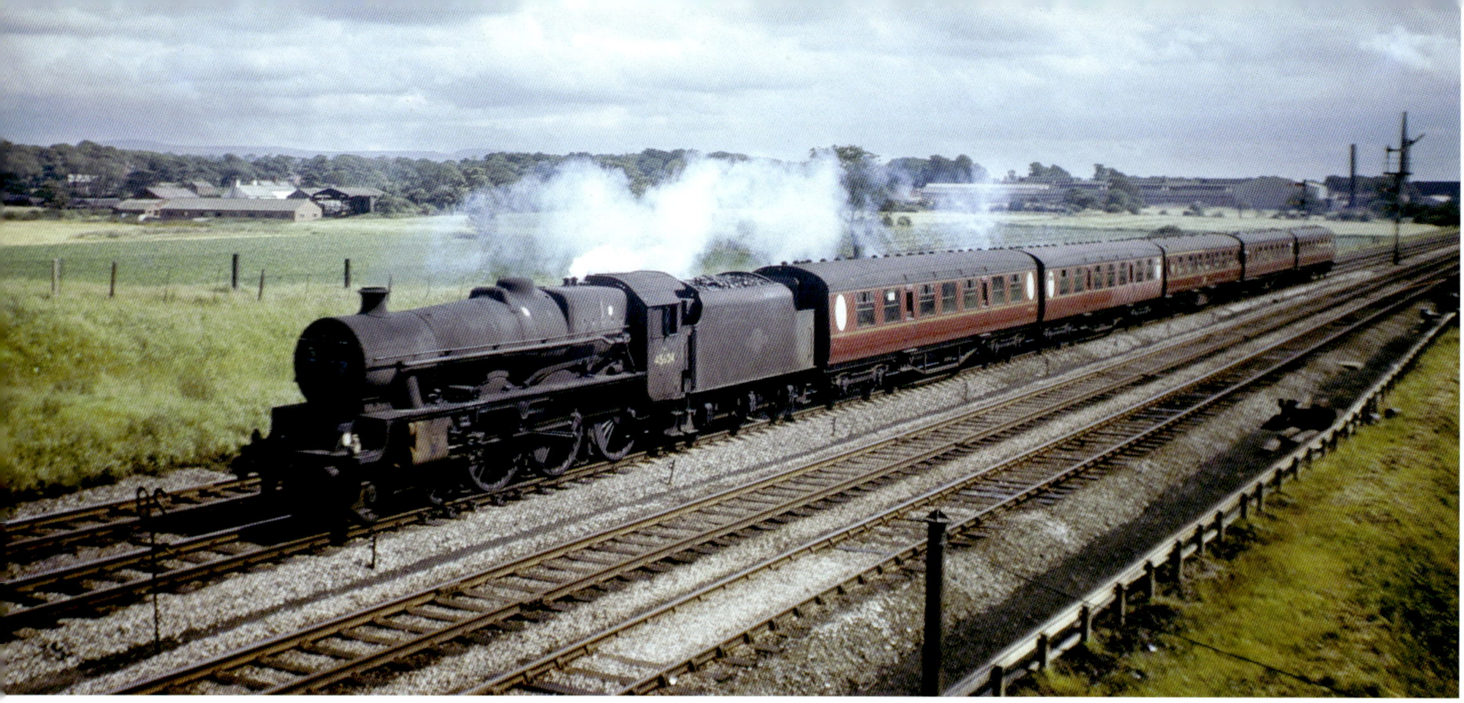

The variety of uses the class were put to meant that they could be seen all across the former LMS system, although the famed Corkerhill allocation did not stray too far from the usual beats. Another lowly job for 45604 Ceylon, now with a Stanier tender, at Farrington on 11 June 1964. ***Chris Forrest***

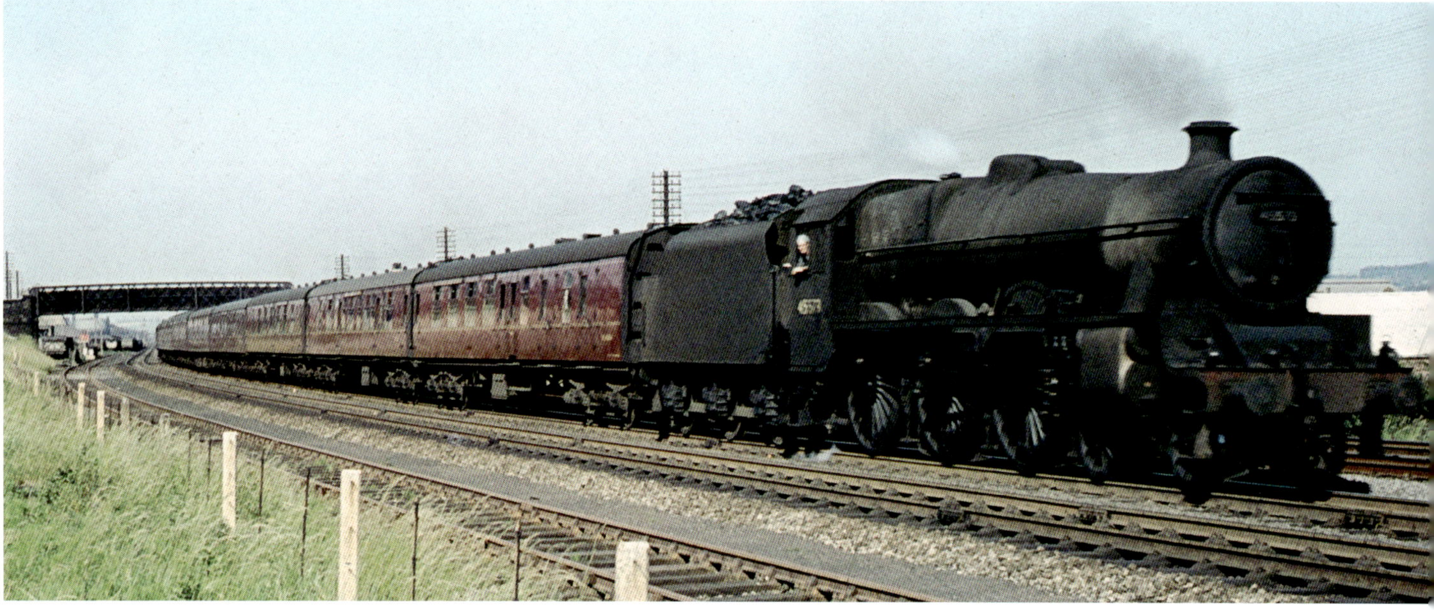

The use of the class on inter-regional and cross country routes gave much employment to the class such as here near Rotherham where we see firstly 45573 Newfoundland and 45599 Bechuanaland in 1958. ***Both: Strathwood Library Collection***

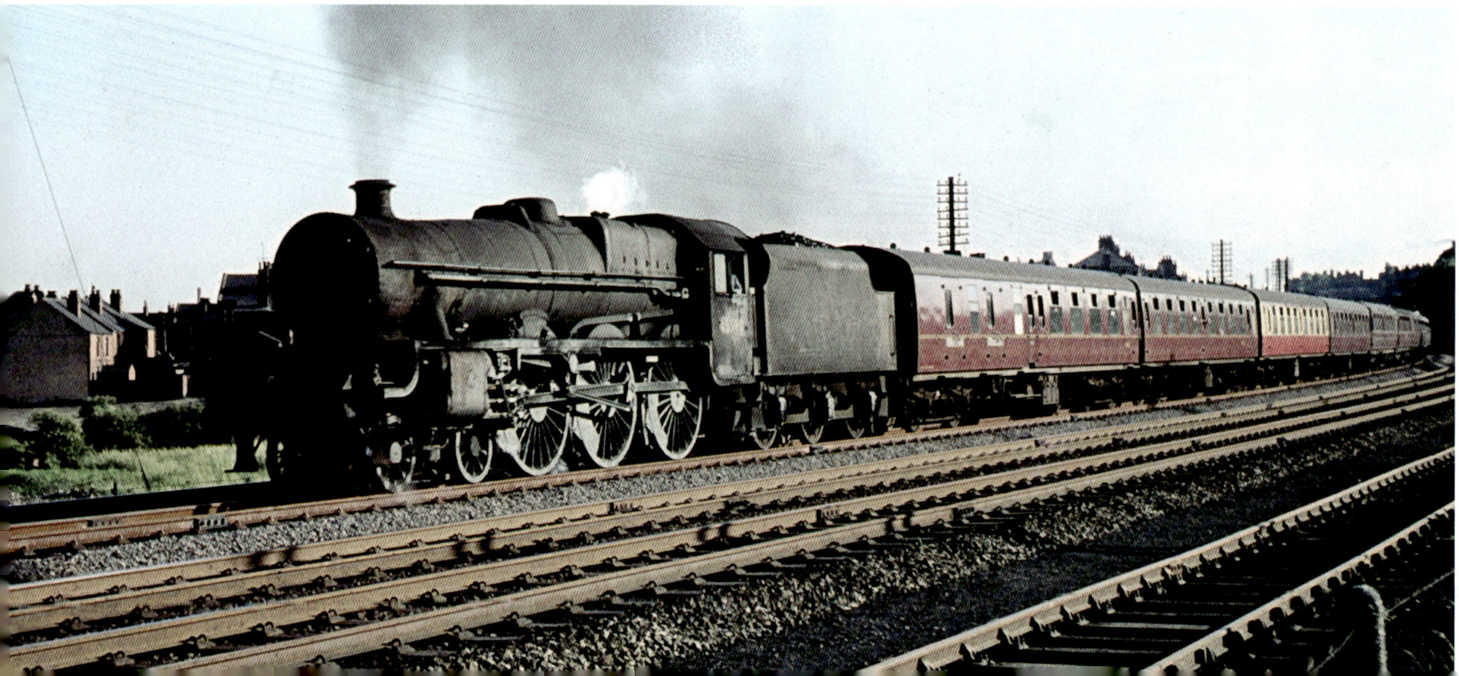

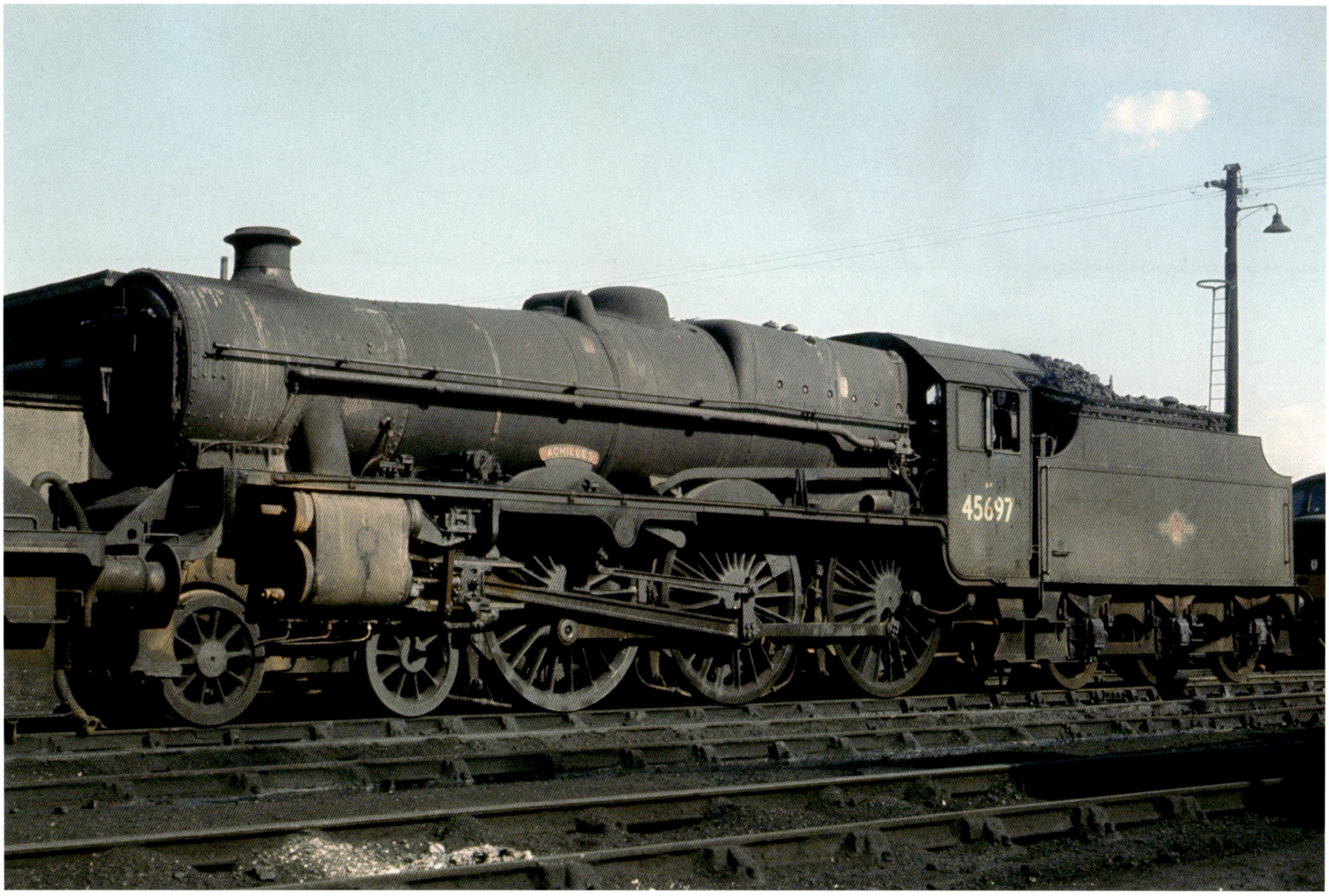

Not all of the class ran with Stanier tenders in the end as seen by 45697 Achilles at Kingmoor on 18 April 1964. ***Strathwood Library Collection***

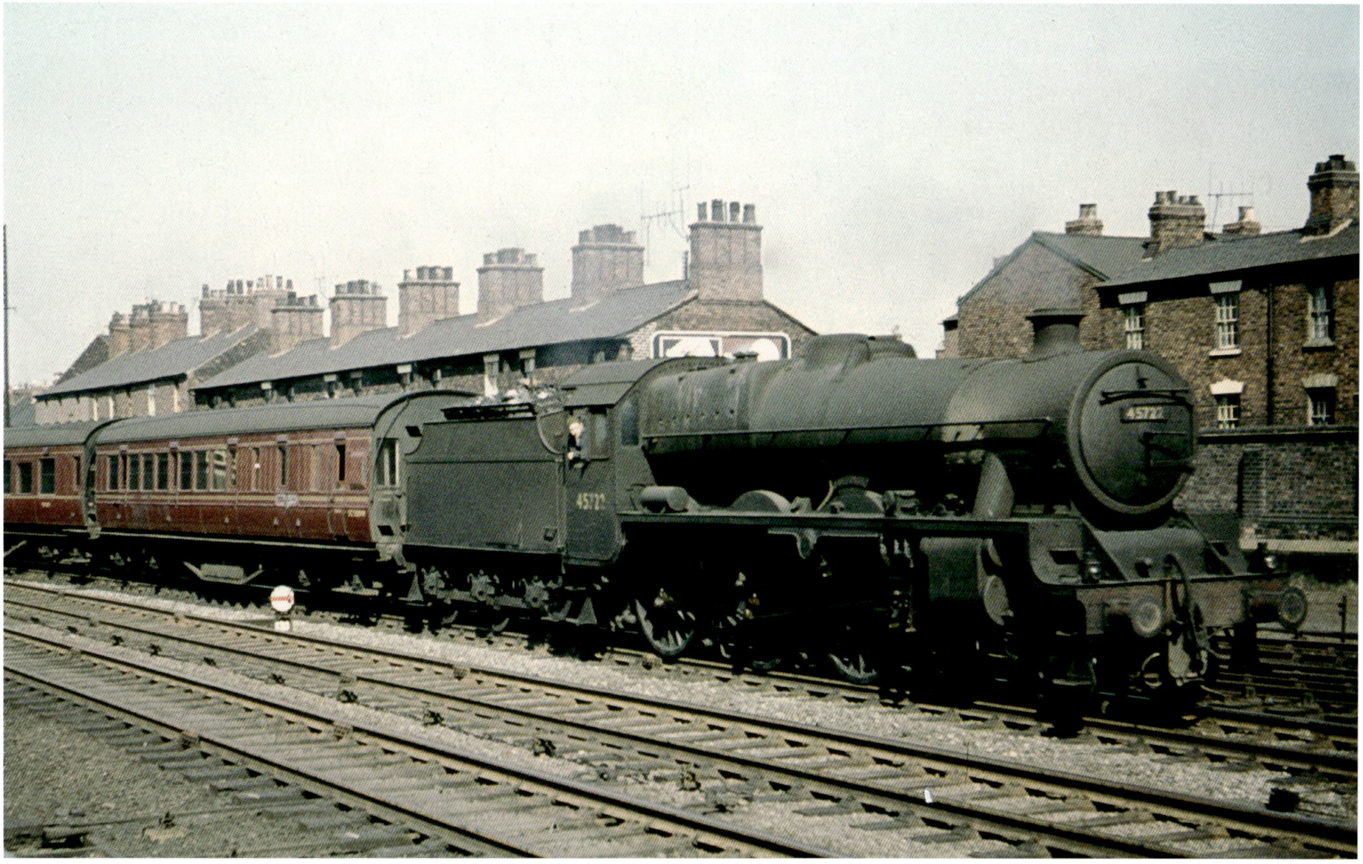

In the late 1950s 45722 Defence enters Stafford. This locomotive was briefly fitted with a double chimney for tests at Rugby Testing Station in 1956 as the class were still plagued by unreliable steaming qualities, in spite of many modifications through their lives. ***Strathwood Library Collection***

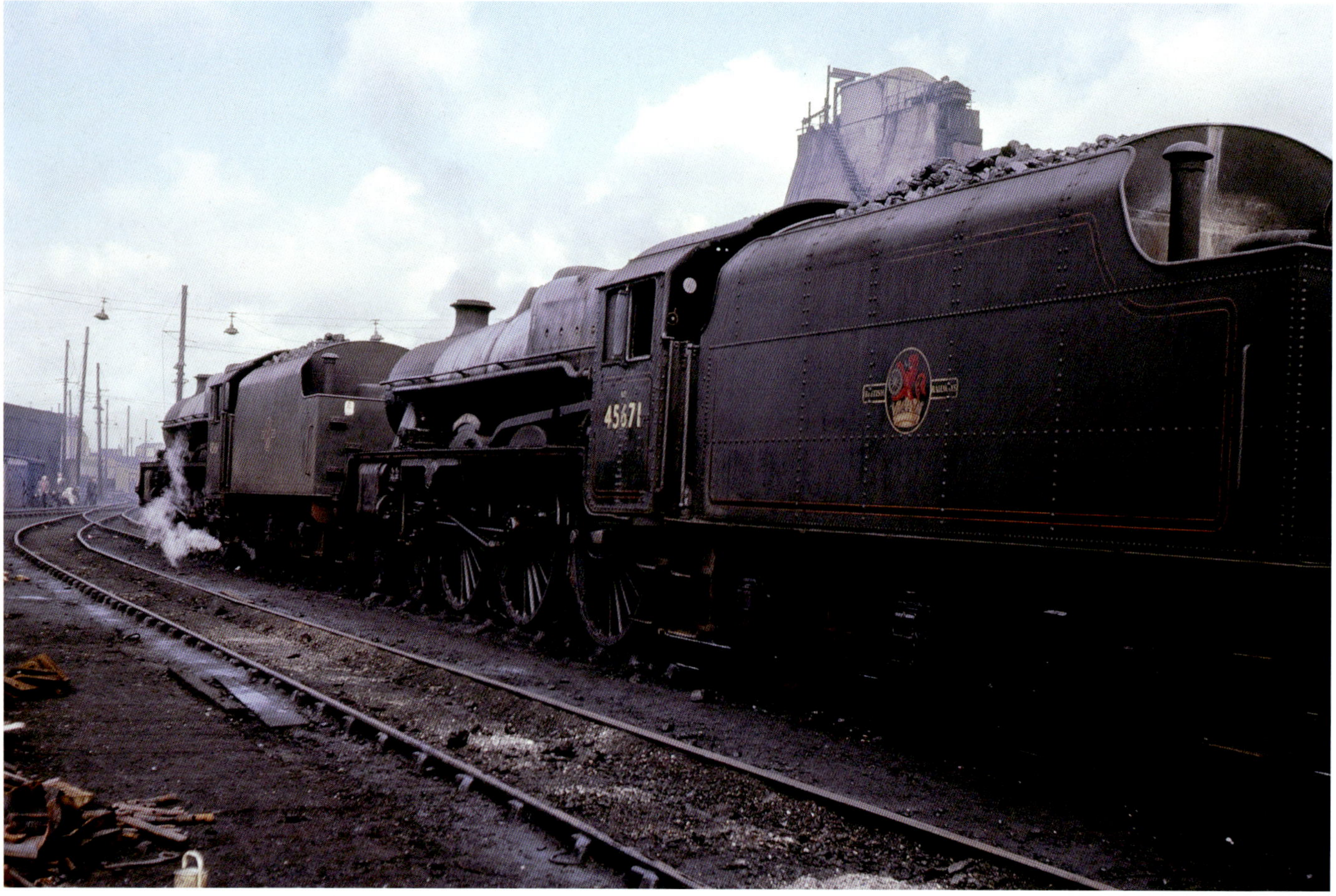

In the early war years 45671 Prince Rupert seen here at Willesden in August 1963 was fitted along with three other examples with manually controlled smoke box ash ejector equipment, which was removed by 1941. ***Win Wall/Strathwood Library Collection***

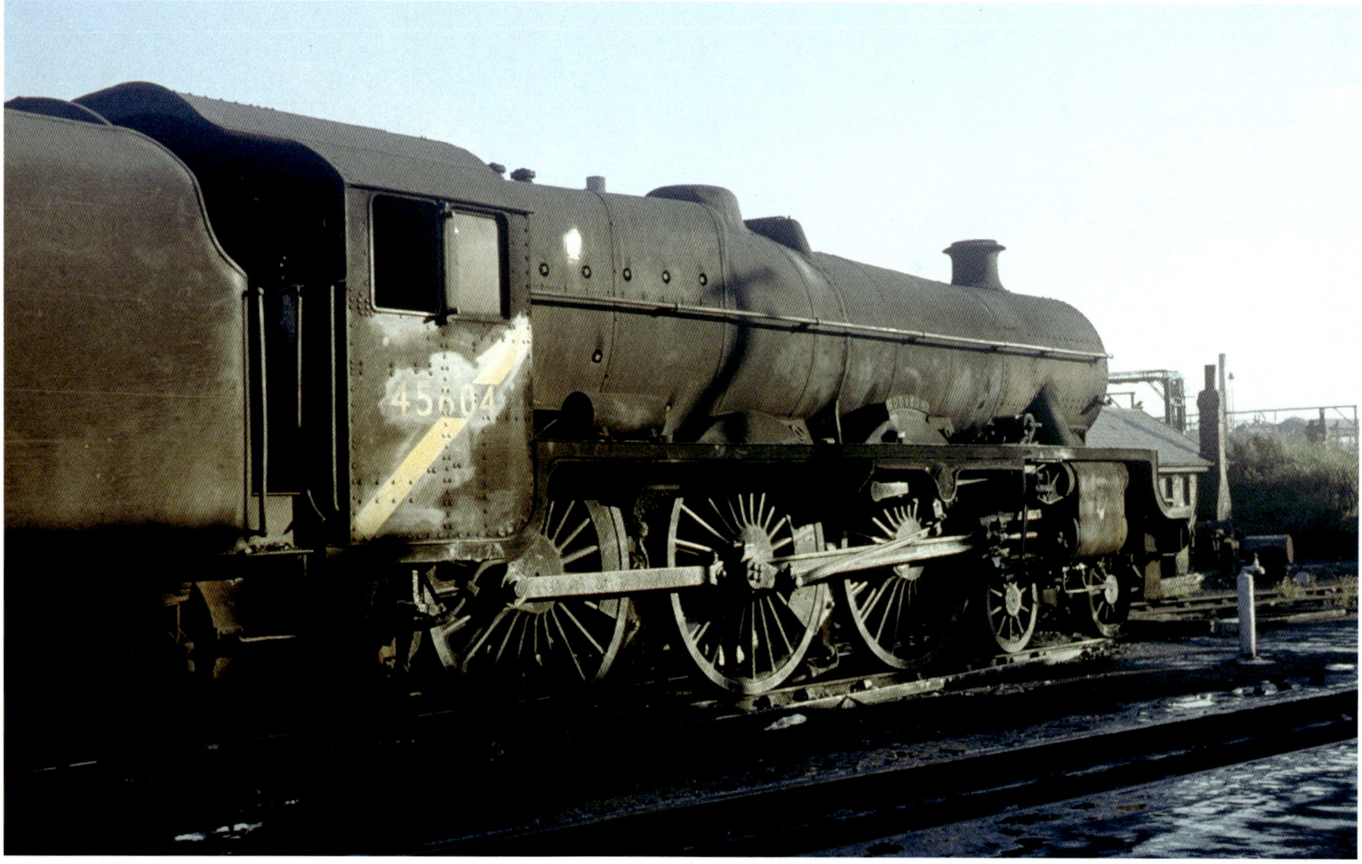

When built 5552-5664 were not originally named choices for names being drawn from the various Dominions, Colonies, Provinces and Dependencies of the United Kingdom, later followed by a selection of Admirals, naval battles and warships. By 26 September 45604 Ceylon was looking very much down at heel at Stockport Edgeley. ***Dave Down***

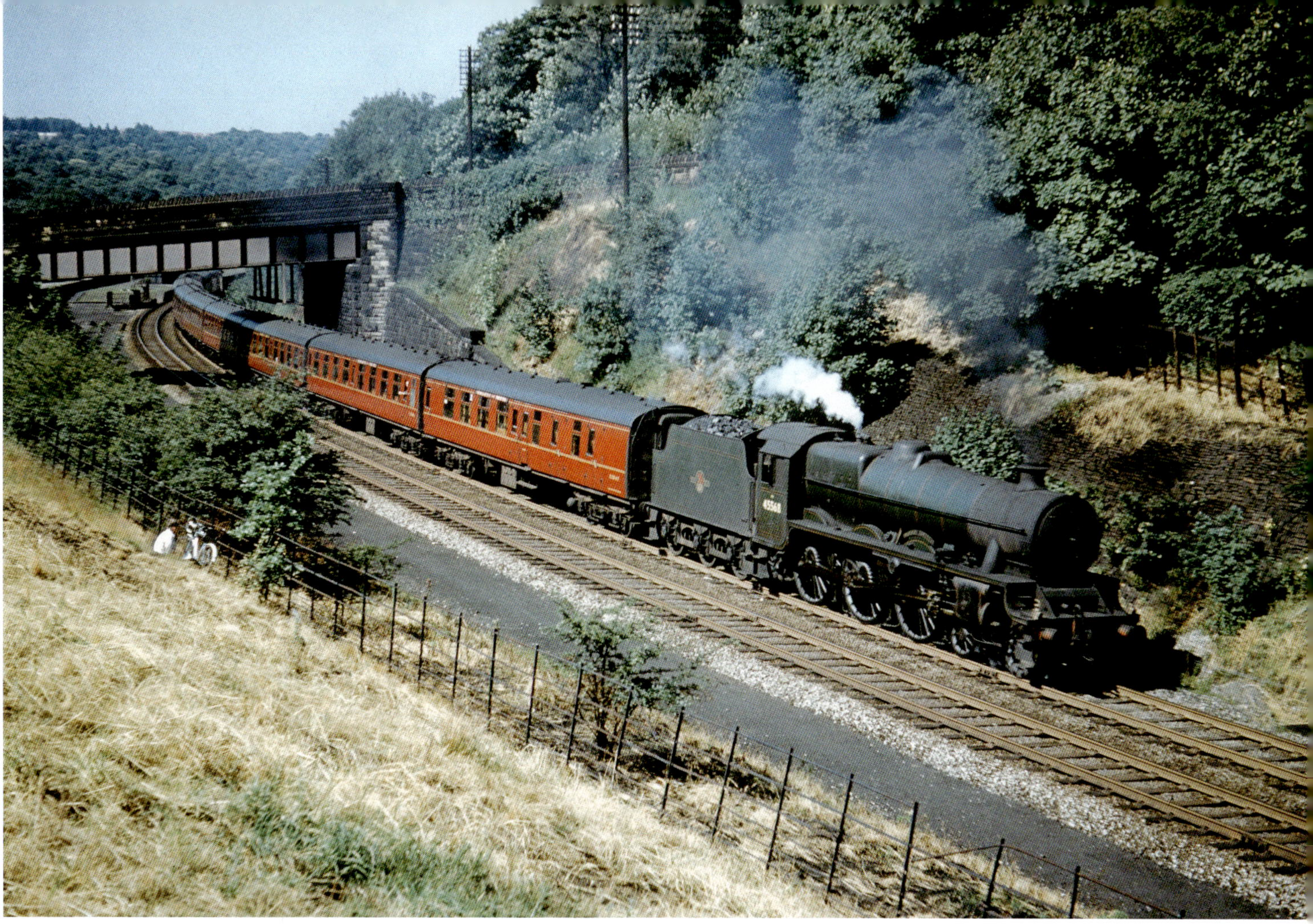

Back to the tender variations at Dore & Totley once again with 45568 Western Australia running with a Fowler high sided 3500 gallon tender, number 45710 Irresistable and 45719 Glorious were also seen with this type of tender in the 1950s. ***Strathwood Library Collection***

Commencing with 5665 built in November 1935 the remainder of the Jubilees were built with a modified boiler giving the appearance of a slightly longer firebox with an increase in the size of the superheater size to 24 elements. One these improved locomotives 45683 Jutland is seen arriving at Rotherham in 1958. ***Strathwood Library Collection***

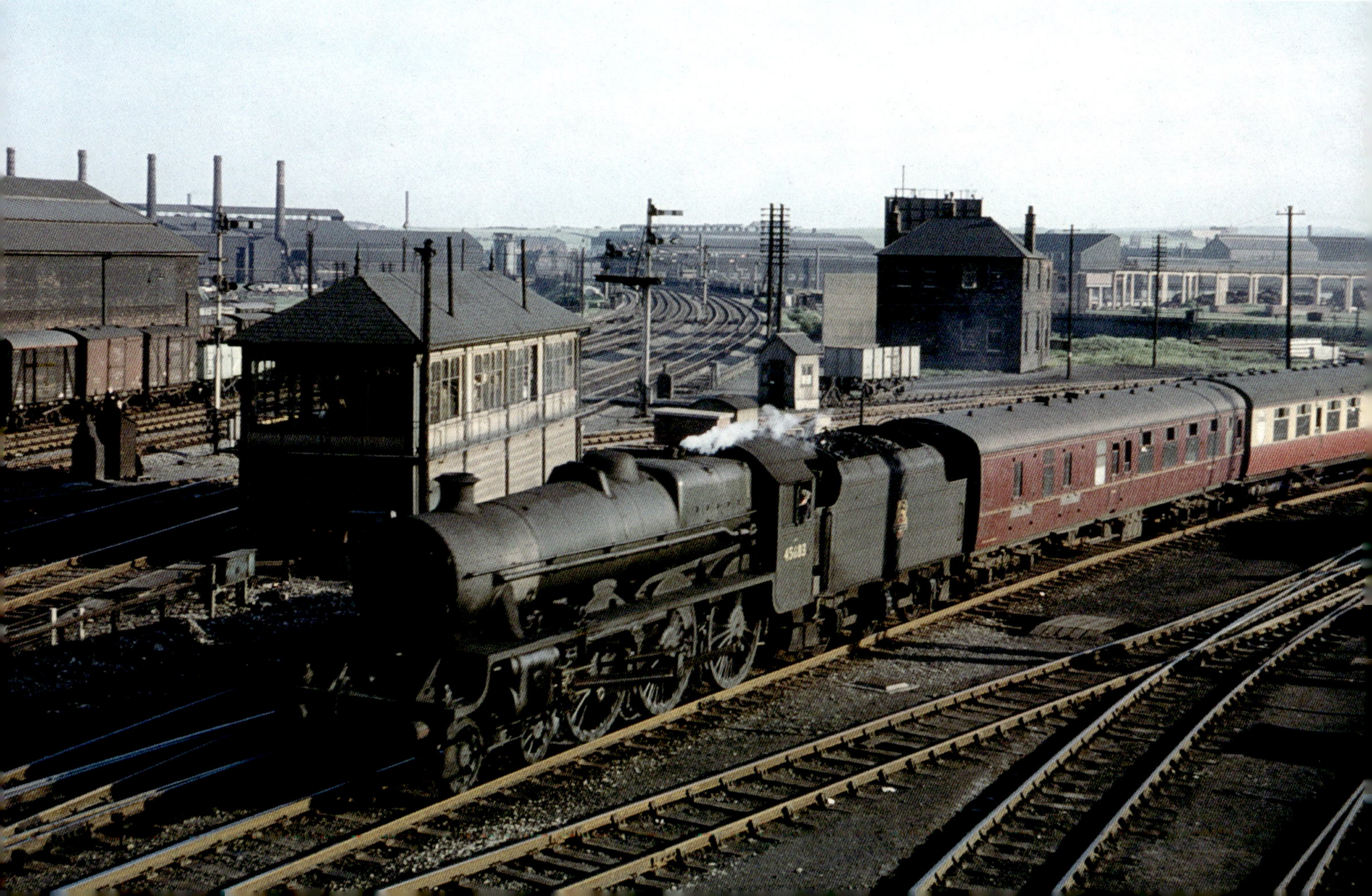

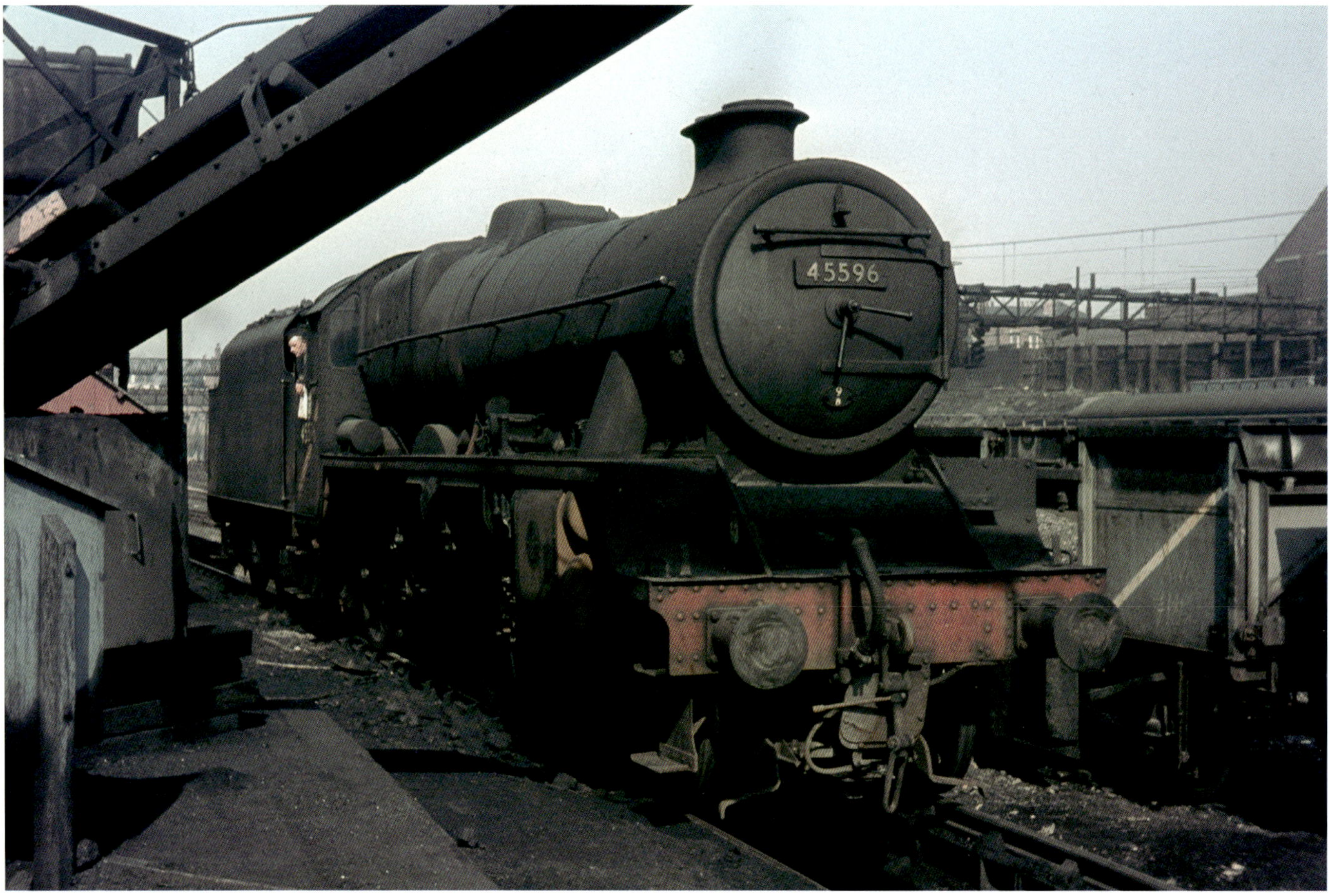

After the experimentation to 45722 mentioned earlier, 45596 Bahamas was fitted with a double chimney in 1958 which the engine retained beyond the end of its British Rail service days. Here we see the engine manoeuvring to take coal at Stockport Edgeley in 1966. ***Dave Down***

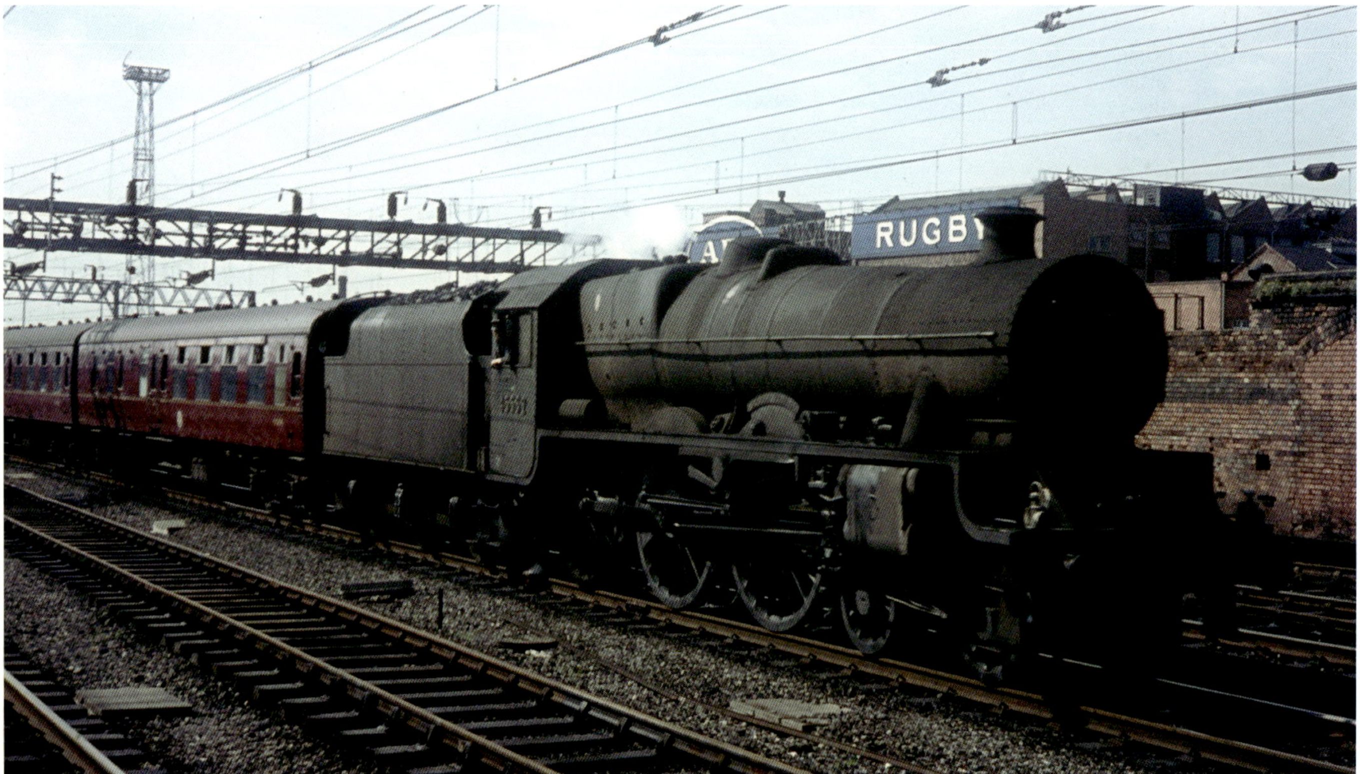

When the LMS management decided it wished to commemorate the Silver Jubilee of His Majesty King George V in May 1935 it wanted the first of the class to bear the name Silver Jubilee. In the event 5552 exchanged identities with the more recently delivered 5642, and was duly adorned with chromed nameplates, numbers, boiler bands and other fittings, set off by a smart plain black high gloss paint scheme for the naming ceremony at Euston. By 1964 the same locomotive was much more world weary although it still retained chromed metal numbers as 45552 when it passed the AEI works at Rugby. ***Jack Hodgkinson***

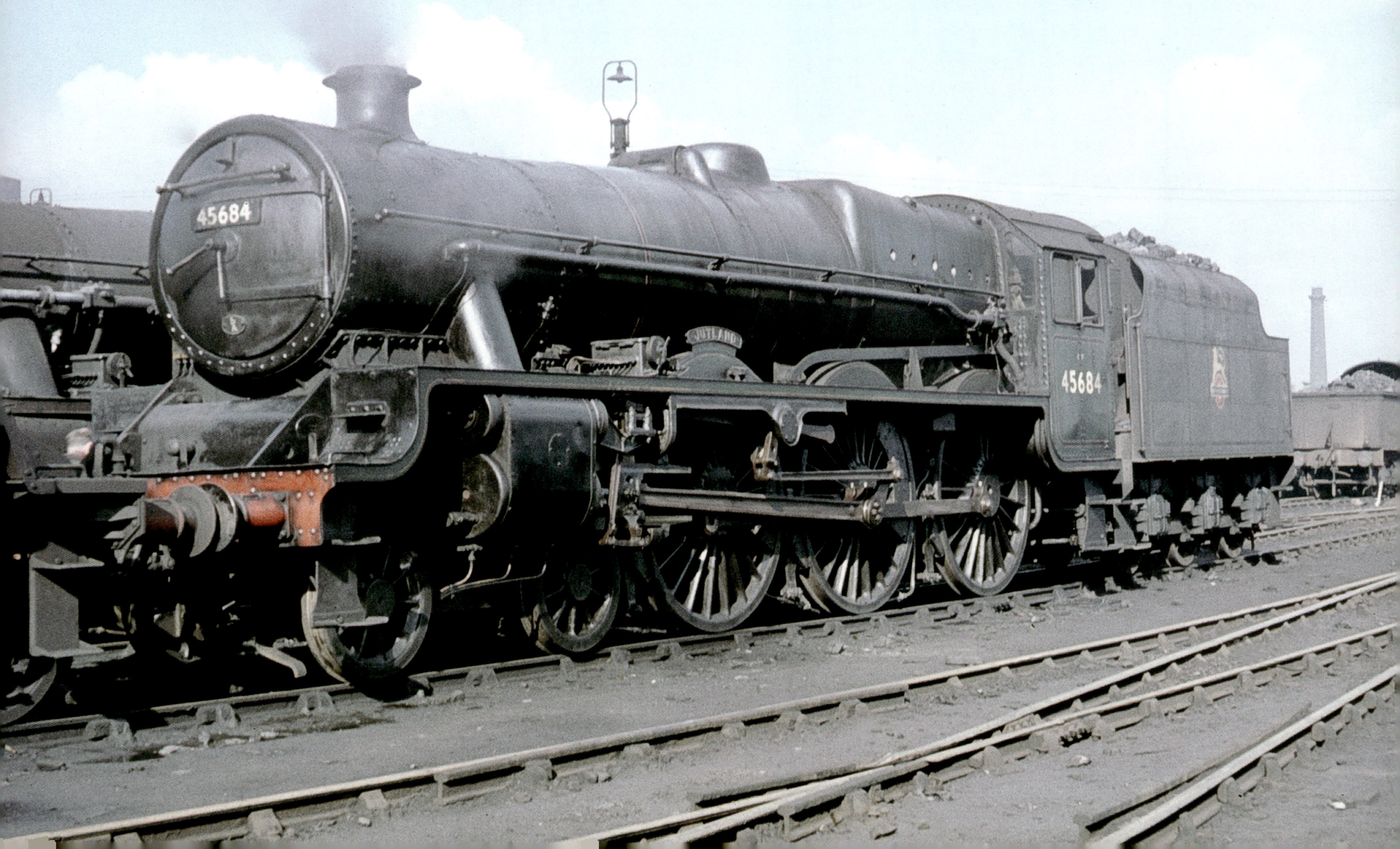

A much smarter external appearance for 45684 Jutland this time seen at Crewe in 1959. ***Strathwood Library Collection***

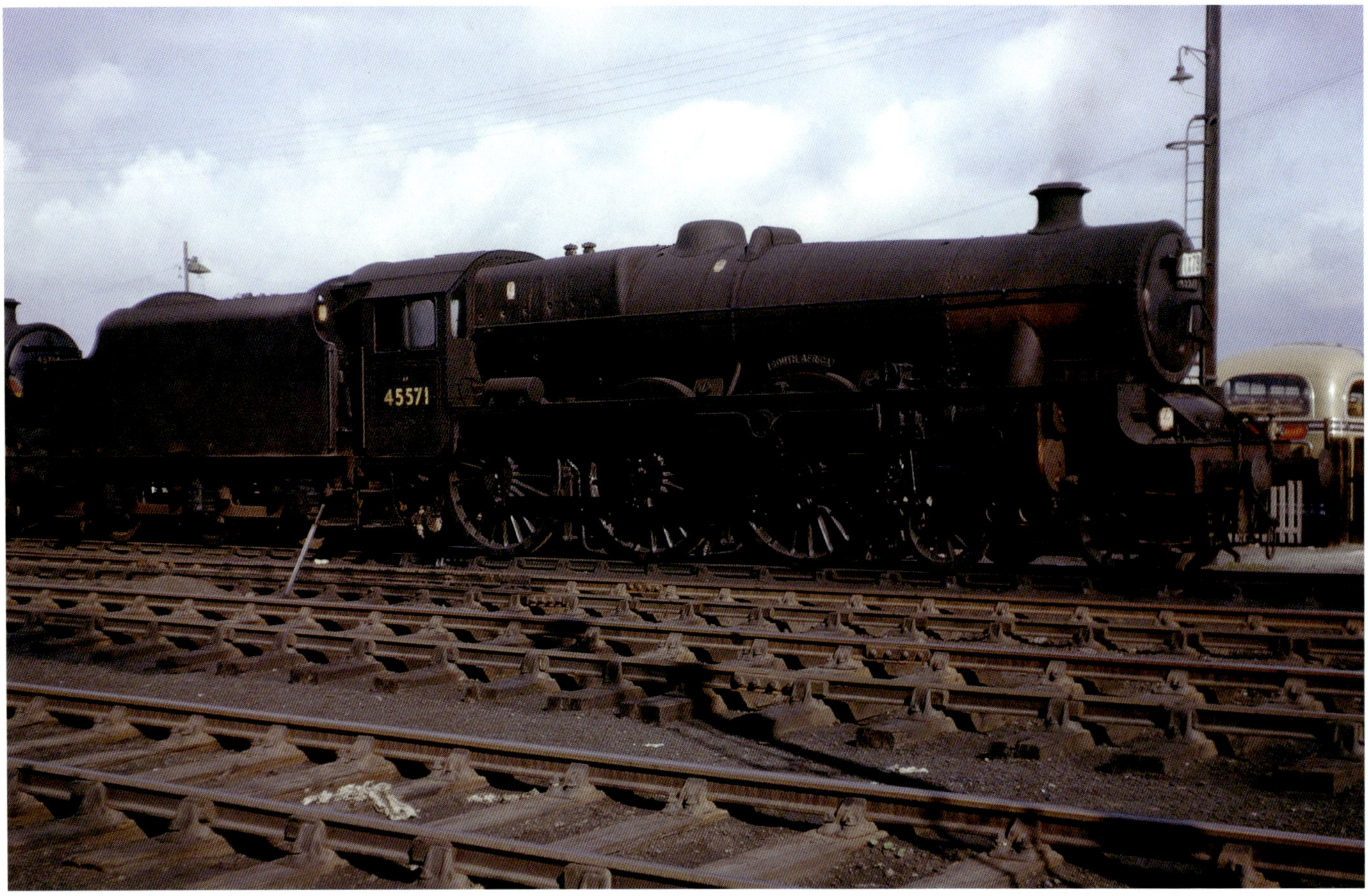

Blackpool was a regular haunt for the class and 45571 South Africa was on shed during a visit in 1964. ***John Rowe***

Photographers and a fortunate young lad were on hand for the visit of 45593 Kolhapur to Edale in 1967 just before being withdrawn. ***Strathwood Library Collection***

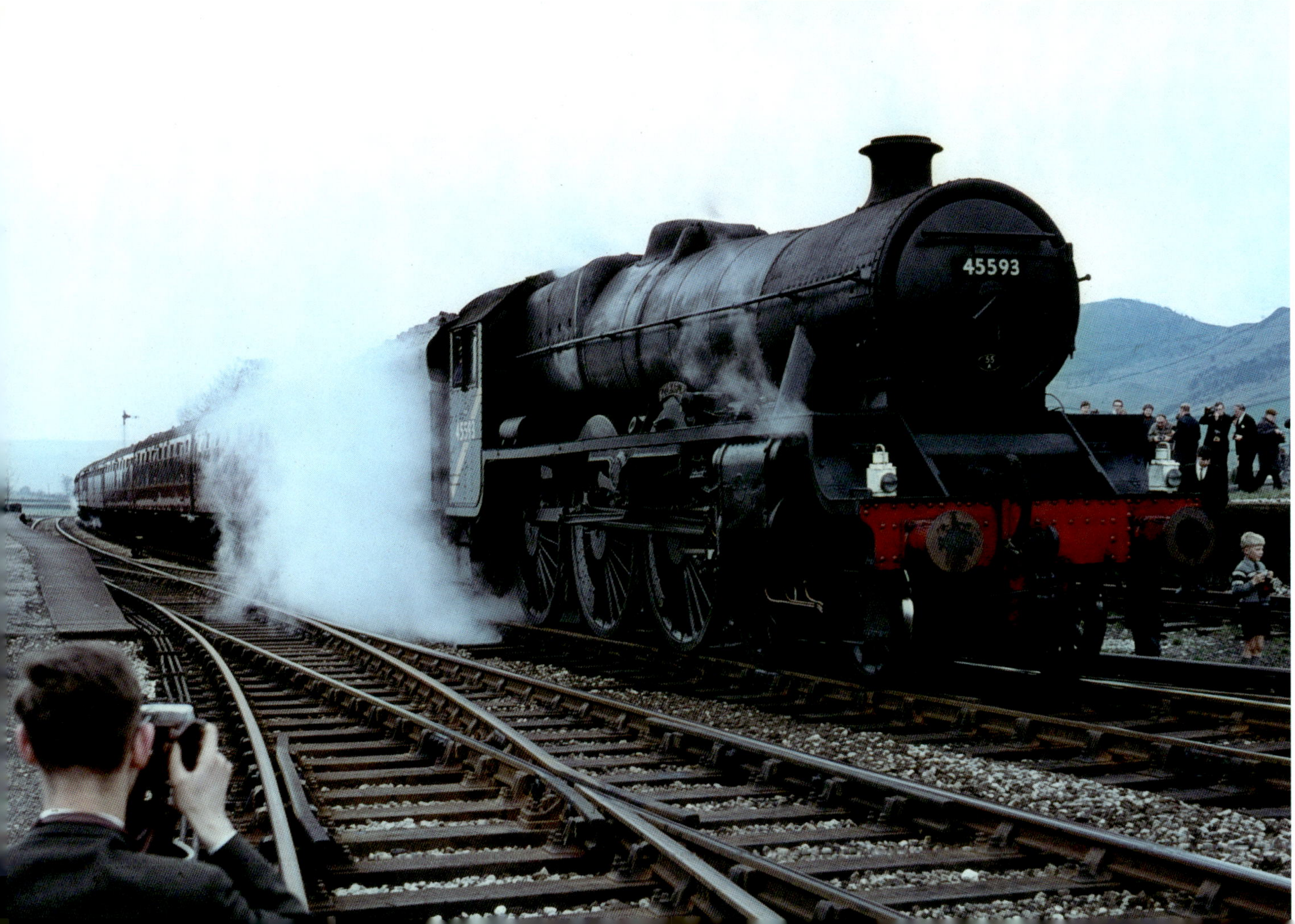

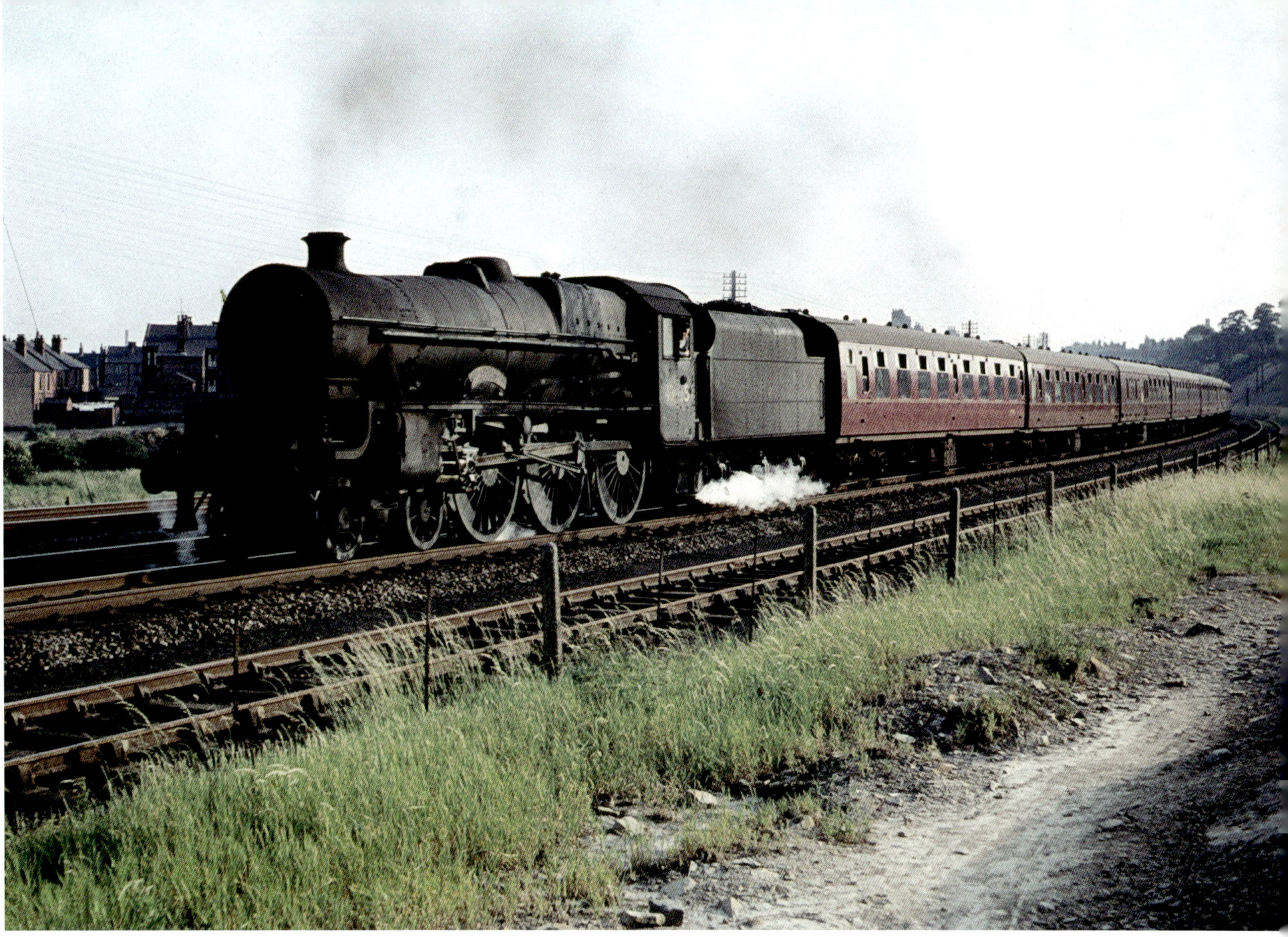

A double line nameplate was fitted to 45665 Lord Rutherford of Nelson as the sun highlights the grime on the locomotive in 1958 near Rotherham as yet a further reminder that so many locomotives ran in this decade with the absence of the attentions from cleaners, and it was not just in the 1960s that standards tumbled. ***Strathwood Library Collection***

That said 45633 Aden puts on a reasonable appearance on shed at Preston in 1960. ***Strathwood Library Collection***

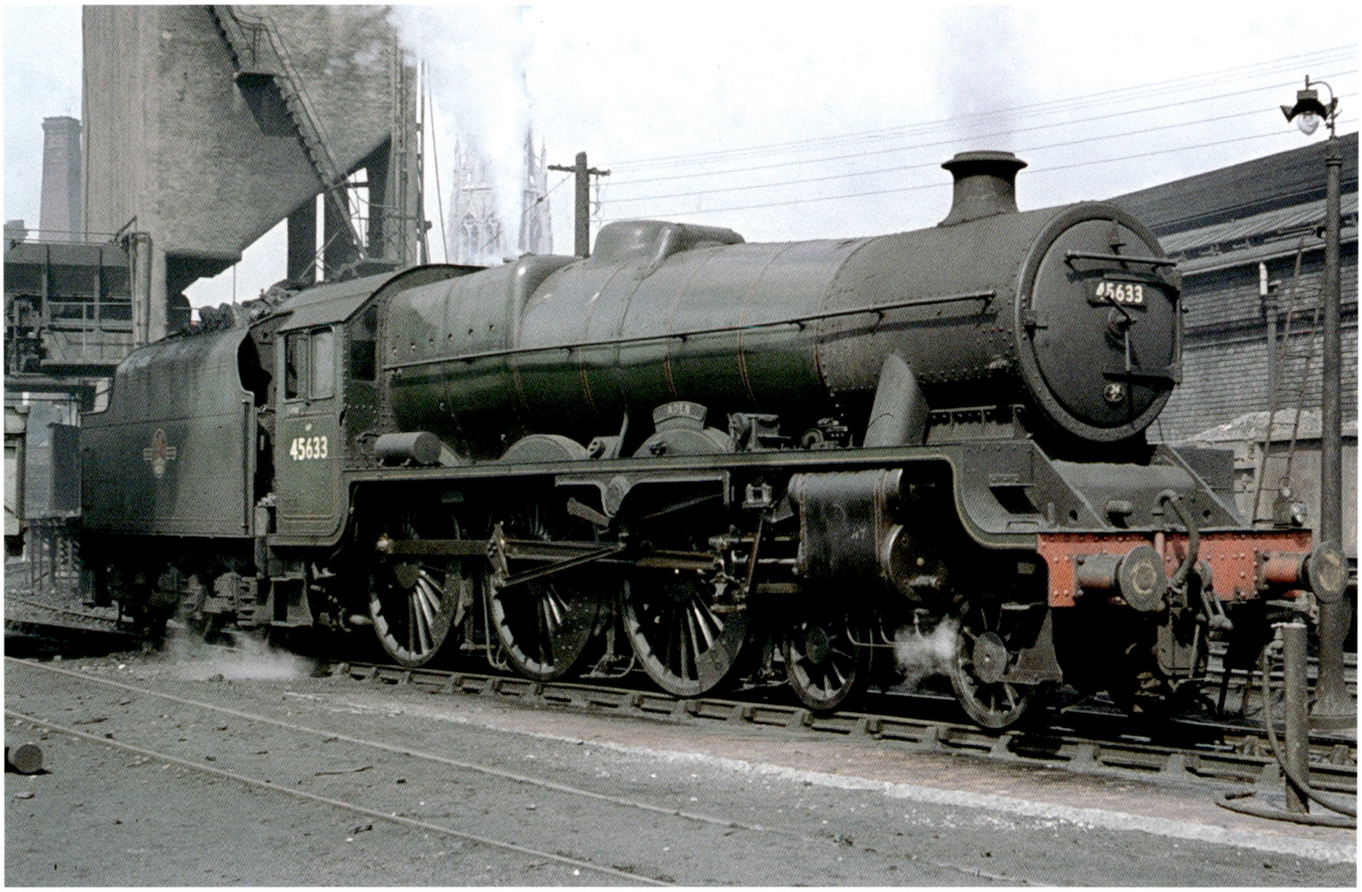

Those Fabulous Fives

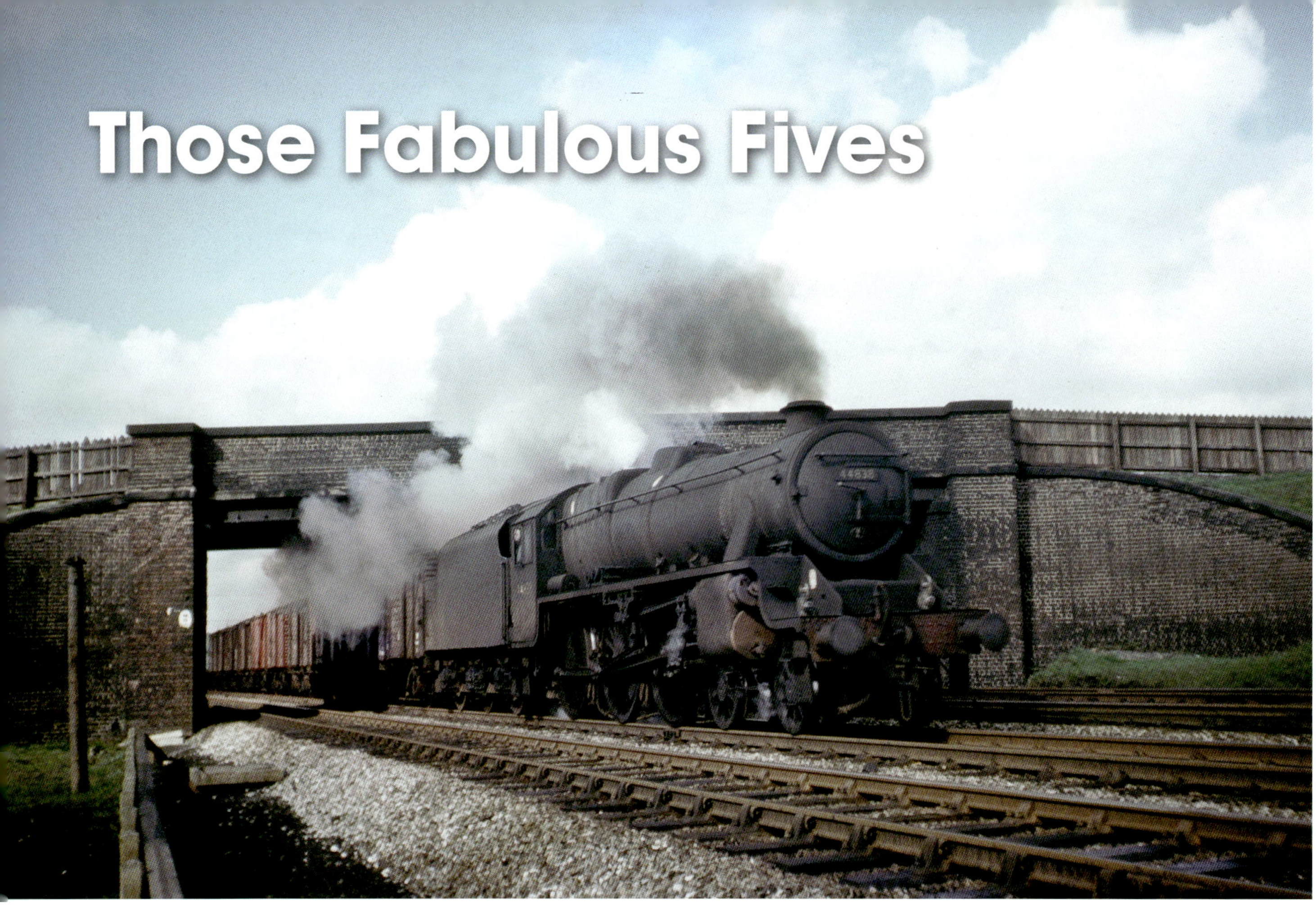

Going well with a fitted freight through Farrington on 7 April 1965 was 1944 Crewe built 44838. ***Chris Forrest***

Just four of the class were named including 45154 Lanarkshire Yeomanry being coupled to the rear of stock at Tyldesley on 24 September 1966. Rumours abounded that 5155 was to have been named Queen's Edinburgh in 1937, but no hard proof exists that it was in the event. One imagines if the LMS had embarked on a similar program to the GWR on naming its mixed traffic 4-6-0s we might have been down to Scout troops by the end of 842 examples. ***Strathwood Library Collection***

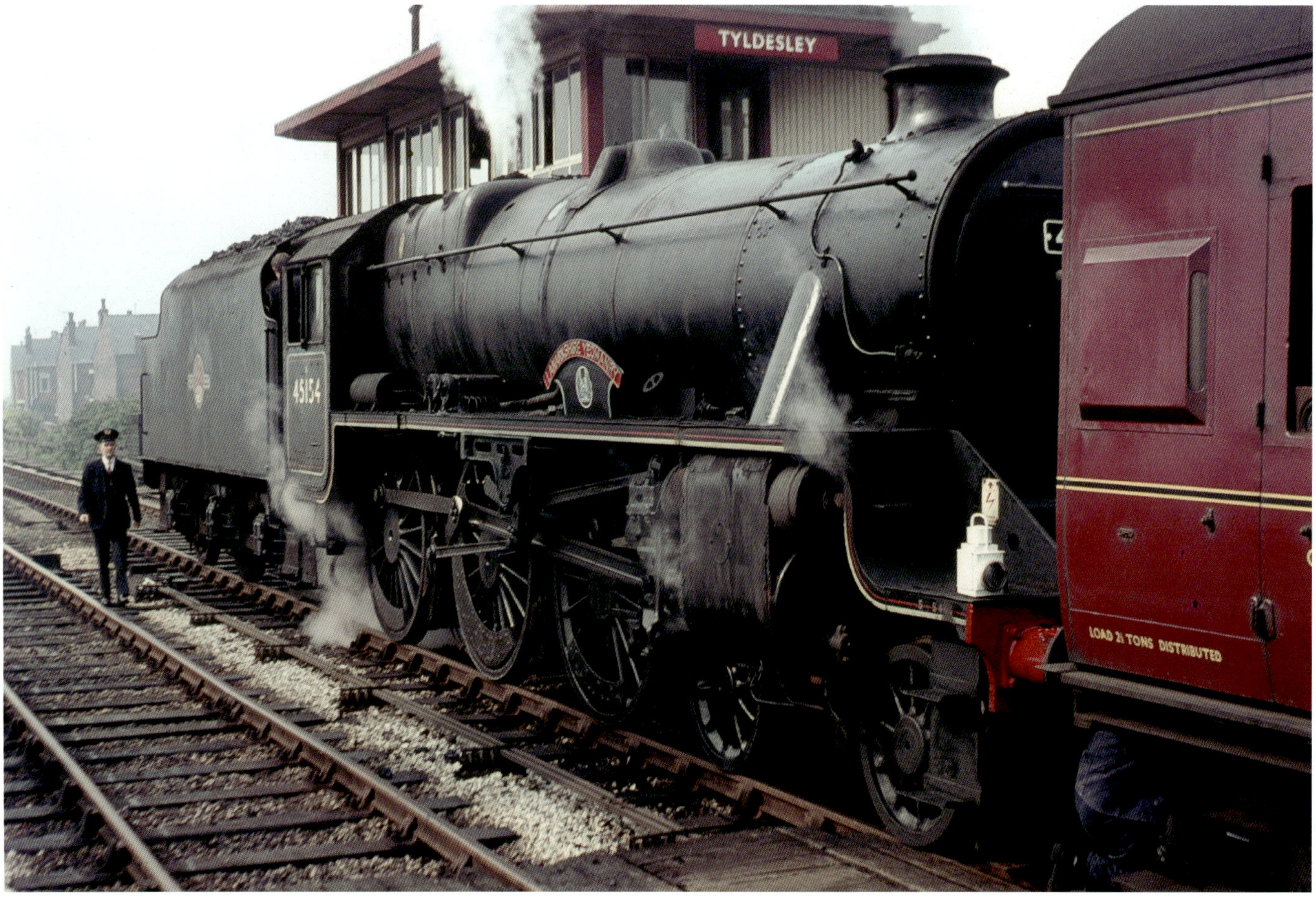

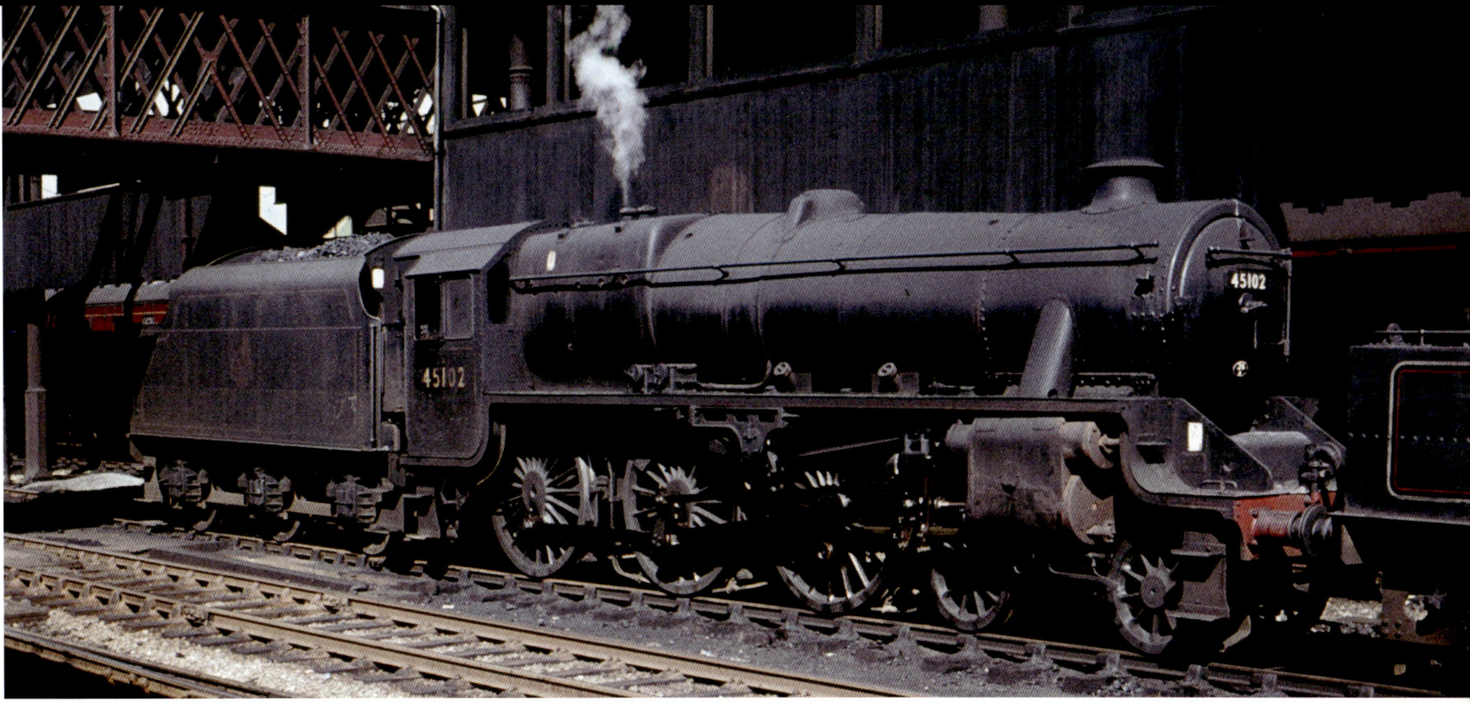

Variations and subtle differences within so many Black Fives would be the work of a lifetime to complete. We will however deal with the Stanier varieties in this volume and refer the reader to the accompanying book on Riddles and Ivatt locomotives for the later Ivatt adaptations to the basic design. Built at Vulcan Foundry in 1935, 45102 had a combined top feed and domed boiler when posed for the camera at Manchester Victoria in 1959. ***Strathwood Library Collection***

Steam to spare on 10 June 1967 for 45227 with an up parcels at Bolton, this example was built in the works of Armstrong Whitworth in 1936. ***Jerry Beddows***

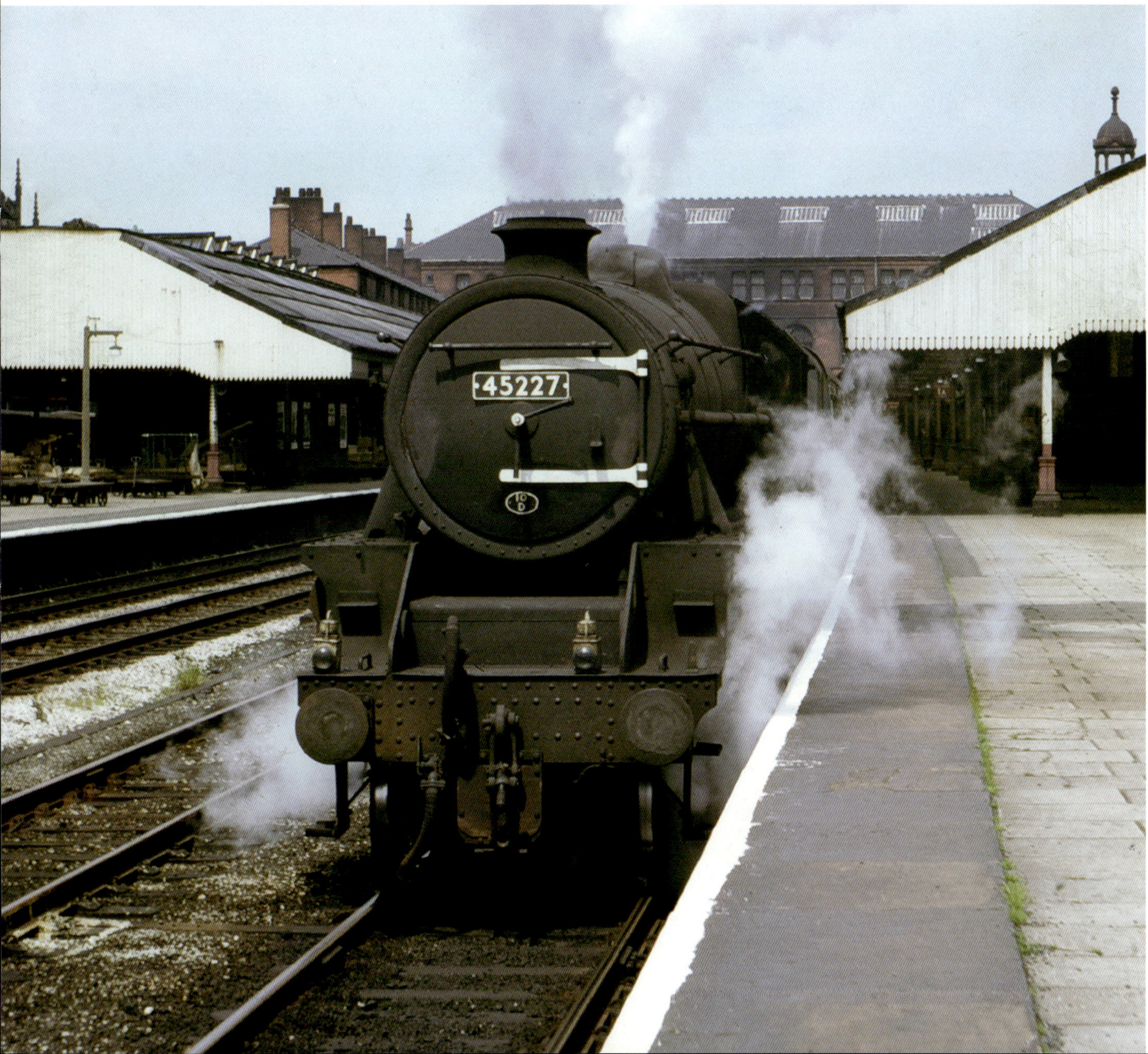

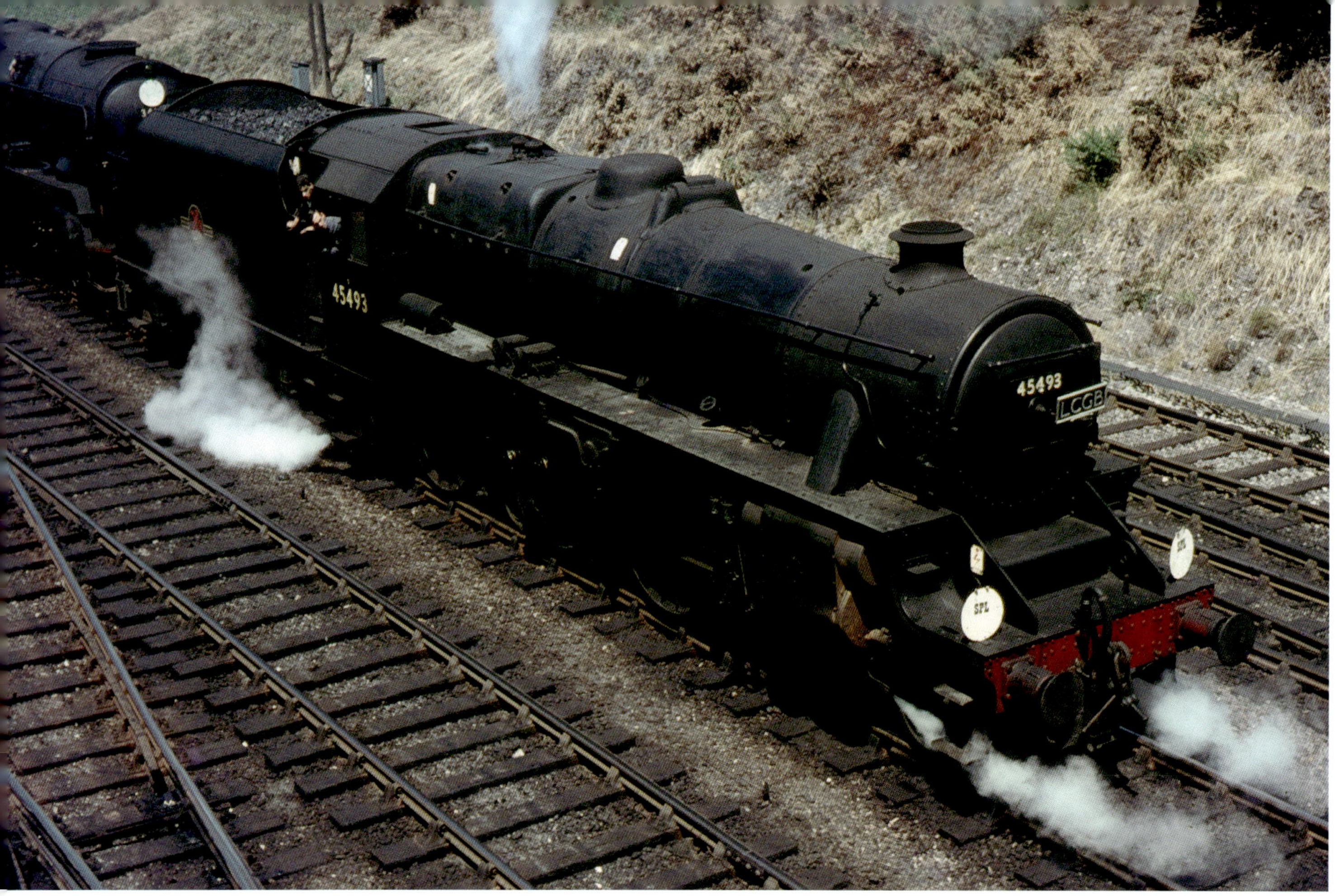

A splendid elevated view for modellers of 1944 Derby built 45493 at Weymouth on 3 July 1964. Note the usual liberal dusting of dry sand around the sandboxes - inevitable to spill some whilst preparing your locomotive on a dark windy night. ***Dave Down***

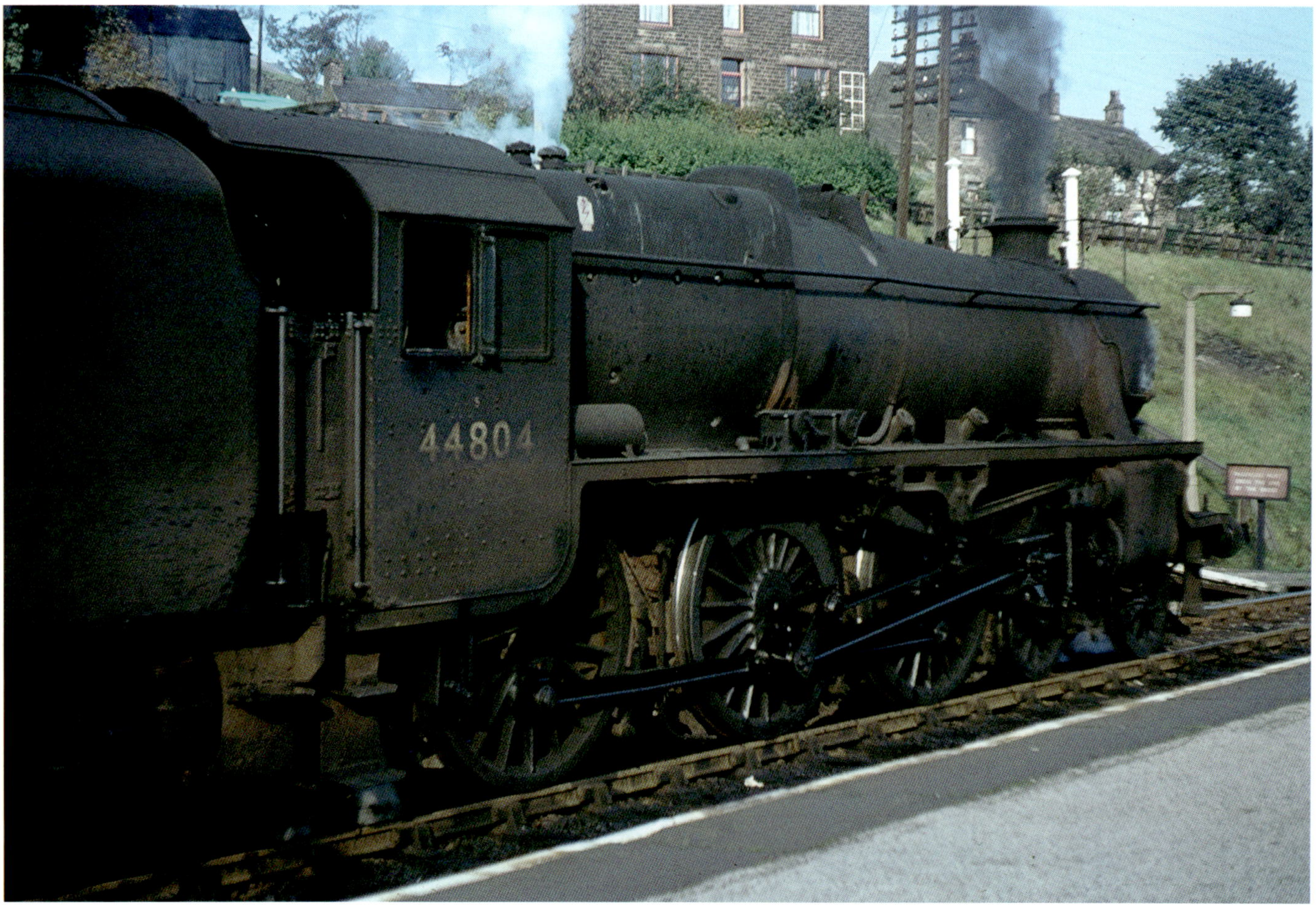

No such steaming problems for the Black Fives as experienced in the more powerful Jubilees as exemplified here again by 44804 paused at Chinley with Sheffield train 20 October 1965. ***Strathwood Library Collection***

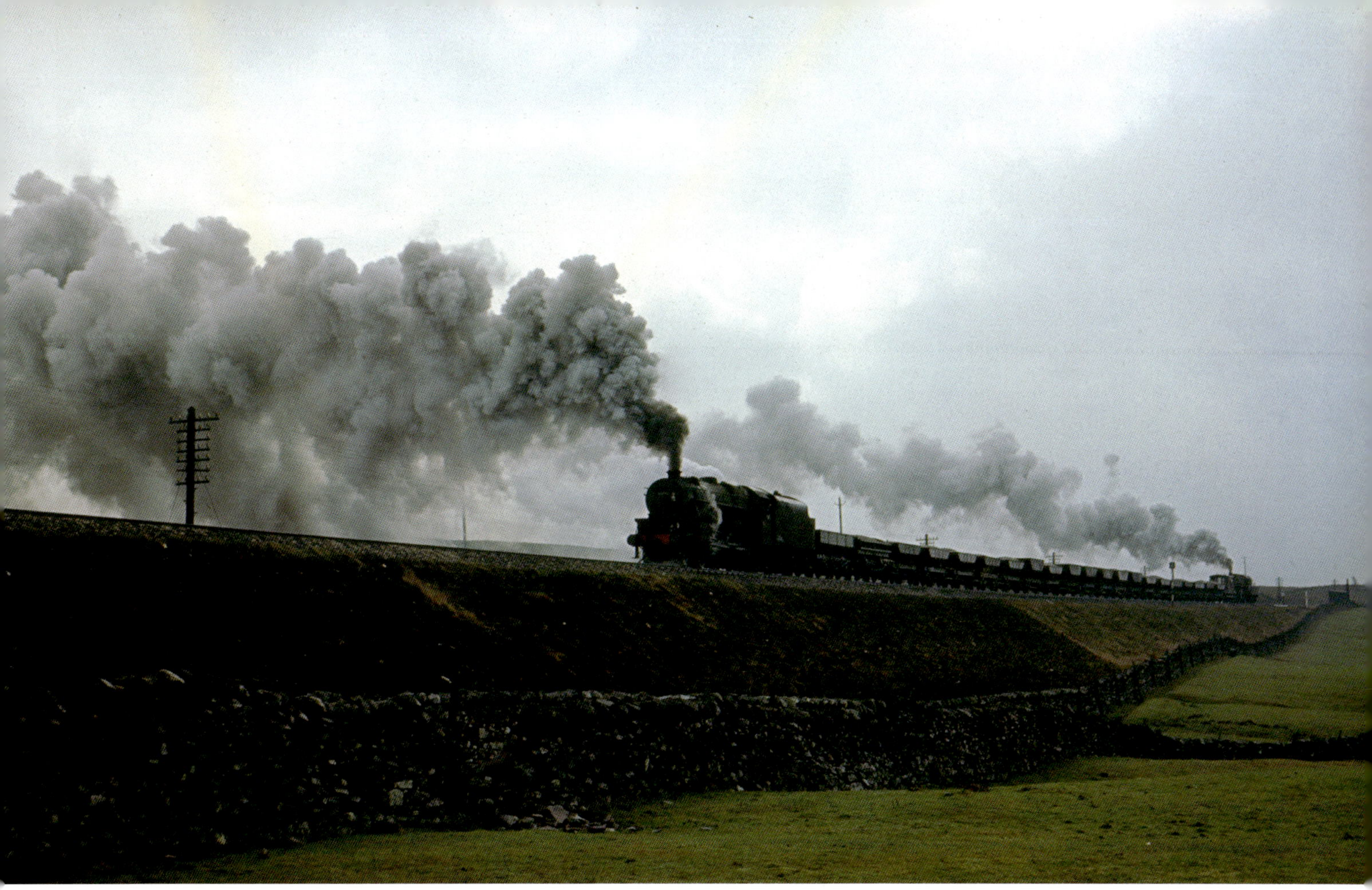

The assault of Shap on greasy rails could be a great leveller to the confidence of a young driver as we see with 44778 being banked on 30 April 1966, clearly working hard. ***Win Wall/Strathwood Library Collection***

Thumping away from Lancaster with an up goods in 1962 was 1945 Crewe built 44868 in some style. ***Late Ray Helm/Strathwood Library Collection***

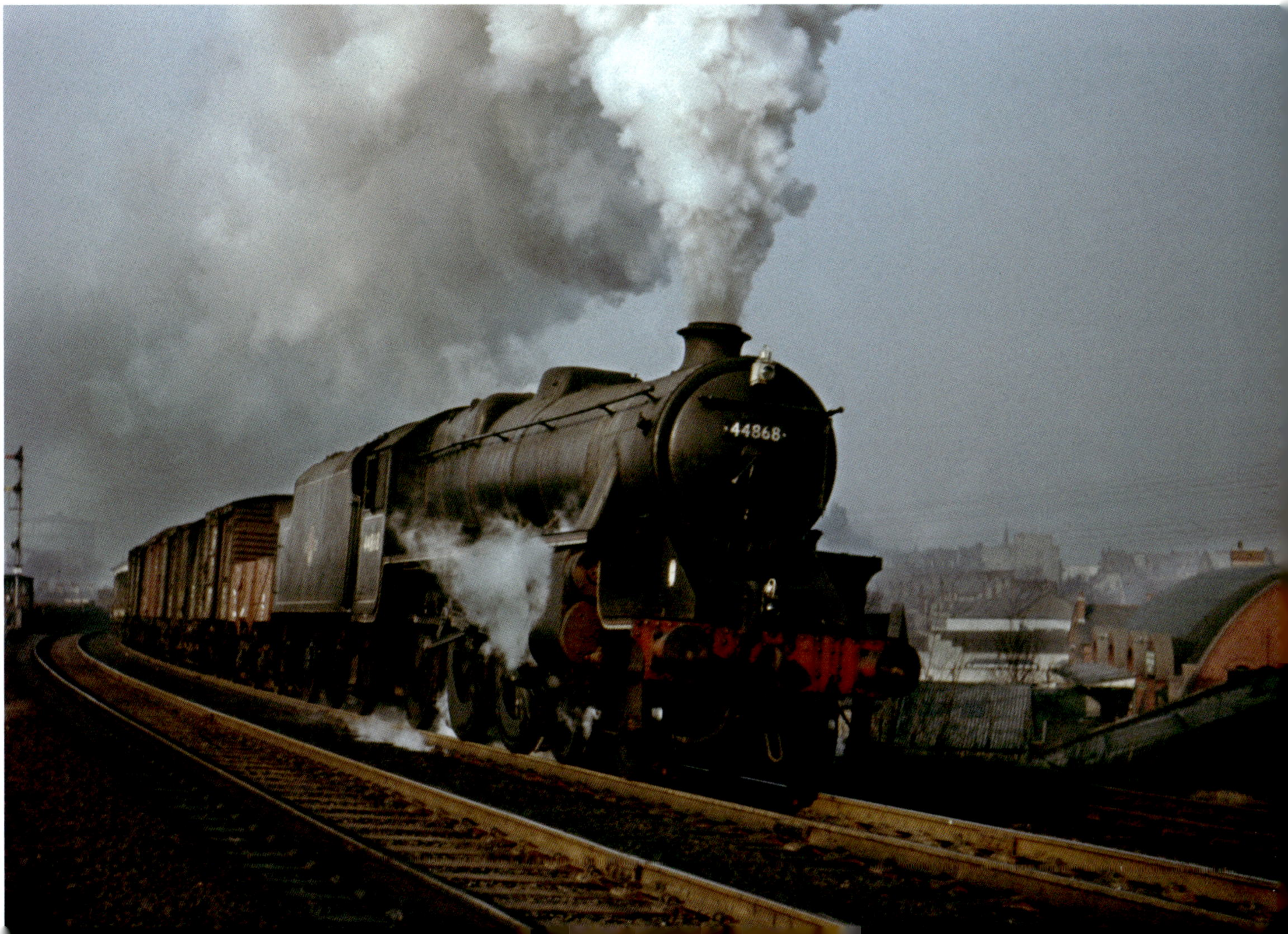

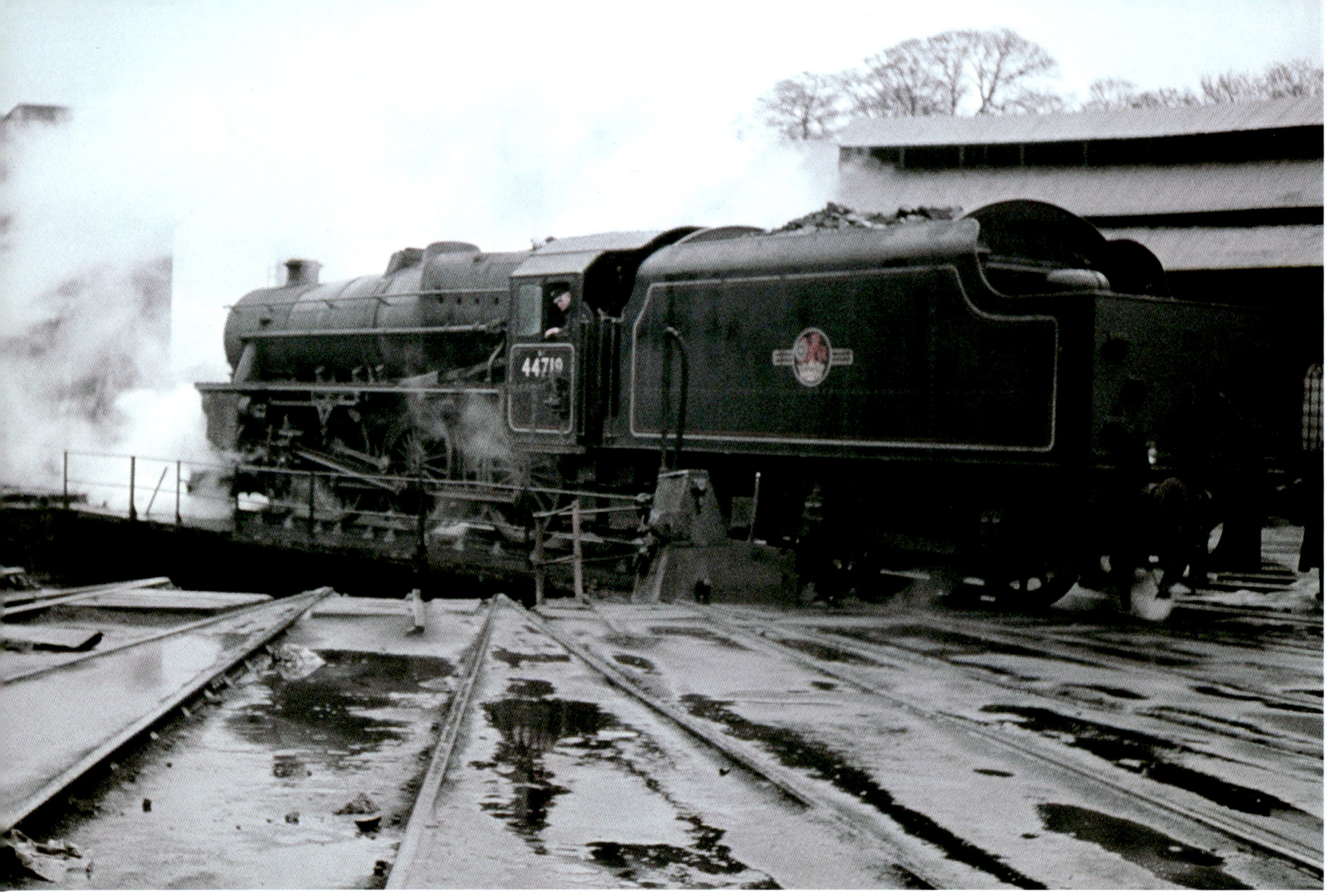

Stanier's Black Fives were well suited to so many of the duties over the Highland main line and north from Inverness. To make life easier on these single track sections protected by tablets, many were fitted with apparatus on the cabside for catching same. Such as 44719 being turned on a rainy day within the open roundhouse at Inverness during April 1961. ***Late Vincent Heckford/Strathwood Library Collection***

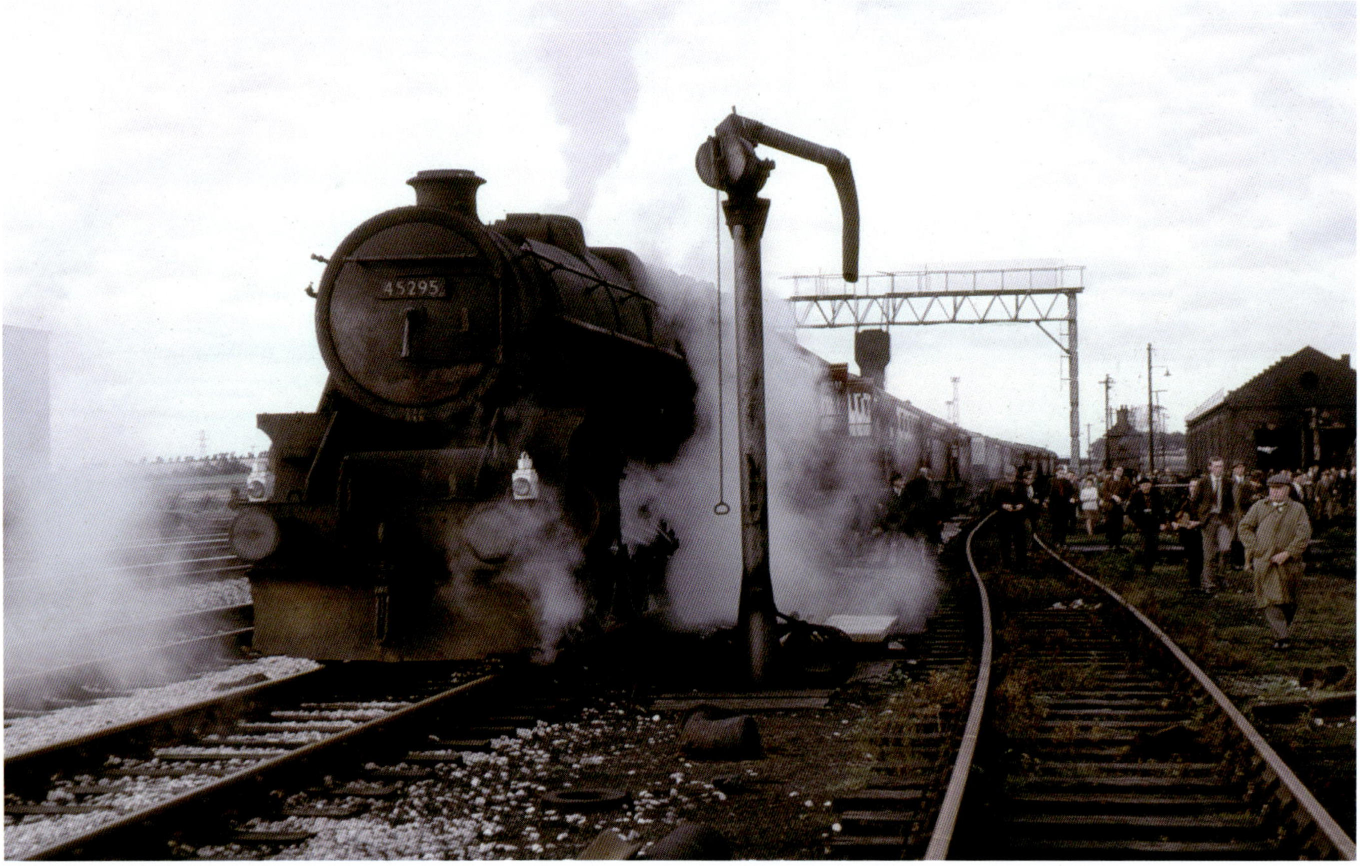

Snow was associated with many of the routes the class could be found on and 45295 is well equipped for action alongside Kingmoor depot in the days when an RCTS special would be allowed to discharge its passengers without a platform alongside the main line to visit the engine sheds as here on 28 October 1967. ***Strathwood Library Collection***

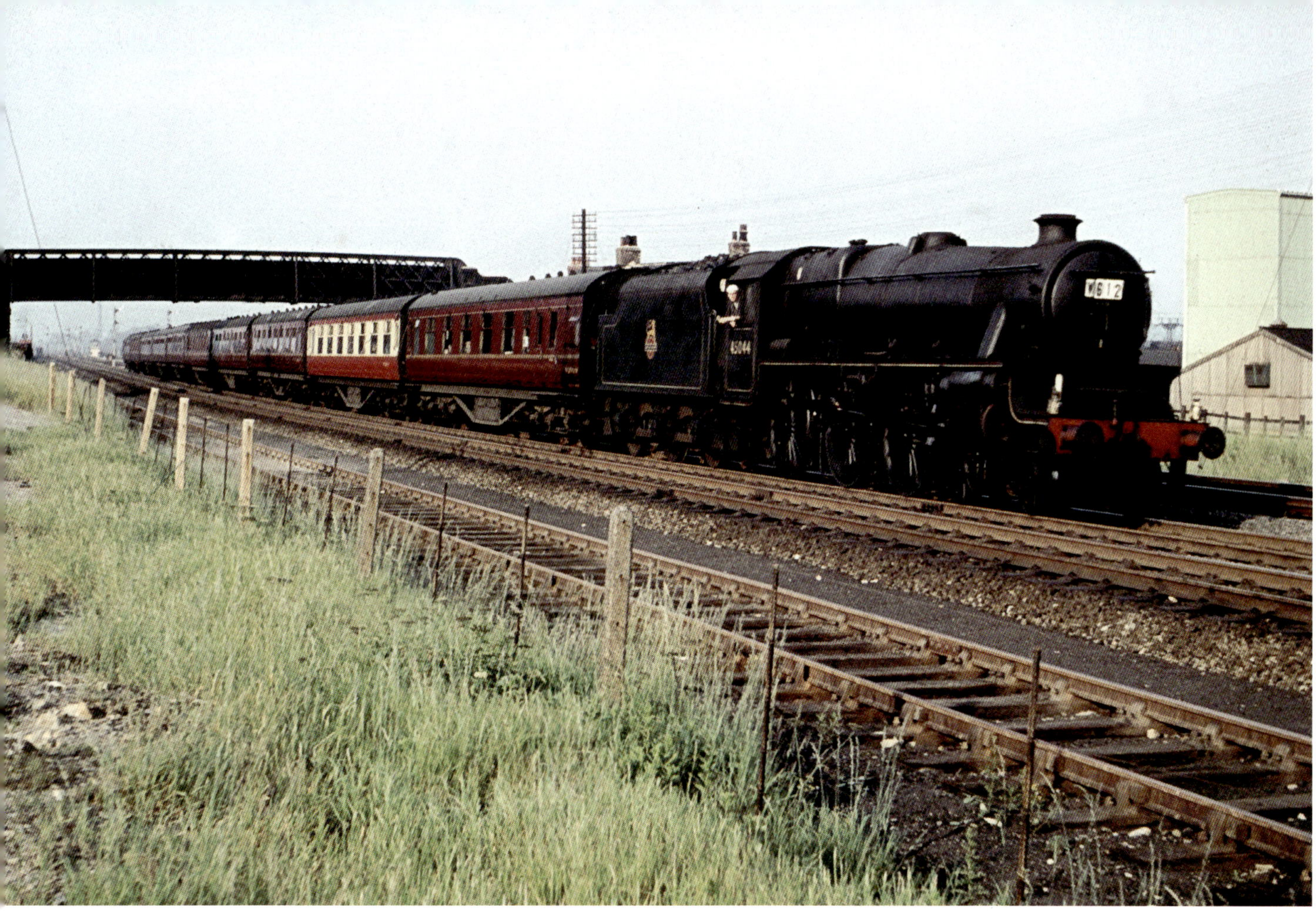

Employment of a nicely cleaned 45044 with a holiday extra passing Rotherham most likely for a seaside destination in 1958. ***Strathwood Library Collection***

Having dropped down from Shap, 45055 slows as it enters Tebay, in the summer of 1967 although both pegs are off for a clear run heading southbound. ***Late Alan Marriot/Strathwood Library Collection***

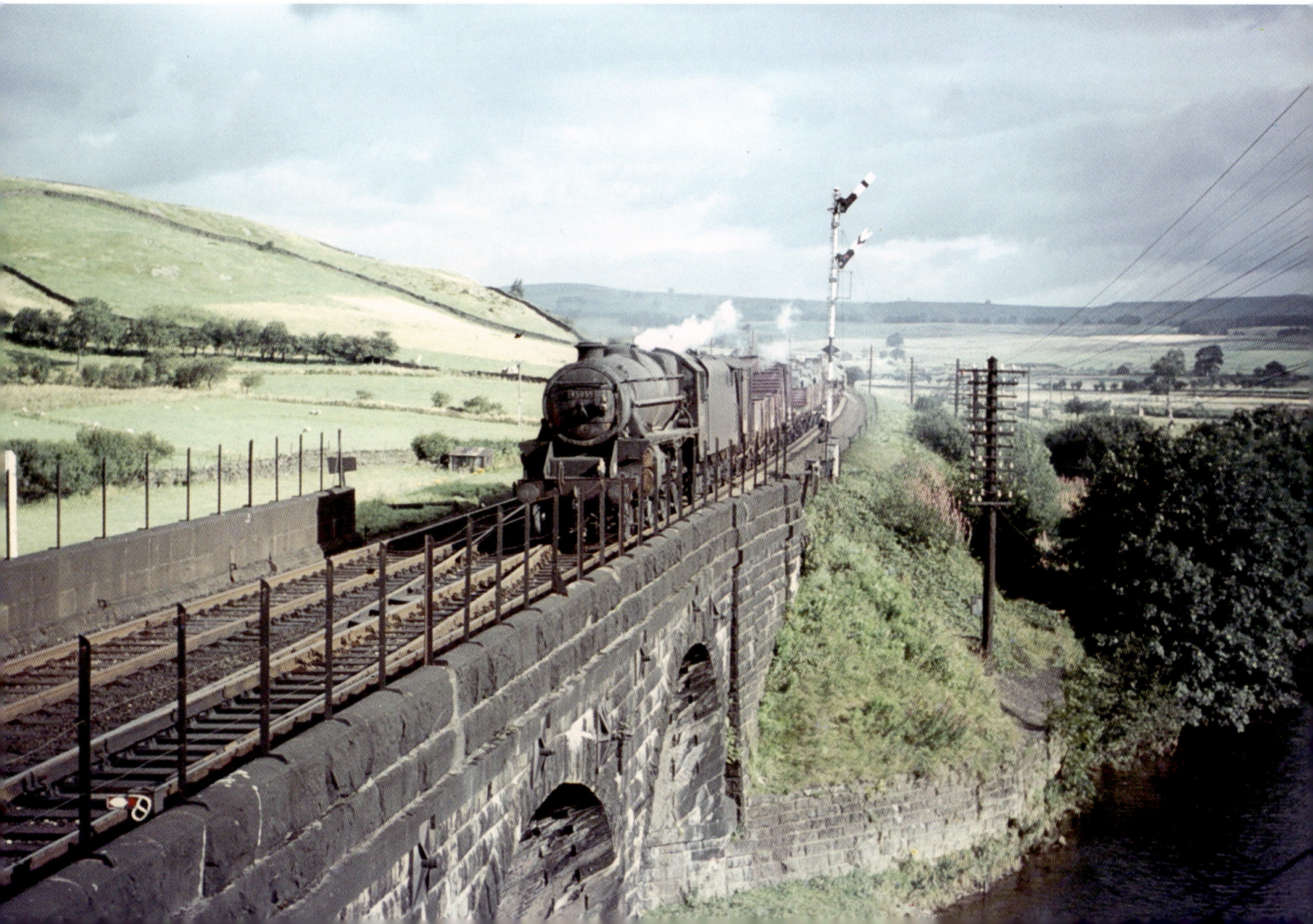

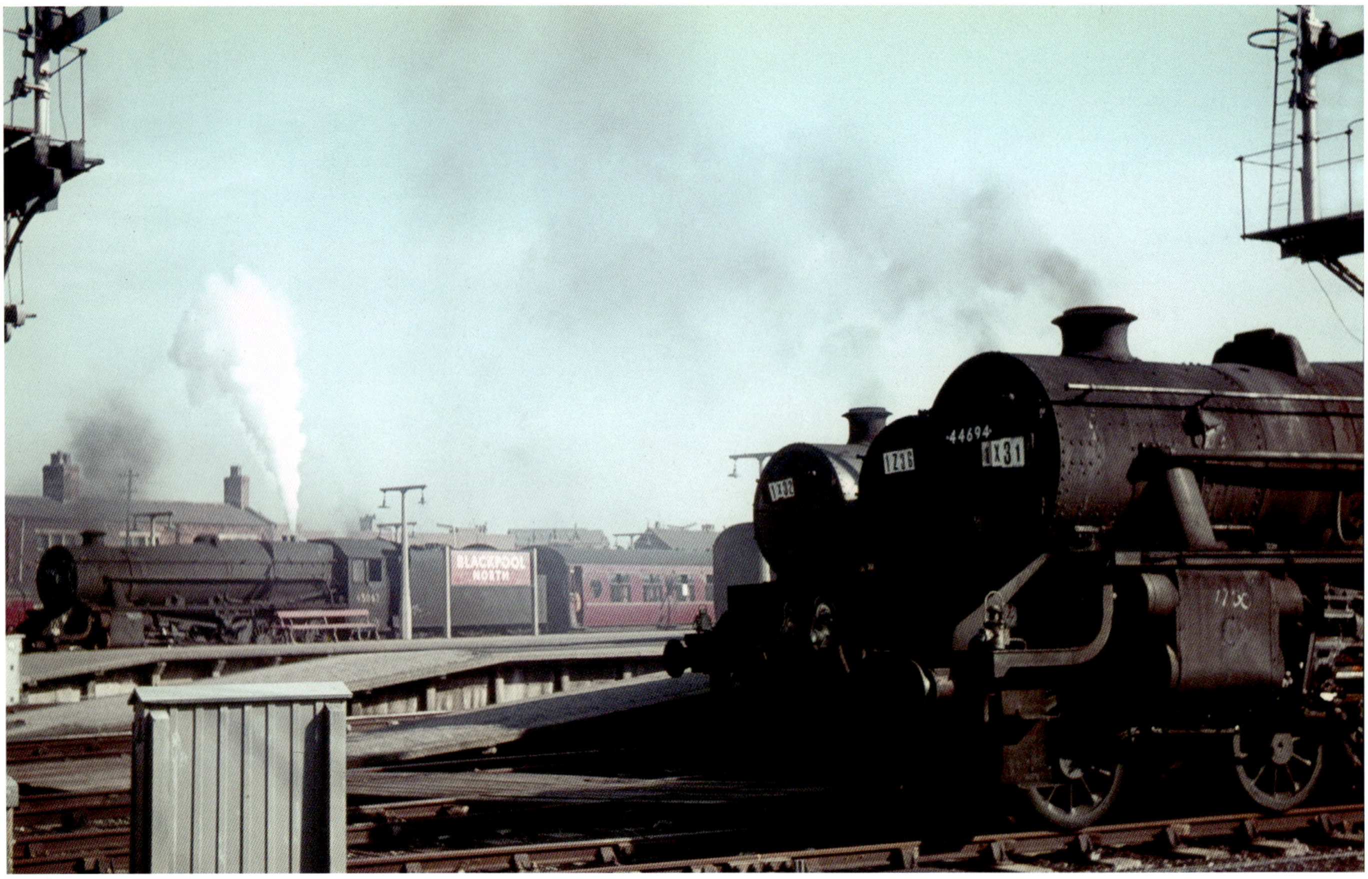

A chance to play spot the Jubilee at Blackpool North amongst the Black Fives on 30 May 1966 with 45063, 45581 Bihar and Orissa, 44906, 44694 all having a day by the seaside. ***Peter Coton***

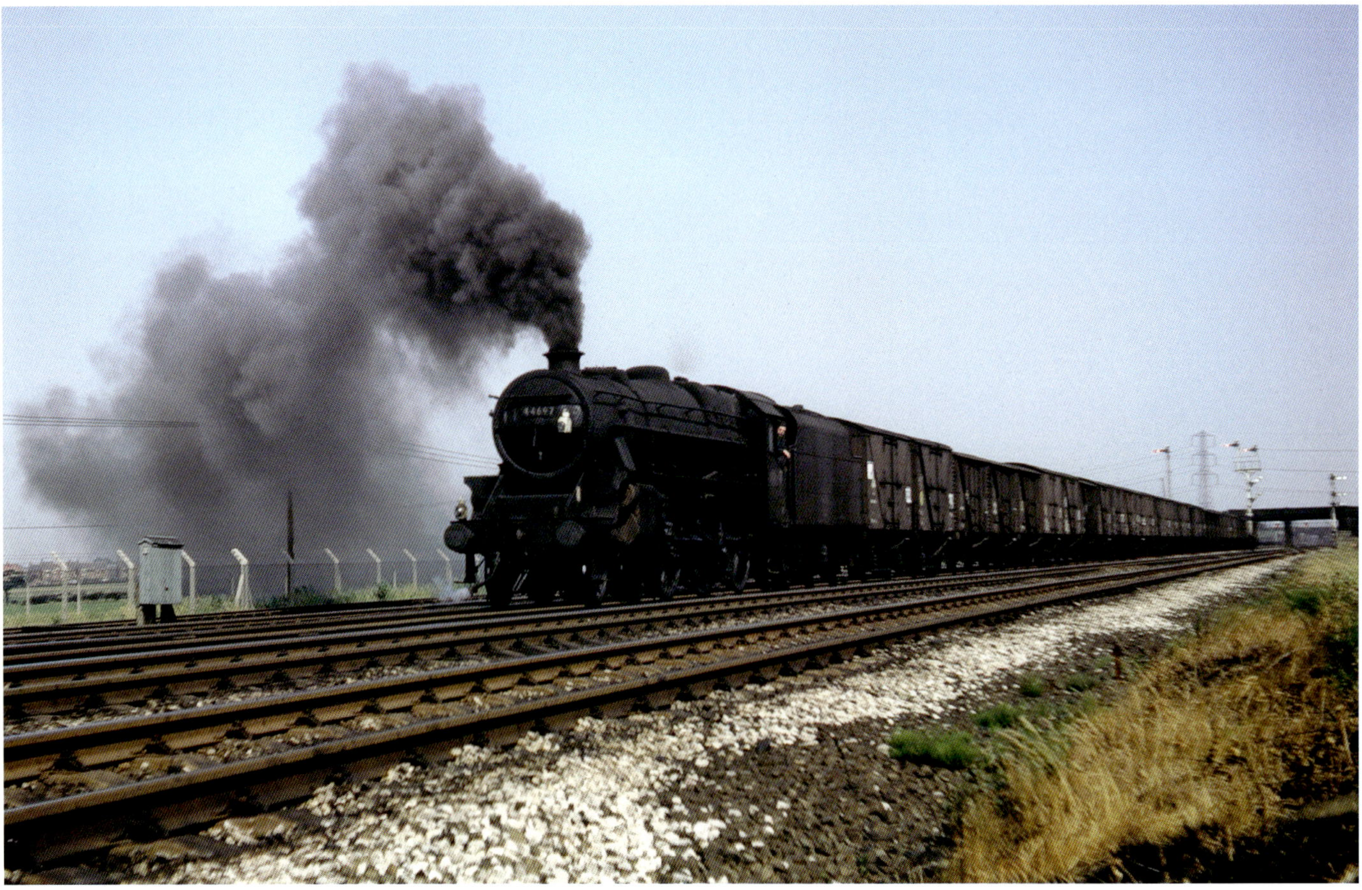

Horwich Works built a number of batches of the class including the last one constructed with 44697 entering service in December 1950 and viewed here in 1967 rolling past Farrington. Those engines built from 1946 enjoyed refinements such as self cleaning smoke boxes, rocking grates, and self emptying ashpans. ***Michael Beaton***

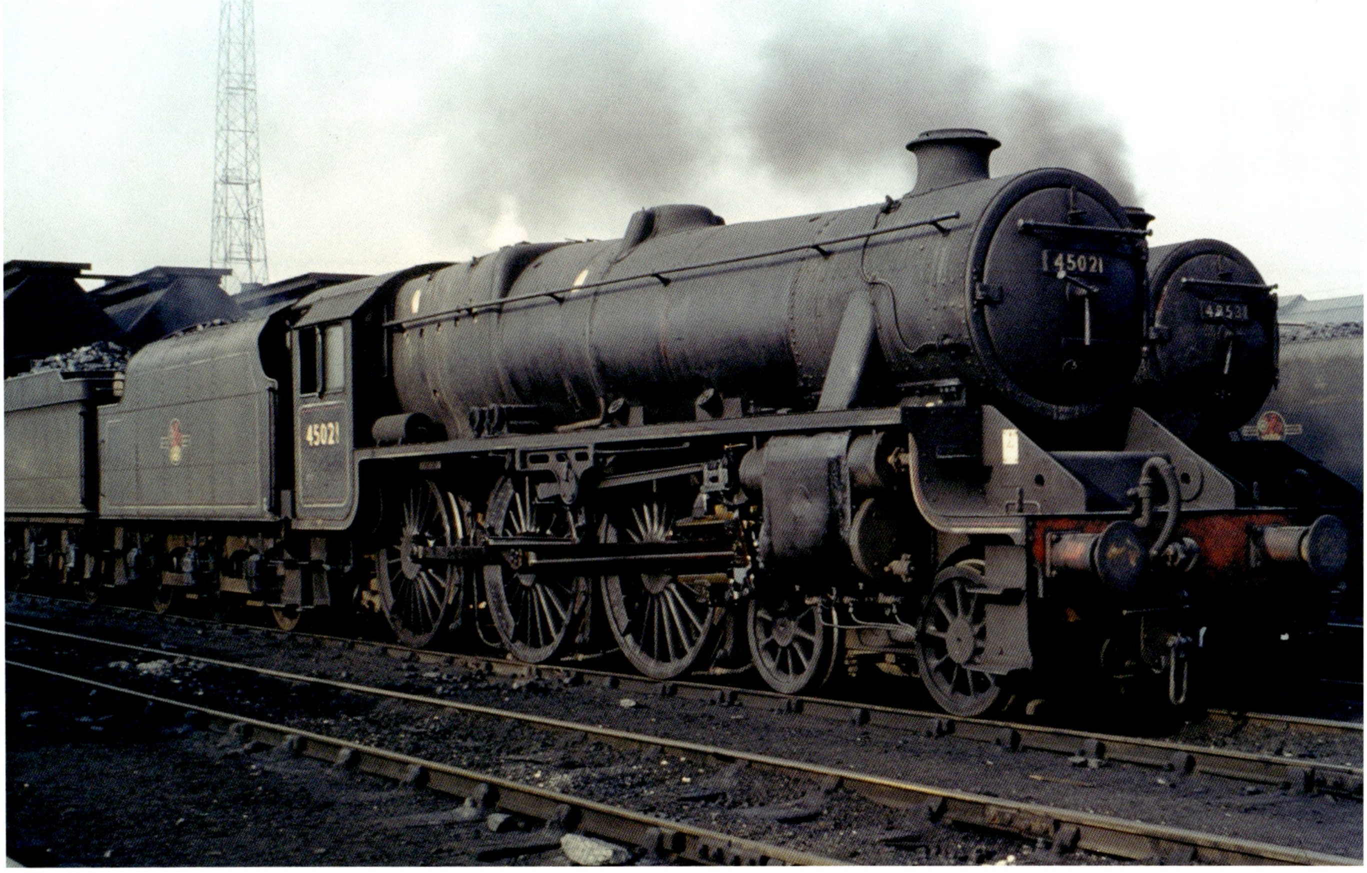

One of the longest service lives would be attributed to 45021 seen at Crewe South on 23 March 1964. This Vulcan Foundry locomotive went into service in August 1934 and remained in use until September 1967. ***Strathwood Library Collection***

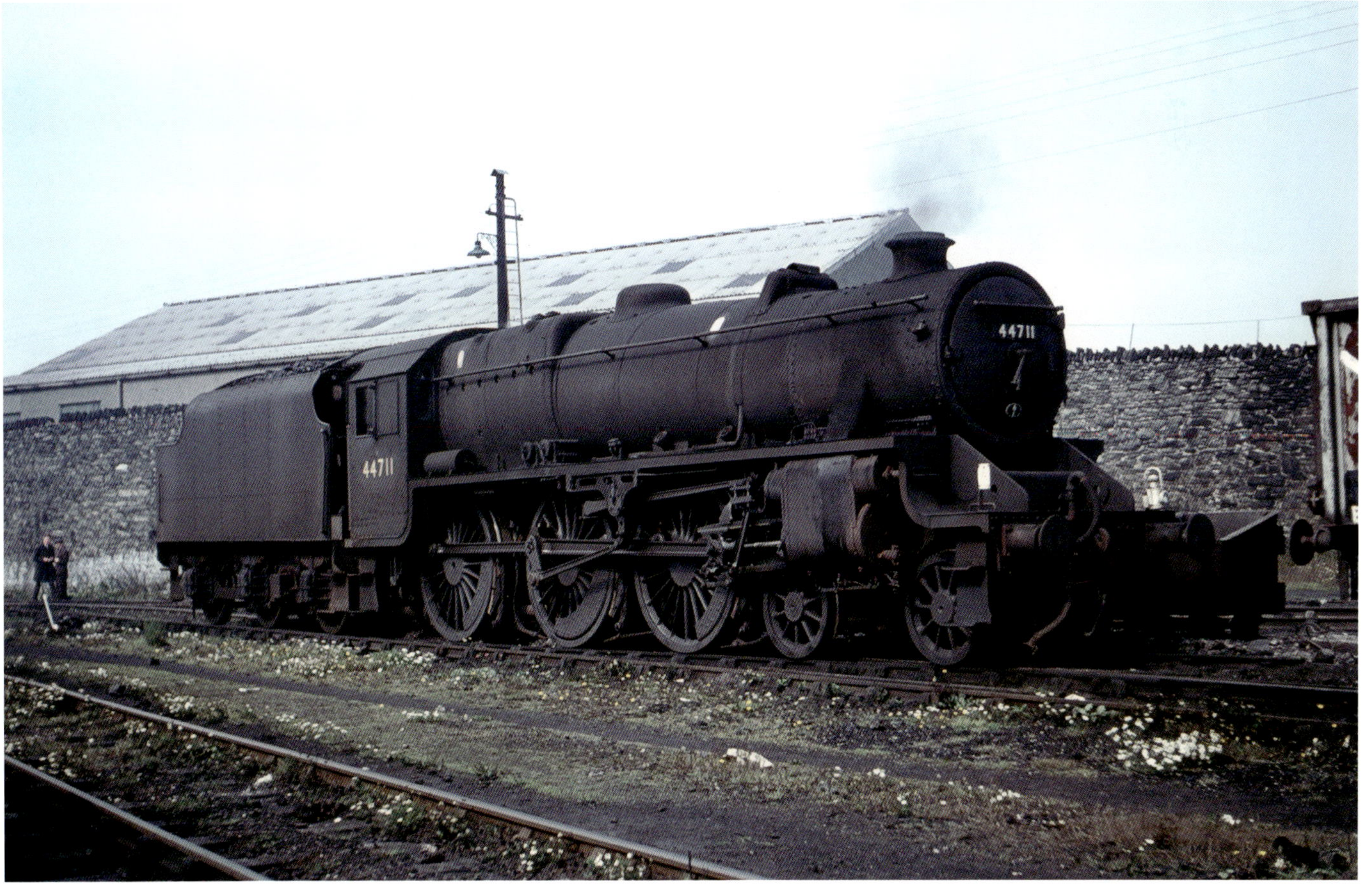

The top feed is much further forward on the boiler of 44711 coming off shed at Holyhead on 21 August 1966. ***Strathwood Library Collection***

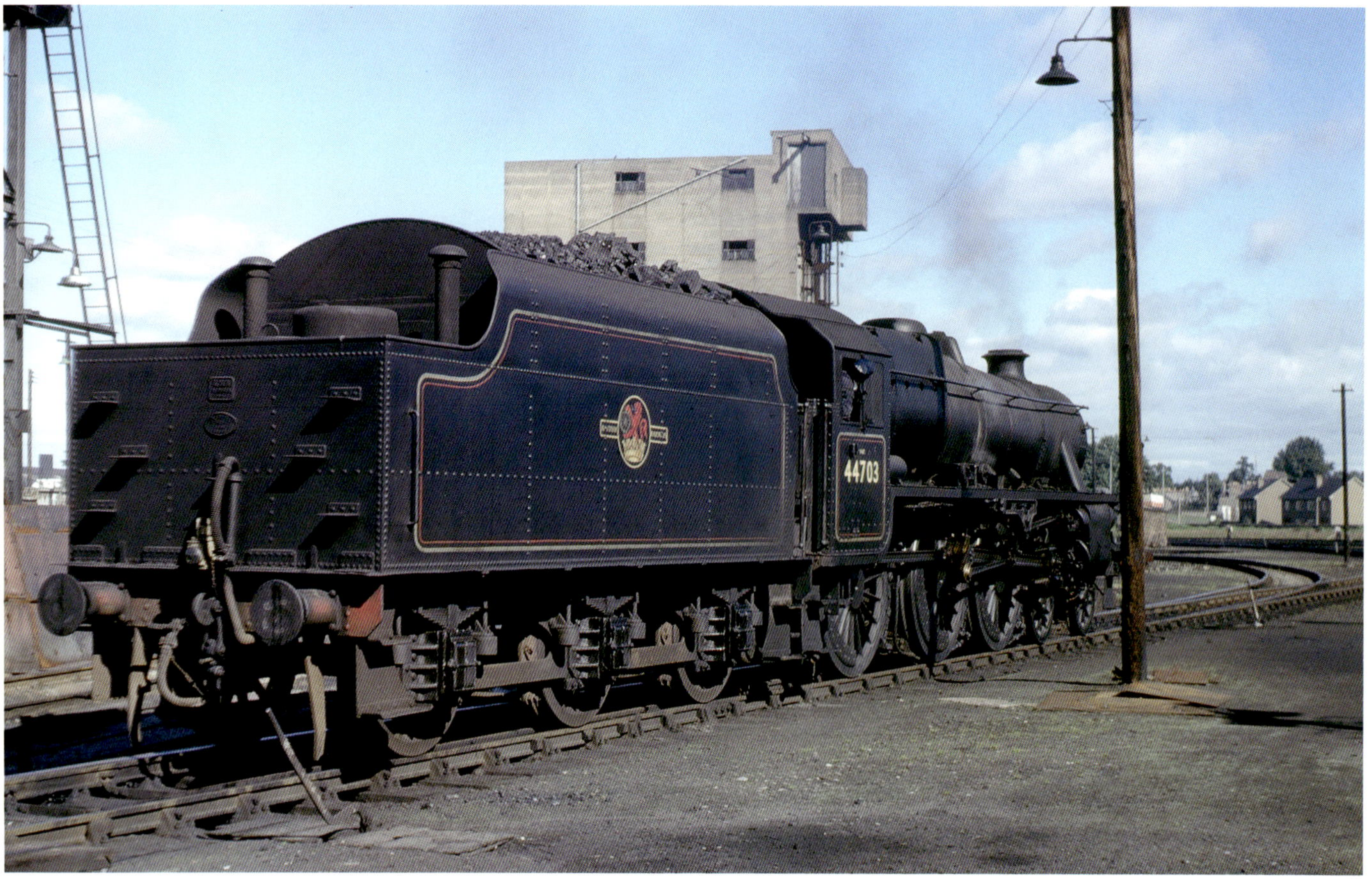

A fully riveted tender is fitted to 44703 in the sunshine at Perth on 24 August 1967. Comparing the water overflow vents with those below and opposite shows these to be higher on this version. ***Jerry Beddows***

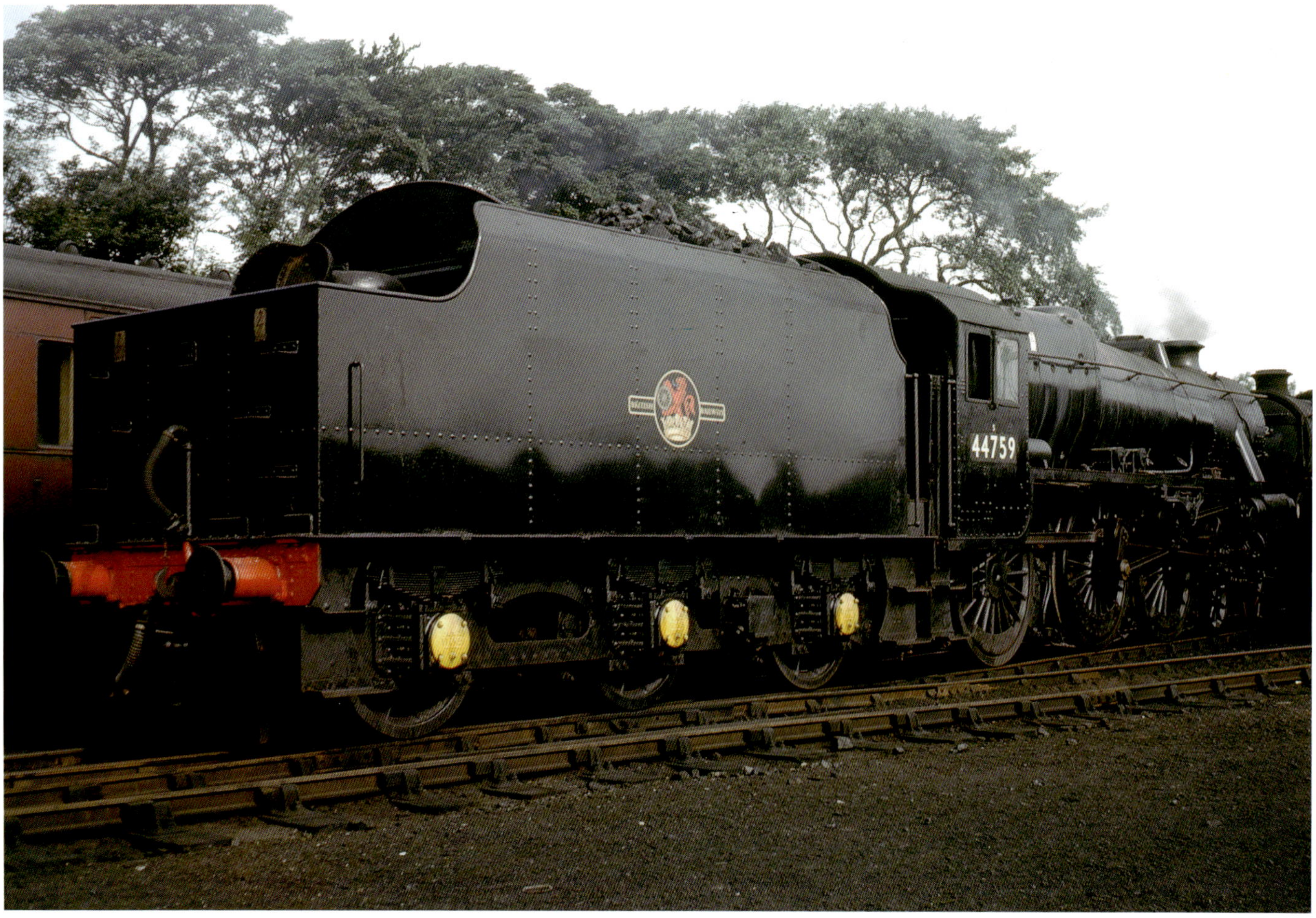

The bright yellow painted Timken bearing axle box covers contrast with the recent basic unlined black repaint made to 44759 stabled at Carnforth in July 1965. ***Win Wall/Strathwood Library Collection***

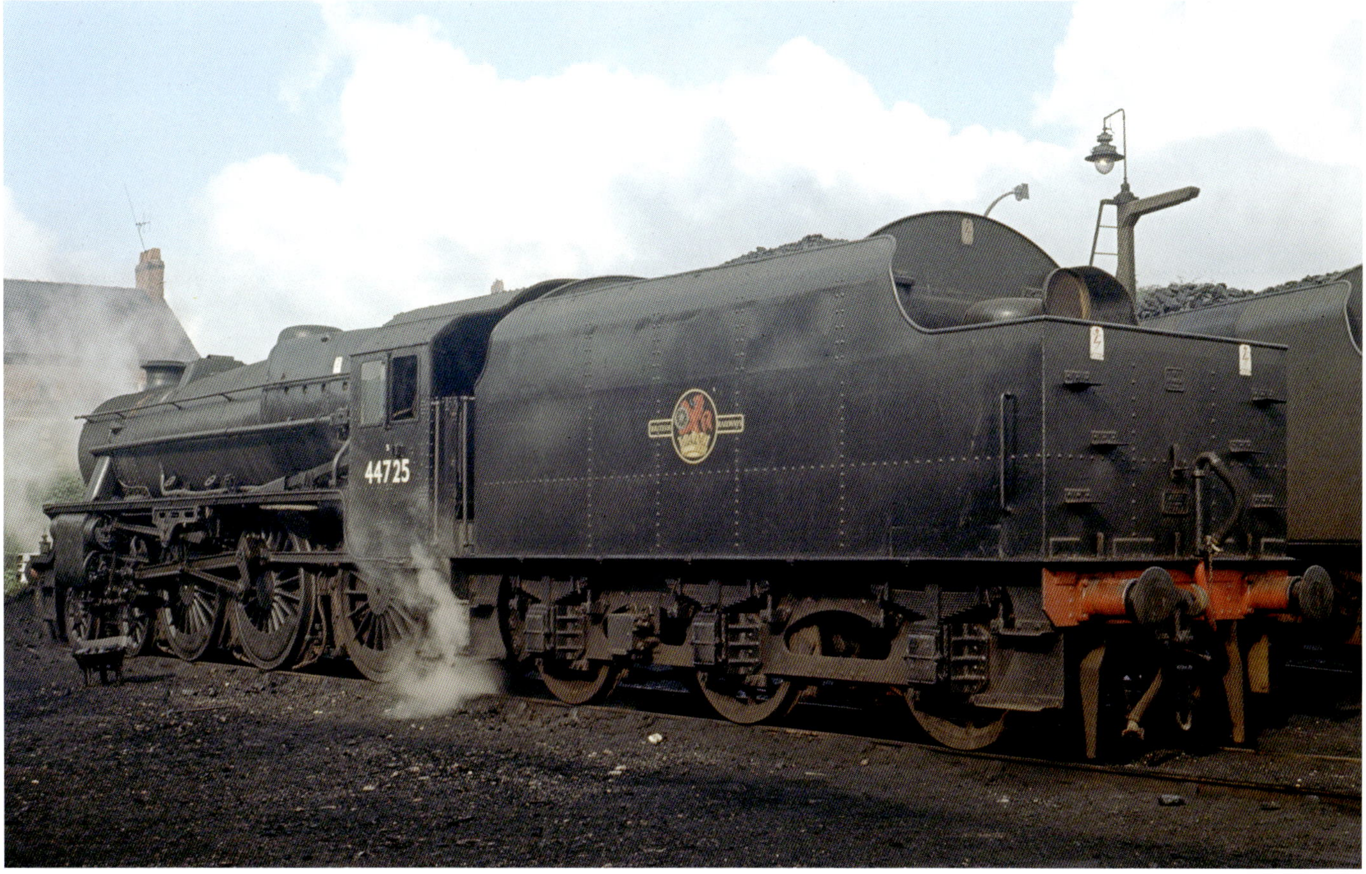

Another economic simple black repaint has been bestowed upon 44725 at Northwich on 30 July 1966 this time to a standard axle box riveted tender variant. ***Win Wall/Strathwood Library Collection***

Maintaining our plain Black Five theme with 44835 near Leaton on 31 July 1964 this time with a welded tender in tow. ***Strathwood Library Collection***

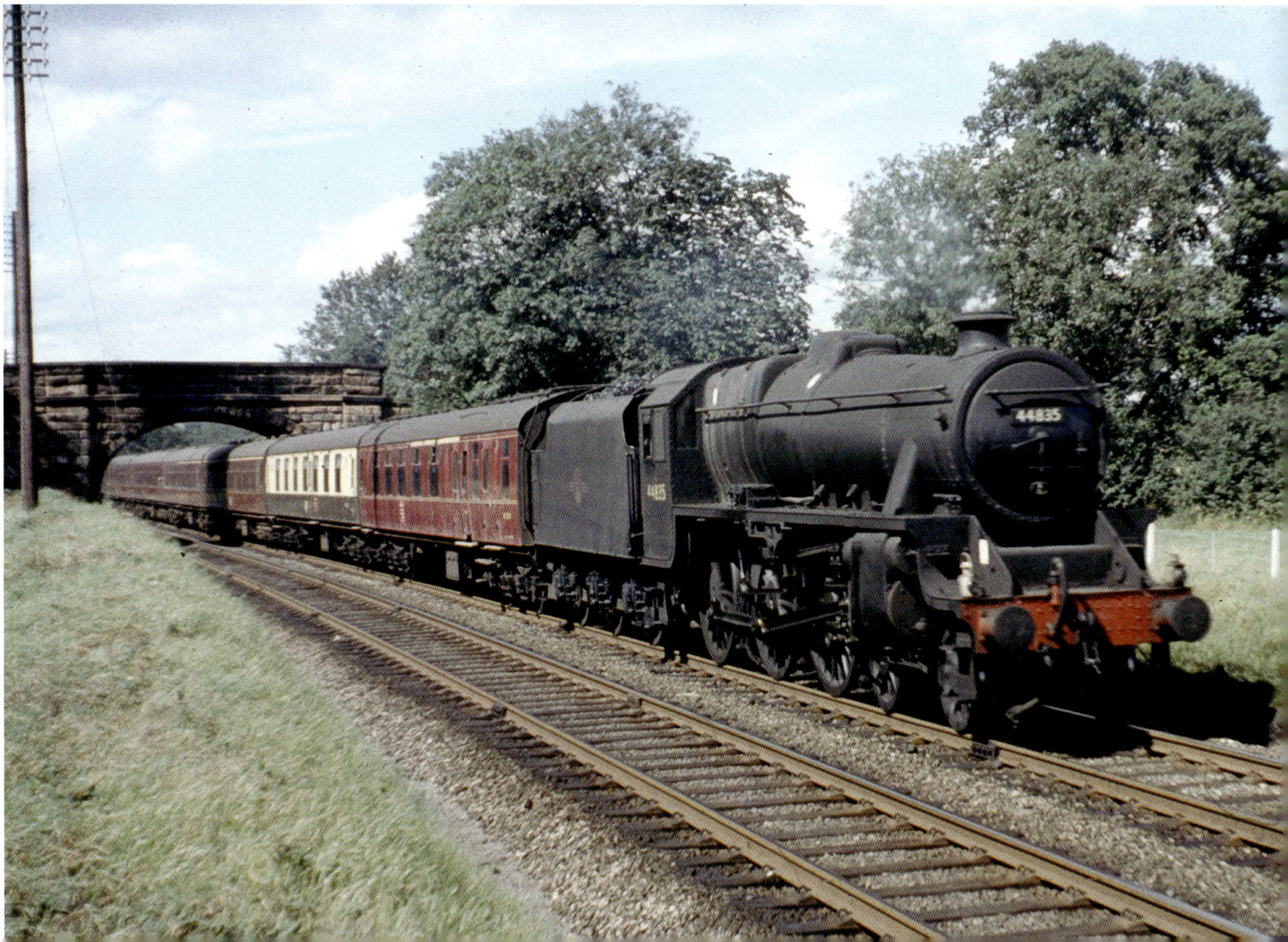

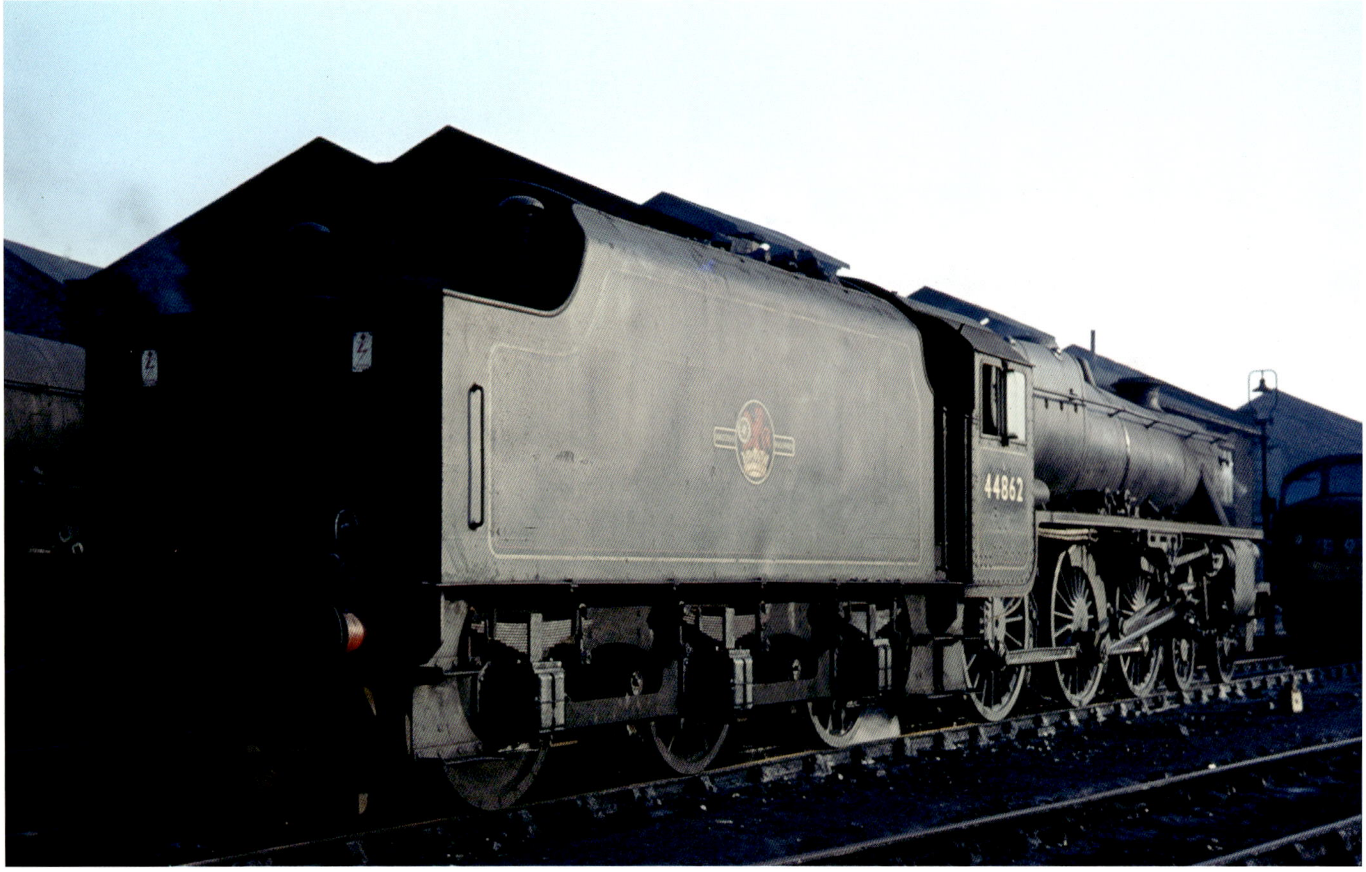

A closer look at a welded tender as fitted to 44862 at Wellingborough on 7 March 1965, and a second glance shows that she has picked up a mix of wheels with the rearmost set being not the usual spoked type but of the disc variety. ***Winston Cole***

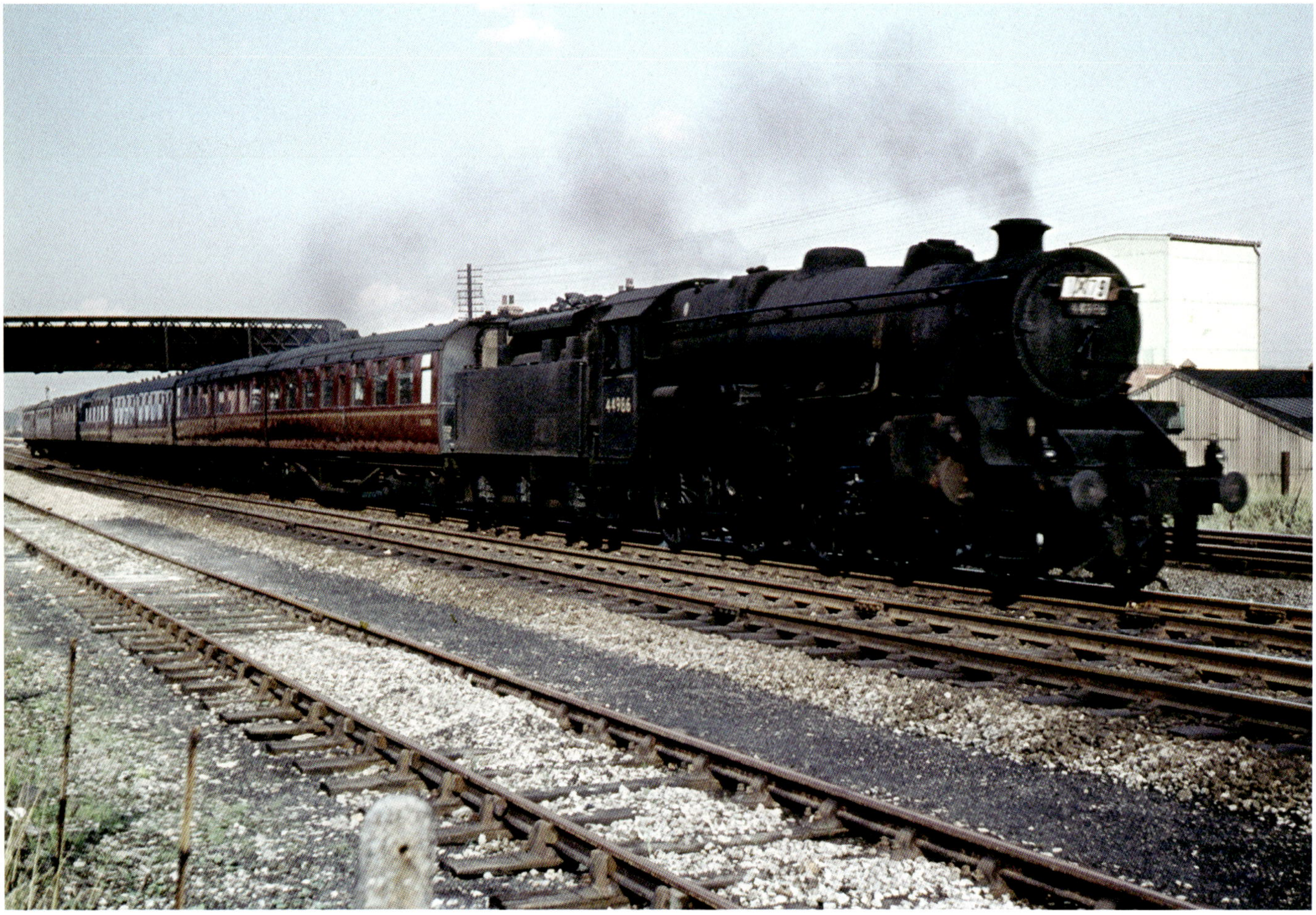

At various times differing class members have been paired with a coal weighing tender such as 44966 passing Rotherham with another holiday extra in 1959. ***Strathwood Library Collection***

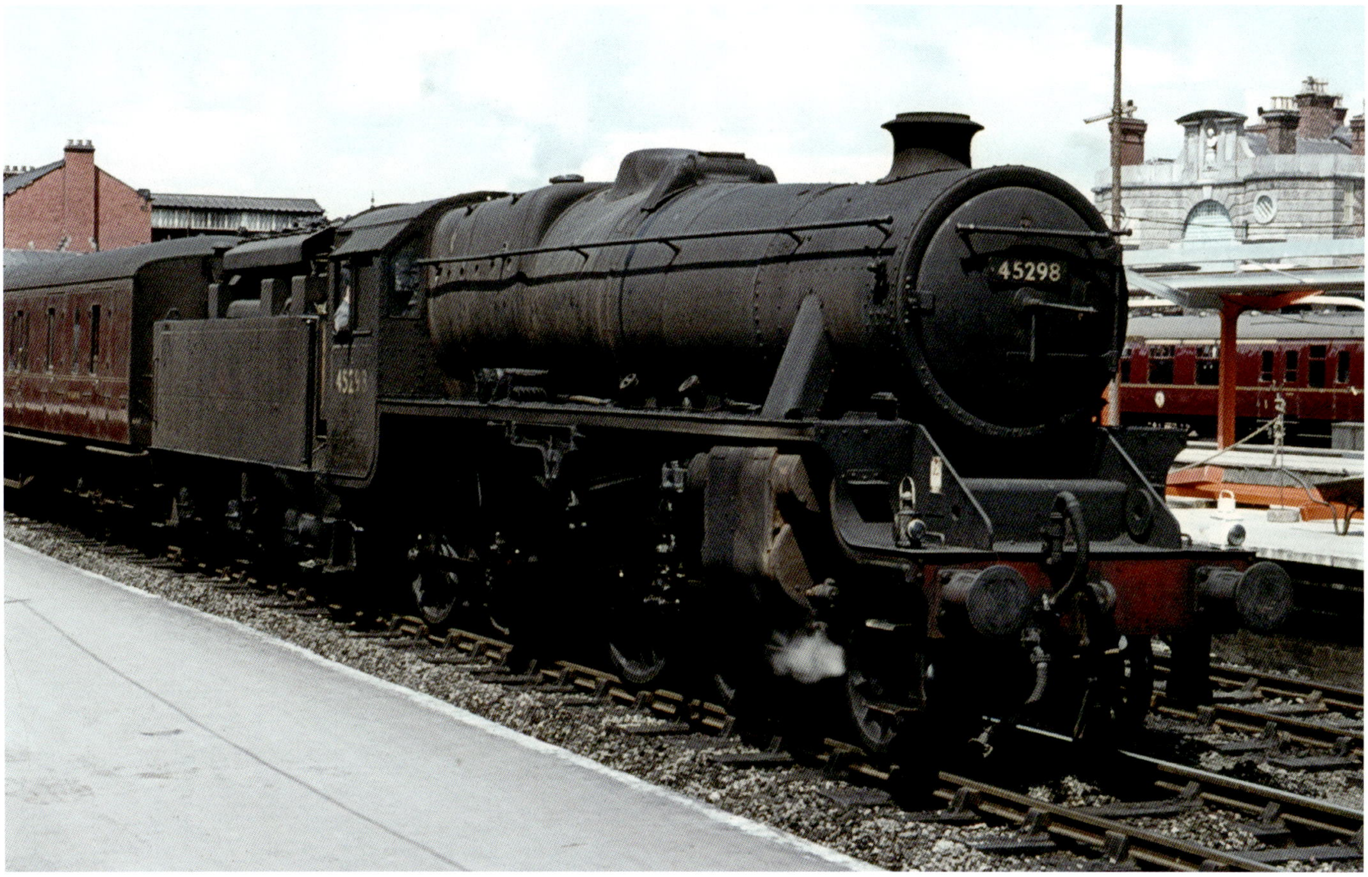

Whilst 45298 is so fitted with one of these Horwich built tenders at Stafford in the early 1960s. ***Strathwood Library Collection***

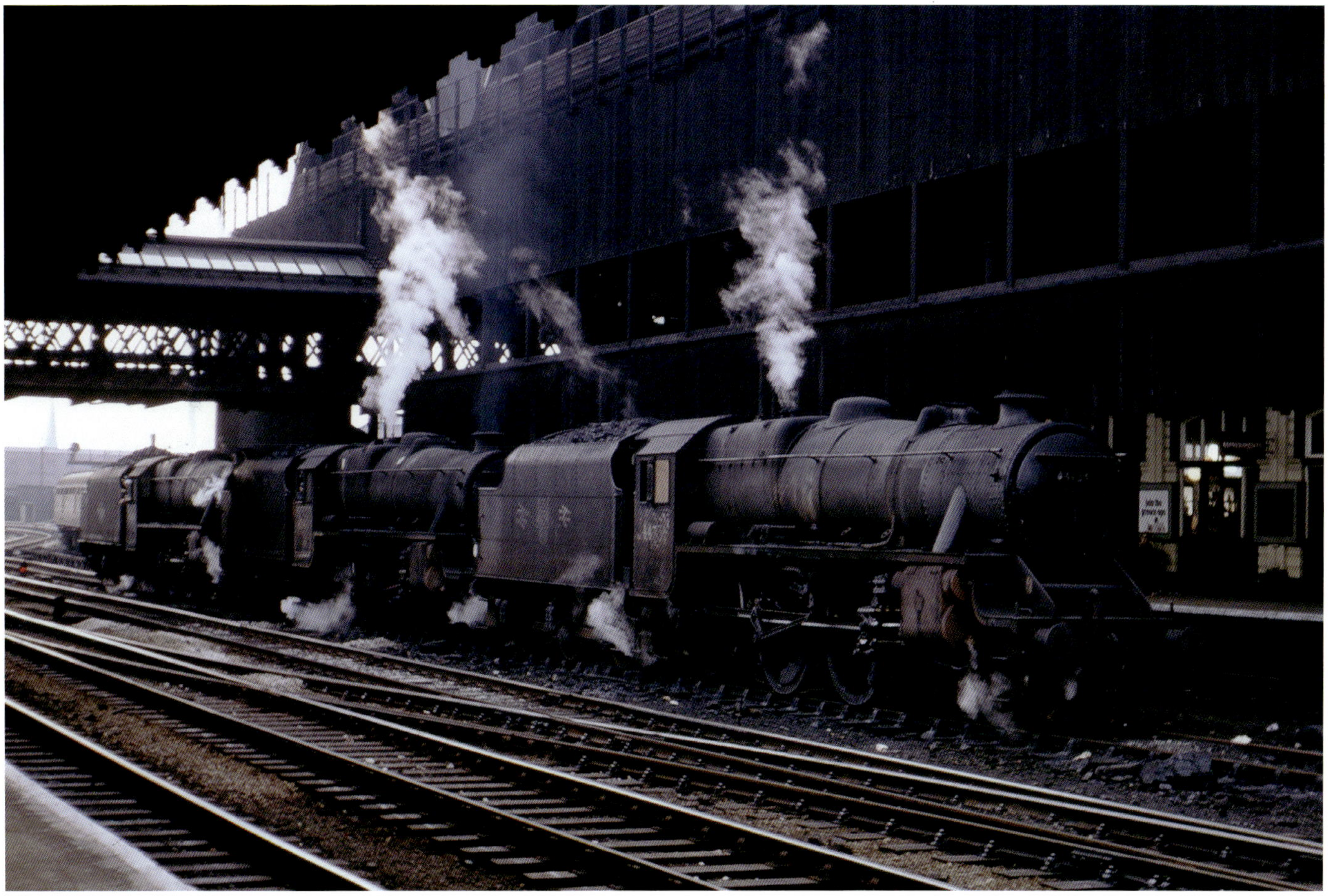

If the use of Inter City arrows had been decreed by British Rail on repaints to steam locomotives after 1966 we can get some idea of how it may have appeared from where some wag has chalked it upon 44734 seen at Manchester Victoria on 10 June 1967 along with classmates 45411 and 45234. ***Jerry Beddows***

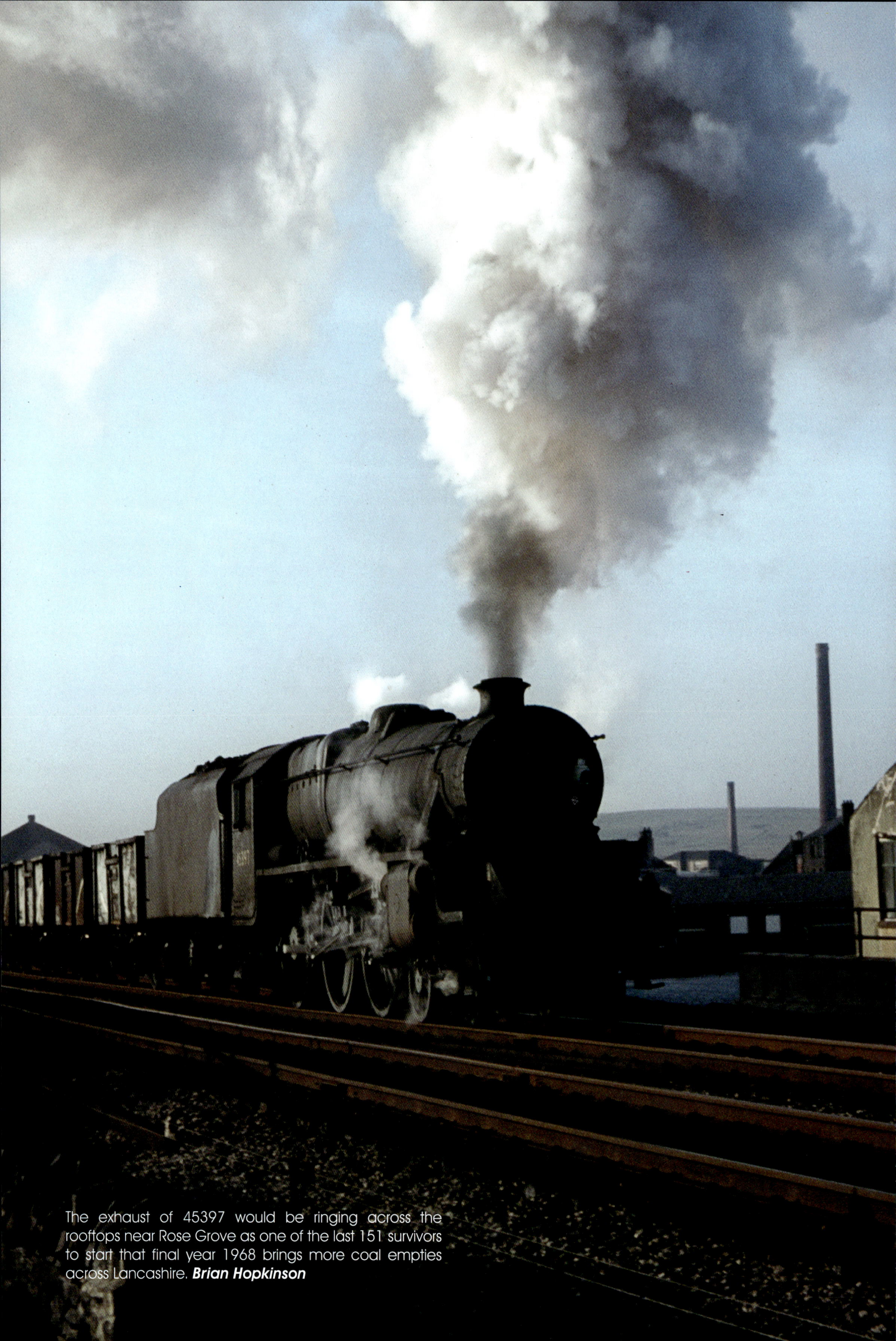

The exhaust of 45397 would be ringing across the rooftops near Rose Grove as one of the last 151 survivors to start that final year 1968 brings more coal empties across Lancashire. ***Brian Hopkinson***

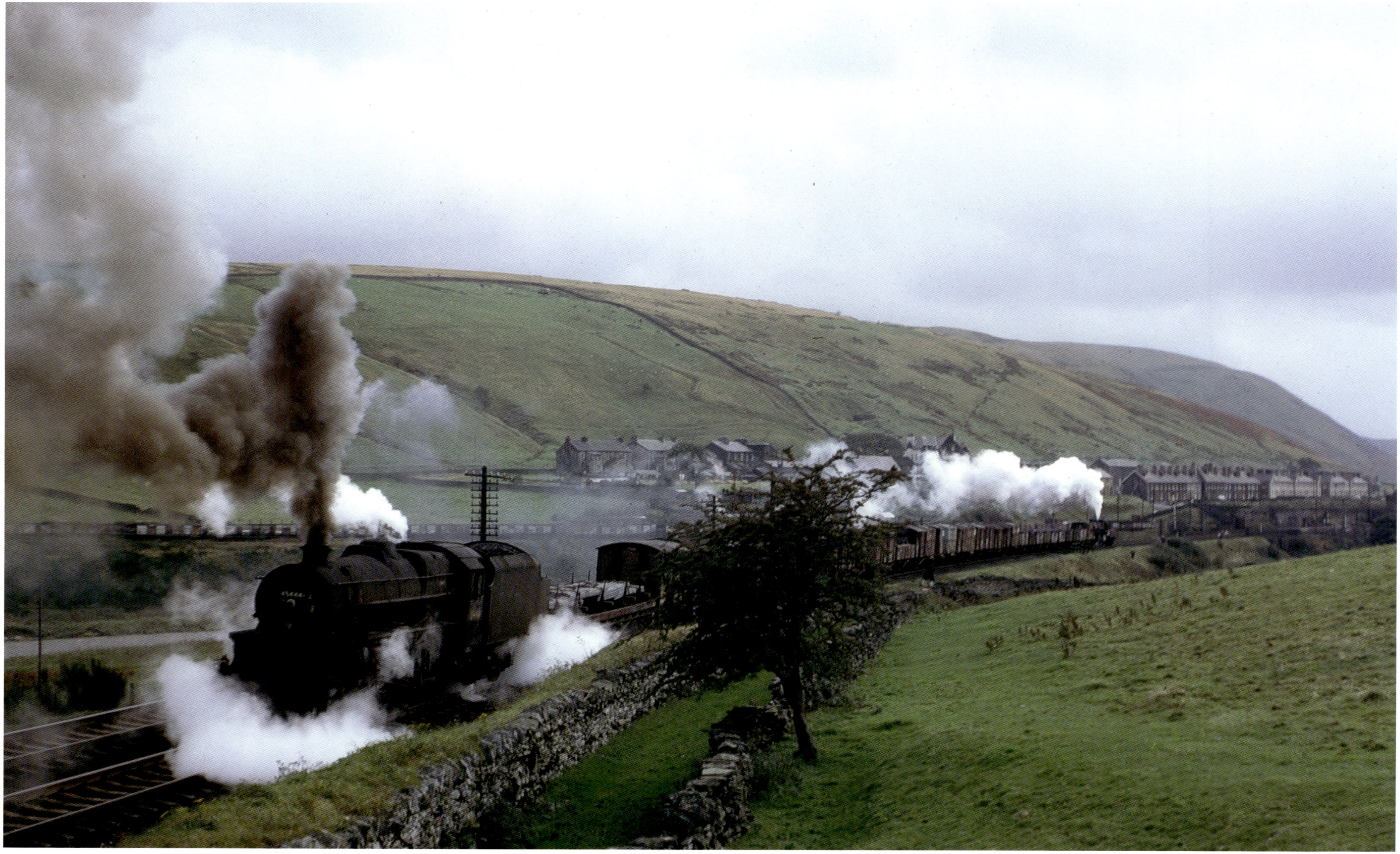

Having taken on a banker, it's blast off for 45444 at Tebay with a down freight 7 October 1967 as they head for Shap Summit. ***Jerry Beddows***

Pairings

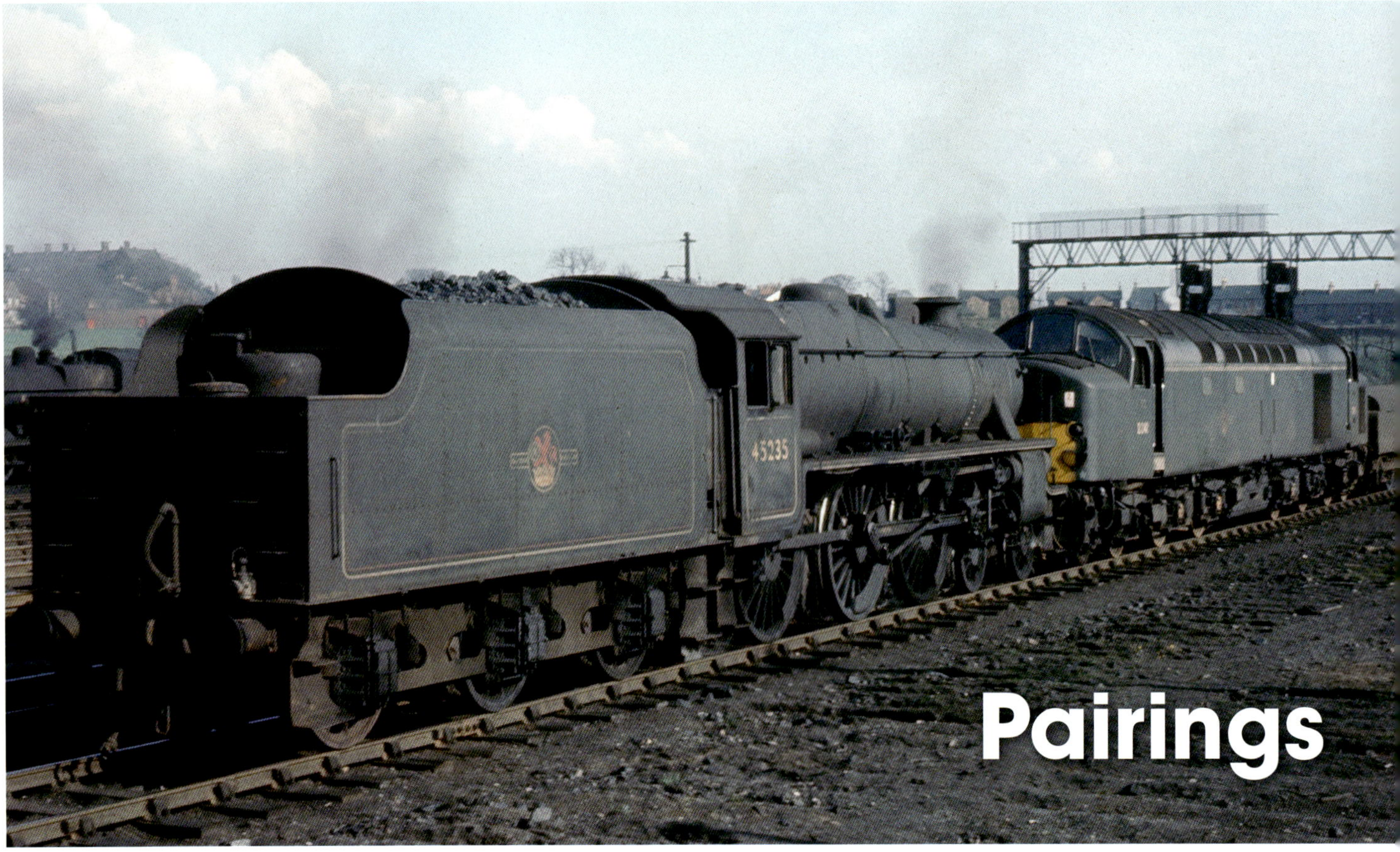

Running tender first Black Five 45235 assists a failed English Electric Type 4 past Kingmoor on 18 April 1964. ***Strathwood Library Collection***

Permanent way working brings Stanier 8Fs 48445 and 48679 together near Leyland. The latter 2-8-0 had been running with a Fowler tender from a Jubilee exchange before, and now has been mated with a Black Five tender. Note the crudely blacked out lining in August 1966. ***Brian Hopkinson***

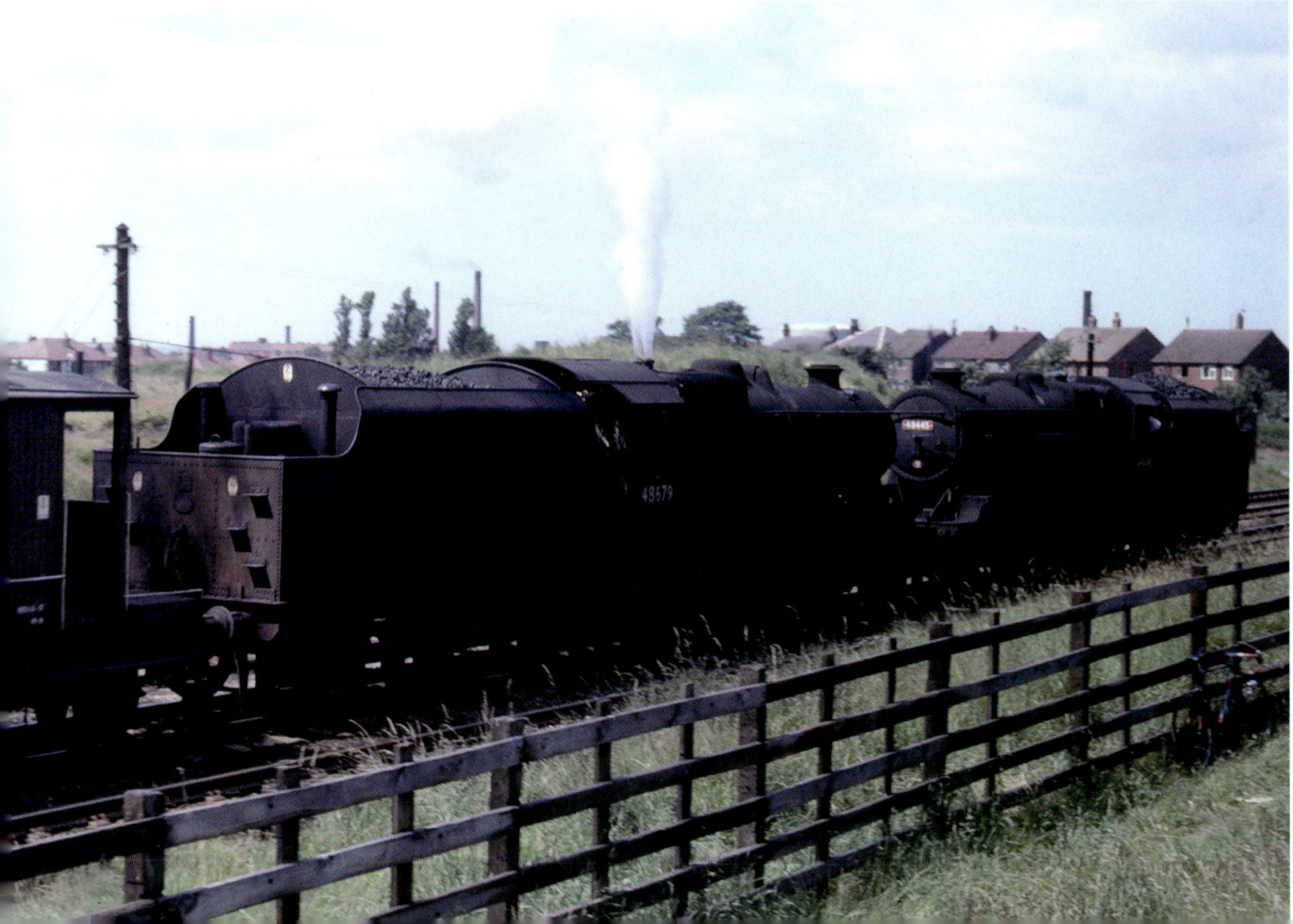

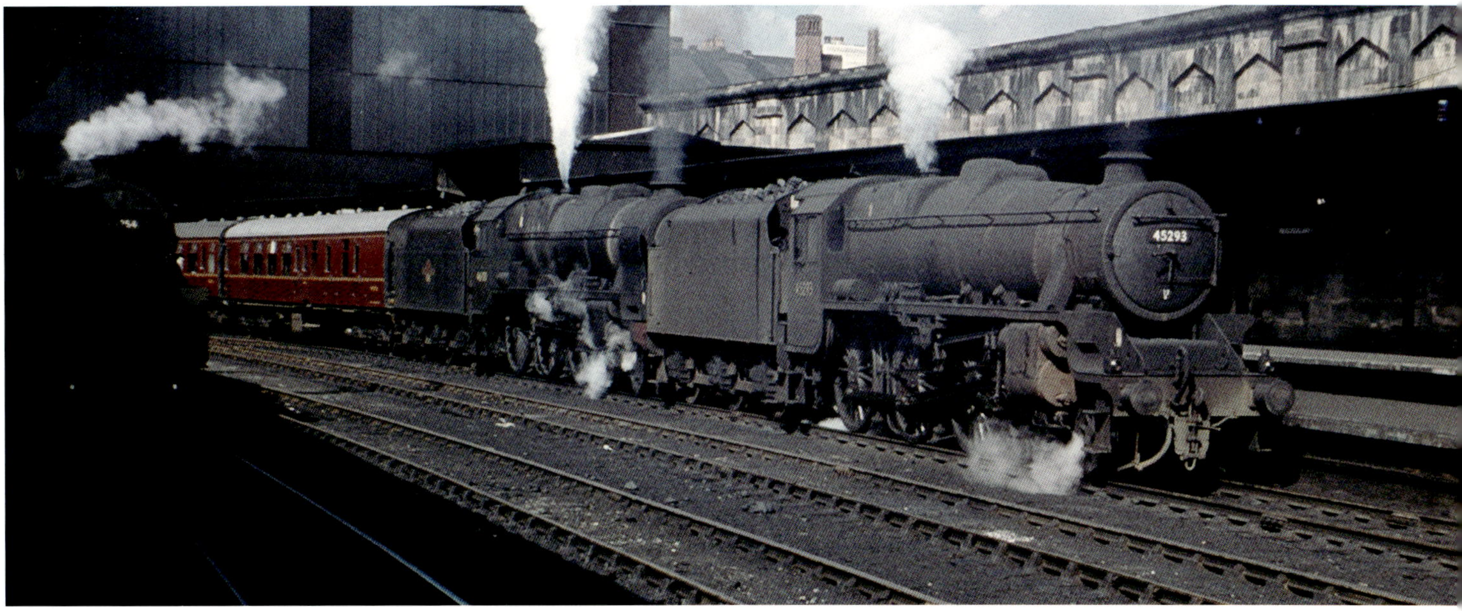

Assisting an unknown Royal Scot at Carlisle across the border was Black Five 45293 in the early sixties. ***Strathwood Library Collection***

A Black Five piloting a rebuilt Bulleid West Country this time with 34100 Appledore and 45493 passing the engine sheds at Weymouth on 3 July 1966 as stand ins for the failed Class V2 60916 on the LCGB Green Arrow Railtour ***Dave Down***

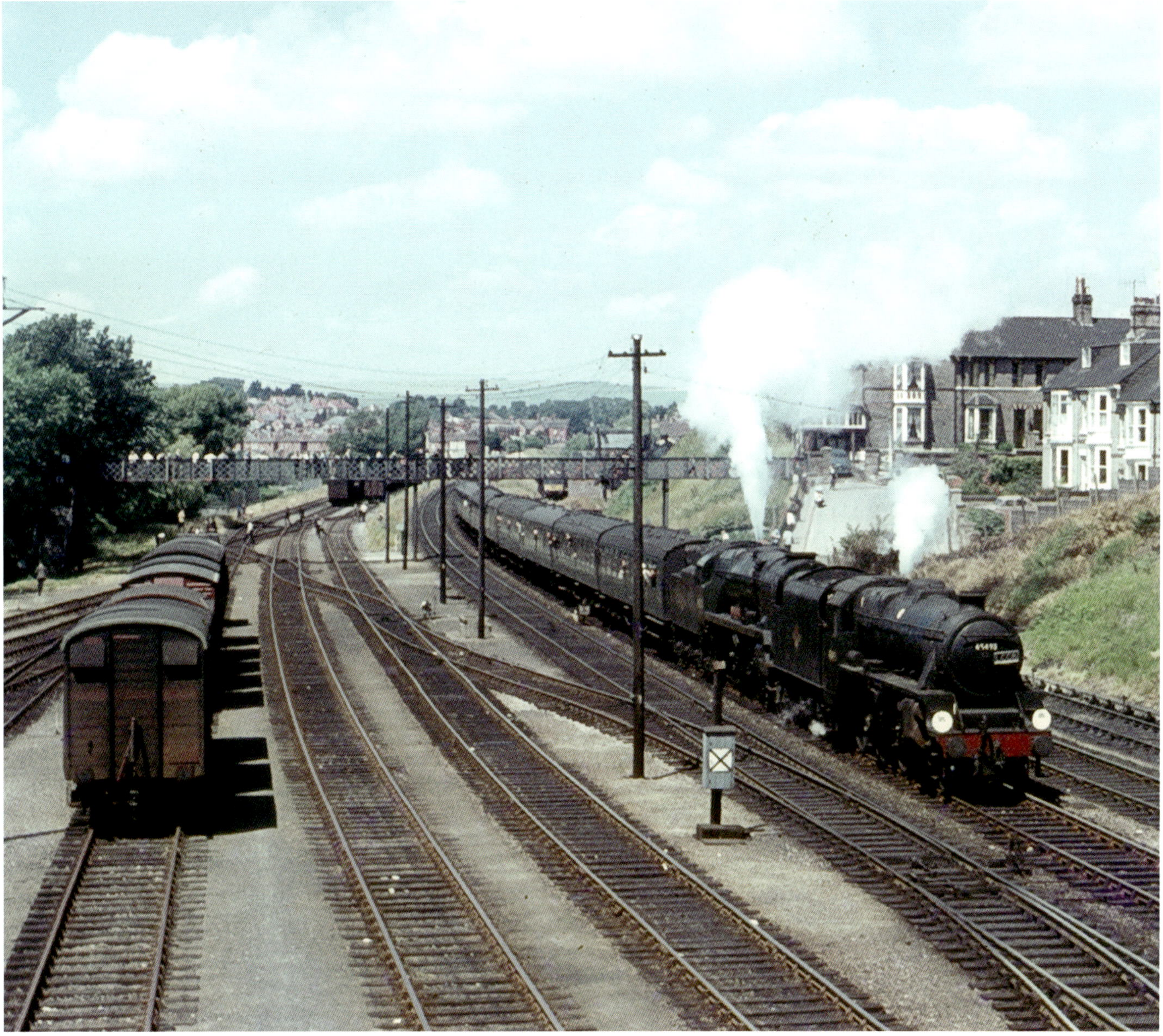

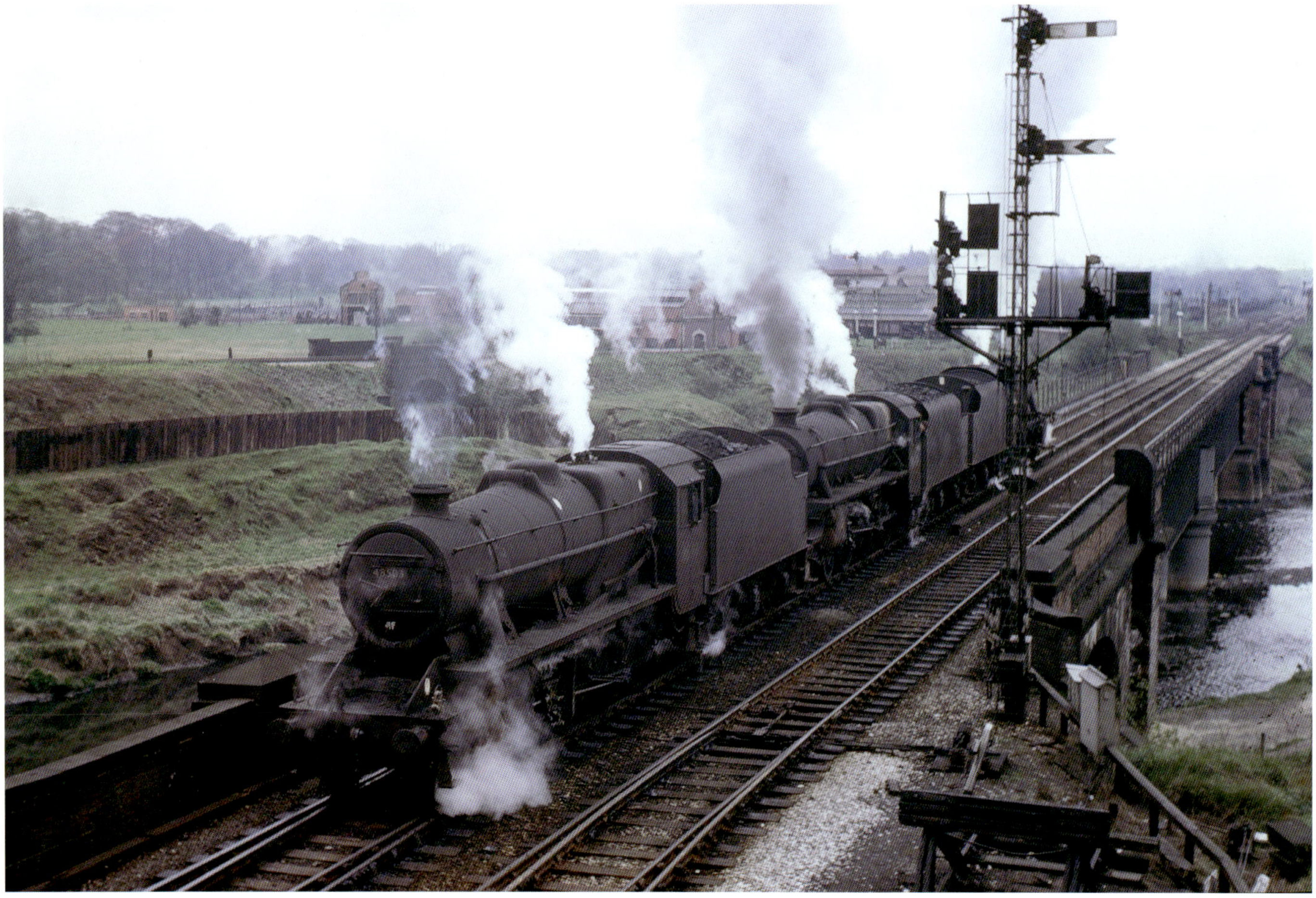

A light engine combo of 48203 45188 and 48504 rumble past Heaton Mersey on 22 April 1967. ***Jerry Beddows***

A congregation of Stanier 8Fs at Preston station on 8 May 1967 as 48553, 48200 and 48742 gather to let off steam. ***Michael Beaton***

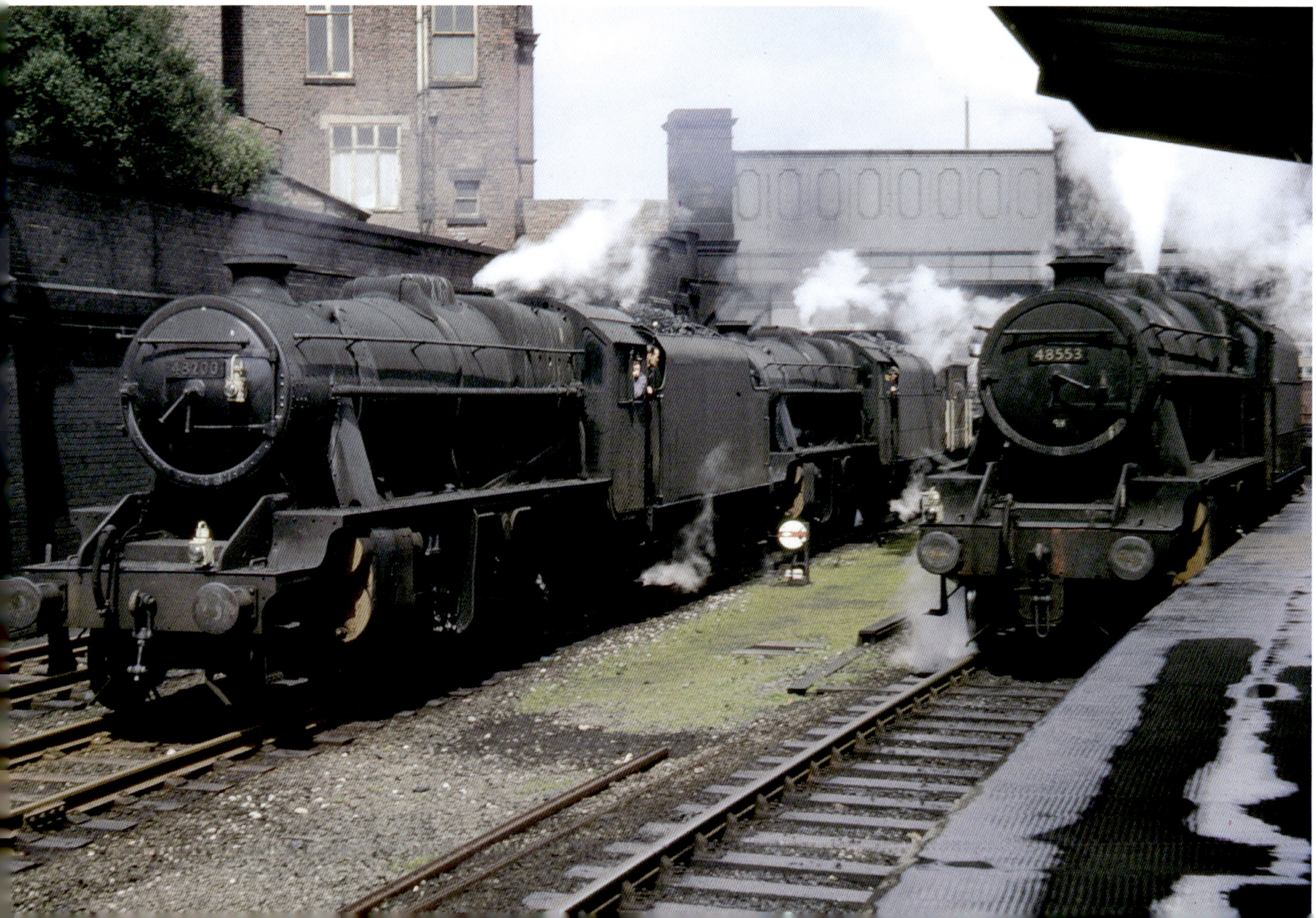

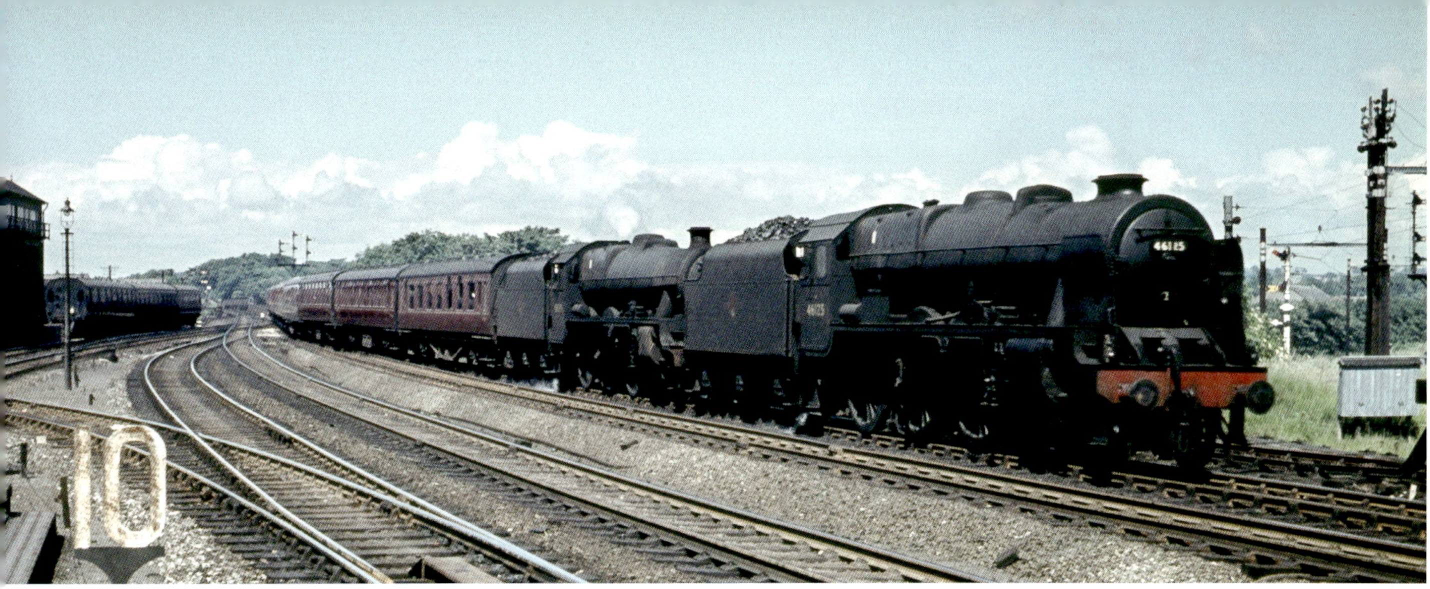

Piloting an unknown Jubilee into Lancaster in 1958 was Royal Scot 46125 3rd Carabinier, was this a failure or a balancing working? ***Strathwood Library Collection***

One of a number of combinations of locomotives on 4 August 1968 involved 44871 and 44894 running smartly across Saddleworth Moor. ***Peter Simmonds***

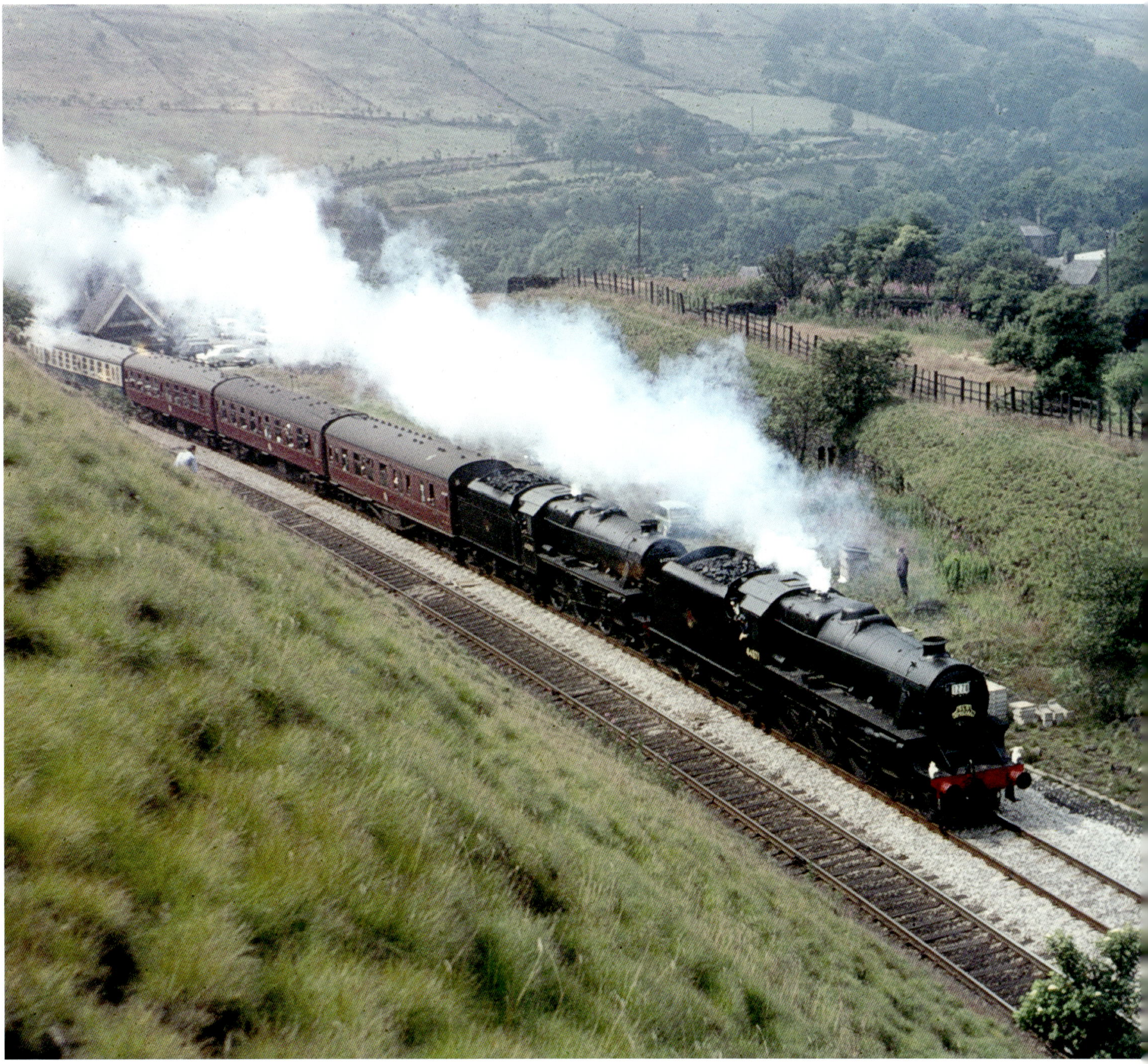

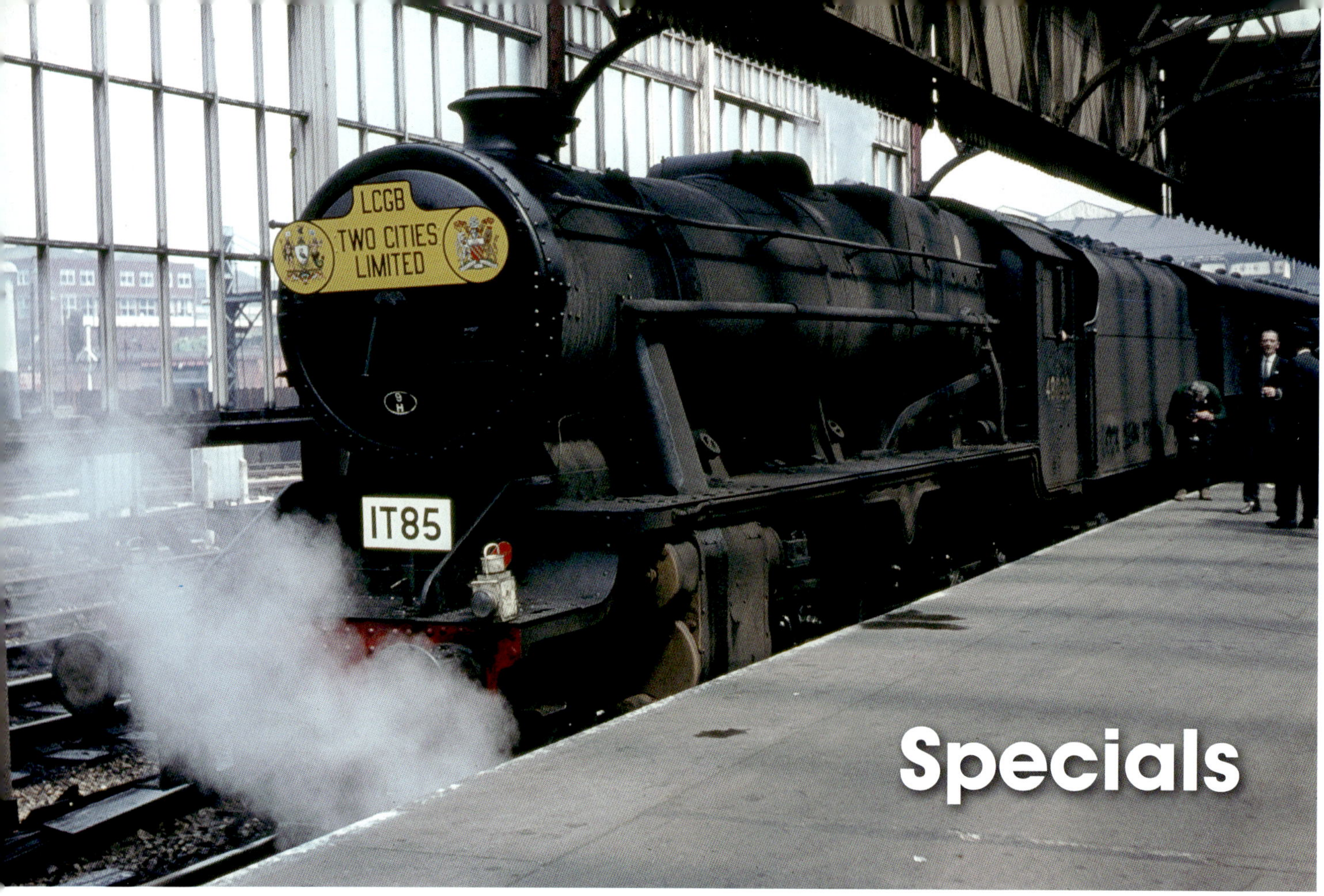

Specials

In earlier days the thought of a lowly Stanier 8F with a headboard on a special may have been incredible, especially if it were during the winter. However by the last summer of steam it was a welcome opportunity for many to travel behind steam as witnessed by 48033 waiting at Manchester Victoria on 23 June 1968. ***Strathwood Library Collection***

Another pairing for Black Fives on 4 August 1968 with 44874 and 45017 charging through Copy Pit. ***Strathwood Library Collection***

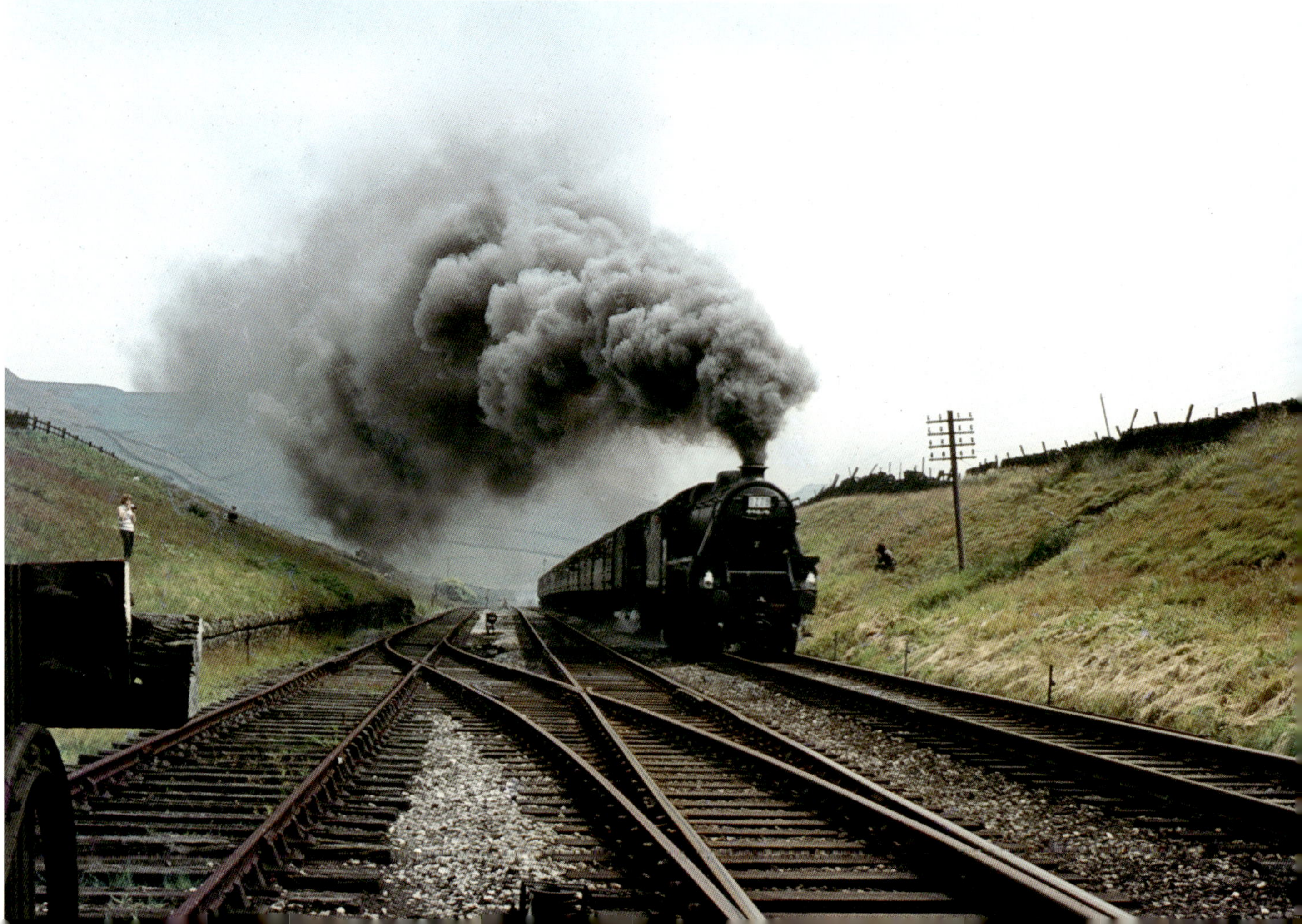

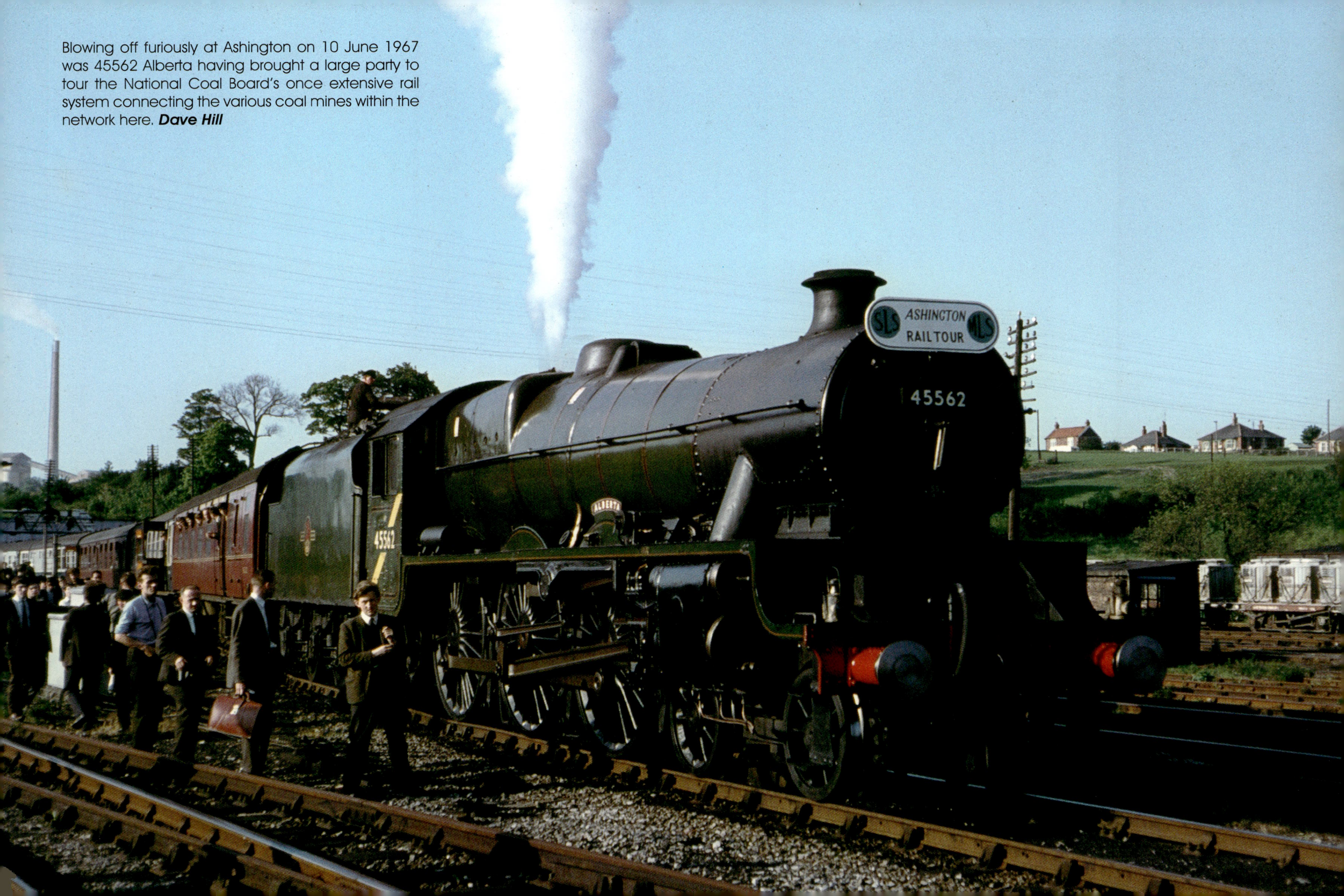

Blowing off furiously at Ashington on 10 June 1967 was 45562 Alberta having brought a large party to tour the National Coal Board's once extensive rail system connecting the various coal mines within the network here. ***Dave Hill***

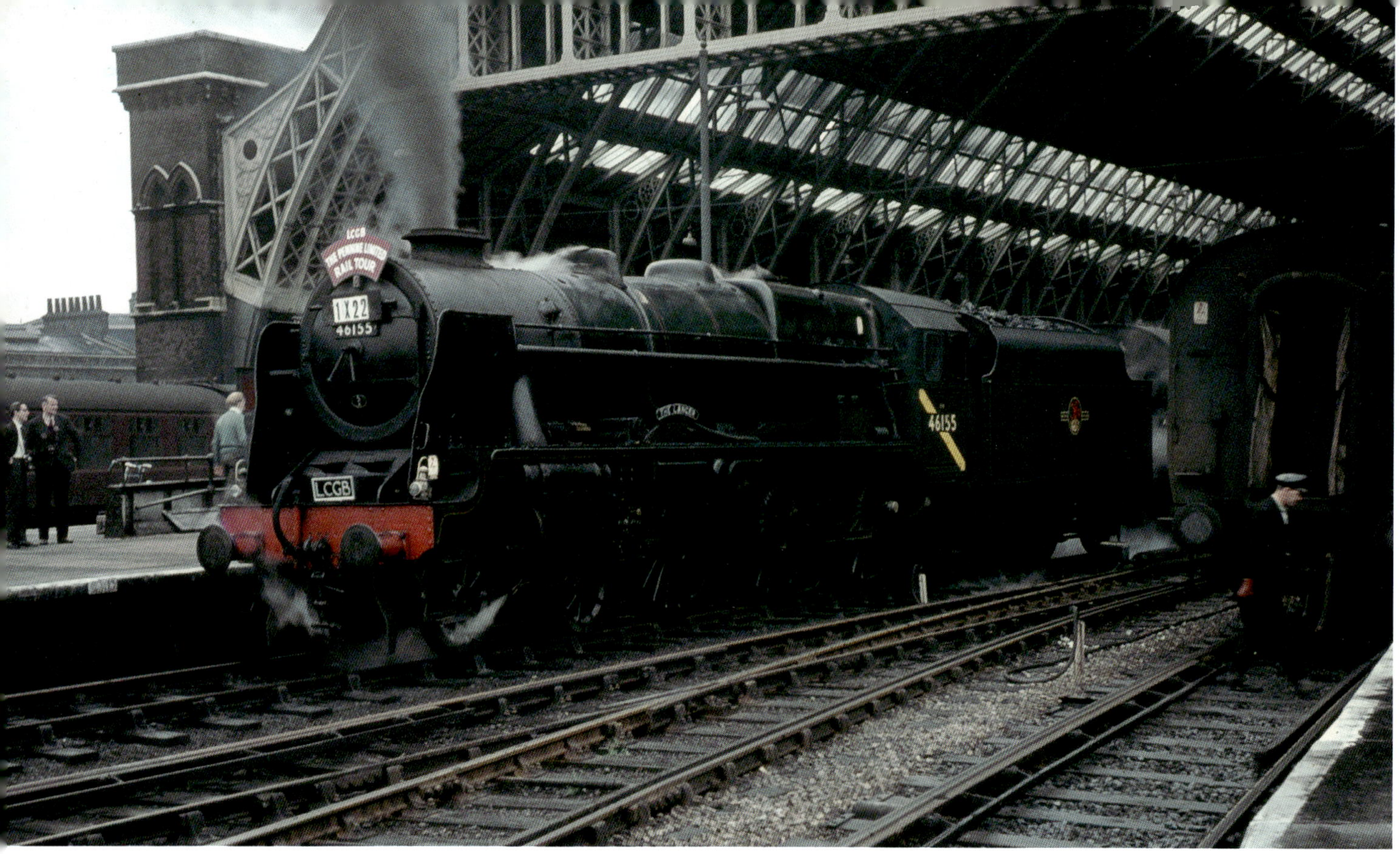

Cleaned and prepared to work the LCGB Pennine Rail Tour on 19 September 1964, Royal Scot 46155 The Lancer backs on at St. Pancras to head the first leg of the tour as far as Peterborough East where Class A1 60128 Bongrace would be waiting. ***Strathwood Library Collection***

The RCTS arranged The Duchess Commemorative Railtour for 5 October 1963 to run from Crewe to Edinburgh Princes Street and return. In the event the intended locomotive 46251 City of Nottingham had been failed the week before with a bogie defect. However it was put right and restored to traffic to be used on the day bring some spirited running at times along the route such as here near Lancaster. ***Late Ray Helm/Strathwood Library Collection***

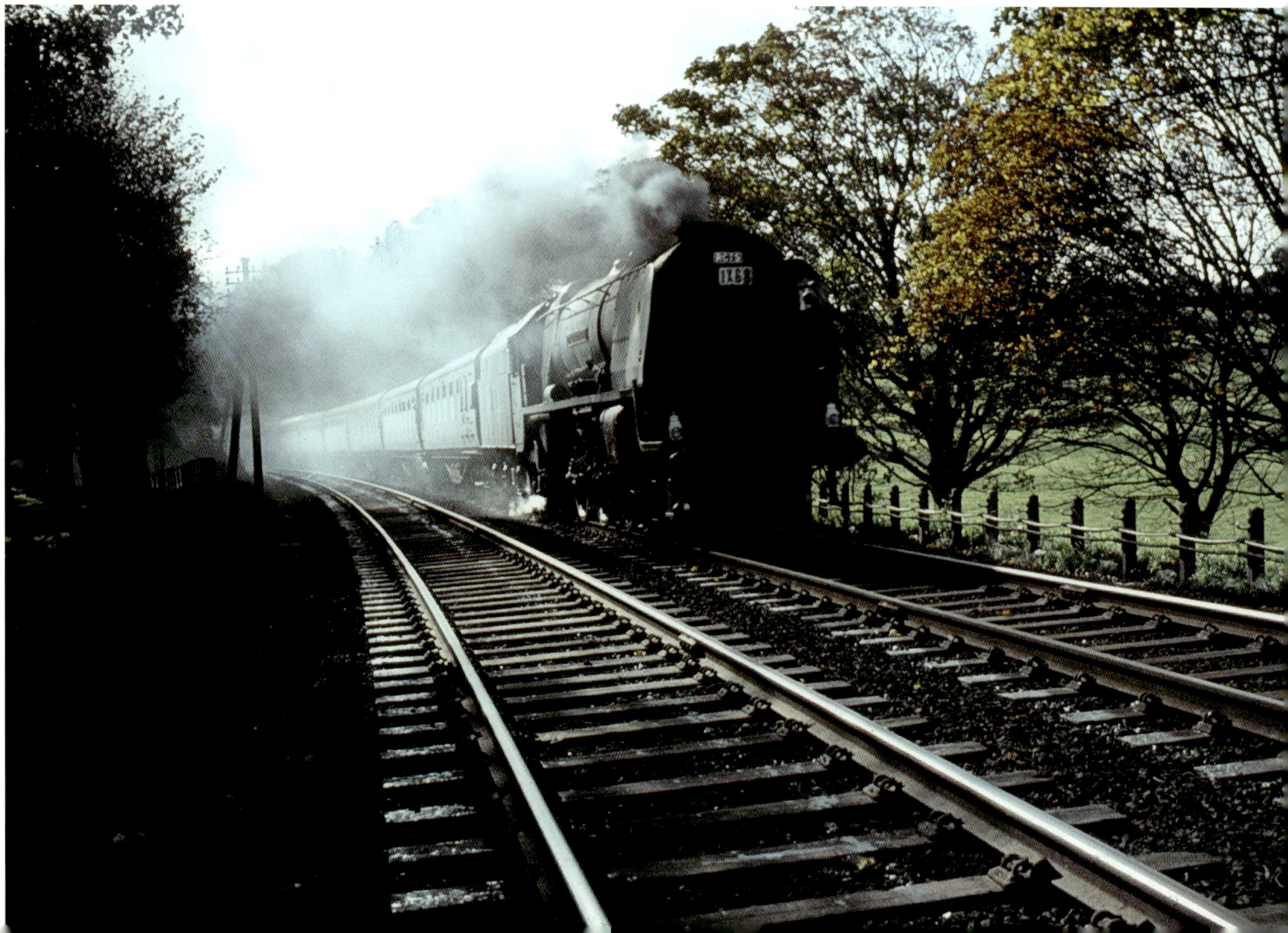

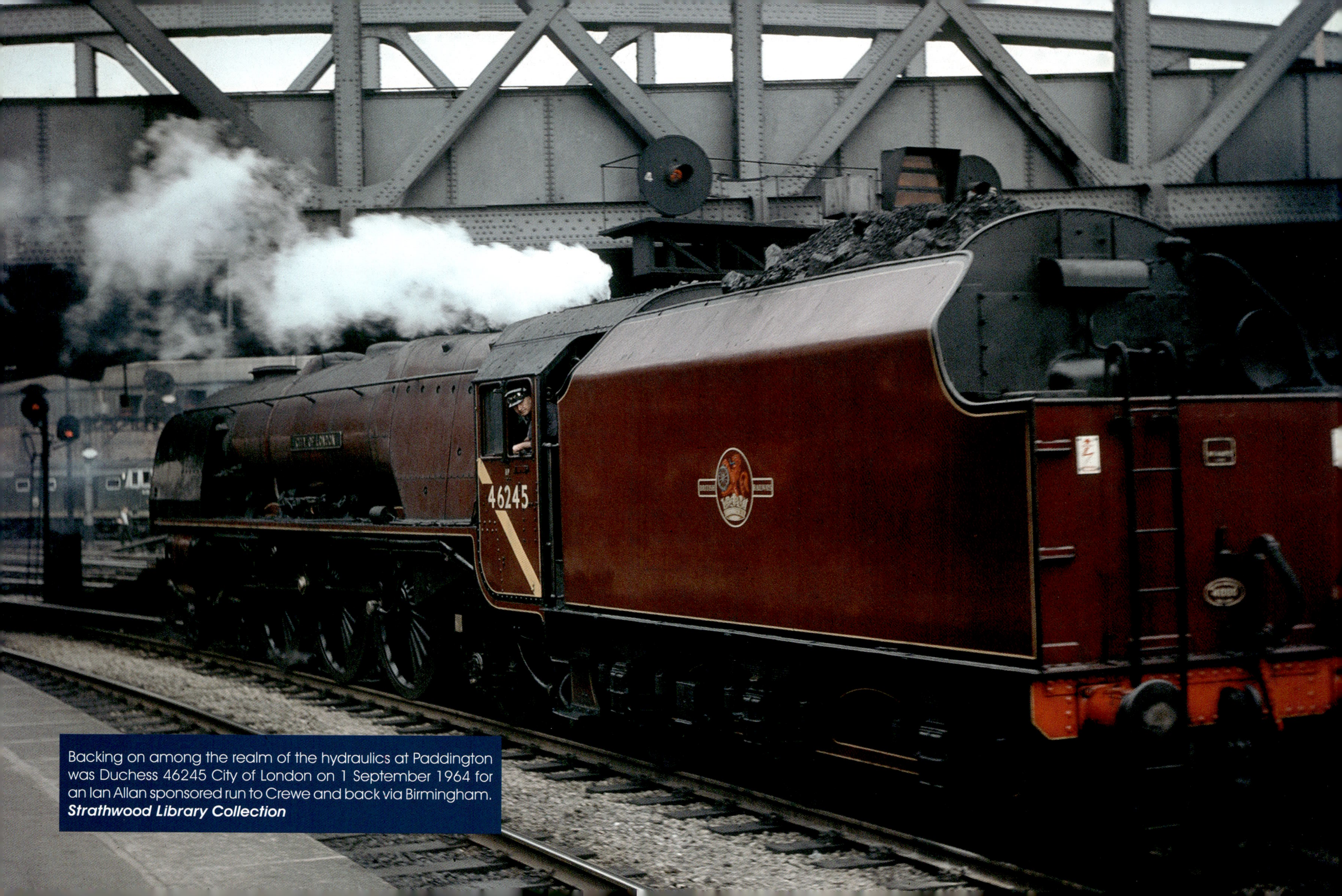

Backing on among the realm of the hydraulics at Paddington was Duchess 46245 City of London on 1 September 1964 for an Ian Allan sponsored run to Crewe and back via Birmingham. ***Strathwood Library Collection***

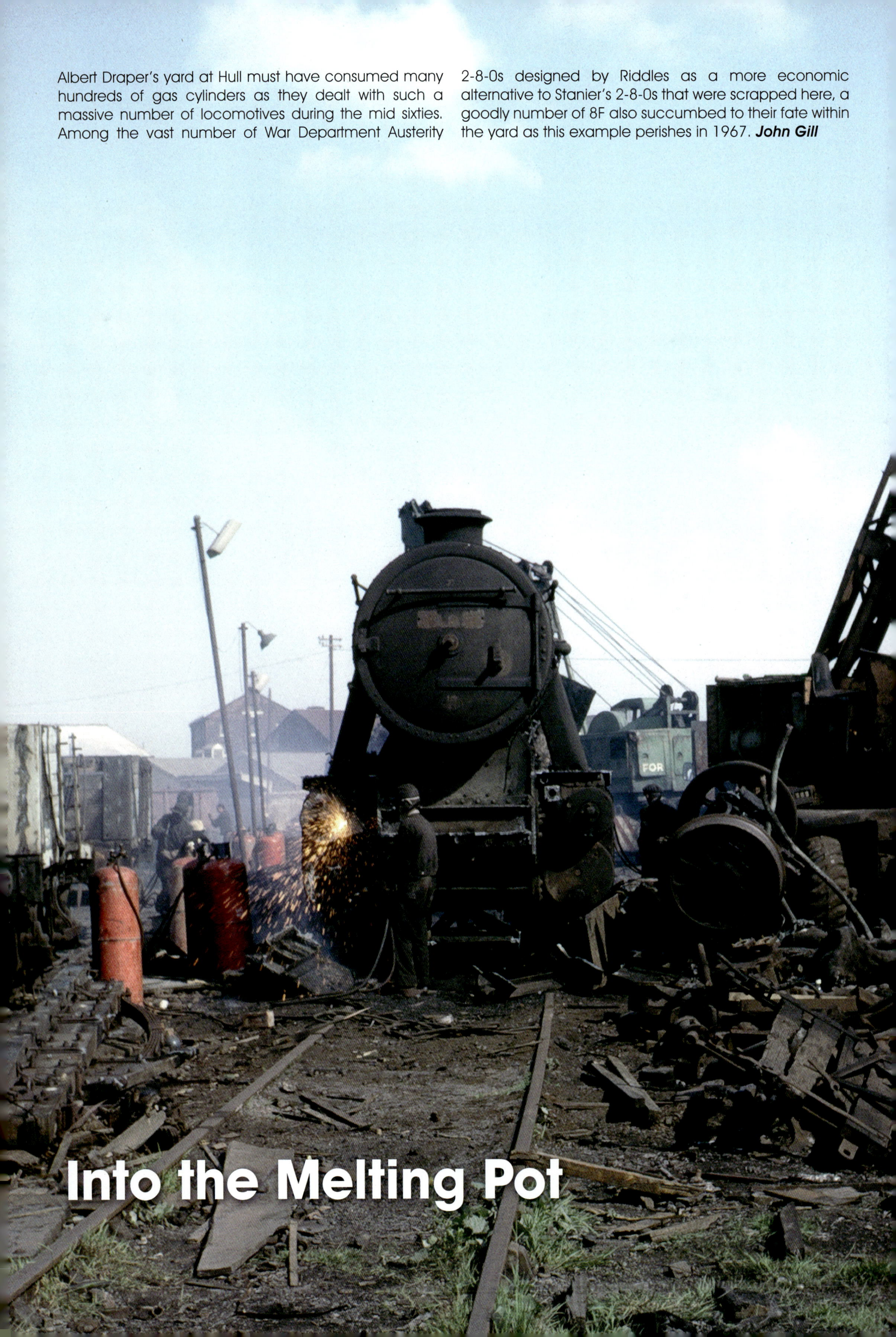

Albert Draper's yard at Hull must have consumed many hundreds of gas cylinders as they dealt with such a massive number of locomotives during the mid sixties. Among the vast number of War Department Austerity 2-8-0s designed by Riddles as a more economic alternative to Stanier's 2-8-0s that were scrapped here, a goodly number of 8F also succumbed to their fate within the yard as this example perishes in 1967. ***John Gill***

Into the Melting Pot

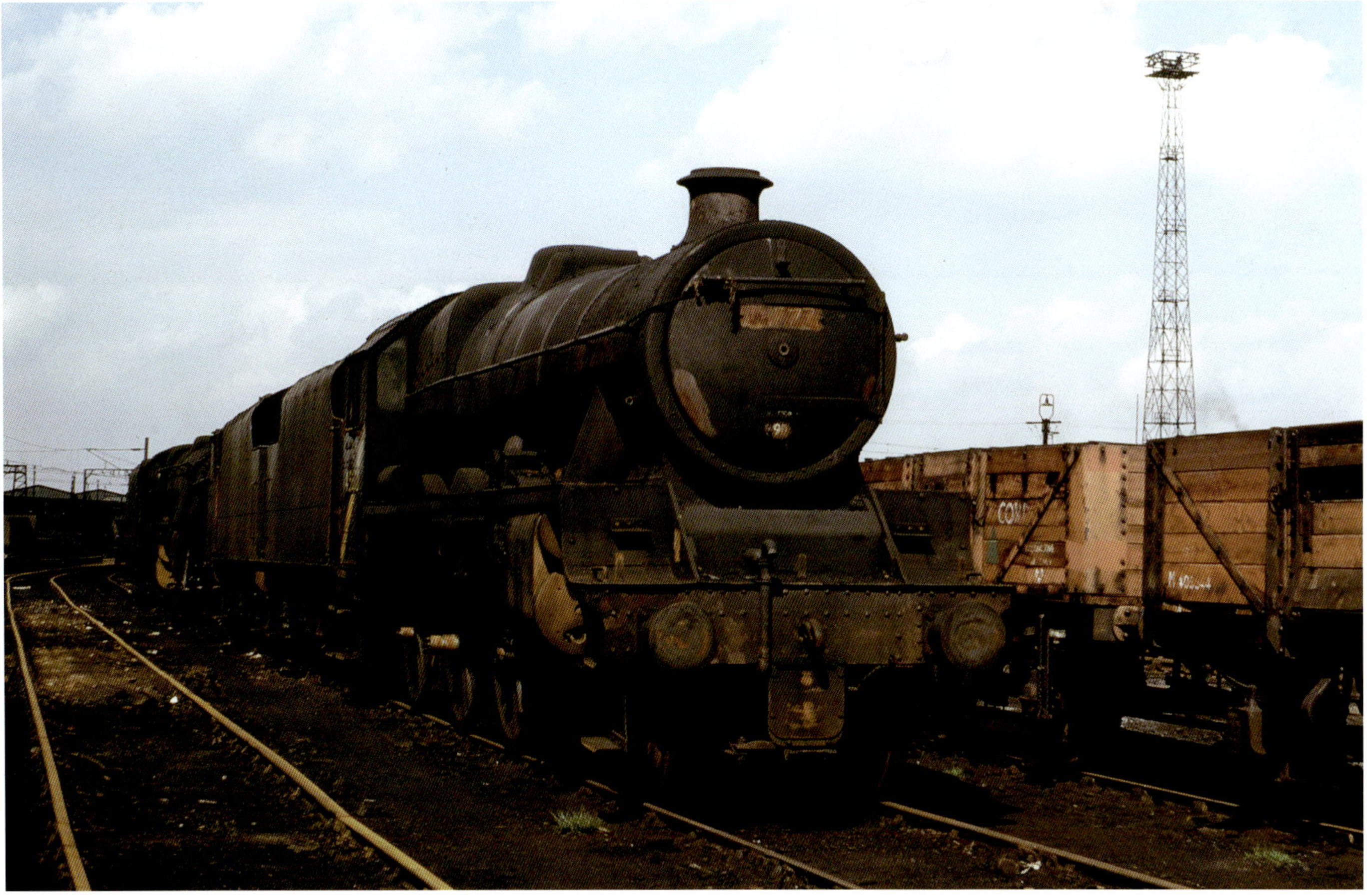

Filthy, rusty and outcast Jubilee 45600 Bermuda lies at Crewe South awaiting the final journey to the breakers on 10 April 1966. ***Jerry Beddows***

Among the line of condemned engines at Lostock Hall on 25 July 1967 could be found 42546 a product from North British in 1936 to Stanier's 2 cylinder design of 2-6-4T. ***Strathwood Library Collection***

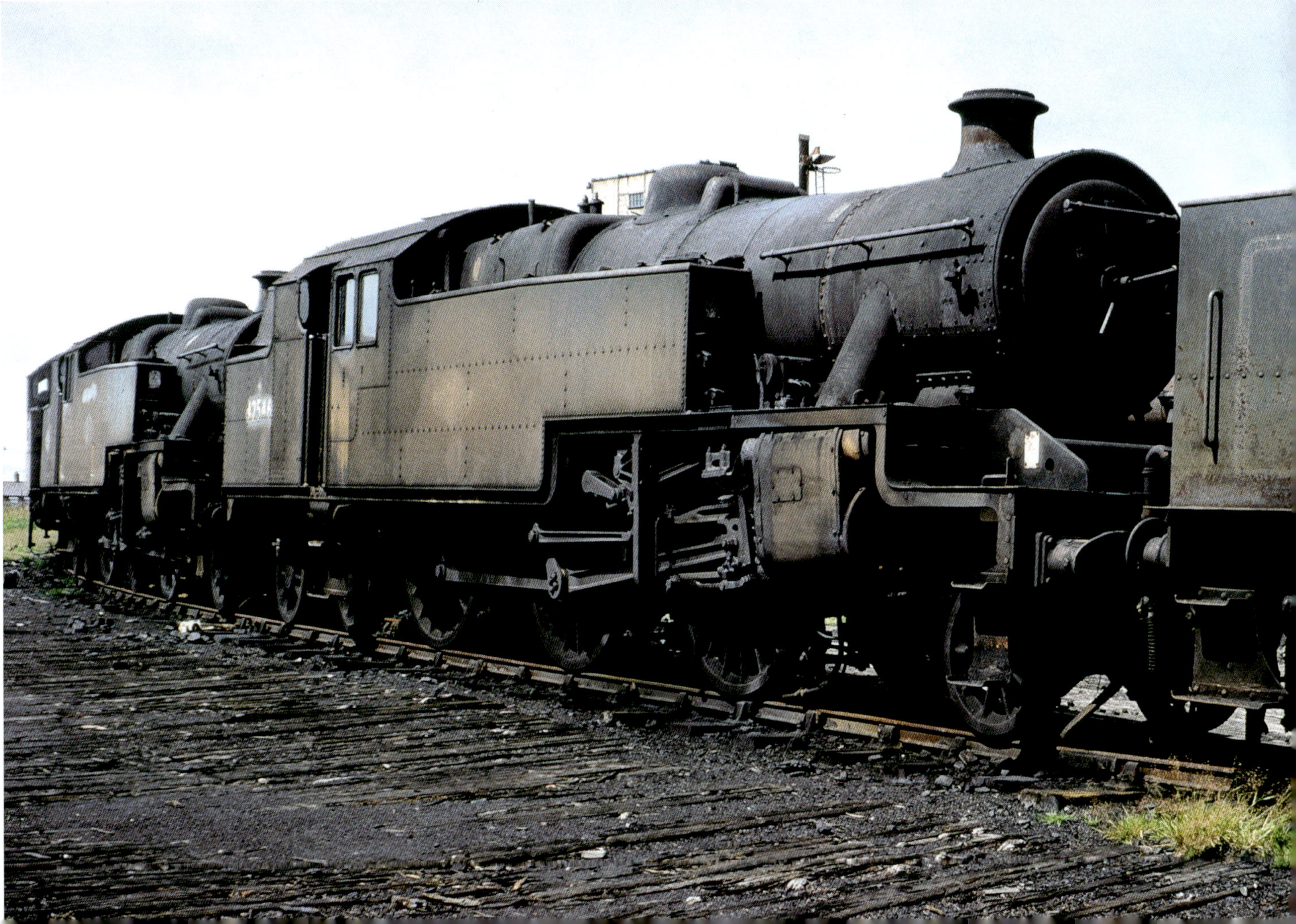

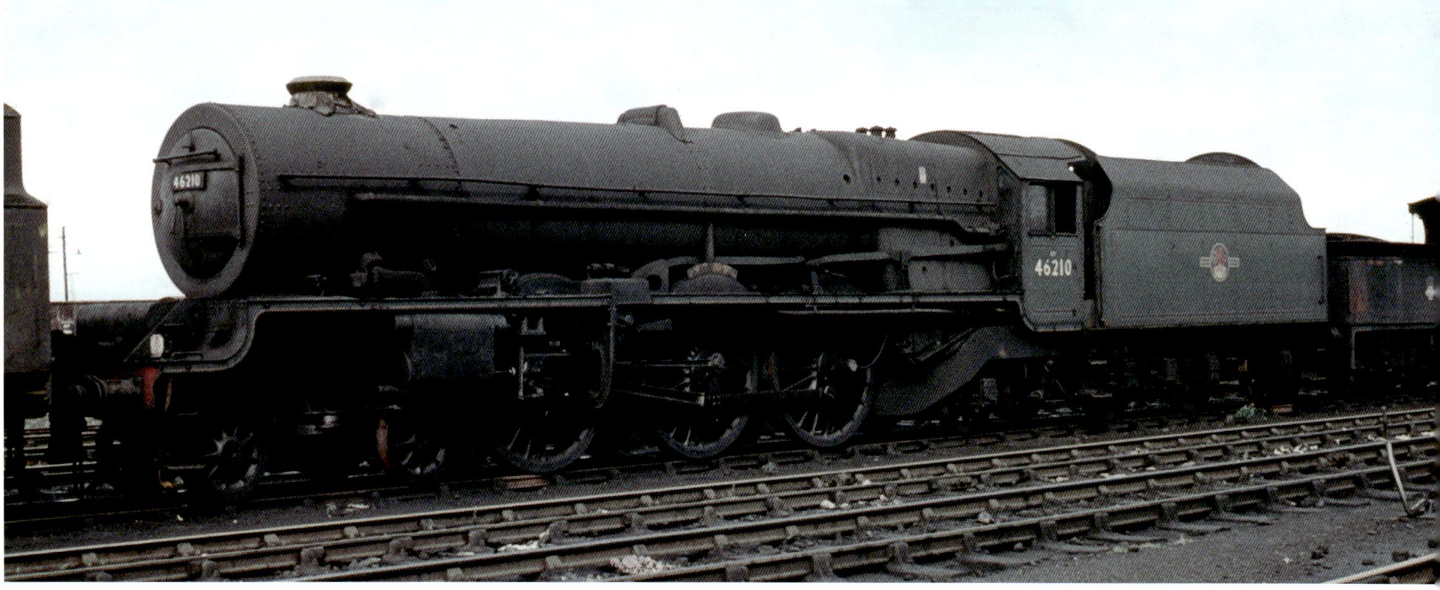

Set aside with cracked frames in 1961 was 46210 Lady Patricia awaiting her fate at Carlisle Kingmoor. ***Strathwood Library Collection***

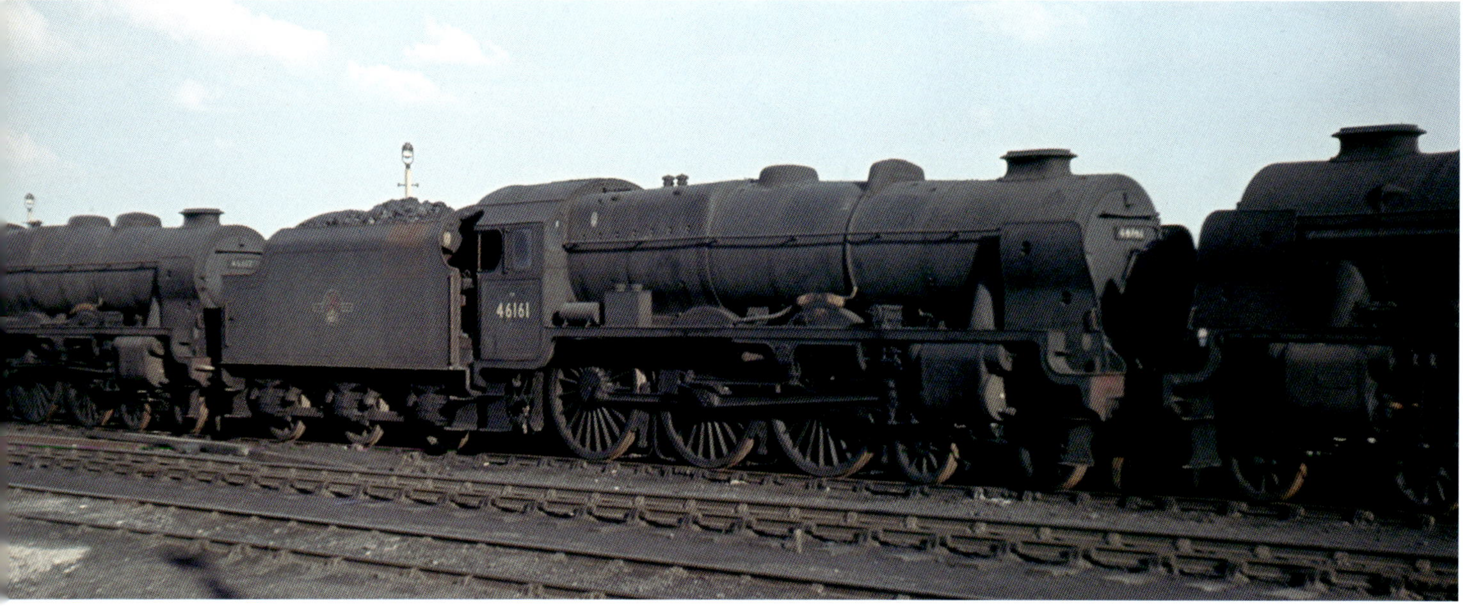

Withdrawn Royal Scots 46161 King's Own and 46117 Welsh Guardsman await dismissal at Neville Hill on 13 July 1963. ***Strathwood Library Collection***

Below: The end is nigh for 46243 City of Lancaster on 2 May 1965 within the Central Wagon Works at Wigan. ***Win Wall/Strathwood Library Collection***

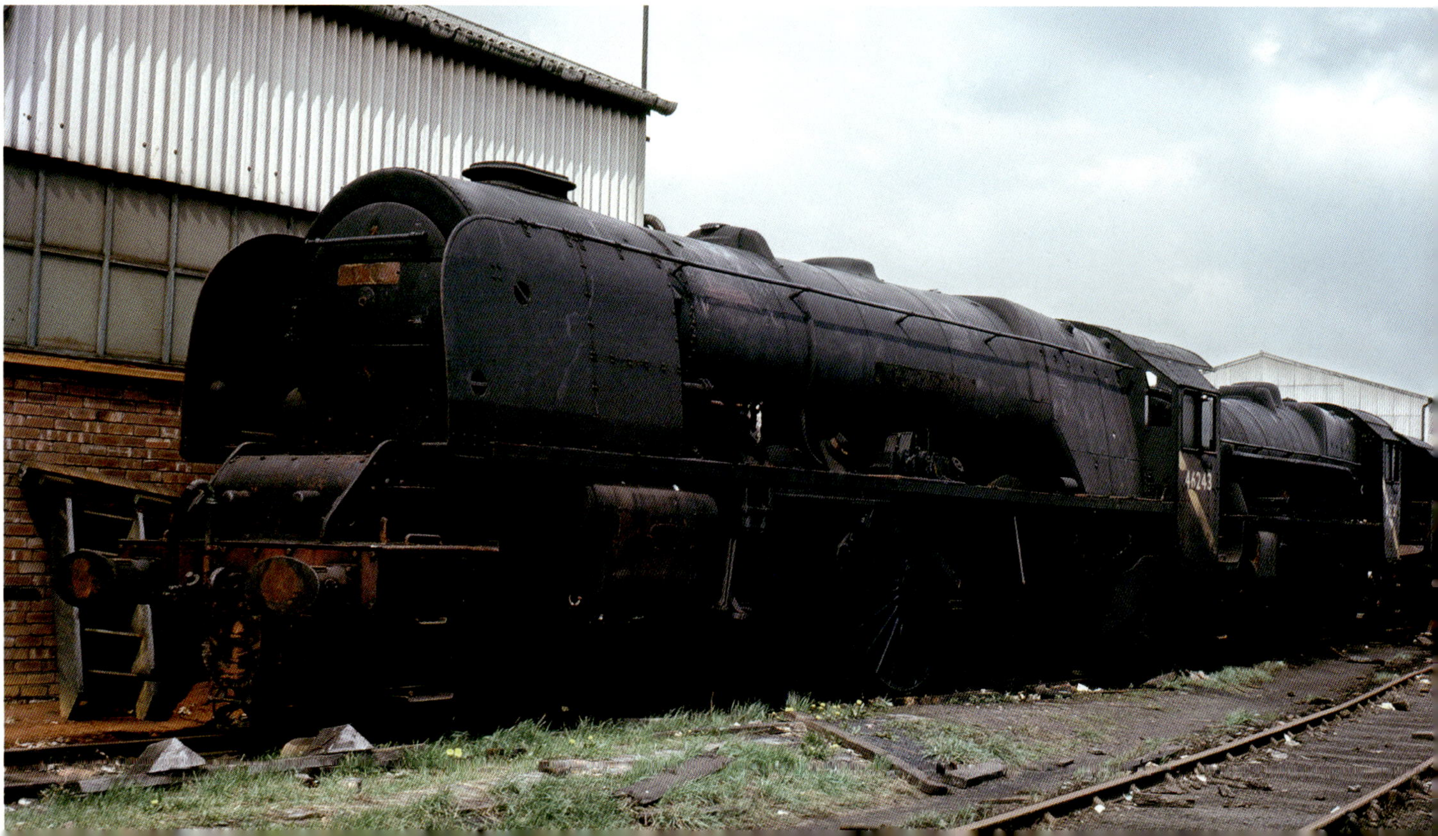

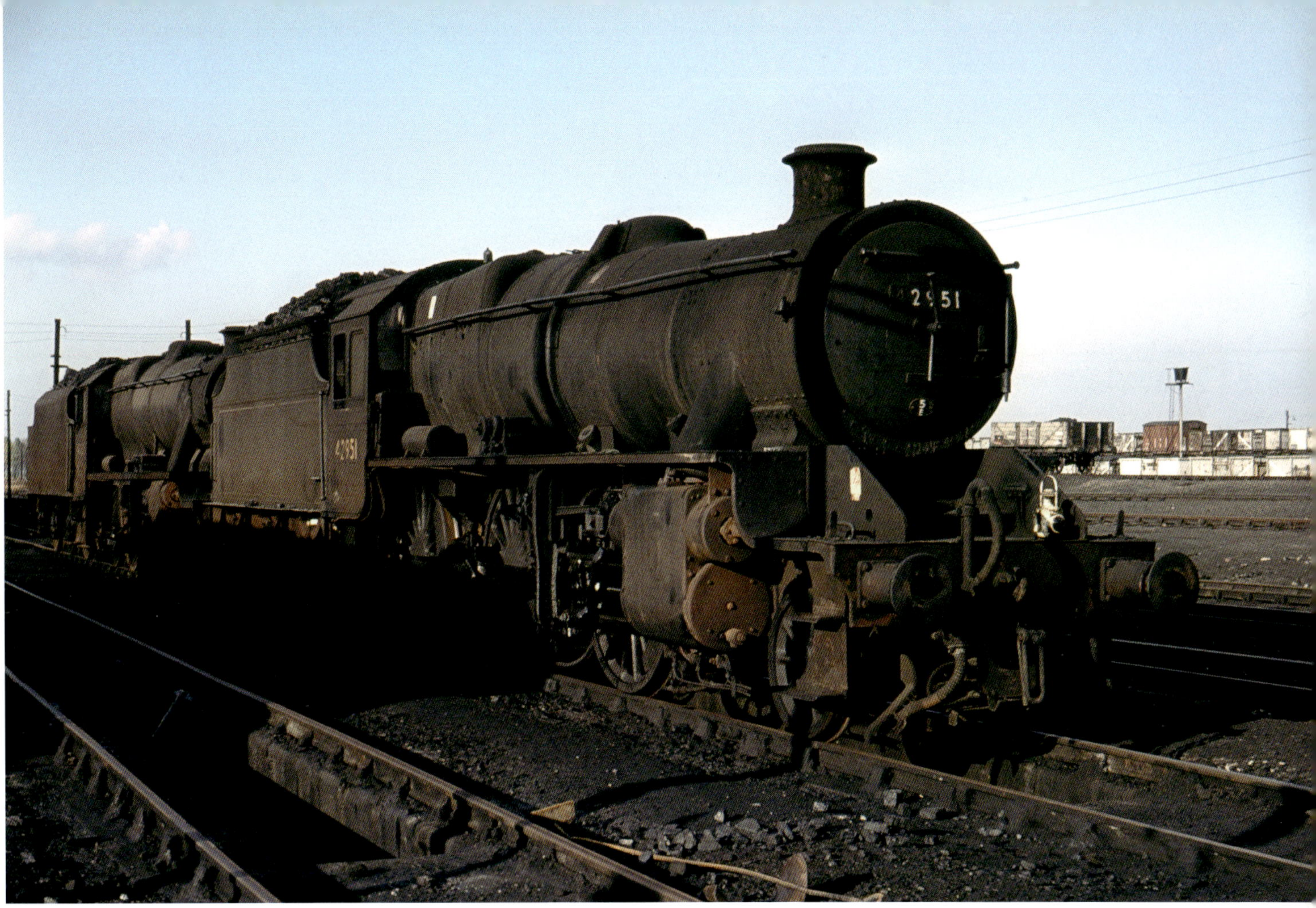

Mogul 42951 is fully coaled and dumped in the yard at March considering what might come next. ***Strathwood Library Collection***

A demise within the works yard at Doncaster for Stanier's 3 cylinder 2-6-4T 42517 in 1962, as all but the prototype of the class were swiftly broken up. ***Strathwood Library Collection***

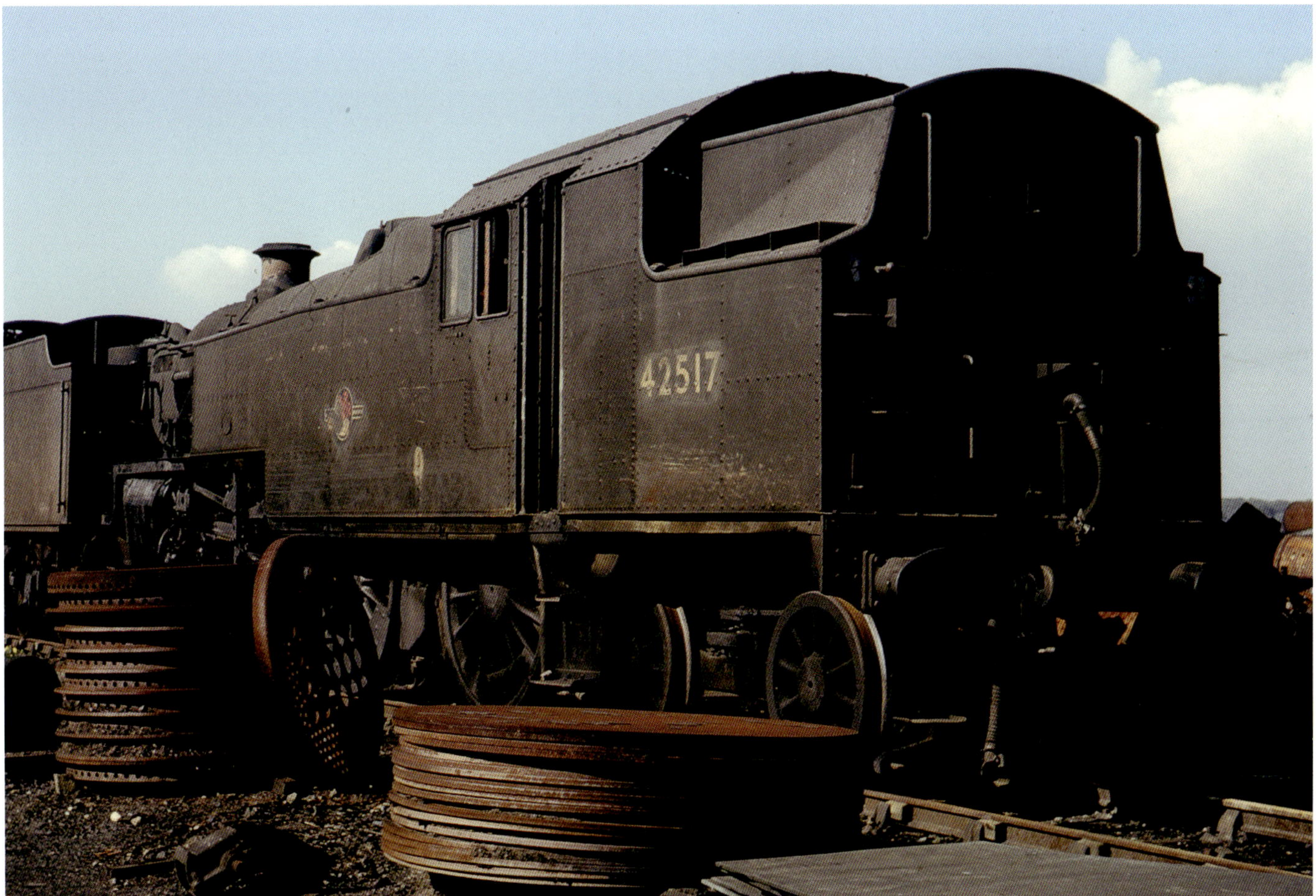

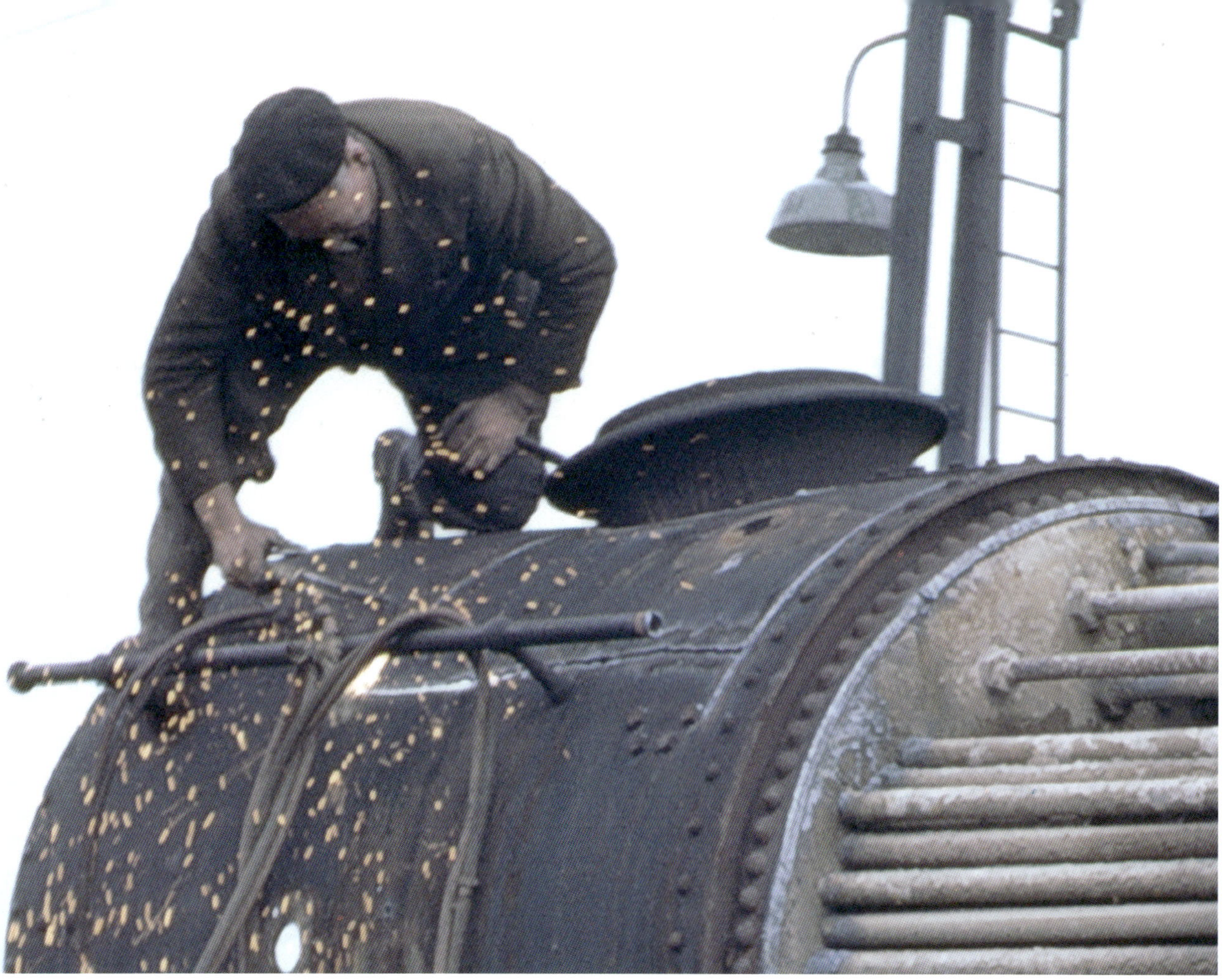

The scrap men don't wait for Stanier 8F 48469 to come to them as they descend upon Bolton depot to conduct their work on 30 March 1968. ***Jerry Beddows***

Drapers Yard in Hull bids farewell to an unknown Black Five in November 1967. ***John Gill***

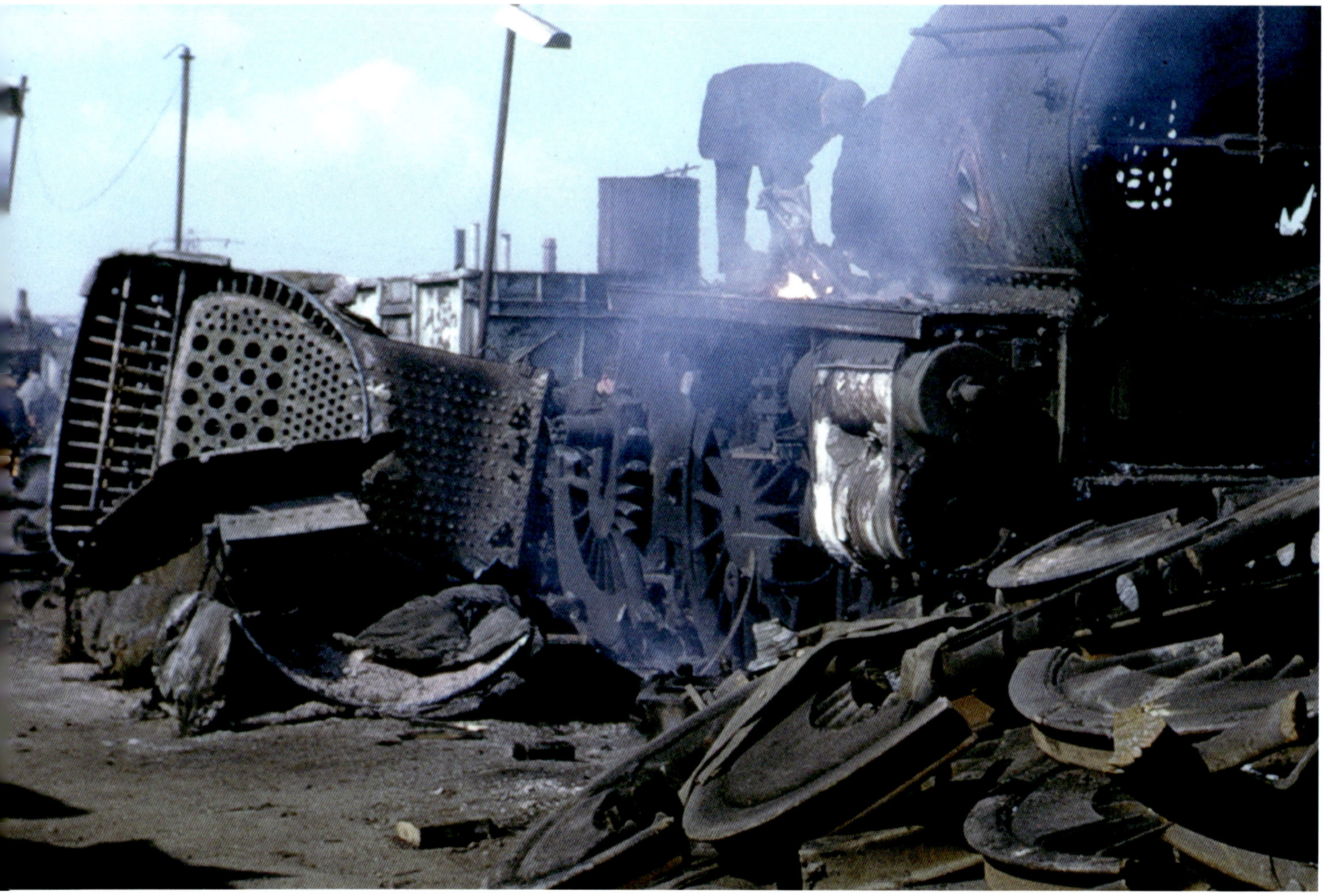

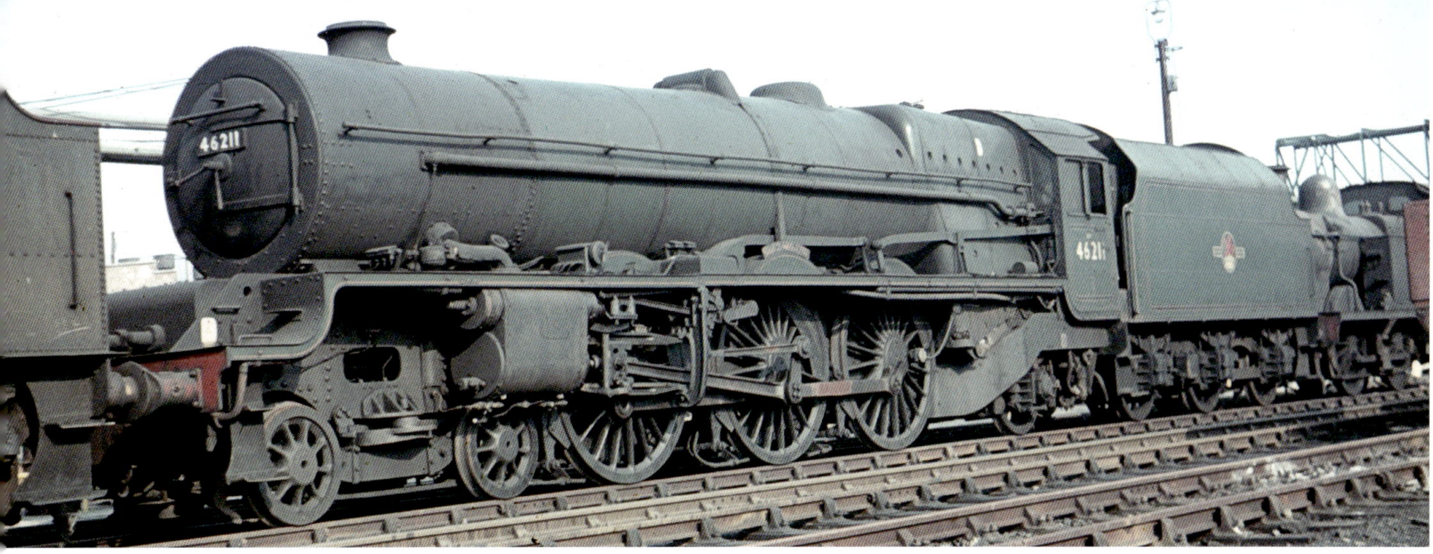

Waiting on death row at Carnforth in June 1961 was 46211 Queen Maud. ***Strathwood Library Collection***

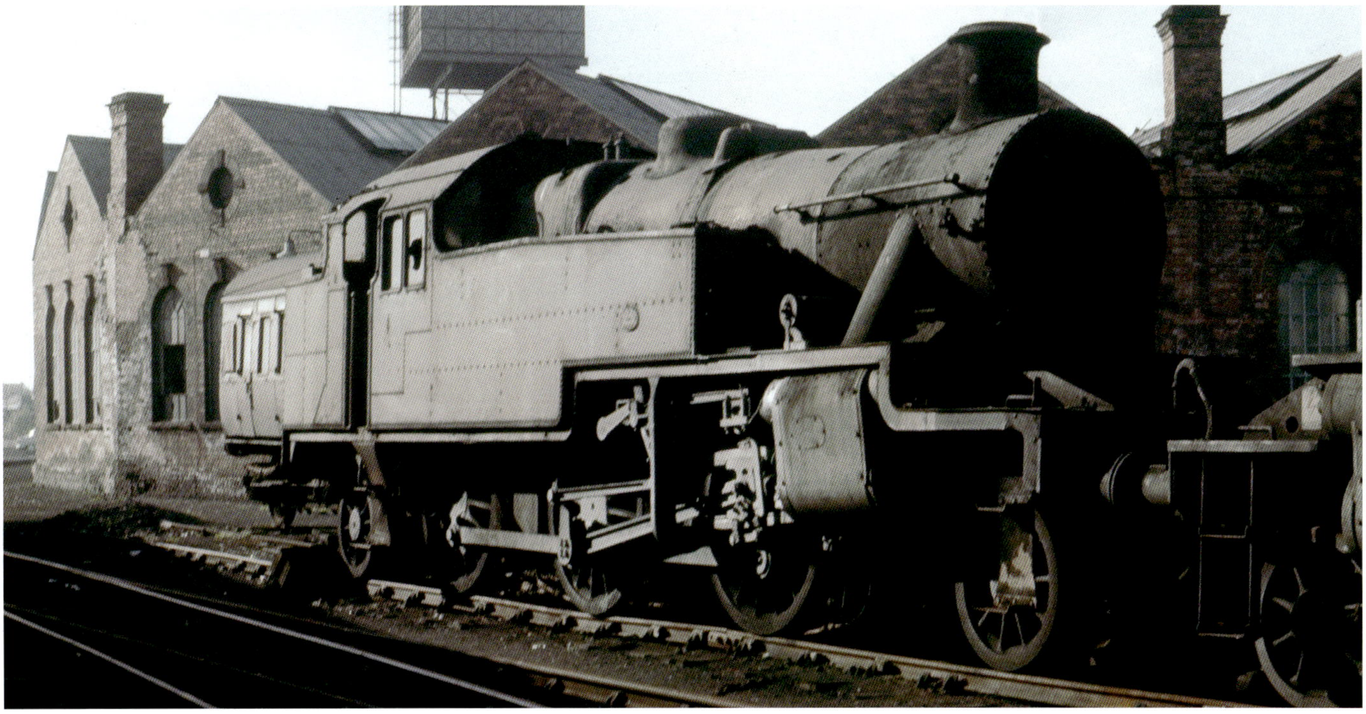

Darlington Works will become the resting place for 3P 2-6-2T 40190 reflecting the past on 20 October 1963. ***Strathwood Library Collection***

The last Stanier push and pull fitted 0-4-4Ts 41900 waits in the cold on 2 January 1962 at Wellington. ***Richard Icke***

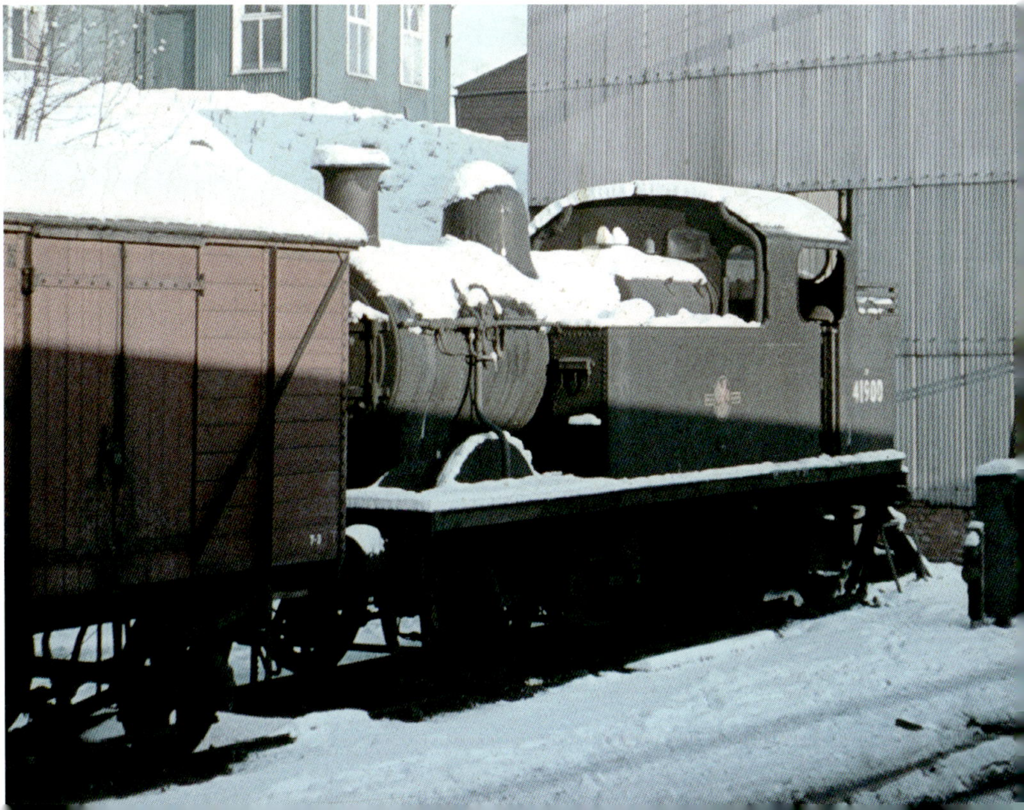

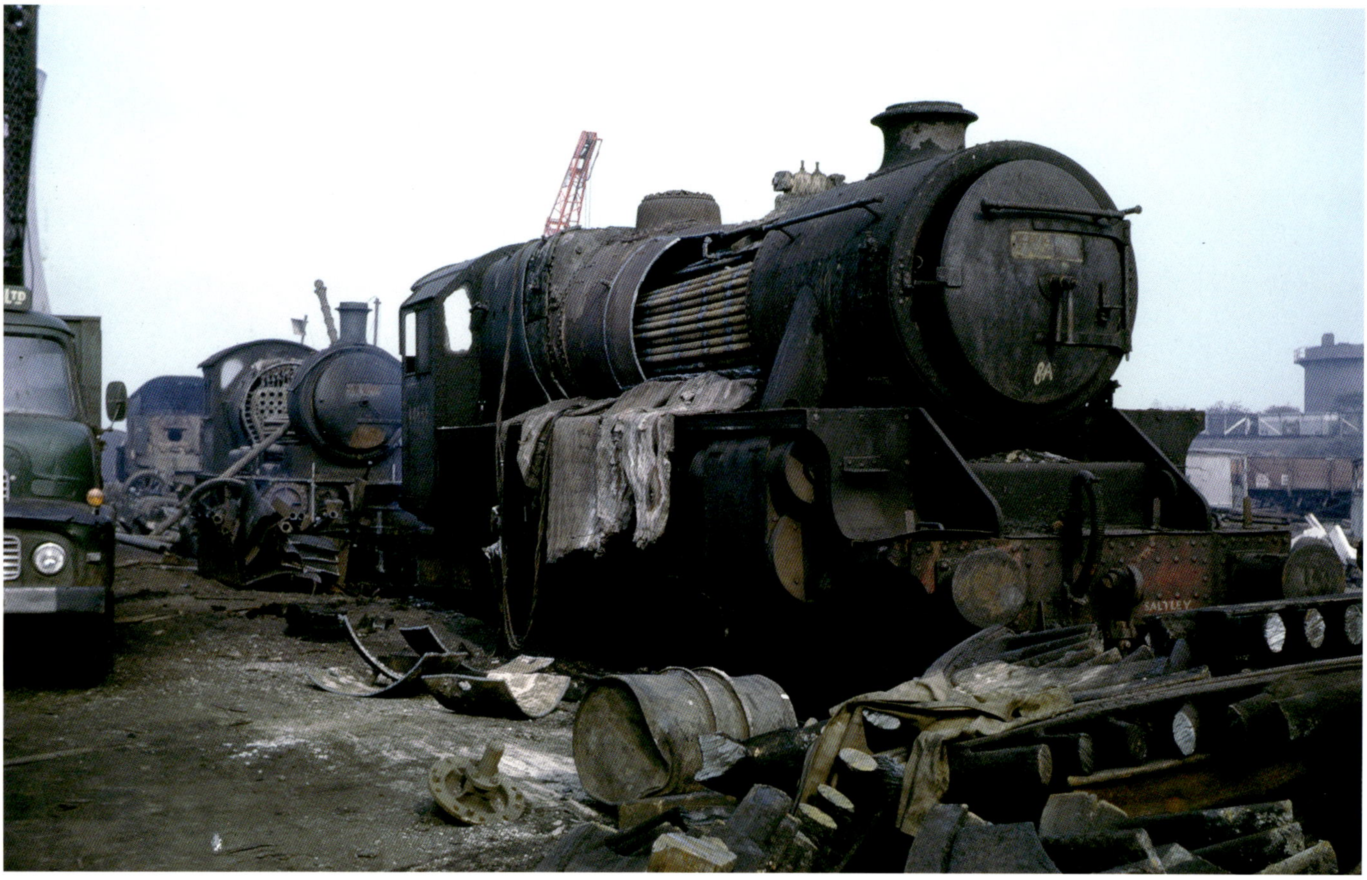

Draper's yard in Hull reduces another Black Five 44658 to its core parts again in 1967. ***John Gill***

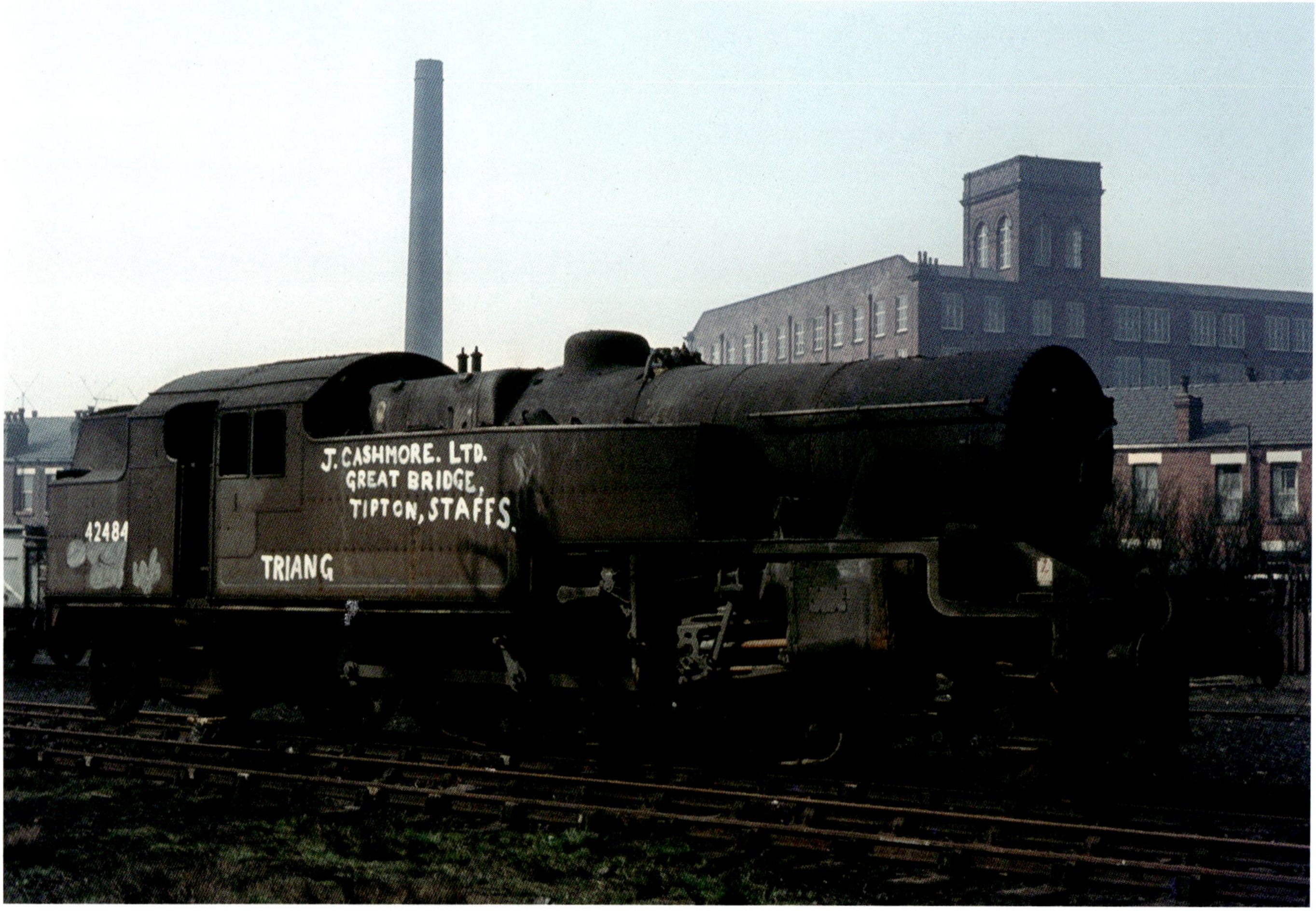

The destination for a chimneyless 42484 at Bolton on 3 April 1966. We doubt Tri-ang would have been interested at the time. ***Dave Down***

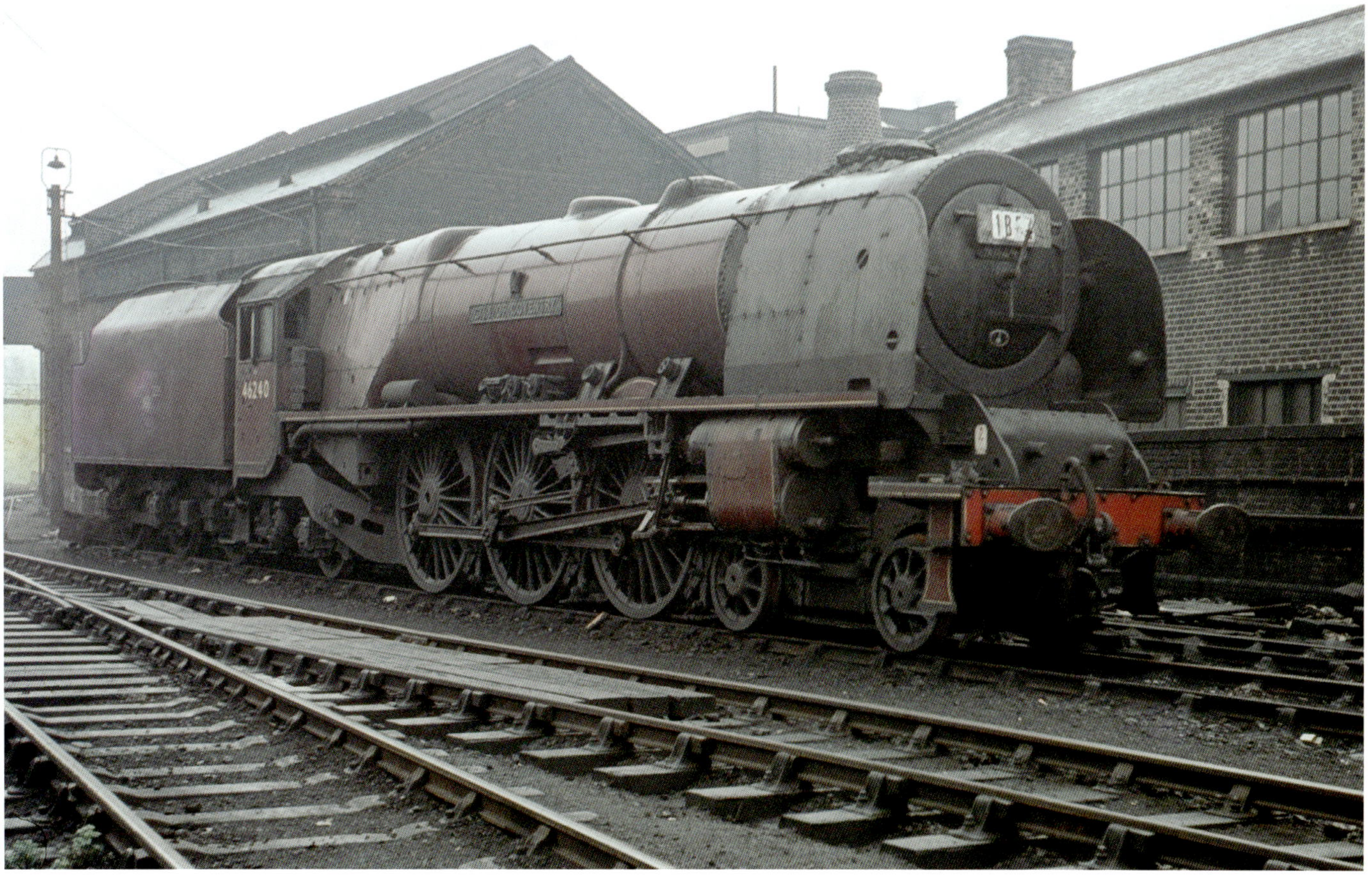

Stored with all of her plates still intact was 46240 City of Coventry withdrawn in late 1964 and seen at Camden. ***Strathwood Library Collection***

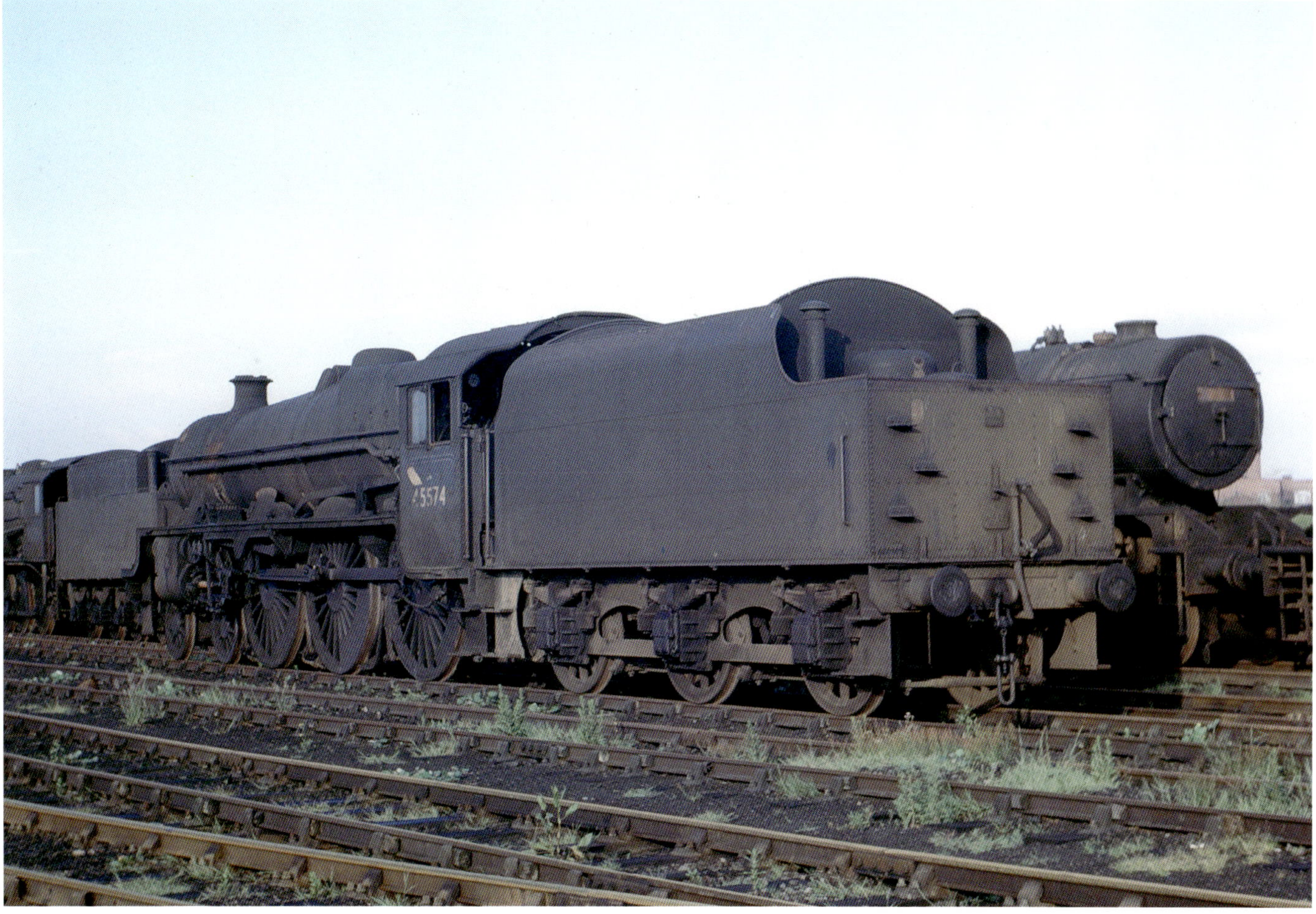

A short trip working from Hull Dairycoates shed across to the yards of Albert Draper awaits Jubilee 45574 India on 14 May 1966. ***Jerry Beddows***

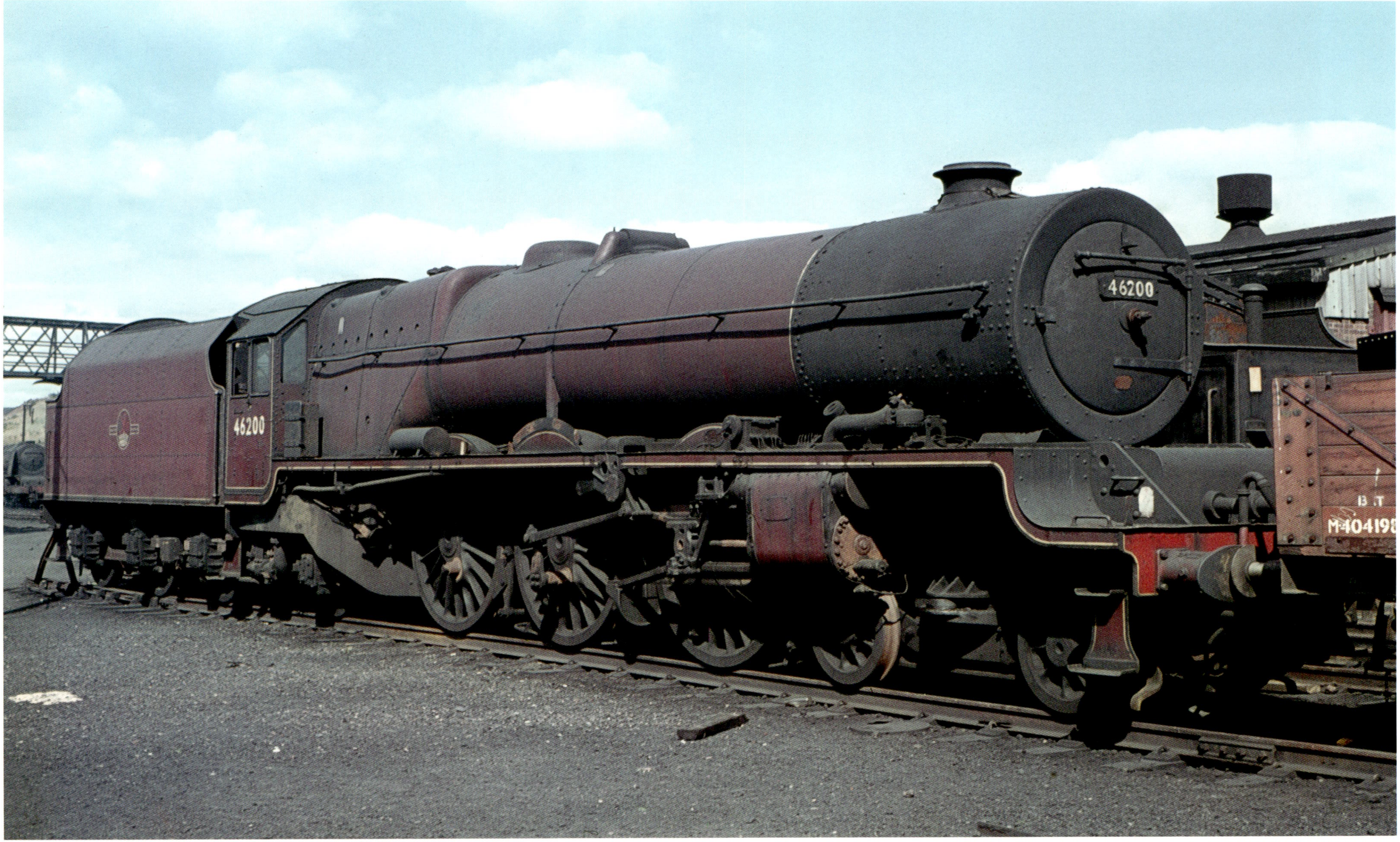

The Princess Royal nameplates have been removed from 46200, seen stored in the open at Carlisle Upperby in 1963 as scrap men all across the country bid for bargains to cut up. ***Strathwood Library Collection***

Almost Lost

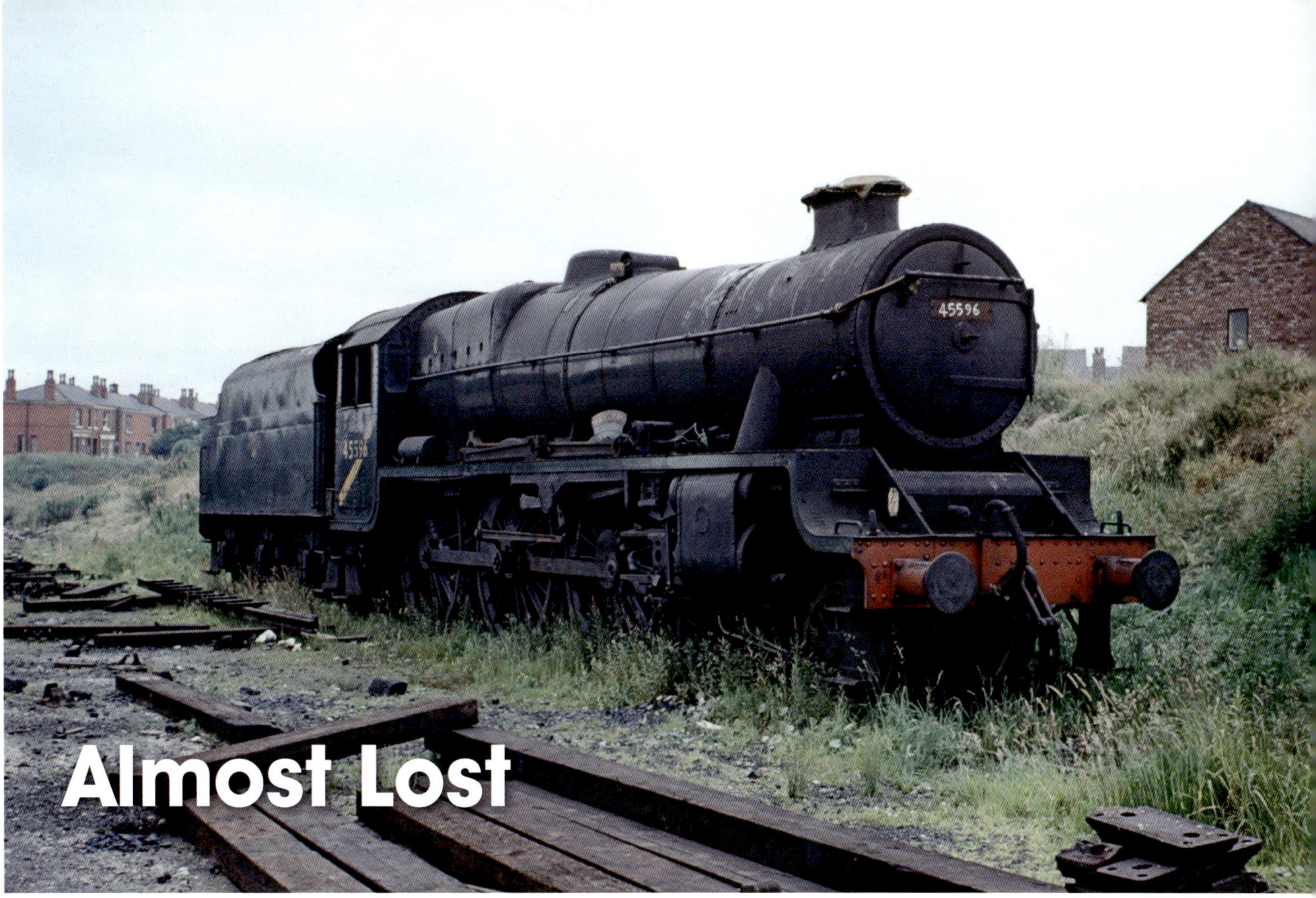

Having been out of service for twelve months, double chimney Jubilee 45596 Bahamas presented a sorry sight stored at the back of Stockport Edgeley on 9 July 1967. ***Strathwood Library Collection***

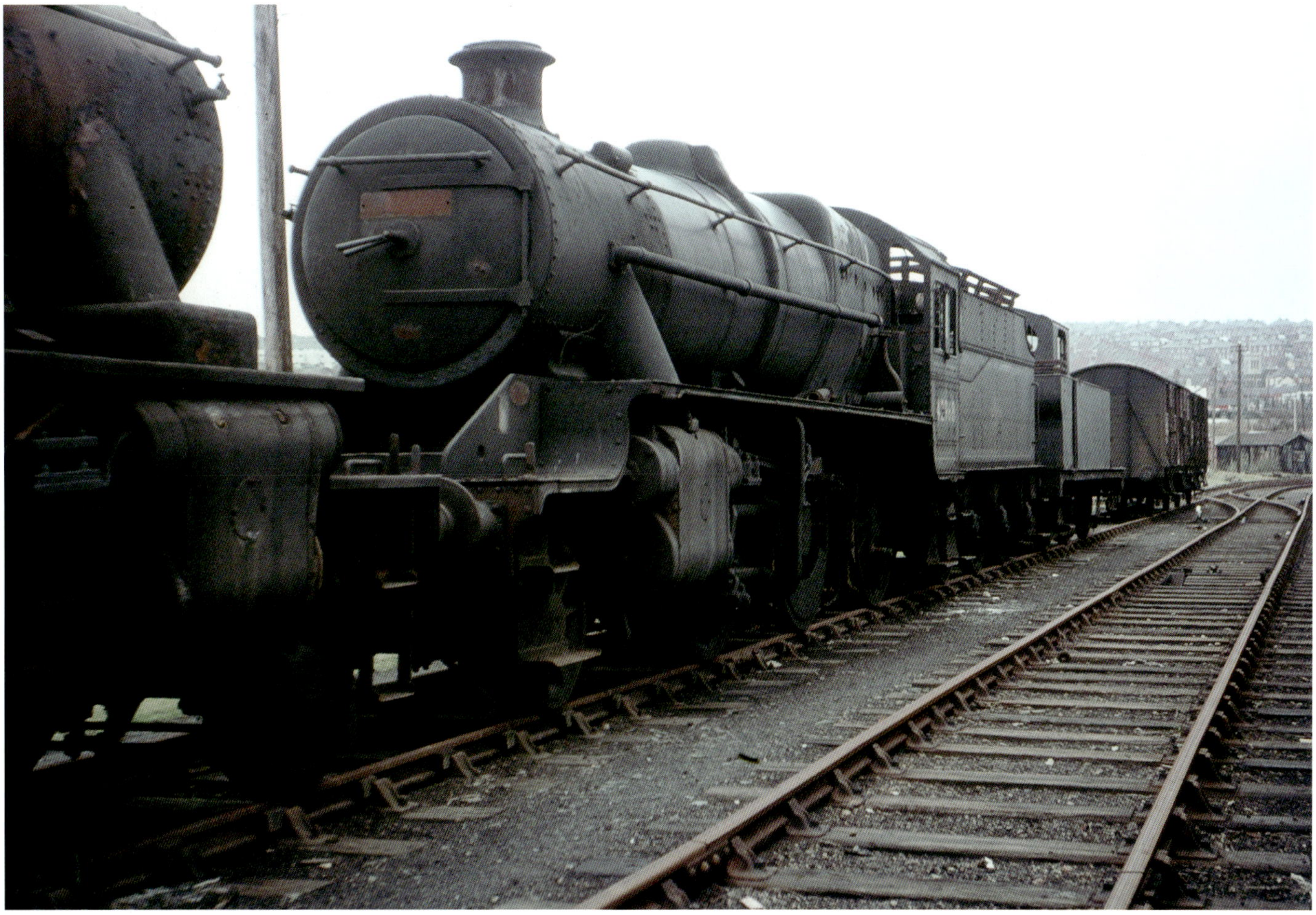

Part of the Barry miracle was the sole surviving Stanier Mogul when photographed in the yard on 16 March 1968. 42968 escaped from Woodham's yard to find sanctuary on the Severn Valley Railway in December 1973. ***Strathwood Library Collection***

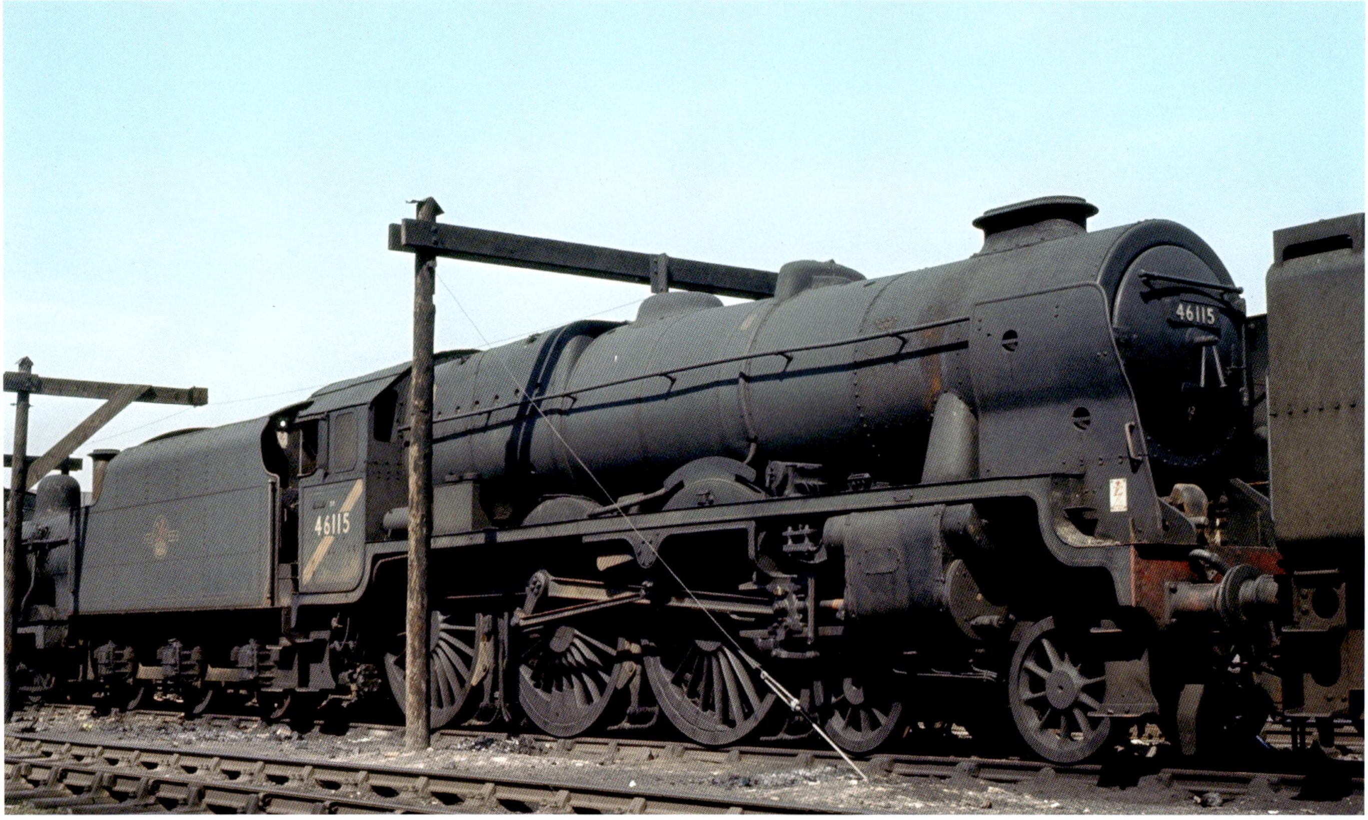

Although 46115 Scots Guardsman had been withdrawn in December 1965 it lingered at Carlisle Kingmoor and was still in use for demonstrating overhead wire safety for enginemen when seen on 30 April 1966. Firstly a berth on the Keighley and Worth Valley Railway and then a spell at Dinting kept this Royal Scot from the scrappers. ***Win Wall/Strathwood Library Collection***

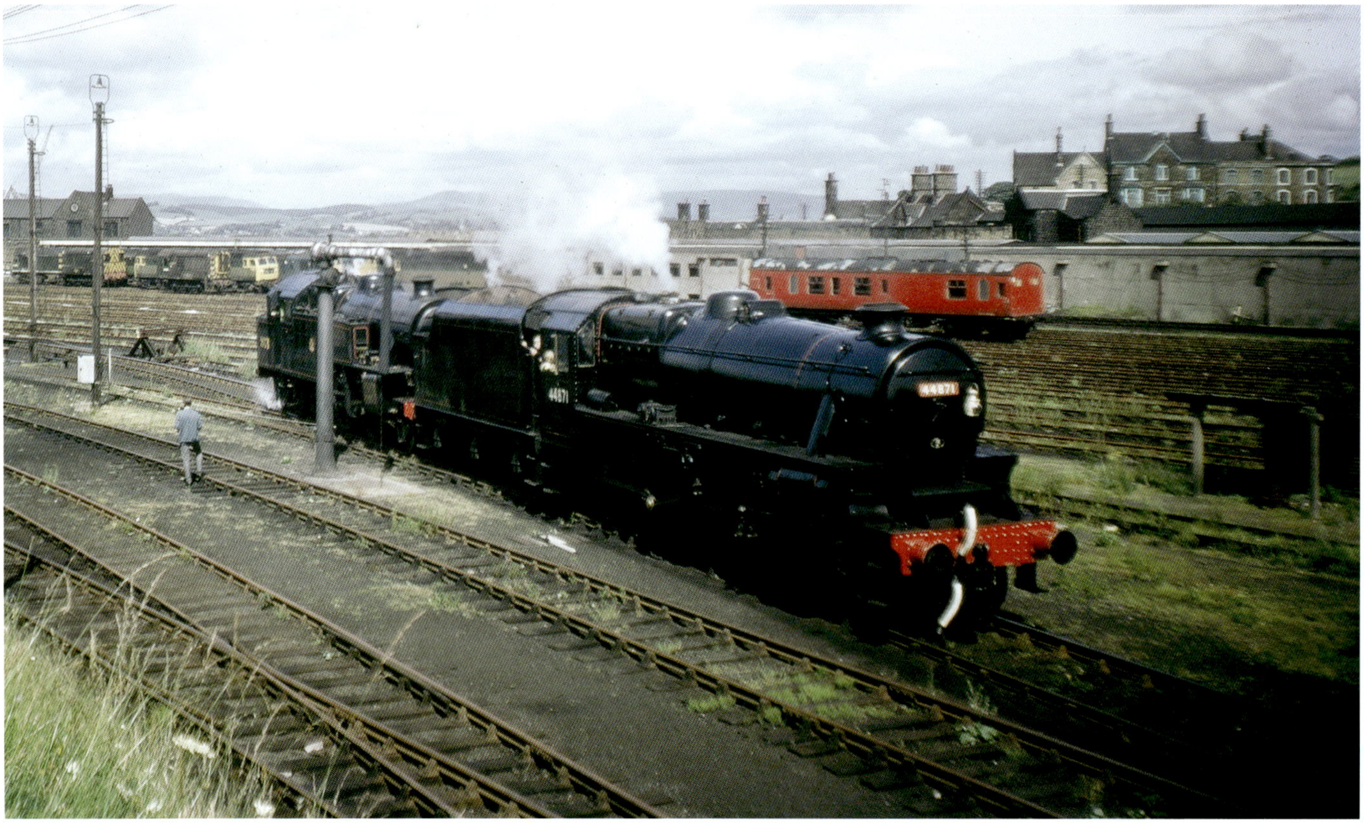

By July 1969 the long lines of stored steam locomotives had departed to the scrap yards from Carnforth depot, but British Rail continued to use the yard for stabling diesels. However the preservationists had moved in to the now grassy former steam shed where Steamtown was born and was host to a number of steam locomotives including Black Five 44871 and one of Fairburn's developments of Sir William Stanier's 2-6-4Ts. ***Chris Forrest***

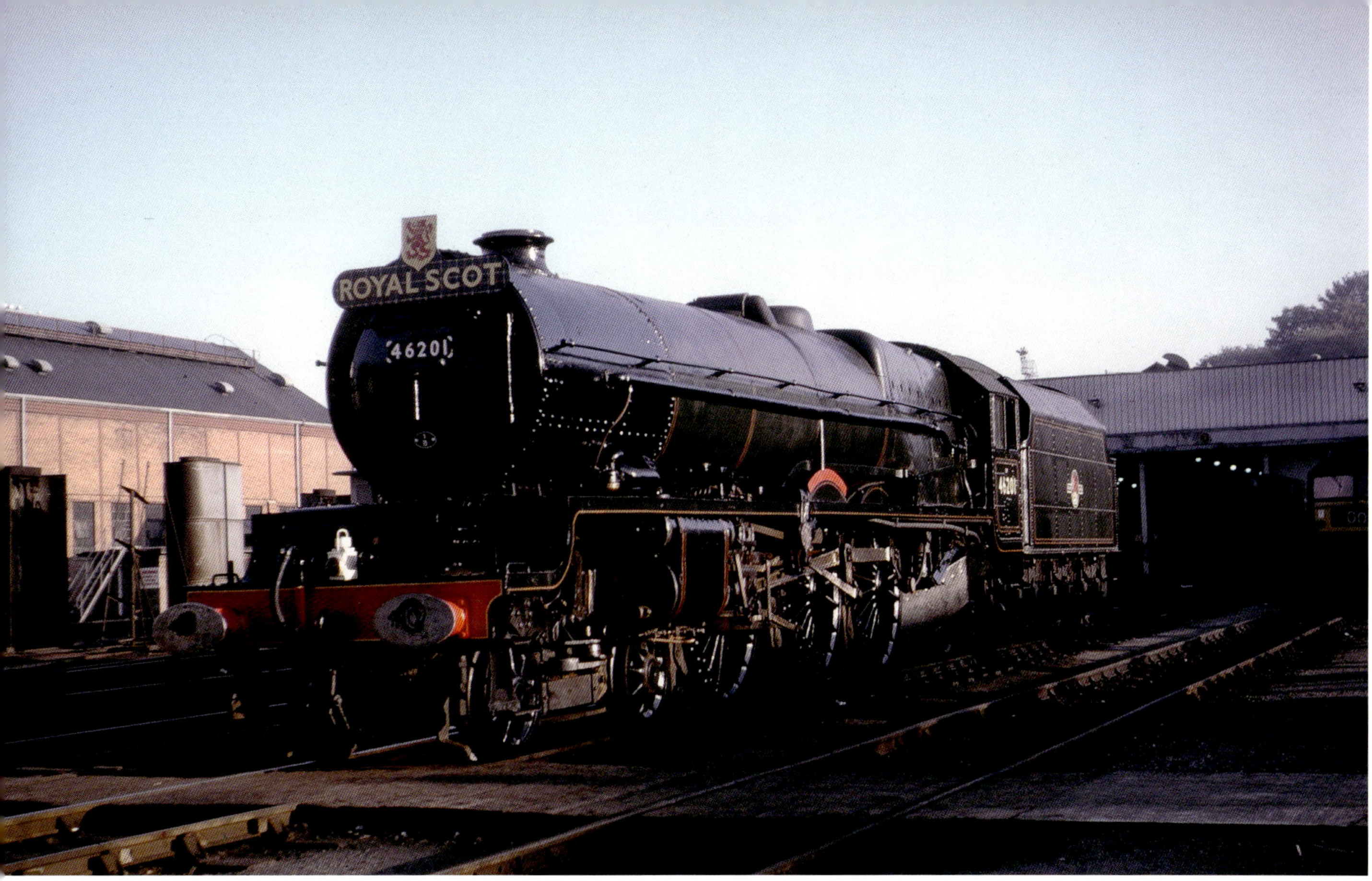

The star exhibit for the Bristol Bath Road Open Day in October 1967 would be 46201 Princess Elizabeth. This fine Pacific was bought by the then Princess Elizabeth Locomotive Society straight from British Railways service when withdrawn in 1962. Initially kept at the Dowty Railway Preservation Society's premises at Ashchurch, and then subsequently at the Bulmers Railway Centre in Hereford until it closed. ***Strathwood Library Collection***

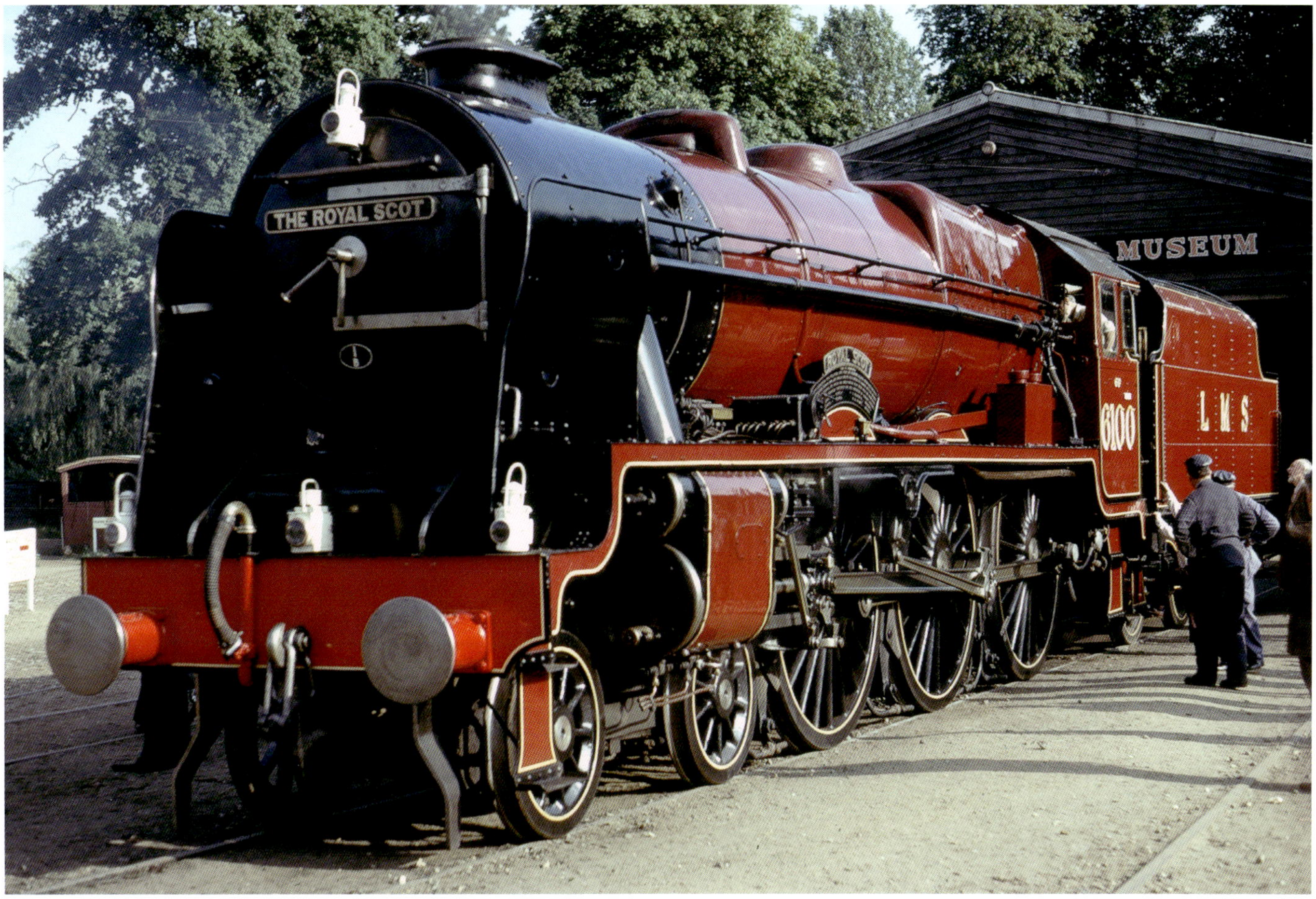

The notable history of 6100 Royal Scot perhaps ensured it was selected for preservation, not as part of the National Collection but instead by an enterprising Billy Butlin who set the locomotive upon a plinth at his Skegness Holiday Camp in 1963. Here it stayed until March 1971 when it moved to a new home at the Bressingham Steam Museum the brainchild of another entrepreneur Alan Bloom. Here it was returned to steam the following year. ***Strathwood Library Collection***

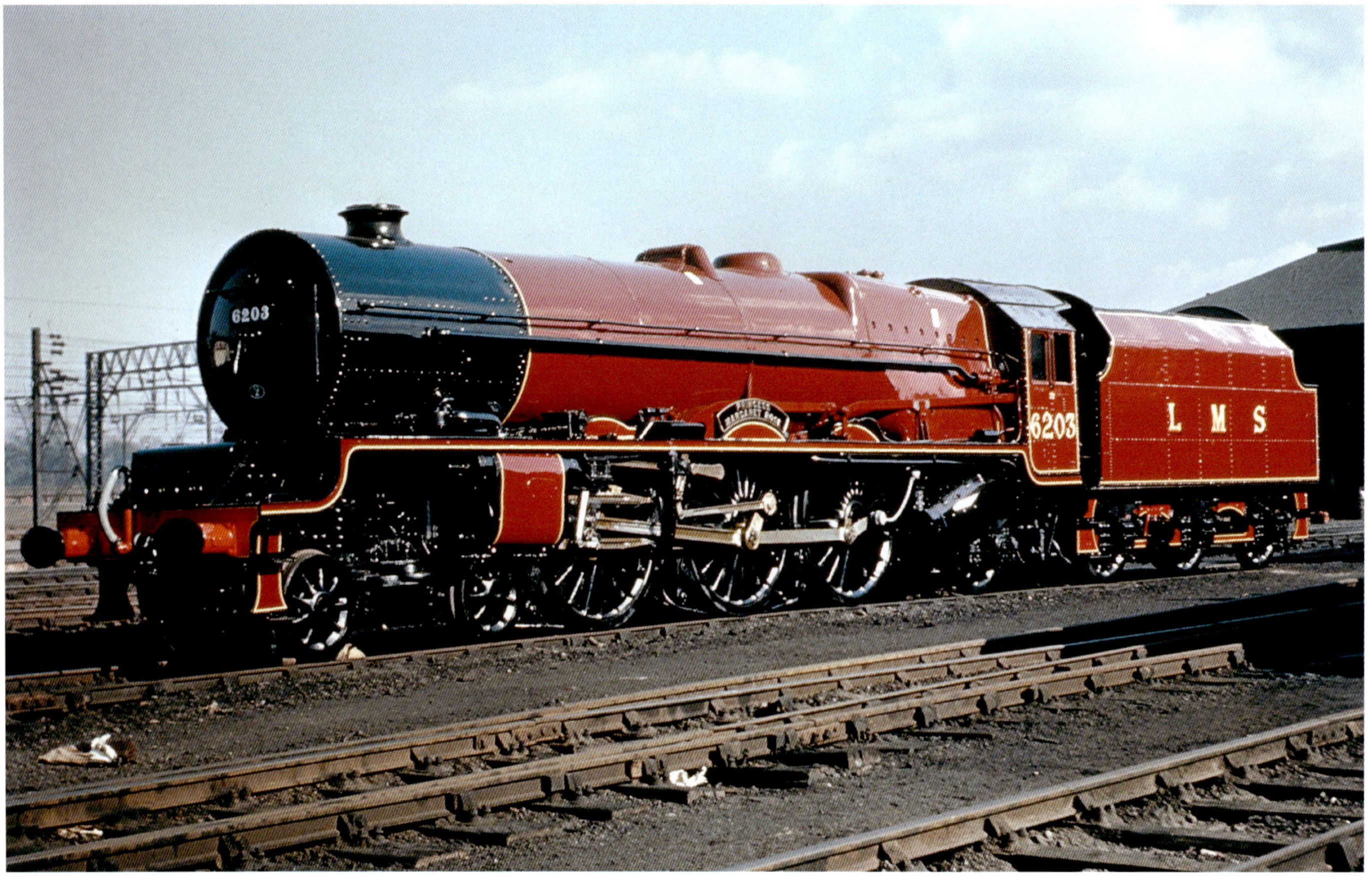

Another of Billy Butlin's acquisitions was 6203 Princess Margaret Rose which was withdrawn in October 1962. The locomotive was cosmetically restored at Crewe where we see it in May 1963, before it was moved to the Butlins camp at Pwllheli. Here it remained as a static exhibit for holidaymakers until 1975 when it left for the Midland Railway Centre at Butterley. ***Strathwood Library Collection***

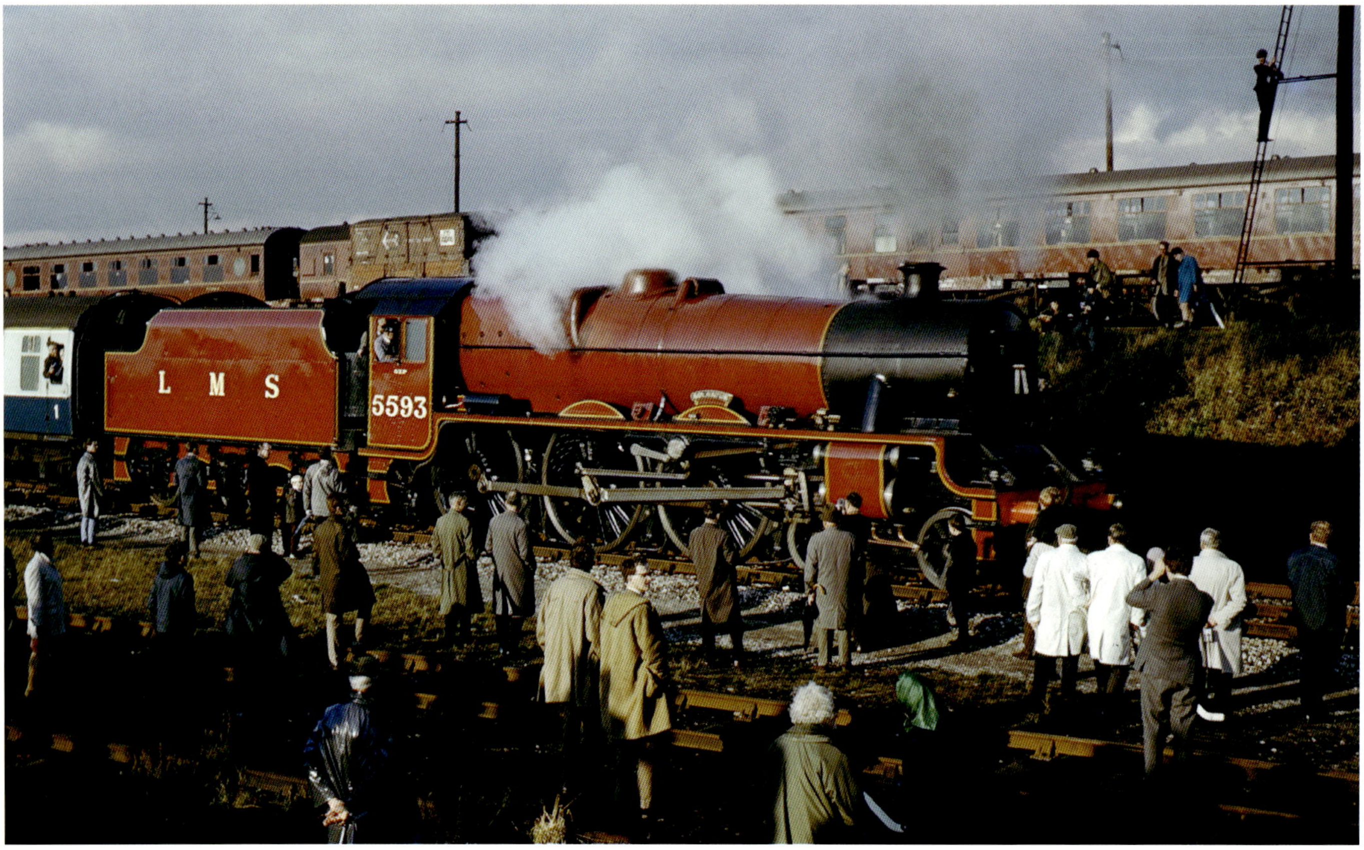

The Standard Gauge Steam Trust raised funds to secure Jubilee 45593 Kolhapur after it was taken out of service from Holbeck depot in 1967. The engine was still in good condition and quickly repainted back into LMS red livery and displayed and run for the public at Tyseley as here in 1968. ***John Gill***

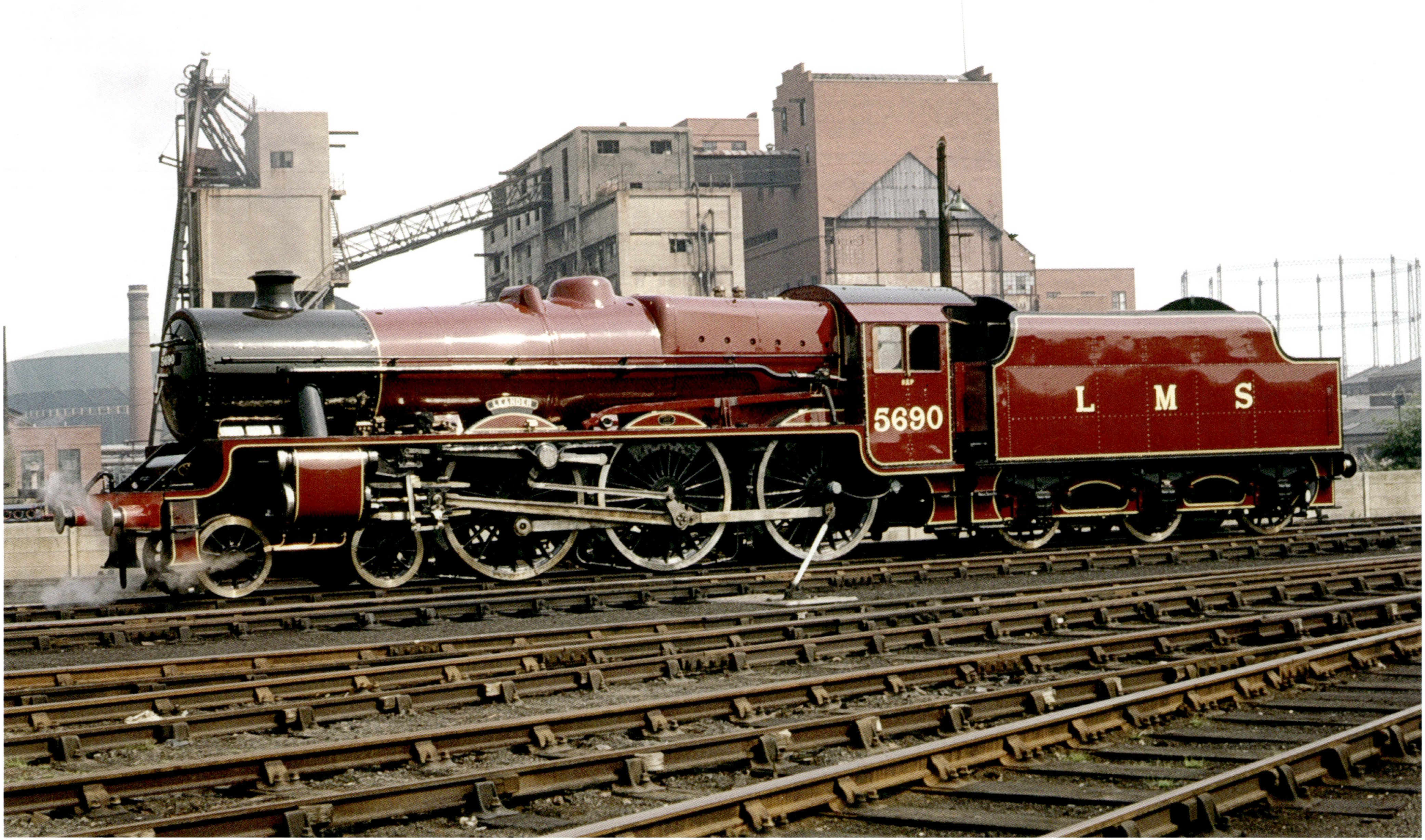

Another Stanier evacuee from Woodhams yard was Jubilee 45690 Leander staying in the yard for eight years before salvation came in 1972. The locomotive was named in respect of HMS Leander which in turn recalled the Greek legend Leander who fell in love with Hero. ***Strathwood Library Collection***

Help To Preserve Our Railway Heritage

Strathwood not only publish books on our railway heritage but have also set up the Railway Photographic Preservation Association as a Charitable Trust to house an archive of images comprising over 200,000 photographic negatives and slides.

The archive was established to not only preserve the collections of over one hundred photographers both living and deceased, but to also make their work available to a younger audience for the future. To achieve this aim, we have begun an energetic programme to publish a considerable number of books. Allied to this we are making as many as possible of the photographs and slides we hold, available as copies to interested enthusiasts, individuals, societies and other publishers.

Many photographers have chosen Strathwood to care for their collections and to publish the best examples of their work for posterity.

If you have negatives or colour slides of transport subjects then we would like to hear from you. We purchase, accept on loan, or welcome donations of material to the archive. Photographers always receive recognition for their work when it is used by publishers (A N Other/Strathwood Library). To answer why so many images are just credited as Strathwood Library Collection in this volume, the reason is we do not know who the original photographer was. This is usually because their collection gets split up via auctions or collectors upon their death with no record of the late photographer for us to credit. Please do not let this happen to your collection. Make contact with us today to discuss what can be done to ensure you work is fully credited and recognised for both today and the future.

Please call us today if you would like to see your work in print, perhaps in a similar fashion to this publication. We also undertake publications to benefit charities and societies on behalf of our contributors. In addition we can store, and catalogue collections on behalf of clubs and societies by way of loan, thereby releasing such groups to concentrate on other aspects of their activities.

Strathwood Ltd,
Glenavon House,
Kinchurdy Road,
Boat of Garten,
Inverness-shire,
PH24 3BP.

Telephone 01479 831139

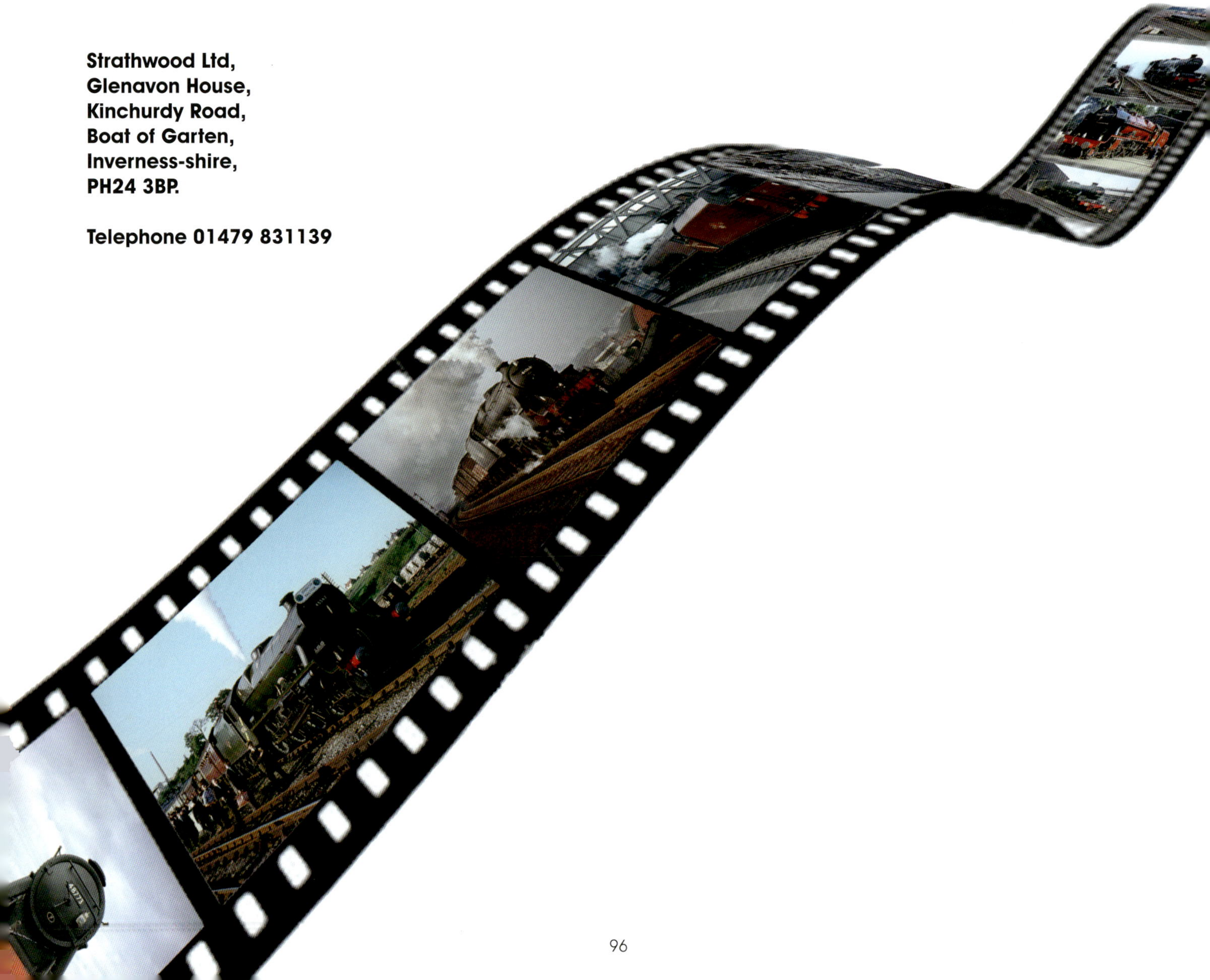